BISMARCK

BISMARCK

The Final Days of
Germany's Greatest Battleship

Niklas Zetterling & Michael Tamelander

CASEMATE
Philadelphia & Newbury

Published in the United States of America and Great Britain in 2012 by
CASEMATE PUBLISHERS
908 Darby Road, Havertown, PA 19083
and
17 Cheap Street, Newbury, Berkshire, RG14 5DD

ISBN 978-1-61200-075-6
Digital Edition: ISBN 978-1-93514-982-8

Cataloging-in-publication data is available from the Library of Congress
and the British Library.

Printed and bound in the United States of America.

For a complete list of Casemate titles, please contact:

CASEMATE PUBLISHERS (US)
Telephone (610) 853-9131, Fax (610) 853-9146
E-mail: casemate@casematepublishing.com

CASEMATE PUBLISHERS (UK)
Telephone (01635) 231091, Fax (01635) 41619
E-mail: casemate-uk@casematepublishing.co.uk

Contents

Foreword

The military career of the battleship *Bismarck* was unusually brief, embracing but nine days at sea, while the interest she has provoked has lasted for more than half a century. Perhaps it is all the mysteries that surround her, despite this single operational journey, which have attracted the curiosity of historians, military professionals and general readers alike. Most certainly, this interest in the *Bismarck* has also been promoted by her size, her speed, her very effective armour belt and the power and efficiency of her armament. When launched, she was, together with the British battlecruiser *Hood*, the largest warship then afloat. As these two giants met during the dramatic battle in the Denmark Strait, posterity was given a gripping tale and a naval story that continues to tantalize many an audience. Radio silence that was broken for reasons still unexplained; fuel tanks not topped up before departure; and the question of whether the crew of the *Bismarck* scuttled her during the final battle, are only some examples of the many unanswered puzzles that followed the German battleship to her grave, and which continue to baffle those searching for answers today.

One of the central issues regarding the short life of the *Bismarck* is why she was sent out on the Atlantic at all. What was the underlying purpose of her deployment there? It may appear as if she was sent out aimlessly onto the open sea, where she was first discovered in the Denmark Strait, fought a major battle in which she was damaged, shook off her British pursuers and turned towards German-occupied France, only to be rediscovered again. And finally went down, damaged, alone, and fighting bitterly to the very end. A partial aim of

this book is to depict the *Bismarck* within the context created by both
the German and the British maritime strategies, which in turn were
mainly dictated by the trade, economy and history of these two nations.
Of course, most of the space in the book is devoted to the *Bismarck's*
dramatic journey, but we will also discuss whether the above mentioned
strategies were sound or mere folly.

While working with the story of the *Bismarck*, it gradually became
apparent to us that chance, coincidence and sheer luck play a great part
in the shaping of maritime events, at least during a single episode like
Operation Rheinübung. Numerous examples spring to mind: misinter-
preted orders, false assumptions, the taking of unnecessary risks. If
grave, just one of these examples could mean the difference between
success and utter failure; and even if minor, a number of these mishaps
could combine to alter the chain of events and lead to an unexpected
outcome. For us, who enjoy the benefit of hindsight, it is easy to see
that sometimes mistakes and misjudgements could even create
advantages. Huge sums of money were spent to build, outfit and crew
the huge ships, and thus responsibility weighed heavily on the vast
numbers of officers and seamen who were entrusted to command and
serve on them. Added to the burden of responsibility were scant intelligence, uncertainty about enemy intentions, lack of knowledge about
other friendly forces, fatigue and many other hardships and ambiguities
which demanded luck to result in victorious battles or operations.

A problem encountered by anyone trying to follow the movements
of ships on the Atlantic is time, as the ships sailed over vast expanses of
ocean, covering several time zones. The *Bismarck* followed daylight-
saving times, which was introduced in Germany in 1940. As the ships
moved further and further west, sunset happened progressively later,
unless the clocks on board the ships were adjusted. Indeed Admiral
Lütjens ordered that *Bismarck* and *Prinz Eugen* should set back all
clocks on board one hour at 13.00 hours on 23 May.[1] Consequently,
the two ships used Central European Standard time. The British also
used daylight-saving time, but unlike the Germans they adjusted the
clock by two hours compared to normal time. Hence, German and
British time on land coincided during this period, while Lütjens'
squadron was one hour behind. British ships at sea may of course also
have adjusted their clocks to suit the time zone they were sailed within.
We have endeavoured to use Central European summer time in our

description of the events, but the reader is asked to keep in mind that the clocks on board the ships may have differed.[2]

An exception is the times given during Operation Berlin (January–March 1941), when virtually all events are described from the point of view of the German squadron. We decided to use the time as it was set on board the two German battleships. During the operation, several time zones were covered, further complicating the issue.

Another time-related problem is encountered when the various messages are dealt with. A message was assigned a time when it was written. However, minutes or hours could pass before it had been coded, transmitted, received, decoded and presented to the commander for whom it was intended, so it can be tricky to settle for a specific time. Sources do not always make it fully clear what is meant when the timing of a message is given. Thus the reader is encouraged not to take all times given in the book too literally. We have tried to limit the problem by not using more exact wording than warranted by the actions described, but it has not been possible to do away with times altogether.

The terminology used at sea can place demands upon writer as well as reader. Many of the words common within naval forces may be difficult to understand for landlubbers like us. We have chosen to use specific maritime terminology to some extent, as the book clearly is about naval warfare, but as we want to reach a broader range of readers, who like us may lack experience with the terminology used by navies, we have strived to reduce the professional terminology to a necessary minimum.

Some of the literature we have relied upon is available in many versions and even languages. Most important is Burkhardt von Müllenheim-Rechberg's book, which has been available to us in Swedish, English and of course German. All page references in our footnotes refer to Müllenheim-Rechberg's German version. As very few of *Bismarck's* crew survived, and even fewer survived from the *Hood*, we have relied heavily on Müllenheim-Rechberg and Ted Briggs, respectively. When, as authors,we worked extensively with the thoughts and impressions of another person, we gradually developed a kind of acquaintance with him. Thus it was with regret we learned, early in June 2003, that Müllenheim-Rechberg had passed away, 62 years after the *Bismarck* hit the bottom of the ocean. Ted Briggs is, at the time of writing, still alive and healthy. He is now the only survivor of the more than 1,400 men that left Scapa Flow with the *Hood* on 21 May 1941.

Prologue

When Prime Minister Winston Churchill left London on a Friday evening in May 1941, to spend the weekend at Chequers Court, he was not in a cheerful mood. The fortunes of war did not favour his fellow countrymen. The British army had been evicted from the continent a year earlier, and France – Britain's most powerful ally – had surrendered shortly afterwards. After the disasters in May and June 1940, Britain had almost been forced out of the war. Only the Royal Navy, the Royal Air Force and the obstacle presented to the Germans by the Channel, allowed her to battle on. Nevertheless, the war so far had been one of setbacks, defeats and disasters.

After the week that had just passed, the situation looked even bleaker. The Blitz still persisted. A bomb had recently wrecked the House of Commons and many surrounding buildings. In the Atlantic, the German submarines became more and more aggressive and a few days earlier a convoy had lost seven merchant ships in a single attack. In North Africa and the Middle East the situation was no brighter. An insurrection in Iraq threatened the vital British supply of oil from the region and in Libya a German general, Rommel (who was yet to become famous), had advanced from the Sirte to the border of Egypt and laid siege to Tobruk.

The latest crisis that had occurred was at Crete, which had been assaulted by German paratroopers and where a violent battle ensued in dust and heat. At first news had reached the British Prime Minister that the German attack might have failed. The enemy had suffered serious losses and initial reports reaching London presented a bright picture.

But the situation changed. Suddenly he had to face the fact that defeat was not only a possibility, but a likely one.

To make matters worse still, news had reached London that the brand new German battleship *Bismarck* had been sighted in the Kattegat, accompanied by a heavy cruiser. She had anchored at Bergen in occupied Norway, only to slip away in the poor weather. For the moment no one knew where she was. Was she heading back towards Germany, after a concluded mission, or did she intend to break out into the vast expanses of the Atlantic? The latter scenario could mean catastrophe to the British convoys that were plodding along the routes over the Atlantic. Churchill was concerned especially about a major troop transport heading for the Middle East.

Churchill's bad mood was not alleviated during the dinner with his family and the invited guests who were at Chequers Court. Almost silently he ate his food, pondering on the gloomy situation for the British Empire. He uttered a few sentences to Averell Harriman, the envoy of President Roosevelt who had come to Britain to administer lend-lease weapons and ordnance, and to generals Ismay and Pownall, who were to stay at Chequers during the weekend. After the meal, Churchill's son-in-law went to the piano and began to play the 'Apassionata' by Ludwig van Beethoven.

Possibly thoughts about the high casualties suffered at Crete were foremost in his mind, when Churchill turned to his son-in-law and said in a high tone: 'Not now, Oliver! The last I want to hear tonight is a funeral march.'

'Why?' asked the baffled son-in-law. 'Don't you like it?'

'No funeral march in my house,' said the Prime Minister, who obviously confused the piece of music with something else. The family and the guests smiled at the situation.

Later in the evening, news reaching the Prime Minister slightly cheered him up. The *Suffolk* had sighted the *Bismarck* on the way towards the Atlantic. The *Suffolk*, assisted by the cruiser *Norfolk*, had immediately begun to shadow the German squadron. Admiral Lancelot Holland was already at sea, with the battlecruiser *Hood* and the brand new battleship *Prince of Wales*. His squadron was on a course to intercept the *Bismarck*. Hopefully the German battleship could be brought to battle sometime after midnight.

Could this be the chance for a victory, to offset the negative political consequences of all defeats suffered thus far? Of course, in a naval battle almost anything could happen, but if the two British capital ships, together with *Norfolk* and *Suffolk*, could attack *Bismarck* and her lone cruiser, the outcome seemed to be clear. Churchill had a direct telephone line to the Admiralty and the First Sea Lord, Dudley Pound, who had promised to stay at the Admiralty until the operation against the *Bismarck* had ended. The Prime Minister would be informed as soon as anything particular happened at sea.

The hours passed without the phone ringing. Churchill's wife and the rest of the family went to bed; Ismay and Pownall too found the hour late. The Prime Minister stayed up together with Harriman for a few hours after midnight, but just before 3.00 am they, too, went to bed.

When Churchill woke up the following morning the sky was grey and unusually strong winds swept over England. Rain rattled on the windows behind the curfew curtains.

Surprised, the Prime Minister blinked at the secretary who had just woken him. Then he remembered.

'Have we caught her?' he exclaimed. 'Have we caught the *Bismarck*?'

The secretary shook his head.

'No,' he answered, 'but unfortunately the *Hood* has been sunk.'

PART 1

CHAPTER 1

Lessons from Previous Wars

The logic behind the expansion of the German Navy during the two decades that preceded World War I is difficult to grasp. In 1871 Germany had been united under the leadership of Chancellor Otto von Bismarck. The young German nation, surrounded as she was by strong land powers, gave priority to the army, but as industry developed, considerable resources could also be devoted to the Navy. In 1898 it was announced that Germany would lay down 12 armoured cruisers; two years later another 20. A few years later it was declared that cruiser forces too would be expanded. The expansion of the Navy was zealously pursued, despite reasons to limit it. With the benefit of hindsight it seems clear that Germany possession of a strong navy would certainly drive Great Britain to oppose her.

At the time, rivalry between France and Britain remained pronounced. France still had a grudge against Germany dating from the Franco-Prussian War of 1870–1871. With France a most likely enemy, it might have seemed natural for Germany to foster good relations with Britain in the future. However, the German naval expansion served to alienate Britain. Command of the seas had been the pillar upon which British foreign policy and military strategy rested. The British economy had long since been adapted to the transoceanic trade, and the import of raw materials and manufactured goods had become absolutely vital to it. The insular nation had gradually increased its influence over the seas and the transoceanic trade since the 16th century. She had been challenged many times, but always emerged with a stronger position than before, and during the 19th century British dominance of the seas reached its height.

With this background it is not surprising that German naval expansion alarmed the British. A wiser strategy might have been for the Germans to curtail their naval programme, to avoid provoking the British to ally with the French against them. Almost regardless of German long-term ambitions, it would have served them better to have Britain as friend rather than foe. The naval arms race contributed to forming two blocks in Europe, fighting against each other in World War I, with Germany dominant on one side and Britain and France on the other.

During World War I Germany possessed a strong Navy, but not strong enough seriously to challenge the Royal Navy. The only major battle at sea was the famous Battle of Jutland in 1916. Both sides tried to claim the battle as a victory, but the outcome of the battle was not clear-cut. The British lost more ships, but on the other hand many German ships had to be repaired after the battle. Furthermore, the Royal Navy had forced the Hochseeflotte to return to its bases, where it was to remain for the duration of the war. This was a major success, as the main British aim was to protect the merchant shipping so vital to her ability to conduct war.

Both sides, of course, analysed the Battle of Jutland thoroughly to extract useful lessons. In Britain, much attention was devoted to the vulnerability of the battle cruisers and to fire control. Before World War I the British First Sea Lord, Admiral John Arbuthnot Fisher, had argued that the battleships should be replaced by battle cruisers. The latter were, at the expense of armour protection, characterized by high speed and a powerful armament. With their efficient armament they were supposed to engage enemy ships at long range, while their high speed would allow them to determine when, where and how the battle was to be fought. Heavy armour would thus be superfluous. Since three British battle cruisers blew up after being hit during the Battle of Jutland, their protection was called into question. The British experts were quite convinced that the German battle cruisers had remained afloat despite receiving several hits.

A problem partly related to the vulnerability of the battle cruisers had been the German ability to score quick hits at long range, usually before the British gunners found their mark. This was a serious disadvantage for British battle cruisers, which had been designed on the premise that they should be able to engage the enemy at ranges long enough to render him unable to return fire effectively. The experiences from the Battle of Jutland contributed to a reduction of the British battle cruiser programmes. Only three British battle cruisers were ever completed after Jutland, two of them the already launched *Repulse* and *Renown*. The third was the battle cruiser *Hood*. There was still much work remaining before the latter was completed and some of the lessons from Jutland were incorporated into her design.

For the Germans, the lessons from Jutland did not revolve mainly around the issue of ship design. Rather, their problem was much more fundamental: how to achieve freedom of action. The strong Royal Navy possessed favourably located bases, which allowed it to prevent the Germans from reaching the Atlantic. Any hopes that production of ships would turn the scales in German favour were unfounded. Admittedly there were heavy naval ships being completed at German shipyards, but even more could be expected to be commissioned by the Royal Navy in the future.

Although the Germans were tactically on the defensive, the strategic roles were actually the opposite. It was the British who defended their merchant shipping and the Germans who tried to attack it. Since the German Navy was confined to a few poorly located bases on the coast of the North Sea, the British Navy could keep the Germans curbed. All German attempts to break out into the Atlantic had failed. The alternative found by the Germans was to go *under* the British blockade, instead of through or around it. The submarine eventually became the principal German weapon to attack British shipping during World War I.

However, although the sinking by German submarines of numerous merchant ships during World War I severely strained the British war effort, they could not knock Britain out of the war. After stubborn resistance from their own top leadership, the British finally adopted the convoy system, which reduced the threat from the German submarines to manageable proportions. German submarine warfare was also one of the chief reasons behind President Woodrow Wilson's decision to declare war on Germany in 1917. The American involvement contributed heavily to the German defeat late in 1918, when she was forced to sue for armistice and then to accept the Versailles Treaty. In an attempt permanently eliminate the threat of the German Navy, the British demanded that the German warships should be surrendered. However, the Germans chose to sink most of their ships rather than give them up to their former opponent. Nevertheless, with the German ships on the bottom of the sea, the main British objective had been achieved.

The Versailles Treaty forced many limitations upon Germany, including reductions to her Navy. She was forbidden submarines completely, as well as any surface ships above 10,000 tons. Such limitations forced German naval strategists to be content with hypothetical speculations on a future war, as a useful German Navy simply did not exist.

Britain had emerged victorious from World War I, but it was an appallingly costly victory, politically and economically, as well as in terms of human suffering. The general public wanted to avoid yet more carnage of the same kind at almost any cost. Due to the general exhaustion after the war, there were strong sentiments in favour of reducing military spending.

The United States and Japan had emerged from World War I stronger and more capable of challenging British dominance at sea. The rivalry between France and Italy was a threatening cloud and a naval arms race loomed ominously. The depleted economies would be severely strained if vast sums of money were spent on large naval vessels. To prevent yet another naval arms race, a conference was held in Washington 1921–22, where size limitations were imposed upon the signatory powers. Germany did not attend, as she was already limited by the Versailles Treaty, but the victors of World War I—the United States, Great Britain, France, Japan and Italy—participated.. During the conference the participants agreed upper limits to the total tonnage of each nation's battle fleet. The Royal Navy was allowed to complete the two *Nelson* class battleships, but otherwise production of battleships and battle cruisers was halted. In some cases battleship projects that were already underway were converted to aircraft carriers.

The Interwar Years

It comes as no surprise that officers in the German Navy had ample reason to reconsider their strategic concepts after World War I, but too had to reconsider their naval strategies. While the limitations enforced by the Treaty of Washington prevented battleship production, resources were devoted to development of aircraft carriers. How and to what extent aircraft would influence naval operations remained uncertain during these years. The effect that the use of mines and submarines might have on the conduct of naval operations was still unforeseen.

For the Royal Navy, it was not only a matter of thoroughly dissem-inating its revised tactical and operational concepts; the strategic situation too might be in a process of change that was decidedly unwelcome. During World War I, Japan had fought alongside Britain, but the course of events in the Far East was ominous, as it suggested that Japan might become hostile to Britain. A conflict with Japan was serious even if British interests elsewhere in the world were not threatened. But if war broke out in Europe and if Japan commenced hostilities in the Far East, Britain would have to depend on support from the United States.

Great Britain imported numerous different products, from cars and crude oil to cereals and tinned meat. Her domestic food production only sufficed to feed about half the population. For obvious reasons, the products had to reach the British Isles by sea. For her trade, Britain possessed 4,000 merchant ships, of which at least 2,500 were sailing at any given moment.[3] The most important task for the Royal Navy was to protect the vital sea lanes. However, the Royal Navy also had many other tasks, as the British Empire covered considerable parts of the globe. During the 1930s, it gradually became apparent that the size of the Empire placed such vast demands on the Royal Navy that it would be strained beyond its capacity if war broke out. As long as France balanced Italy and the United States held Japan in check, the strategy could be maintained, but if support from France or the United States were to disappear, the situation would become intolerable.

Since the British trade routes from the United States and Canada converged as they approached the home country, it was particularly important to protect the Northern Atlantic. But at this time few dangers seemed to threaten the North Atlantic trade routes. Neither Japan nor Italy could seriously threaten British trade routes in the North Atlantic, and the German surface forces were far too small to effectively challenge the Royal Navy. German submarines posed a more serious threat; here, the British placed high hopes on a technological solution. With a clear memory of the German submarine attacks during World War I, the British developed ASDIC, a system that could detect submerged submarines. Aided by ASDIC, the Royal Navy confidently believed the threat from German submarines could effectively be countered. When Germany began re-arming after Adolf Hitler came to power in 1933, British superiority in the North Atlantic seemed more than adequate. To build major warships required time and in this period the German Navy had no such vessels in service. It would require less time to build submarines, but the Royal Navy felt confident that the ASDIC system could handle the submarine threat.

Other problems than British superiority at sea were discussed among the German naval staff. In Germany, the Navy had always been considered secondary to the Army. When the Luftwaffe was created as a separate force, the Navy became the third priority. This was not surprising. Germany's most dangerous enemies were the Soviet Union, Poland, Czechoslovakia and France, all land powers with strong armies. Until the middle of the 1930s, Poland, Czechoslovakia or France would probably have been able to defeat Germany. Even later the three powers could probably have defeated Germany, had they cooperated effectively. The Russians should also be included in these strategic considerations. Although the Soviet Union did not have a land border with Germany, it could nevertheless interfere in a war involving Poland or Czechoslovakia. In this context, Germany had no realistic alternative to a strong army and an air force that was developed to cooperate with the Army. Neither a strategic air force nor a strong navy could be expected to produce decisive results, except during a long war, the kind of war Germany was not expected to win anyway.

Like Britain, Germany had few domestic raw materials. In the event of war, import across the seas would be impossible and inevitably all imports would have to travel via land. Thus, the primary task for the German Navy was not to protect her own sea routes, but to attack the trade routes of other belligerents. Exactly how this was to be achieved, remained an unanswered question. During World War II, German naval warfare would eventually be directed first and foremost against Great Britain, but in fact a war against Britain had never been something Hitler strived for. Rather he hoped that Britain would not participate in a war on the continent. All the other countries that Germany could face in war had, with the exception of France, no major interests on the seas. To attack France with naval forces from Germany was highly impractical. Altogether it was not clear what role the German Navy should have in case of war.

Within the German Navy itself hopes for a more prominent role had never been extinguished. Should the necessity arise, German naval

officers held that the main responsibility for waging war against the
British would fall on the Navy. How to do it was of course more difficult
to say. Admiral Karl Dönitz, commander of the German submarines,
believed he had found a solution. If the German submarines attacked on
the surface during the night, it would be very difficult for the ASDIC
system to detect them, since it was designed to detect submerged
submarines. Under cover of darkness, the low silhouette of the submarine
would make it almost invisible to observers on board surface ships, while
the submarine would find it easier to find merchant ships, whose high
silhouette would be clearly visible against the lighter night sky. If the
submarines also operated in groups, Dönitz believed they would be able
to attack convoys even if the latter were escorted by enemy warships.
Small-scale tests, conducted in the second half of the 1930s, suggested
that he might be correct. However, most high-ranking German naval
officers were not willing to spend large sums of money on submarines, as
they believed strongly in the value of the major surface ships.

The first major German ships built after World War I were three
vessels that have proved difficult to classify. They have alternately been
called pocket battleships, armoured cruisers and heavy cruisers. Their
names were *Deutschland* (later renamed *Lützow*), *Admiral Graf Spee*
and *Admiral Scheer*. The ships were armed with 28cm guns and were
fairly well protected. They had diesel engines, which limited their speed
to 26 knots but their radius of action was exceptionally large. It was
intended that they should attack enemy shipping on the Atlantic. If
confronted with an enemy battleship they would use their superior
speed to evade it, while they could use their heavy artillery if they met
faster adversaries. Their excellent radius of action would enable
operations in areas far from home bases, including the southern
Atlantic and the Indian Ocean. The Germans called this strategy
Kreuzerkrieg, cruiser warfare.

The design of the pocket battleships had certain shortcomings. The
British battle cruisers *Repulse*, *Renown* and *Hood* were faster, better
protected and more heavily armed. Furthermore, the French battle
cruiser *Dunkerque* was completed about the same time as the Germans
constructed the three pocket battleships. She was also faster, better
protected and carried more powerful armament than the German
pocket battleships. It was unlikely that the German pocket battleships
would face any of these adversaries, since the French as well as the

British Navy had other tasks than chasing German pocket battleships. In the future however, more ships would be introduced and they were almost certain to be quicker and more powerful than the German pocket battleships. The Germans themselves had such ships on the drawing table, to go into production soon.

Nonetheless, the pocket battleships were indicative of future maritime strategy for the Germans. They could operate alone or in small groups on the vast expanses of the oceans. By staying outside the main shipping lanes, they could unexpectedly attack lonely merchant ships or convoys that lacked strong escort. A prerequisite for this strategy was supply ships, which the Germans stationed in desolate areas of the oceans, where few ships sailed. From the supply ships the warships could refuel, replenish ammunition and get various stores. Furthermore, it was necessary to move from the home bases to the Atlantic undetected, that is, beyond the line Northern Ireland – Iceland – Greenland. This would be especially difficult if war had already commenced, since the Royal Navy would then be in an excellent position to block the routes between Great Britain and Norway. However, if the ships had already sailed before war broke out, they could be ordered by radio to begin cruiser warfare as soon as war had been declared. Nevertheless, sooner or later the pocket battleships would still have to return to Germany, to rest their crews and to provide maintenance or repairs to ships damaged in battle. They would be forced to travel through waters dominated by the Royal Navy in order to return to Germany, and then again as they made their way back to the Atlantic. No matter how the Germans thought about the problems, there was always some inherent disadvantage.

In the 1930s the naval arms race began in earnest. After the three pocket battleships, in 1935 the German Navy began building two heavy ships, the *Scharnhorst* and *Gneisenau*. They are sometimes called battle cruisers, but that is actually quite inappropriate, as a battle cruiser was characterized by high speed at the expense of protection. The two ships were indeed fast, capable of 32 knots, but also well protected. However, their armament was weak, as they did not receive the six 38cm guns that had been intended for them, but were rather given nine 28cm guns. Undoubtedly these ships were more suited to cruiser warfare on the Atlantic, compared to other German ships, although they did have one weakness. The *Scharnhorst* and the *Gneisenau* were powered by a new type of high-pressure steam turbine that, despite low weight and small space requirements, generated much power. Unfortunately these were not as reliable as the older machines, which of course was a serious disadvantage during prolonged operations on the Atlantic.

Before the *Scharnhorst* and *Gneisenau* were commissioned, construction on the *Bismarck* and *Tirpitz* were begun. With the latter two ships, the German constructors expected to be ahead of all other navies. Like the *Scharnhorst* and *Gneisenau* the Bismarck-class had a few characteristics suggesting their usefulness against allied merchant shipping on the Atlantic. They had 12 15cm guns, well suited to engaging merchant ships or transports and the lighter naval vessels expected to escort convoys. The heavy guns could thereby be spared until a more equal opponent emerged on the horizon. It was important to use the 38cm guns as sparingly as possible, since the barrels of these high performance guns quickly wore out.

During the second half of the 1930s, many high ranking German naval officers became increasingly convinced that surface ships attacking convoys would be a major element in a war with Great Britain. The British were of course resolved to protect their crucial merchant shipping, which could be done in many ways. The British Home Fleet with its base at Scapa Flow in the Orkneys, could quickly reach waters between Norway and Scotland. This area could also be mined, to prevent German ships from reaching the Atlantic. The only remaining alternative for the Germans was the Channel, but this narrow strait was even easier to block and it seemed highly unlikely that the Germans would try to sail through the Channel with surface ships.

The British Navy was indeed very large, but it also contained many ships that were fairly old. In particular the battle fleet was quite old, as many of the ships originated from World War I. When World War II began in September 1939, the *Nelson* and *Rodney* were the most modern British battleships, despite the fact that they were almost 15 years old, and their speed of 23 knots was hardly sufficient to cope with the kind of warfare the Germans envisaged. Five new battleships were under construction, but the first of them was not expected to be in commission until late in 1940.

Despite the age many of its ships, the mere size of the Royal Navy was such that the Germans had to avoid battles between major ships. Speed was, as mentioned before, one way to avoid engagement; another was of course to avoid detection. In this respect two factors were particularly important: air power and the development of radar. Both the Germans and the British made considerable progress in radar development, but it was difficult to assess its effect on naval warfare. Air power was, by this time, a fairly mature technological system, but there was no agreement on how and to what extent it would affect naval warfare. Furthermore, in Britain as well as in Germany, the Navy and the Air Force often became absorbed by petty rivalry. Almost since its inception, the Royal Air Force had focused on forcing an opponent into submission by bombing industrial areas and cities. Naval warfare was almost regarded as an unnecessary waste by the commanders of the Royal Air Force. This was a serious disadvantage to the Royal Navy, as aerial reconnaissance could be extremely useful in detecting German ships trying to break out into the Atlantic. Certainly it was assumed that the Germans would try to use the cover of darkness and poor weather to avoid being detected, but it required quite some time to move from the German North Sea ports to the waters north of the British Isles. Luck was needed to cover the entire distance under conditions wholly unsuitable for reconnaissance aircraft. Coastal Command was the part of the Royal Air Force that was responsible for cooperating with the Navy. It was allotted aircraft, but often old models and not in abundant numbers.

The situation was hardly better on the German side. Admittedly, the Germans, in specific operations, managed to improvise very good cooperation between the Navy and Air Force, but this was accomplished rather by the initiative of local commanders, than as the result of a sound doctrine formulated by the top commanders of the respective branches. Hermann Göring's Luftwaffe showed no inclination to conduct long-term development work to produce the kind of equipment, units and techniques necessary effectively play an effective part in naval warfare on the Atlantic.

The difficulties encountered by the British and German naval strategists during the interwar period, when they pondered on how to fight the next war, were hardly unique. Military forces in peace time have to rely on many assumptions on what the future has in store. The purpose of a war and its actors can vary considerably. Swift technological progress, as was evident during the interwar period, makes it even more difficult. It was by no means obvious how submarines, aircraft, mines, carriers or battleships would develop.

CHAPTER 2

The First Attempt

On 1 September, 1939 the *Deutschland* and *Admiral Graf Spee* were at sea and awaited orders to attack British and French merchant shipping, while *Admiral Scheer* lay in dock, as her machinery needed maintenance. Furthermore, German supply ships were stationed in the Atlantic. One of them was the *Altmark*, who was detailed to support the *Graf Spee*. But the Germans also had other intentions for their supply ships. Warships aimed to capture their prey rather than sink them, so that they could take possession of the valuable cargoes merchant ships carried. German crews could then be transferred to the merchant ships, to sail them to Germany. Prisoners were then transferred from the German warships to the supply ships.

During the first days of the war, Hitler hesitated to permit cruiser warfare. He seems to have nurtured hopes that there would be no war with Great Britain and was unwilling to do anything that could push the British into a more hostile attitude towards Germany. His hopes were frustrated however, and towards the end of September 1939 the German warships on the Atlantic were instructed to initiate operations. The two pocket battleships accomplished little. The *Graf Spee* sank nine merchant ships and the *Deutschland* sank or captured only three. This was enough to make the allies deeply concerned about the threat from the raiders and they organized several task forces to chase the German ships out of their waters. It was not an easy task. The German ships were equipped with powerful radio transmitters that could jam the alarm signals from the merchant ships. With scant useful information, the Allies were hard-pressed to locate the German raiders.

Often the loss of a merchant ship was not recognized until several days after the actual sinking. The British Admiralty was therefore forced to rely on information that was outdated. It was also unclear to the Allies how many German raiders were at sea.

One of the British task forces finally located the *Admiral Graf Spee* off the coast of South America. It was one of the weaker groups, consisting of one heavy cruiser and two light cruisers. All of them were faster than the German ship, which could hardly avoid battle. The British commander, Captain Henry Harwood, did not hesitate to attack. The British heavy cruiser *Exeter* was seriously damaged in the ensuing action and forced to withdraw from battle, but the light cruisers continued the action. The *Admiral Graf Spee* was damaged too and the commander of the ship, Captain Langsdorff, decided to set course for Montevideo in Uruguay and put in at the neutral port. The two British light cruisers followed closely.

Once he had reached the port of Montevideo, Captain Langsdorff faced difficult decisions. He did not know whether the two British cruisers outside the port were the only enemy ships nearby, or if more ships were on the way. Finally he decided to blow his ship up, and committed suicide. The loss of the *Admiral Graf Spee* was a set-back for German maritime strategy. She had only scored limited success before she was lost. The *Deutschland* took advantage of poor weather to return to Germany and reached port on November 15, also without achieving significant results. After this operation, the ship was renamed the *Lützow*.

It was not only the pocket battleships that were used for cruiser warfare early in the war. The *Scharnhorst* and *Gneisenau* finished their period of testing and training early in the autumn of 1939 and were sent on a foray against British merchant shipping. The two ships had recently been fitted with secret equipment called Dete or E.M. II, later known as radar.

On 22 November 1939, the two battleships left Wilhelmshaven, with the *Gneisenau* as flagship. The force was commanded by Admiral Marschall. After passing through the lanes created in the German mine fields outside the North Sea coast, the squadron increased speed to 27 knots, while the new radar searched for enemy ships. Nothing was seen on the screens. At noon on 22 November the two battleships passed between Scotland and Norway, without noting any British counter measures. The weather became rougher. The wind got stronger and the seas became higher and higher. Even the battleships began to roll and several sailors on board the ships suffered from sea sickness, while wave after wave hit the decks. Late in the evening the ships set course towards Iceland. Later in the night, the gale abated, to the relief of many on board the two battleships. [4]

At dawn on 23 November, the weather was clear and visibility excellent. Nothing was seen along the horizon until late in the afternoon, when a merchant ship could be discerned at a position half-way between Iceland and the Faeroe islands. It was the British auxiliary cruiser *Rawalpindi*, an armed merchant ship that was patrolling the area. She had been sent out to assist in the search for the pocket battleship *Deutschland*, which was expected to head towards her home bases. [5]

On board the *Rawalpindi*, the commander, Edward Kennedy, saw the winter sun set on the horizon. The sea was calm and in the north a bank of fog drew nearer. It drifted towards a few distant icebergs that had recently gleamed white in the approaching twilight.

'Bridge!' the lookout in the foremast shouted. 'Ship starboard aft!'

Kennedy shifted his attention from north to south, where he discovered the silhouette of a major warship. It was the *Scharnhorst*, heading straight towards *Rawalpindi*. After briefly studying it through his binoculars, Kennedy incorrectly assumed that it must be the *Deutschland*. The captain ordered 'Action Stations!' followed swiftly by a command to alter course to port. His ship turned north, while smoke floats were lit. Thereafter a signal officer reported to Home Fleet that an enemy ship, probably the *Deutschland*, had been sighted. In situations like this, auxiliary cruisers were not expected to engage the enemy but were supposed to assist the heavy units of the Royal Navy to attack the enemy.

While the alarm bells rang in the ship and the *Rawalpindi* approached the bank of fog far too slowly, Kennedy saw how the German ship signalled to him with a signal light.

'Heave to!' one of the signalmen reported.

The German request was followed by the blast of a gun, and soon a column of water shot up in front of the auxiliary cruiser. Kennedy ignored the request. He continued towards the bank of fog, but he knew he would not make it in time. The gravity of the situation became even more apparent when he was informed that the smoke floats had died down. Kennedy quickly gave orders for a new course, this time

Scharnhorst and Gneisenau's Sortie

November 21–27, 1939

Jan Mayen

ARCTIC CIRCLE

ICELAND

24 Nov
25 Nov

23 Nov

Faeroe Isles

NORWAY

Shetland 22 Nov

26 Nov

27 Nov

Wilhelmshaven

IRELAND

ENGLAND

Set sail 21 Nov
Return to port 27 Nov

GERMANY

FRANCE

towards an iceberg that could provide some cover.

Suddenly another major warship was observed, further east, and for a short while the crew on board the *Rawalpindi* hoped it was a British cruiser. In fact, it was the *Gneisenau* and she was soon identified as a German battleship. Kennedy fully realized that his ship was doomed. While *Scharnhorst's* signal lamp sent yet another message, Kennedy turned towards his officers on the bridge.

'We'll fight them both, they'll sink us – and that will be that. Goodbye.' He shook the Chief's hand, turned on his heel and cleared the decks for action. Kennedy had been moulded by the traditions of the Royal Navy and surrender was unthinkable to him. The auxiliary cruiser was made ready for battle.

On the *Scharnhorst's* foretop, Captain Hoffmann watched incredulously how the *Rawalpindi* turned to starboard. 'What is she doing?' he exclaimed in astonishment. 'She can't intend to attack us?' But as the *Rawalpindi* completed her turn and approached on a south-southeasterly course, it indeed seemed as if the auxiliary cruiser was attacking. Three times Hoffman requested the *Rawalpindi* to stop and take her crew into safety, but the auxiliary cruiser showed no inclination to comply with the requests. The range was quickly reduced and soon amounted to little more than 5,000 metres. Finally, Hoffmann decided to sink the wilful ship, but the *Rawalpindi* opened fire first. Her port 15cm guns fired a salvo against the *Gneisenau*, which hit but failed to cause any damage. Shortly afterwards, the British ship fired a starboard salvo at the *Scharnhorst* and again scored, but without causing any damage. The protection of the German ships seemed too strong.

Nevertheless, the *Rawalpindi's* fire was not harmless and the Germans soon responded. The first shell from the *Scharnhorst* hit the boat deck just beneath the bridge. The radio room was destroyed and splinters from the explosion penetrated the floor of the bridge, killing most of the men there. It was the beginning of a quick execution of the poor *Rawalpindi*, as the Germans could hardly miss at the short range. The fire control was knocked out, thereafter one of the starboard guns. The electrical power to the ammunition lifts was put out of action. Kennedy, who had survived the massacre on the bridge, ordered the seven remaining guns to fire individually and ammunition to be carried to the guns.

The *Rawalpindi* suffered further hits. Her steering system was destroyed. Fires covered her from fore to aft and her guns were silenced one after the other. Somebody yelled that the captain was dead and the struggle against the German battleships gradually became a struggle to survive. A life boat turned upside down when it was lowered down to the sea. On the deck a number of shells had began rolling away from a knocked-out gun and a few seamen threw them overboard, to prevent them from reaching the flames and exploding. One of the loaders bellowed at his comrades to help him—he was so confused and shocked that he could not understand that the men he shouted at were already dead.

The inevitable end came as a shell from the *Scharnhorst* hit one of *Rawalpindi's* magazines. The ensuing explosion tore the hapless auxiliary cruiser apart and she sank quickly. A few life boats had already been launched and some of the crew had saved themselves. The men who remained on board the *Rawalpindi* dived into the ice-cold water. Unfortunately the *Scharnhorst* had come so close that her backwash turned some of the life boats upside down. The Germans stayed to help save British seamen, and this rescue work was in full swing when suddenly an unknown ship was sighted. The initial report from the *Rawalpindi* had reached Home Fleet and the light cruisers *Newcastle* and *Delhi* had been dispatched, together with their heavier sisters *Suffolk* and *Norfolk*. The *Newcastle* was the first to arrive on the scene. The Germans broke off the rescue when they saw the British warship and turned away in the twilight. The British cruiser vainly tried to follow them, but she could not match their speed. She had to turn back and save the survivors of the *Rawalpindi*. Only 38 men from her complement of 276 survived.[6]

Admiral Marschall seemed to believe that the British would be able to order warships to the area far more swiftly than was actually the case and consequently he ordered his squadron back to German bases. Soon visibility deteriorated, thus facilitating his attempt to return undetected. The barometer fell and a gale began to blow. The *Scharnhorst* and *Gneisenau* scarcely reduced their but proceeded at 27 knots in the violent weather. On 27 November they reached Wilhelmshaven.[7]

After these fumbling efforts to initiate cruiser warfare in the Atlantic, the strategic situation changed to such an extent that further German attempts to reach the Atlantic were temporarily abandoned. Scandinavia suddenly attracted Hitler's attention. Several factors were behind his newly awakened interest in northern Europe. The commander-in-chief of the German Navy, Admiral Raeder, advocated an invasion of Norway, arguing that the German Navy might find far better bases along the Norwegian coast. Such bases could not easily be blockaded by the Royal Navy and could be used for submarines as well as surface vessels. There were also strong fears that the Royal Navy might block shipments of Swedish iron ore, which was shipped from the port at Narvik to Germany. The iron ore was crucial to Germany's ongoing war efforts. At first Hitler was indifferent to the warnings, but after he had met the leader of the Norwegian fascist party, Vidkun Quisling, and seen reports that the allies planned to attack Scandinavia, he decided to occupy Norway and Denmark. The preparations for this operation, code named Weserübung, called for a halt to the cruiser warfare in the Atlantic.

When Germany attacked Norway and Denmark on April 9, most of her Navy was involved. Several of the assumptions upon which the Germans had based their plans quickly proved wrong. Among other things, Norwegian resistance was tougher than expected. The hopes that tankers would reach Norwegian ports undetected turned out to be unfounded. The German Navy suffered serious losses: one heavy cruiser, two light cruisers and ten destroyers. Further, two battleships, one heavy cruiser, one light cruiser and one pocket battleship were damaged and required several months in shipyards before again being capable of operations. During the summer of 1940, only the heavy cruiser *Admiral Hipper* was available for operations in the Atlantic. The recently conquered bases were of little value when hardly any ships were available.

Plans for cruiser warfare had to be postponed further during the summer of 1940. The German Navy was expected to take active part in Operation Sealion, the planned invasion of Great Britain. The Kriegsmarine had to keep its few heavy units ready if the operation were initiated. Not until 17 September, when Hitler shelved Operation Sealion, could Raeder and his colleagues seriously begin to reconsider forays into the Atlantic.

The Royal Navy had also been prepared for Operation Sealion. A significant portion of her destroyers and escort ships were tied up in the Channel ports, in case of a German invasion. The German submarines were able to attack weakly protected British convoys, while many of the escort ships were awaiting a German invasion of Britain. Although the

British could not know what Hitler had decided, from mid-September they grew increasingly confident that there would be no German invasion during 1940, not least because of the difficult weather that could be expected during the autumn. As the Germans lacked real landing craft, they had to rely on prams and various other vessels of limited seaworthiness, so calm weather was a prerequisite for invasion. Furthermore, their inferiority at sea forced the Germans to rely on air support from the Luftwaffe, which also required good weather in order to operate effectively.

From mid-September onwards, there were likely to be long periods when the weather would not be appropriate for an invasion. When the Battle of Britain failed to weaken the RAF significantly, so that it remained a force to be reckoned with, it was clear that the imminent danger of invasion was over. The Royal Navy was able to send many of its ships to escort the convoys on the Atlantic. Consequently, losses of merchant ships declined during the latter part of 1940. Thus Raeder had good reason to use his surface ships to increase the pressure on the shipping lanes in the Atlantic. In short, he wanted to use the German Navy in what he regarded as its primary role, that of attacking British imports over the sea.

Both sides began to devote a larger share of their resources to the war in the Atlantic, but a few factors favoured Germany, making her prospects look brighter compared to the situation one year earlier. France had been knocked out of the war, while Italy had entered it, which meant that the situation in the Mediterranean had changed dramatically. The Royal Navy had to send many ships to Alexandria and Gibraltar to counter Mussolini's ambitions. The Home Fleet was further strained by the fact that larger areas had to be patrolled after the German conquest of Norway.

The time had come to begin operations against the British sea trade.

CHAPTER 3

Preparations

During a rainy day early in June 1940, Lieutenant Burkard von Müllenheim-Rechberg arrived at Hamburg to begin his duty on the battleship *Bismarck*. The German armed forces had achieved triumph after triumph and the German army was about to complete its greatest victory since the beginning of the war. France had lost her army and the British had already evacuated their expeditionary force from Dunkirk. Despite this, in a speech on national radio, Winston Churchill declared: 'We shall never surrender.' However, at the time, there was little to suggest that the Allies would emerge victorious in the war.

Müllenheim-Rechberg arrived one day ahead of the time appointed and decided to stay at a hotel. Thirty years old, and with a long family tradition of serving in the armed forces, he had served 11 years with the German Navy. His father had been killed in action during World War I, at the Argonne in France. His younger brother, a Luftwaffe officer, died in Poland on the second day of the war. Müllenheim-Rechberg was a gunner and had served on the *Scharnhorst* when she sank the *Rawalpindi*. He was to serve on the *Bismarck* as fourth artillery officer.

After his breakfast, Müllenheim-Rechberg went to the harbour, where he saw the battleship *Bismarck* for the first time. Not even the army of workers swarming the deck and the superstructures, or the tools, machinery, cables and welding equipment which concealed substantial parts of the ship, could diminish the impression of an enormously powerful ship. The silhouette strongly resembled that of the *Scharnhorst*, but everything was larger, longer and much wider. The main artillery was the most powerful ever carried by a German battleship and she was cluttered up with lighter guns and anti-aircraft weapons. From a distance, Müllenheim-Rechberg contemplated his new home for a few minutes, before going on board and asking for the captain's cabin. He could not avoid feeling somewhat nervous when he met the man who commanded the battleship that was soon to be the most powerful in service.

'Lieutenant Müllenheim-Rechberg reporting aboard for duty, as ordered.'

Captain Ernst Lindemann was 16 years older than Müllenheim-Rechberg, delicately built, but with strong willpower. He was an ambitious man, but he never let his ambitions affect those around him. The crews that served under Lindemann respected him as a selfless and skilled leader. Such impressions filled Müllenheim-Rechberg already during the first seconds, when Lindemann inspected the young officer without letting his bright blue eyes turn away. The commander of the *Bismarck* smiled and said: 'Welcome on board.'

Lindemann quickly made Müllenheim-Rechberg acquainted with his duties on board the ship. 'I regard it as my objective,' the captain said, 'to make this powerful and beautiful ship ready for action as soon as possible. I expect your complete participation.'

Müllenheim-Rechberg answered that he intended to do his duty to the best of his ability.

'As you already know,' continued Lindemann, who like Müllenheim-Rechberg was a gunner, 'as you are trained to direct fire from heavy guns, your battle station will be in the aft fire control centre. But as it will not be sufficient to keep you fully occupied until the ship is commissioned, I have decided to make you my aide.'

Müllenheim-Rechberg was pleasantly surprised by the appointment. It would make his work much more interesting.

'Oh, yes, there was one more thing,' Lindemann added after completing his instructions. 'In the future, I would prefer to hear people talk about *Bismarck* in the masculine form. A ship as powerful as this can only be a *he*, not a *she*.'

Language puritans may shudder at this breach of the traditional naval language, but undoubtedly the *Bismarck* was a very powerful ship. Yet, the battleship era was not old when World War II broke out. As late as the time of the American Civil War (1860–1865), wooden ships fought alongside early metal vessels. Subsequently, naval technology developed at an accelerated pace, but the British *Dreadnought* was the first really modern battleship. She carried a uniform armament and was commissioned in 1905. Most other heavy ships became obsolete, although the Royal Navy was not alone in the development of similar ships. During World War I, further advances in naval technology led to bigger and more powerful ships. Even more impressive designs existed when the war ended in 1918, but the ensuing peace and the Washington conference brought production of battleships to a standstill. It was not until the 1930s, when war began to seem possible, that governments began to increase spending on naval ship construction. As a consequence, many navies had two generations of battleships in World War II.

After World War I, the German situation differed markedly from the British. Germany had been deprived of all her heavy ships by the Treaty of Versailles, and had to rebuild the Navy from scratch after Hitler's seizure of power. Therefore, unlike the Royal Navy, the Kriegsmarine mainly consisted of modern vessels when war broke out in 1939. Still, the German Navy had only relatively few ships, and still lacked carriers and battleships with powerful armament. Matters seemed to be improving though. Construction of the *Bismarck* and her sister ship the *Tirpitz* had proceeded well. These two ships, much anticipated by the German Navy, had been laid down in 1936.

According to international treaties, battleships were not allowed to exceed 35,000 tons. When the *Bismarck* and *Tirpitz* were designed, the limit was neglected from the very beginning, but the Germans were by no means alone in doing that. The *Bismarck* had a design displacement of 41,700 tons (over 50,000 fully loaded). The British battleships of the *King George V* class also exceeded 35,000 tons, but not by as much as the *Bismarck* and *Tirpitz* did. Battleships constructed in the United States, Italy and France at the time also also exceeded treaty commitments.

The two German battleships were bigger than their contemporary rivals in the Royal Navy and all the extra weight was devoted to armour protection. Altogether, armour made up 41% of the weight.[8] In the *King George V* class, armour protection made up 32% of the weight.[9] Of course the protection of a battleship also depends on the layout and the quality of the armour steel, but the percentages indicates how highly protection was prioritized when the *Bismarck* was designed.

Such immense ships involved an expenditure of vast amounts of money. Overall cost for the *Bismarck* was almost 200 million

Reichsmark, an enormous sum in those days. To put it into perspective, the same amount of money could have bought the Germans almost 1,700 main battle tanks, or a similar number of fighter planes. Another impressive figure is the number of working hours needed to build the ship. It was estimated that the shipyard spent almost six million working hours on the project, and further time was of course spent at the subcontractors.[10]

Even a major power like Germany had relatively few companies that could undertake a project of these dimensions. The contract for the *Bismarck* was given to Blohm & Voss in Hamburg, while the Kriegsmarinewerft in Wilhelmshaven was assigned the project to build the *Tirpitz*. On 1 July, 1936, the *Bismarck* was laid down, followed four months later by the *Tirpitz*. For almost three years, the two ships lay on their slipways, while they gradually assumed the shape designed. The Germans wanted to build more battleships, ships even larger than the *Bismarck* class. However, as long as the *Bismarck* and *Tirpitz* were on the slipway, these projects had to wait.

On 14 February, 1939 many of the leading figures in the Nazi machinery of power arrived at the Blohm & Voss shipyard in Hamburg, among them Hitler, Heinrich Himmler, Hermann Göring, Joachim von Ribbentrop and Martin Bormann. The commander-in-chief of the German Navy, Grand Admiral Raeder, attended as well. The time had come to launch and christen the battleship. The latter honour was given to Dorothea von Loewenfeld, grandchild of the 'Iron Chancellor,' Otto von Bismarck. Before a crowd numbering several thousand, Hitler delivered a speech where he urged the crew of the battleship to show the same resolve and spirit as Chancellor Bismarck had exhibited.[11]

Immediately afterwards, the *Bismarck* began to slide down majestically into the Elbe River, but much work remained to be done on her before she could be taken over by the Kriegsmarine. In fact, another year and a half remained before the Navy could begin testing the brand new ship.

Besides the cost, the long construction time indicates the enormity of the project. Almost five years passed from the day work on the *Bismarck* was begun, until the Kriegsmarine had a combat-ready ship with a fully trained crew. In addition, the construction of the ship had been preceded by years of discussions, studies, drafts, sketches and plans before the final design was approved.

A battleship was like a small community. The crew on board the ship numbered about 2,000 men and they needed enough room to endure weeks or months at sea. They had to take care of their hygiene, so facilities such as numerous showers had to be included on the ship. Also, they needed some amusement. On the *Bismarck* there was a pub where beer could be served. The battleship had its own bakery and a laundry. Dirty clothes amounting to several hundred kilograms could be cleaned in a single day. Doctors were needed too, and there were operating theatres where surgery could be performed. Similarly a dentist served on the ship, fully equipped to attend the dental problems suffered by the seamen. A tailor's workshop repaired and modified clothes, a necessity on a journey extending over several months. Specialists like tailors, bakers and launderers had further duties during battle, such as assisting the medical orderlies.

To all of this was of course added everything that had to do with the firepower and survivability of the ship. *Bismarck* had eight 38cm guns in four twin turrets. Each gun barrel was almost 20m long and weighed over 100 tons, while a complete turret, with all its armour, weighed over 1,000 tons. The turrets revolved on a bearing ring, but they were not actually fixed. Rather they had just been lifted into place on the barbettes. Once in place their considerable weight would keep them there.

In future actions, it was vital to enter combat from an advantageous position, which required good intelligence. Radar had been fitted to some British and German warships (although, oddly, both sides seem to have doubted that their opponents had radar) but was yet not in widespread use. Radar technology was at an early stage of its development, which meant that its performance could vary greatly from ship to ship. Many of the early systems were fragile and it was necessary to have skilled technicians on board, who could quickly repair any damage.

Another important source of information was hydrophones, which were used to listen for noise, for example from propellers. Skilled operators were needed to extract as much valuable information as possible from the hydrophones.

Many other positions required specialised skills. The machinery fitted to the *Bismarck* was of an advanced type, constructed to generate

138,000 horsepower, but during trials it exceeded the intended output. Figures ranging from 150,000 to 163,000 horsepower can be found in different sources.[12] Whatever the final number, it was sufficient to propel the *Bismarck* at speeds exceeding 30 knots, surpassing the designer's calculations. Machinery of this kind required considerable expertise on behalf of the men who operated it. As the machines were specifically designed for the *Bismarck* and *Tirpitz*, familiarity with them was needed. At sea the engineers and technicians were responsible for the ship's ability to move at high speed, which was vital to its ability to survive. The knowledge needed to locate any defects or damage that might occur at sea, and repair or confine them, was indispensable.

A battleship also had various teams responsible for damage control. Most important was to fight, prevent and extinguish fires and to keep the hull reasonably watertight. Despite the metal construction, fire was a major hazard. There were many flammable substances on a ship, for example electrical components, fabric, wood, paper and various fluids. Furthermore, the *Bismarck* carried about 1,000 tons of ammunition and about 8,000 tons of fuel oil at full load. Consequently, there was serious danger of fire, especially as the ships were intended for battle. Ammunition for the heavy guns was stowed in armoured compartments and hoisted to the guns mechanically, as the rounds were far too heavy to be manhandled. The ships had many anti-aircraft guns, and due to their very high rate of fire, some ammunition had to be kept near the respective guns. Even hits from lighter weapons could cause fires near the anti-aircraft guns.

Despite her 18,000 tons of armour, plus the armour on the gun turrets, the *Bismarck* could not be entirely protected.[13] First and foremost, the armour was concentrated around the most vital components, such as machinery and ammunition compartments. Thus in common with other vessels in all navies, large areas of the ship lacked armour protection.

It was assumed that combat might well result in water entering the hull. To a significant degree it was the task of the damage control teams to handle such situations. As soon as leaks occurred, the damage control parties attempted to seal them, work that might be difficult as well as dangerous. To cope with inflow of water, large sections of the ship could purposely be filled with water to restore trim. If water entered the starboard side, pumps could fill compartments on the port side with water. In the same manner, water could be pumped into the aft, if a leak had occurred in the bow. The pumping systems were elaborate and were sufficient to keep minor leaks in check.

If the sea was reasonably calm, the bow could be filled with water to such an extent that the propellers came up above the waterline, allowing repairs to propellers or rudders. A ship as large as the *Bismarck* could take in thousands of tons of water, without being seriously affected, partly because she was divided into 22 watertight sections, which were further subdivided. It seemed that nothing relating to her survivability had been left to chance.

Enemy shells were not the only threat to the battleships. Torpedoes from surface vessels, submarines or aircraft were another serious threat. During the interwar period, aerial bombs had been emphasized as a major threat against heavy warships. The infamous American Air Force officer Billy Mitchell had arranged a trial where bombs from aircraft sank one of the German battleships handed over to the victors after World War I. During World War II however, it would become apparent that it was difficult to hit ships with heavy bombs while they moved at sea. Dive bombers were more accurate, but they could not carry the heavy bombs needed to cause serious damage to modern battleships.[14] Torpedoes were a different matter, though. They could be launched by smaller aircraft, including those operating from carriers. As the torpedo detonated beneath the waterline, it could cause serious damage. The large underwater surface of a battleship precluded all ideas to use armour for torpedo protection. Rather, the underwater protection system was designed to bring the torpedo to detonate as far as possible from the vital parts of the ship. Also, the careful subdivision into watertight compartments was an important element in a ship's ability to absorb torpedo hits. A wide beam created opportunities for an effective underwater protection and the *Bismarck* had an unusually wide beam of 36 metres, which was four metres wider than the largest British battleships.[15]

The *Bismarck* had other advantages over her British counterparts. Her protection was better, and her speed slightly superior to the British battleships, although the actual speed a ship was able to attain could vary with the amount of fuel on board. Another important advantage was her superior radius of action, especially at speeds exceeding 25 knots, when she could cover twice the distance before having to re-fuel, a most important characteristic during operations in the Atlantic.

The main artillery of the *Bismarck* was eight 38cm guns mounted in two twin turrets fore and two aft, as had been employed many times before, by British battleships as well as German ones. Most British capital ships launched before 1920 and still in service at the outbreak of World War II carried exactly this armament, for example, the battlecruiser *Hood*. The *Bismarck's* guns were more modern though, with greater range, a higher rate of fire and her shells could penetrate thicker armour.

Evidently the *Bismarck* had several advantages compared to the ships she was likely to confront and expectations of her performance were high. However, success in naval battles did not depend on the performance of the ships alone. The crews had to be well trained and the commanders had to possess the necessary experience. Most of the seamen serving on the *Bismarck* were about 21 years old, all of them had volunteered. First they were given basic military training and education for the specific positions to which they had been assigned, which was conducted while Blohm & Voss completed the *Bismarck*. Some of the crew also assisted at the shipyard, in particular those who were responsible for various technical systems. For example, many of those who were eventually to serve in the machinery assisted when turbines, high-pressure steam pipes and fire extinguishing systems were fitted to the battleship. Similarly some of the gunners attended the mounting of guns. Also, some crewmen were sent away to subcontractors, to gain knowledge about generators and other electrical components.[16]

By the summer of 1940, the *Bismarck* was almost complete. On 24 August she was officially taken over by the Kriegsmarine. It was a cloudy day. Cold easterly winds swept over Hamburg and created small waves with white crests on the River Elbe. The crew of the *Bismarck* had assembled on deck, from the forecastle to the quarterdeck, while Lindemann addressed his men. Müllenheim-Rechberg was present, as was Commander Hans Oels, the second-in-command, the Lieutenant Commanders Adalbert Schneider and Helmut Albrecht, 1st and 2nd artillery officers respectively, Lieutenant Commander Wolf Neumann, the navigation officer, and Lieutenant Commander Walter Lehmann, the Chief Engineer.

When Müllenheim-Rechberg began his service on board the *Bismarck* almost two months earlier, it had seemed likely that the war would end soon and the guns of the battleship would not have to be fired in anger. But German hopes for a peace with Great Britain gradually faded as the summer months passed. Early in July, the Royal Navy attacked and sank part of the French Navy at Oran, a clear demonstration of British resolve. Shortly afterwards, the Luftwaffe, commanded by Reichsmarschall Hermann Göring, intensified attacks on England, but the Royal Air Force offered harder resistance than expected. When Lindemann addressed his officers and seamen, there was no doubt that he expected his ships to be committed to combat.

'Soldiers on the *Bismarck*,' he began. 'The awaited day when our beautiful, great ship is commissioned has arrived.' He expressed his thanks to the Blohm & Voss shipyard for its extensive effort to deliver the ship and added that he expected every man to do his utmost to make the *Bismarck* an instrument of war. The German nation was in a momentous period requiring a military solution.

'Politics is not created by speeches, shooting displays or songs,' he said and quoted the man whose name the battleship carried. 'It is only created by blood and iron.' The German Navy colours were hoisted. The *Bismarck* was now officially a warship.[17]

CHAPTER 4

Cruiser Warfare

As Operation Sealion petered out during the autumn of 1940, Admiral Raeder and his colleagues in the Kriegsmarine began to focus on the kind of warfare they believed in. Following the damage sustained in the spring of 1940, a sense of optimism was renewed when many ships returned from the shipyards. Among the ships expected to be fully serviceable soon were the battleships *Gneisenau* and *Scharnhorst*. They had formed a task force during the attack on Norway in April 1940, when Admiral Marschall had been in command. If sent to the Atlantic together, they would form a powerful group, menacing British merchant shipping. The long winter nights would also improve chances of them being able to break out undetected into the Atlantic. Finally Raeder could embark on the large-scale warfare against merchant shipping that he had advocated for so long. His intention was not only to sink merchant ships; Raeder hoped that the countermeasures that the Royal Navy would be forced to take would also disrupt British trade.

The German Navy had deployed surface ships against British merchant shipping since spring 1940, but these were not regular warships. Instead, the Germans had employed *Hilfkreuzer*—armed merchant ships not unlike the British *Rawalpindi*.[18] By fitting the weapons behind doors and other forms of cover, they could be effectively disguised, yet quickly made ready to fire on prey as it appeared. Mostly, the ships sailed under false colours, to avoid recognition. Their combat capabilities were far too low to engage regular warships and the German Navy did not expect any grand achievements from them. However, by sailing outside normal convoy routes, the *Hilfzkreuzer* could search for merchant ships sailing alone, approach disguised and when they had approached close enough, sink or capture them. Usually the Germans preferred to employ their armed merchant ship in areas like the Indian Ocean and the South Atlantic, where many ships sailed unescorted. Protected convoys were left to the regular German warships, which had not appeared in the Atlantic since the autumn of 1939.

The first German warship to reach the Atlantic Ocean in 1940 was the pocket battleship *Admiral Scheer*. She had been at Wilhelmshaven when the war broke out, as she needed a major overhaul. Her anti-aircraft artillery shot down a Wellington bomber while she was at the yard, but otherwise she took no part in combat during the first year of the war. When she was at last fully refitted, her crew needed training to attain combat readiness. She was sent to the Baltic for a month of intensive exercise, before finally being declared ready for operations. On 23 October, 1940 she weighed anchor at Gdynia and steered west on the Baltic. After passing Denmark, she sailed north. Undetected she continued towards the Atlantic and a week after departing from Gdynia, she passed through the Denmark Strait between Greenland and Iceland. The first phase, regarded as the most difficult part of the operation by the Germans, had been successfully completed. The *Admiral Scheer* could begin searching for prey.[19]

She did not have to wait long. Early on 5 November she discovered the lone *Mopan* and promptly sank her. A few hours later the lookouts on board the *Admiral Scheer* caught sight of an even more tempting quarry, the convoy HX84—a British convoy numbering no less than 37 merchant ships. The escort consisted of only a single ship, the armed merchant ship *Jervis Bay*. Since the sun was about to set, the commander on board *Jervis Bay*, Captain Edward Fegen, decided to accept battle with the *Admiral Scheer*, hoping that the convoy could scatter and as many merchant ships as possible disappear in darkness before the German ship got too close. Fegen's decision doomed his ship. The battle was hopelessly uneven. A sailor in the convoy thought the action resembled a bulldog attacking a bear. The 40 year old, 152mm guns fitted to *Jervis Bay* did not even have the range needed to success-fully engage the German warship. Nevertheless, the British fired incessantly, while laying smoke to protect the ships of the convoy. The battle could only end in one way and after 24 minutes it was over. The

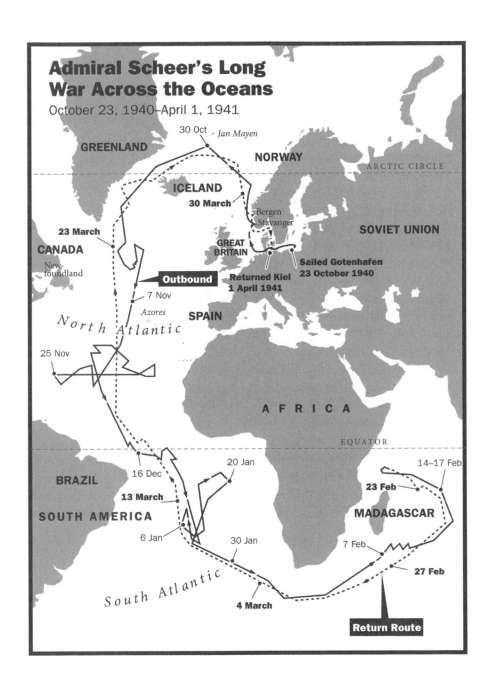

Admiral Scheer's Long War Across the Oceans

October 23, 1940–April 1, 1941

Jervis Bay had become a burning wreck. *Admiral Scheer* sank five merchant ships and another three were damaged, but the rest of the convoy escaped. Later, 65 men from the gallant crew of the *Jervis Bay* were saved by the Swedish freighter *Stureholm*.[20]

A few uneventful days followed, until on 12 November *Admiral Scheer* met with the tanker *Eurofeld* and the supply ship *Nordmark*. A few days were spent bunkering diesel oil and taking on supplies. Also, 68 prisoners from the *Mopan* were transferred to the supply ship, before the *Admiral Scheer* resumed her search for prey. The results were not impressive. After almost a month had passed, she had only been able to add another two ships to her tally. Again, the pocket battleship met with the supply ship to bunker. On this occasion, the opportunity was used to perform some maintenance on her diesel engines, before the *Admiral Scheer* set course for the southern Atlantic on 15 December.[21]

While the *Admiral Scheer* operated in the Atlantic, the heavy cruiser *Admiral Hipper* was prepared for the same purpose. In fact, she had sailed already on 24 September, with the intention of reaching the Atlantic, but before passing the Skagerrak she had problems with her machines. She was forced to return to Germany and spent two months in the yard, until she was finally fit again. On 30 November she left harbour, commanded by Captain Wilhelm Meisel, to attack convoys in the Atlantic. The operation was called *Nordseetour*. At first she searched in vain for Allied shipping and had to survive extremely bad weather. Problems with her machinery ensued, but they could at least be temporarily repaired. The *Admiral Hipper* bunkered fuel oil from German supply ships, first on 12 December, then on 16 and 22 December, but after three weeks at sea not a single enemy ship had been seen. However, on the night before Christmas Eve, her radar finally picked up an echo. She had found the British troop convoy WS5A about 600 miles west of Cape Finistere. Unlike HX84, which had been attacked by *Admiral Scheer* seven weeks earlier, the WS5A was escorted by regular British warships: the heavy cruiser *Berwick* and a few smaller ships. Captain Meisel did not become aware of the British escort, and shadowed the convoy with the intention of attacking it after dawn. While it still was dark, Meisel closed the distance to the convoy and fired a number of torpedoes, but none hit. The German commander was not deterred and pursued his intention to attack at dawn, this time relying on his guns. Almost immediately the lookouts on the *Admiral Hipper* found the *Berwick*. Meisel decided to attack the British cruiser. In the ensuing battle, *Berwick* was damaged and forced to withdraw from the battle, but enough time had passed to allow the convoy to scatter and all merchant ships evaded the *Admiral Hipper*. The German cruiser had not been hit, but nevertheless Meisel decided to break off the operation and steer towards Brest. His decision was based mainly on the defects in the machinery, which he wanted to correct. On Christmas Day the lone freighter *Dumma* was found and sunk. It was the only success scored by the *Admiral Hipper* during Operation Nordseetour. She reached Brest on 27 December.[22]

Operation Nordseetour and the battle between the *Admiral Hipper* and the *Berwick* exposed shortcomings in the German Navy's concept of cruiser warfare. Although the German ship came out unscathed, the action had certainly put her at risk. When encountering an escort of equal strength, the German ship might at least suffer damage and impaired mobility. This was a serious risk, considering the kind of warfare Raeder intended to conduct.

On the very day the *Admiral Hipper* reached Brest, a meeting took place in Berlin, attended by Hitler, Raeder and a few other high ranking naval officers. The German Navy was already planning for the *Admiral Hipper's* next voyage and Hitler wanted to know the purpose. Raeder explained that the *Admiral Hipper* was only to attack enemy supply lines, concentrating on the convoys as the main target but avoiding the escorts. She should only accept battle with the escort if it was clearly inferior in armament. Hitler concurred. It is possible that this discussion resulted from discontentment with Meisel's decision to engage a British heavy cruiser.[23]

The *Admiral Scheer* spent the last weeks of 1940 without much drama. The only exception was on 18 December, when her floatplane found the refrigerator ship *Duquesa*, which carried food, including about 15 million eggs and 3,000 tons of meat. She was captured and her cargo came in handy for the German ships operating in the Atlantic. In addition to the *Admiral Scheer* and the *Admiral Hipper*, the armed merchant ships *Thor* and *Pinguin*, several blockade runners and captured ships were also operating in the Atlantic. The *Duquesa* supplied several German ships with food, before she was finally sunk after two months.[24]

While the *Admiral Scheer* and *Admiral Hipper* ravaged the Atlantic, the two battleships *Gneisenau* and *Scharnhorst* also prepared for an operation in the same waters. They sailed on 28 December, but very bad weather caused damage to the *Gneisenau* and both ships had to return at an early stage. The *Gneisenau* was quickly repaired, but the operation was postponed for a month.

Meanwhile the *Admiral Scheer* patrolled the South Atlantic. She did not score any notable successes. No convoy was found, but a Norwegian tanker was captured and sent to Bordeaux on 17 January. Three days later two freighters were sunk, but subsequently the

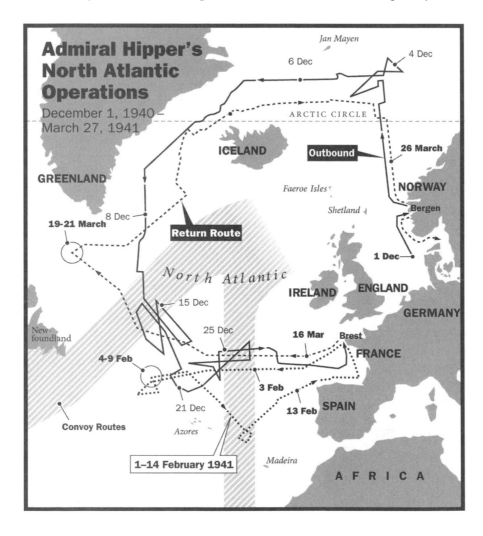

Admiral Hipper's North Atlantic Operations
December 1, 1940–
March 27, 1941

Admiral Scheer ran out of luck. Late in January she set course for the Indian Ocean, hoping to find better opportunities for success there. On 3 February the *Admiral Scheer* passed south of the Cape of Good Hope.[25]

Major accomplishments had thus far eluded the German naval ships in the Atlantic, but Raeder indulged in expectations of more success when the *Scharnhorst* and *Gneisenau* reached the transatlantic convoy routes. Due to the mishap with the *Gneisenau*, Admiral Lütjens, who commanded the squadron, was given more time to think about the best way to use his two battleships. As they were much more powerful than the *Admiral Hipper* and *Admiral Scheer*, Lütjens could attack escorted convoys without hesitating. When Meisel had attacked WSA5, despite the cruiser included in its escort, his action had bordered on the foolhardy. Considering the scarcity of German heavy vessels, it was imperative to keep them ready for action, or else it would be impossible for the German Navy to maintain the threat against the British convoy routes. With two battleships at his disposal, Lütjens would be in a very different position, as the British could hardly be expected to include stronger ships than cruisers in their escorts. However, damage to the German ships still had to be avoided. Prudence suggested that combat had to be conducted at long range, to avoid the menace from torpedoes.[26]

Lutjens did not have to answer the question of how to attack convoys until his squadron reached the Atlantic, and he had a difficult journey ahead of him. The main problem was the ice in the Baltic, the Danish Belts and the Kattegat. The severe cold in January 1941 had resulted in ice with a thickness of about 30cm in the Danish Belts. Under normal conditions, Lütjens would have preferred to pass through the Belts in darkness, to avoid being seen from the coast, but in the present icy conditions it seemed impossible to sail through the narrow straits during night. The German squadron would have to make the passage in full daylight, when Allied agents as well as men and women from the Danish resistance could easily see the ships. When he had passed through the Great Belt, his two battleships would sail towards the Skagen, where escorts would join them, before continuing in the direction of Norway.

The forthcoming operation was given the name 'Berlin' and was a much more whole-hearted attempt to implement the cruiser warfare concept, compared to the small-scale operations conducted so far.

Lütjens was a good choice to lead Operation Berlin, since he was the German naval officer with most experience at sea. In 1914 he commanded a torpedo boat unit and saw frequent action in World War I. When the Germans invaded Norway in April 1940, Lütjens commanded the *Gneisenau* and *Scharnhorst*, which had been tasked with the mission to protect the landings at Narvik and Trondheim.[27]

Lütjens was a purposeful and calculating commander who carefully considered his alternatives. He preferred to retain freedom of action for as long as possible and was not given to impulsive decisions. Rather, he carefully weighed risks and opportunities. Success in Operation Berlin would depend greatly on the squadron's ability to remain unobserved on the high seas and to maintain the element of surprise. The commander would have to display good judgement in estimating when the British convoys left ports, what course they followed and how fast they sailed, so as best to assess the risks of attack. Errors of judgement would severely curtail prospects of sinking a significant amount of British shipping.[28] Lütjens seemed to possess exactly the traits needed to plan and conduct the kind of operation envisaged.

Operation Berlin provides the best example of the realisation of the German concept of cruiser warfare. The first phase of the operation was the actual break out into the Atlantic.

The passage from Kiel and, further on, the Kattegat and Skagerrak were narrow, icy and partly mined, requiring coordination with icebreakers, minesweepers, antisubmarine units and other escorts to get the squadron through safely, without jeopardizing secrecy. Tankers and supply ships had to be stationed in the Atlantic, to enable the battleships to remain there for months. Rendezvous places and signals had to be established well in advance, in order to minimize radio communication that could be intercepted by the British.[29]

Radio traffic was a major concern. To reduce the risks of British interception the Germans used a large number of code names for various coordinates. A number of locations at sea had been assigned brief codes, such as 'black 3' or 'red 15'. Without the specific tables needed, it was impossible to interpret the content of the messages. Furthermore, the actual transmissions could be briefer with the aid of the codes, making it more difficult to obtain bearings and estimate the position of the sender.[30]

Several frequencies and types of transmitters were used. The two battleships used ultra short wave for communication between them, as it was very difficult to intercept at longer distance. For reporting between the ships and the shore staffs, other frequencies were used. The weather forecasting used its own specific frequency band, as did communication between the ships and the Luftwaffe. Considering the geography, it was unlikely that the battleships would cooperate with the Luftwaffe far out on the Atlantic, but during the initial and the final phases of the operation, coordination with air power might be needed. Communication with the supply ships was governed by special regulations, as was the use of special crews that were to sail captured ships to German-controlled harbours in the Bay of Biscay. All of these details had to be specified and included in the orders issued before the operation began.[31] However, once the battleships had reached the north Atlantic, Lütjens emphasized that he would make the decisions as the events unfolded. [32]

CHAPTER 5

'Now you pretend to be dead'

On 14 September, 1940 the *Bismarck* turned her bow towards the Elbe. Few people on the brinks of the wide river noted her departure and in the evening she anchored at Brunsbüttel, where the Elbe meets the North Sea. During the night, Bomber Command attacked the harbour and the anti-aircraft guns on board the *Bismarck* opened fire. [33]

The air attack was hardly new to the Germans. At this stage of the war, British aircraft repeatedly attacked German ports during the dark hours. Bomber Command tried to disrupt the German build-up for Operation Sealion and the German North Sea coast was well within range of its aircraft. But although transport shipping was the target, there remained a risk that the *Bismarck* would be hit, with possible delays caused by damage from bombs. However, the Germans were fortunate to have a large area where their ships could be almost safe from enemy aircraft—the Baltic. They were also fortunate in that their ships did not have to sail around Jutland because the Nordostsee-Kanal could be used to move ships from Brunsbüttel to Kiel. This was the route that the *Bismarck* took to the Baltic on 16 September. The voyage through the channel was not without suspense. No air attacks were noted, but the narrowness of the passage meant that the ship travelled at action stations. The crew had to stand by at full alert and all hatches and doors were closed. It was not an easy task to manoeuvre the large ship, with its powerful machinery, but everything went according to plan and in the evening of 17 September the battleship berthed at Kiel.[34]

The *Bismarck* remained at Kiel for a week to adjust the gunnery, before setting course towards Gdynia. In the Baltic, the crew were able to test the ship thoroughly and train so as to make the best use of her qualities. To a battleship, firepower was of course of particular importance. In November 1940 comprehensive firing exercises began, an activity that was repeated many times in the future. Exercises were important in ensuring that the crew gained proficiency, but also in revealing any defects, before the *Bismarck* was sent into battle. Firing exercises involved the men serving the guns, as well as those who were responsible for fire control, observation, range finding and many other tasks. The comprehensive training actions required men to master more than their own tasks, such as the exercises designed to train them in emergency procedures used, for example, when parts of the fire control system had been put out of action. This knowledge could prove invaluable in real combat conditions. Obviously the crew was also trained to manage a number of lesser tasks: signalling, encryption, quickly reaching battle stations at alarms, damage control, caring for wounded and so on. All shortcomings and frictions had to be eliminated before commencing operations.

Testing the *Bismarck*

To hit an enemy ship at long range, many factors had to be considered. The *Bismarck's* heavy guns could hurl an 800kg shell more than 36km. At such distances even a 250m long battleship was a small target and several circumstances had to be taken account of. To begin with, the firing ship's own course and speed, roll and pitch affected her firing. The range to the target had to be correctly assessed, but as it could take up to a minute for the shells to reach the target, the projectile's speed and course had to be properly estimated. When firing at long range, the shell travelled through high trajectories where air conditions might be different than those at sea level. Air density, wind direction and other characteristics had to be accounted for.

To make these calculations quickly and consistently, sensors fed data to calculation machines, which were a sort of mechanical forerunner to modern computers. Manual routines provided a back up in case the calculation machines were damaged or received incorrect data. The first salvo was not expected to hit the target, but if the shells did not land too far away, a minor correction might suffice. Observers usually noted the splashes where shells landed, which could be as high as multi-storey buildings. This made them easy to see, at least when the number of ships was not so great that splashes from different ships became confused.

Despite all the technical devices, man remained a crucial component in the overall firing system. Range finding is an example. The Germans used stereoscopic rangefinders, which were very accurate, but placed heavy demands on the operators in the early stages of battle, causing the operators to tire earlier. The British used a slightly simpler system, which was less taxing for the operators over the course of the battle.

During firing exercises, sub-calibre inserts were mostly used for the heavy guns, a method mandated by the wear imposed from full-calibre firing. The *Bismarck's* 38cm guns had an estimated barrel life of about 200 to 250 rounds, before accuracy dropped due to the imposed wear.[35] With the inserts, range was reduced, but was nevertheless sufficient for training. Recoil was also much reduced by using inserts. Some of the strains of battle were therefore not imposed during the exercises.

However, at last the day came when the heavy guns would fire full calibre shells for the first time. Excitement filled the crew on board the battleship. No one knew with certainty how the ship would react to the stresses of fire. Full steam was ordered and heat mounted in the boiler rooms. The pressure was 56 atmospheres. Everything related to *Bismarck's* mobility had to withstand the shock of firing, as the ship would probably move at high speed during battle. Suddenly the sounds caused by the sea were drowned by an enormous crack. *Bismarck* trembled sideways, as eight 800kg shells left the guns at a velocity of 3,000km/h. It took less than 5ms for the shells to travel through the barrels, but in this brief period of time the guns developed more than 60 million Hpw.[36]

The broadside was a violent strain even for a large battleship, but the machines continued to work flawlessly, as did everything else on the *Bismarck*. A few minor items that had not been sufficiently secured dashed around and a few light bulbs went out, but the ship was quite stable in the sea, a result of her unusually large beam. She was ready for a new salvo as soon as the guns had been reloaded, a process of about 20 seconds. The crew had already held great confidence in their ship, but it was boosted even further by the live fire exercise.

Success in battle was heavily influenced by the officers' ability to make correct decisions, for example by making weather, wind and light into factors that worked to their favour. The *Bismarck* had several highly qualified artillery officers, like Schneider, Albrecht and Müllenheim-Rechberg and the test results were very encouraging. Captain Voss, commander of the training department, made a visit to the battleship. When Voss took leave, he approached Schneider last and confided the parting words to him: 'My highest wish to you is that the first enemy ship to appear before the *Bismarck's* guns is the *Hood*—and you will sink her.'[37]

In addition to firing exercises, it was important to learn how the ship behaved in various weather conditions and tactical manoeuvres. The *Bismarck* was a good sea boat, with moderate pitch and roll. Even during sharp sheers, she heeled fairly little. Of course her speed at full steam pressure was tested too. At most 30.8 knots were measured, an impressive speed for such a colossus and sufficient to steam away from most capital ships at the time.

At an early stage the crew tested whether it would be possible to steer the ship by using propellers only. The rudders were locked in a midship position, whereupon different numbers of revolutions were tried on the three propellers. Usually it was possible to steer a ship with proper combinations of speed on the different propellers, but on the *Bismarck* it did not work well. She could not maintain course, was caught by the wind and moved uncontrollably. The problems were caused by the proximity of the three propellers, which produced too little leverage. There seemed to be little risk of it ever having consequences in battle, so probably few on board bothered about it.[38]

Nevertheless, there was a risk that the steering system could be damaged and a recurring exercise was 'measures after being hit in the steering system.' Müllenheim-Rechberg later recalled a particular moment during this drill. The exercise assumed that some of the compartments had been flooded. According to the directives, the men who occupied these compartments were assumed to have perished in the explosion or to have been drowned by the inrushing seawater. During the exercise, many seamen had turned their hats back to front, as was usually done to indicate that they were playing the role of the dead.

'But if it happens in real life,' one of the seamen asked, 'would we be killed?'

'Of course,' the leader of the exercise, a Lieutenant named Friedrich Cardinal, answered, 'so, now you turn your hats and pretend to be dead.' A few seconds later, perhaps after he realized the effect his words could have on the men, he tried to gloss over them. 'But of course,' he said and smiled at the seamen, 'the probability of such a hit is perhaps one in a hundred thousand, virtually nil.'[39]

Many would later remember his assurance with bitterness.

During the period of training, testing and evaluation, the *Bismarck* developed close ties with a much smaller ship: the submarine *U-556*. Both ships were built at the same shipyard, Blohm & Voss, and they had often been moored in the same harbour. *U-556* was commanded by Lieutenant Herbert Wohlfarth, who was known as 'the knight Parsifal' within the German Navy and was also regarded as an inveterate prankster. In January 1941 he had left the shipyard for a testing tour, when he sighted the *Bismarck*, which also was at sea for testing. Wohlfahrt got a humorous twinkle in his eyes and semaphored a brief message to the *Bismarck*. To begin with, he had the impudence to address Lindemann as an equal, which was a breach of etiquette. The second half of the message did not improve matters, as it read: 'What a nice boat you have.'

Considering Lindemann's feelings for the *Bismarck*, the use of the word 'boat' instead of 'ship' was not the most appropriate choice. The *Bismarck* soon signalled back an acidic reply: 'What boat, Lieutenant?'

Wohlfahrt was not discouraged. He semaphored: 'I can do this, can you?,' whereupon *U-556* submerged and disappeared from the sight of the officers on *Bismarck's* bridge.[40]

To mitigate the effects of the incident, Wohlfahrt invited Lindemann and some of his officers to dinner a few weeks later and when *U-556* was officially declared ready for operations, he asked Lindemann to grant him a service. A small submarine did not, of course, have musicians in its crew, but Wohlfahrt wanted to give the ceremony more splendour. He asked Lindemann if he could use the battleship's orchestra. As a sign of gratitude, the crew of *U-556* presented the *Bismarck* with a homemade certificate that promised support:

We U556 (500t) declare before Neptune, ruler of oceans, seas, lakes, rivers, creeks, ponds and rills, that we will stand by our big brother, the battleship Bismarck (42,000t), everyday, on the water, on land and even in the air.

It was dated 28 January,1941, at Hamburg, and signed 'commander and crew of U-556'. It included two illustrations. The first showed the knight Parsifal, who used his sword to protect the *Bismarck* from attacking British aircraft and stopped approaching torpedoes with his left hand. The other illustration showed how the godfather towed the battleship, whose machinery had broken down.[41] Lindemann acknowledged the godfathership by placing the certificate in the mess room, next to photographes of Adolf Hitler and Otto von Bismarck. At the time it was regarded as a kind gesture between two warships, but it would prove to be a very bad omen

CHAPTER 6

'For the first time in history...'

While the *Bismarck* and her crew still worked to become fully ready for operations, the first major step towards an escalation of the German cruiser warfare was taken. At 04.00 hours on 22 January, 1941 the *Scharnhorst* and *Gneisenau* weighed anchor at Kiel. They did not hurry. After about an hour and a half, they passed the lightship outside the harbour. Three hours later the two battleships anchored again, just outside the southern mouth of the Great Belt. This evening, the first on a long voyage, went by without any mishaps, as did the following night. Before sunrise, the two ships again weighed anchor.

From the Admiral's bridge on the *Gneisenau*, Lütjens watched over the passage through the Great Belt. Thus far everything had gone according to plan. No mechanical defects had occurred and only German aircraft and sea birds could be seen in the sky. In the afternoon there was a slight mishap. A mysterious scrunching noise was heard on the *Gnesienau*, creating concern that the ship had grounded. The fears did not prove justified. Half an hour before midnight on 23 January, the squadron anchored about eight miles north of Läsö, after having completed the passage through the Great Belt.[42]

Very careful planning had preceded the operation, but of course there were matters that could not be predicted. On the morning of 24 January the first problems were enountered. Minesweepers and submarine chasers were expected to attach themselves to the squadron as an escort. Four minesweepers appeared, but no other vessels. The two battleships were forced to remain at anchor, a delay that was not welcomed by Lütjens and his staff. An officer was sent ashore to find some kind of explanation. He learned that the submarine chasers had been unable to leave port because of the icy conditions. A 24-hour delay proved inevitable, with all the attendant risks of exposing the operation to the enemy. As if this was not enough, a message reached Lütjens, telling him that two British cruisers, together with several merchant ships, had been observed near the Norwegian coast. This was a surprise, but the most plausible explanation for the observation was a British mine-laying operation. While Lütjens pondered on the consequences of the delay and the British activities, he received yet another message, this time from Marinegruppe Nord. It told him to return, because of the enemy's activities. The same message instructed him that lighthouses had been lit along the southern coast of Norway, to guide his squadron into Kristiansand. Consternation beset Lütjens. Did Marinegruppe Nord really believe he had left the Skagen without the destroyers? [43]

Obviously information was not communicated well between the land staffs. At 19.00 Lütjens decided to break radio silence. He informed those concerned that the two battleships still remained at the Skagen and that he intended to continue Operation Berlin, although not until 25 January when the submarine chasers had joined him. To break radio silence was a difficult decision, which suggests that Lütjens regarded the confusion on land as serious.[44]

On the morning of 25 January, Lütjens' squadron finally set course towards Skagerrak, without any more mishaps. According to the original plan, his battleships should already have passed Stadlandet on the western coast of Norway, but as yet there were no indications that the whereabouts of his squadron had been discovered. Lütjens chose to focus on the next stage of the operation, which was how to get past the Scotland – Greenland line. He had two alternatives. The first was to try to reach the Atlantic as quickly as possible, the second was to go for the Arctic Ocean before trying to break out. If he chose the latter alternative, he could refuel his ships from the tanker *Adria*, which was waiting at a rendezvous point near Jan Mayen. [45] Thereafter he could try to break out through the Denmark Strait.

When the sun rose above the horizon on 26 January, it revealed a clear sky. Such weather was not propitious for a break-out attempt and Lütjens decided to go for the *Adria* and bunker oil. However, during the night a weather forecast told him to expect poor visibility south of

Iceland. Lütjens decided to seize the opportunity and altered his previous decision. Early on 27 January the two battleships, which had reached a position midway between the Lofoten Islands and Iceland, altered course towards southwest, which would enable them to pass between Iceland and the Faeroe Islands. As his ships had not yet covered much distance, they still had plenty of fuel oil on board. Thus, they could just as well bunker from tankers south of Greenland.[46]

So far the operation had proceeded well, except for the confusion at the Skaw, but at this point the lack of useful intelligence information began to have an effect. Was the whereabouts of the German squadron still unknown to the British, or was the Admiralty in the midst of organizing countermeasures? Usually the Luftwaffe dispatched reconnaissance aircraft to see which vessels were at anchor in Scapa Flow, but poor weather had hampered the efforts of the German air force. Lütjens did not know if the Home Fleet's ships were at sea or in their bases. The interception of radio communications had produced little substantial information for Lütjens, although there were reports of freighters south of Iceland. The reports also hinted at unidentified warships in the same area, news that was too unclear to be of much guidance. Lütjens interpreted the information as indicating a reinforcement of the British surveillance in the area, but he could not be sure. The bad weather would at least render any efforts to search for his squadron difficult. There was no clear-cut alternative for him to choose, so in the present situation, the weather forecast persuaded him to make an attempt to break out south of Iceland.[47]

On the evening of 27 January, visibility was still quite good. The battleships increased speed from 25 to 27 knots, while a beautiful display of Aurora Borealis illuminated the arctic night. At midnight Lütjens' ships reached the area where the distance between Iceland and the Faeroes was the shortest, and where the risk of detection appeared greatest. The lookouts strained every nerve, while their binoculars searched along the dim horizon. Imagination could play tricks with them in the darkness. Clouds at the horizon could appear like the silhouettes of ships and white swells could be mistaken for the surge caused by periscopes. At the same time the radar operators focused on their screens. The radar was the best means of finding possible enemies and it was especially alarming to Lütjens when *Gneisenau's* radar suddenly malfunctioned at 05.00 hours with several hours of darkness remaining. The technicians immediately began to search for the problem, which turned out to be a damaged transformer caused by a broken earth connection. The transformer could be replaced in a few hours, but while waiting for the radar to be repaired, the *Gneisenau* would be wholly dependent on her lookouts. Lütjens might have chosen to let the *Scharnhorst* take the lead, while he waited for *Gneisenau's* radar to be fully operable again, but instead he kept the positions in the squadron the same.[48]

More than an hour had passed while the technicians on board the *Gneisenau* worked to repair the radar. Suddenly one of the lookouts warned that he had observed a shadow on the port side. Lütjens immediately ordered a change of course, from southwest to west. The two battleships turned to starboard and began to sail along the southern coast of Iceland. At the same time, contrary to the weather forecast, visibility improved. Undoubtedly prospects of a successful break-out were reduced, particularly as dawn was imminent.[49]

Somewhat later, at about 06.20 hours an echo appeared on the *Scharnhorst's* radar and immediately afterwards the shadow once more became visible on the port side. Again the German reaction was prompt—a sharp, starboard turn. It was difficult to determine the kind of ship observed. It seemed too large to be a destroyer; maybe it was a light cruiser. After six minutes another shadow was observed on the port side by *Gneisenau's* lookouts. It approached quickly. Either it was a modern destroyer, of *Tribal*-class, or a light cruiser. Lütjens' squadron turned 90° to starboard, while he forbade any firing. He was not certain that the enemy had yet become aware of his presence; chances of an undetected break-out might still remain.[50]

A few minutes later, two lookouts observed what appeared to be torpedoes approaching. The battleships made a slight turn to starboard. By now, all the turns had put the two German battleships on a north-easterly course, with a speed of 28 knots. Three minutes later, at 06.33 hours, the squadron made a further slight turn to starboard, whereby the pursuing ship got astern. Subsequently the Germans held their course, but Lütjens wanted to increase speed further and ordered 30 knots. On the bridge, it seemed that the speed did not get as high as ordered and the men in the engine room were asked: 'What speed does the ship make?'

'It is making 28 knots,' was the immediate reply.

'When can we make 30 knots?'

'In ten minutes. The sharp turns caused a loss of speed.'[51]

However, it proved more difficult to reach 30 knots than expected. A safety valve to one of the turbines was released and limited the *Gneisenau's* speed. Lütjens ordered the two ships to make smoke for two minutes, beginning at 07.15 hours. This was a prudent measure, as *Gneisenau's* radar, which had just been put back in working order, detected four objects on the starboard side, and before 08.00 hours it detected a ship approaching quickly on the port side. Lütjens wasted no time. He immediately ordered a turn to starboard. Meanwhile the safety valve in the engine room had been fixed and *Gneisenau* was able to make more than 30 knots. The distance to the enemy ships gradually increased and soon they were outside the range of the German radar. When the sun began to illuminate the area, at about 09.30 hours, the sea around the German ships was empty. [52]

All the manoeuvres had brought Lütjens' squadron far to the east. After the initial contacts, Lütjens had considered trying to outflank what appeared to be some sort of patrol line, but his hesitation grew with every contact. He knew precious little about enemy intentions and was no better informed as to which British ships were, or were not, in Scapa Flow at the time. It was certainly possible that one or even several powerful enemy squadrons were in the vicinity. If he persisted, he might very well encounter enemy ships in full daylight. Furthermore, a break-out attempt would involve the risk of meeting enemy ships on a collision course, and thus could at least initially deprive the Germans of taking advantage of the greater speed of their ships. Accordingly, he preferred to sail northeast, find the tanker *Adria*, bunker fuel oil and then try once again. [53]

The Germans continued on their northeasterly course for most of the day. Nothing remarkable happened before noon. The radar once again failed on the *Gnesienau*, but as visibility was excellent, it mattered little. At noon, mastheads became visible on the horizon. The distance was 34 kilometres and the Germans could not determine the type of ship. Possibly it was a cruiser of *Dido* or *Gloucester* class. In any case the ship was larger than a destroyer. Lütjens gambled that his ships would be more difficult to discern against the darker sky in the northeast, but as a precaution he also ordered a slight turn. The mysterious ship seemed to hold its course and soon its mastheads disappeared. During the afternoon a Sunderland aircraft was seen, but it did not seem to observe the two German ships. Everything seemed well and Lütjens sent a very brief radio message to Marinegruppe Nord: 'Towards *Adria* at rendezvous Karl.'[54]

While the two battleships headed towards the *Adria*, Lütjens had plenty of time to reflect on what had happened in the morning. The behaviour of the British had surprised him, as it had been irresolute and lethargic. Perhaps they had not been searching for *Scharnhorst* and *Gneisenau*. Something completely different may have caused their presence in the area south of Iceland. In that case it might have been a mere coincidence that they had been barring his way to the Atlantic. Maybe ships from the Home Fleet were in the area to receive a convoy, a kind of operation believed to be common by the Germans.

In fact, the Royal Navy had received information suggesting that the German battleships would attempt to break out onto the Atlantic a week earlier. Upon receiving the intelligence, Admiral John Tovey, the commander of the Home Fleet, decided to reinforce his patrolling of the waters between Iceland and the Faeroes. He was informed that the *Gneisenau* and *Scharnhorst* had passed through the Great Belt on 23 January and two days later he sailed with the battleships *Nelson*, *Rodney*, the battlecruiser *Repulse*, eight cruisers and 11 destroyers, to assume a position south of Iceland. Air reconnaissance was also directed to cover the area between Iceland and the Faeroes. Tovey estimated that a German break out was most likely on the nights between 25 and 27 January.[55]

Tovey's assessment was quite accurate. However, the friction that is typical to military operations upset Lütjens' plans and therefore, Tovey's estimates. First, the unintended delay off the Skagen caused Lütjens to lose a day. His wavering between an immediate break out and refuelling from the *Adria* meant further loss of time, again almost a day. Consequently he arrived at the area south of Iceland later than he had intended and also later than Tovey had calculated. Thus, when the German ships finally reached the British patrolling area, the Home Fleet crews were already tired and Tovey had began to nurture doubts about the German break-out. Perhaps this is at least part of the reason that Lütjens found British reactions awkward. Also, the German radar proved very valuable; despite the temporary breakdowns, on several occasions it detected Royal Navy ships. The British on the other hand seem to have observed the Germans only once.[56]

Lütjens now had plenty of time at his disposal in which to consider his next course of action after bunkering fuel oil. Should he once more try to break out south of Iceland, or would it be better to try the Denmark Strait, between Greenland and Iceland? The disadvantage with the latter alternative was the narrow passage between the north-western tip of Iceland and the pack ice along the coast of Greenland. On the other hand, British air reconnaissance was less likely to jeopardize the secrecy of the break out. Near the pack ice, fog was often created when the humid air was cooled by the ice. This was a clear advantage to Lütjens' plans. Finally, no convoys would sail through the Denmark Strait, which reduced the risk for a chance encounter with other ships. Early on 29 January, Lütjens reported to Marinegruppe Nord that he intended to break out through the Denmark Strait, after topping up his ships from the tanker *Adria*.[57]

Towards the evening the two ships approached the rendezvous point Karl, where the *Adria* was waiting. To avoid reaching the tanker before dawn, the battleships gradually reduced speed until they sailed at only 5 knots. Simultaneously the temperature fell sharply, and when the *Adria* was finally found, the thermometer indicated −15° Celsius, while the wind caused the falling snow to whirl around. Visibility was so poor that the tanker would probably not have been found, had the battleships not been equipped with radar. Bunkering proved to be a hazardous undertaking. The sharp cold and the icebergs floating in the area caused hardship and danger. On several occasions bunkering had to be interrupted and ice-free areas had to be found before resuming. The men on the ships worked as hard as they could, but inevitably the procedure required more time than Lütjens had hoped. Finally, at 23.00 hourss on 1 February both the *Gneisenau* and *Scharnhorst* had completed refuelling and Lütjens' squadron was ready to make another attempt to reach the Atlantic.[58]

Lütjens not only worried about British forces searching for him, with the intention of forcing him to battle. He also had to consider the activities of other German ships and the consequences they might have for Operation Berlin. He knew that the *Admiral Hipper* had put in at Brest, for an overhaul of her machines, which had almost been completed. The cruiser would soon put to sea for another voyage on the Atlantic. If the *Admiral Hipper* reached the convoy routes before

Lütjens' squadron had passed through the Denmark Strait, British countermeasures might affect his chances to successfully break out.[59]

Lütjens' concerns were well founded. The *Admiral Hipper* conducted testing on 29 January, which showed that the ship was fully operational. She left Brest on 1 February. Her commander had been instructed to avoid the major convoy routes. The supreme command of the German Navy had understood what Lütjens intended to do and instructed *Admiral Hipper* accordingly. Captain Meisel, was told first to bunker oil from a tanker on the Atlantic and then to await a signal to commence operations against British shipping. [60]

These instructions suited Lütjens' plans. In the evening of 3 February his two battleships approached the Denmark Strait. The weather was not unfavourable, but neither was it ideal. Initially, clouds covered the sky, but visibility on the sea was fairly good. Gradually, fog increased along the ice edge, as Lütjens had expected. It was a critical phase of the break out operation. The Germans lacked up-to-date information on the ice conditions in the strait and large blocks of ice floated around and made navigation difficult. The radar scanned the area around the ships. Lookouts were on tenterhooks and the battleships were ready to fire immediately. Although no other ships were sighted, Lütjens ordered a speed of 23 knots, a swift pace considering the large ice floes drifting around, and set course towards a point ten miles north of the most northwesterly point of Iceland.[61]

At 03.30 hours, the alarm was sounded in the ships. The *Gneisenau's* radar had found a ship ahead, at a distance of 15 kilometres. Lütjens ordered a 30 degree starboard turn. Soon after he ordered yet another turn to starboard and decided to proceed. If the ship held its course, the Germans would pass on the western side behind the enemy ship. Gradually the distance lessened to 7,200m, but nothing suggested that the enemy had sighted the two German battleships. The Germans assumed the vessel was an armed merchant ship, which by now was located on the port side amidships, whereupon the range began to increase. The danger of being discovered was for the moment over.[62] The wide Atlantic was ahead of the squadron and Lütjens informed the crews:

'For the first time in history, German battleships have reached the Atlantic!'

Cruiser warfare could begin.

CHAPTER 7

Operation Berlin

After the successful break out, Lütjens' primary concern was to bunker fuel oil. At a certain point, about 100 miles south of Cape Farewell on the southern tip of Greenland, the tanker *Schlettstadt* waited. This point had the code name 'Schwarz' and Lütjens ordered his battleships to steer towards it. As Lütjens' squadron passed through the Denmark Strait, it left the area of Marinegruppe Nord and moved into the area controlled by Marinegruppe West. Lütjens radioed a brief report to Marinegruppe West, in which he declared his intention to commence operations against British shipping after 10 February. He not only wanted to report that he had reached the Marinegruppe West area, but also to ensure that the *Admiral Hipper* did not begin operations against British convoys too early. It was important to maintain the element of surprise.[63]

While bunkering proceeded, Lütjens and his staff planned future operations. The Germans had a fairly accurate picture of how the British convoys sailed. Convoys from the United States assembled near Halifax in Canada. From there they proceeded along the coast of Newfoundland and then continued along a northerly arch towards Britain. The route was chosen as it roughly followed a so-called great circle, which is the shortest route from one point to another on the globe, as the distance between meridians is shorter closer to the poles. The Germans suspected that convoys from Britain to America, usually consisting of empty ships, followed a route further south.

Lütjens' intelligence also told him that two British battleships, the *Ramillies* and *Revenge*, were based at Halifax. They were two of the

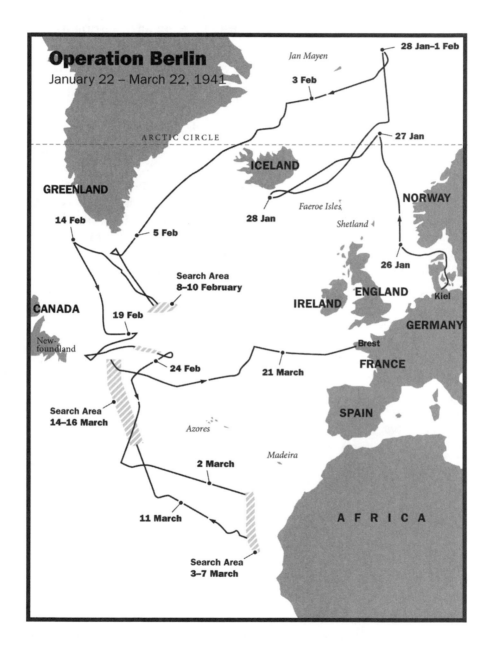

Operation Berlin
January 22 – March 22, 1941

28 Jan–1 Feb

Jan Mayen

3 Feb

27 Jan

ARCTIC CIRCLE

ICELAND

GREENLAND

NORWAY

14 Feb

5 Feb

Faeroe Isles

28 Jan

Shetland

26 Jan

Search Area
8–10 February

ENGLAND

Kiel

CANADA

IRELAND

GERMANY

19 Feb

New-
foundland

Brest

24 Feb

21 March

FRANCE

Search Area
14–16 March

SPAIN

Azores

Madeira

2 March

11 March

A F R I C A

Search Area
3–7 March

oldest battleships in service with the Royal Navy, but they were armed with 38cm guns, more powerful than the 28cm guns constituting the main armament of the *Gneisenau* and *Scharnhorst*. The intention had been to arm the two German battleships with six 38cm guns, divided into three twin turrets. However, the gun was still not fully developed when the *Scharnhorst* and *Gneisenau* were built. Instead, they had to put up with nine 28cm guns in triple turrets.

The *Ramillies* and *Revenge* followed convoys during the initial part of their voyage east, before turning back to Halifax and leaving the merchant ships to the protection of other vessels. With this weaker escort the convoys continued across the Atlantic, until they reached a point where units from the Home Fleet could meet them and assume responsibility for the final part of the voyage. Thus, Lütjens believed there was a sector in the Atlantic where the convoys lacked protection from heavy ships, which meant they would be very vulnerable.

A heavier armament would have been preferable, in case the German ships encountered the *Ramillies* or *Revenge*, but even with heavier guns it is doubtful that Lütjens would have issued fundamentally different instructions, compared to those he actually gave. He made it clear that opponents with firepower equal to that of the German ships should be avoided under all circumstances. The most fundamental prerequisite for cruiser warfare was the high speed of the German ships. Without it, the Royal Navy would be able to gather forces and sink the few German men-of-war. Compared to the *Ramillies* and *Revenge*, the German ships had an advantage of more than ten knots. As long as they were not damaged, *Scharnhorst* and *Gneisenau* could decline battle.

Lütjens estimated that the *Ramillies* and *Revenge* could escort convoys to a point about 1,000 miles east of Halifax. He intended to search for convoys east of that position. Close upon 10.00 hours on 6 February, the German battleships parted from the tanker and set course towards the area where Lütjens wanted to begin searching. He received an intelligence report stating that a convoy was assembling off Halifax, probably a fast convoy designated HX109. Also, a slow convoy, probably SC22, had just left Cape Breton.[64]

At dawn on 7 February the German battleships began searching for prey. They split and sailed across the route expected to be followed by the convoys. If nothing were found during the first day, the battleships would rapidly move east, to resume searching on the following day. Lütjens believed this scheme would optimize his chances of finding a convoy.

The first day passed without anything but sea birds being observed, but the following day offered far more drama. At 08.34 hours, lookouts on the *Gneisenau* observed a masthead towards the west. Funnel smoke rendered observation difficult, but the mast seemed to belong to a warship. Lütjens decided to proceed cautiously. He let the *Gneisenau* sheer towards the northeast, while sending a radio message to *Scharnhorst*. Lütjens informed Captain Cäsar Hoffmann, who commanded the *Scharnhorst*, about the position and course of the enemy observed, and instructed him to attack from the north at 10.30 hours, while the *Gneisenau* would attack from the south.[65]

At about 09.00 hours the masthead disappeared, but at 09.45 hours the *Gneisenau's* ultra shortwave radio sent a message: 'Fleet Commander to *Scharnhorst*. Convoy with at least five ships in quadrant 8435.'

The *Gneisenau* reduced speed to 15 knots and altered course to get into position for attack, but just before 10.00 hours her radio operators picked up a message: '*Scharnhorst* to Fleet Commander. Enemy battleship in quadrant 8198.'

Lütjens immediately called off the attack and gave orders to reassemble. The *Gneisenau* fled south and the *Scharnhorst* sailed north. What had initially appeared to be a promising target turned out to be too dangerous to pursue. [66]

Obviously it was a great disappointment to turn away from the convoy. Also, it was a surprise to encounter a battleship so far from the Canadian coast. This convoy had to be left to submarines for the time being. Instead, Lütjens intended to go for SC22. Lütjens believed the British had not yet identified his ships and that he still had the advantage of surprise. When the two German battleships met in the evening, Hoffmann reported to Lütjens that the *Scharnhorst* had approached the enemy battleship and tried to lure it to the north. At its closest, the enemy battleship had been within a range of 23 kilometres of the *Scharnhorst*. Hoffmann's intention had been to give the *Gneisenau* an excellent opportunity for attacking the convoy.[67]

Lütjens was perplexed. Hoffmann had ignored his instruction to avoid equal opponents; worst of all, the element of surprise was lost. Lütjens signalled that in the future he demanded strict obedience to his orders.[68]

It is fully understandable that Lütjens was angered by the loss of surprise, but it cannot be ignored that he had ordered Hoffmann to attack. Nor had the *Scharnhorst* closed the range to such an extent that the battleship was jeopardized. The question was to what degree Operation Berlin had been compromised. No clear answers could be found. The encounter with the enemy battleship, which in fact was the *Ramillies*, could very well have provoked a forceful reaction from the Royal Navy, but there was also a chance that the British had interpreted the incident incorrectly and not realized the magnitude of the danger to the convoy. Furthermore, Lütjens could not be certain that he had enjoyed the benefits of surprise before the encounter with the British battleship. The very fact that the *Ramillies* had sailed so far east might be an indication of British awareness of the German squadron.

Although he did not know it himself, Lütjens had been lucky. On board the *Ramillies*, the *Scharnhorst* had not been correctly identified. It was clearly understood that a German warship had been sighted, but it had been mistaken for a cruiser of the *Hipper* Class. Thus, the Royal Navy was still not aware that Lütjens' two battleships straddled the convoy routes. Probably the British expectation that either the *Admiral Hipper* or *Admiral Scheer* was heading towards bases in Germany contributed to the incorrect conclusions. Tovey believed that the *Ramillies* had indeed observed one of these two German ships and he sailed to block the approaches to Germany. Lütjens now had a free hand in the area where he searched for the convoys, save for any ships that escorted them.[69]

Despite the incident, and its possible consequences, Lütjens decided to resume searching on the following day. At 10.00 hours he received confirmation that the British had indeed become alarmed. An intelligence report from Marinegruppe West told him that a British unit at sea had sighted one or more ships, probably hostile. There was however a gleam of hope. The British might believe they had sighted the *Admiral Hipper*.[70] Lütjens hoped that Marinegruppe West would soon instruct the *Admiral Hipper* to initiate operations against convoys. He waited for a confirmation while searching along the assumed convoy routes east of Halifax, but no new messages reached him. At 21.56 he sent the short message: 'Operation disclosed by enemy.' As he had hoped, Marinegruppe West understood what he meant. A few hours later, the *Admiral Hipper* was instructed to take action.[71]

At dawn on 10 February the two battleships were at the positions from which they would begin searching. Almost immediately a grave problem was discovered on board the *Gneisenau*. Her machines had been contaminated with salt water, which caused her middle propeller shaft to be unusable. Her speed was reduced to 27 knots. The problem could be corrected at sea, but she could not generate full speed until the afternoon. At the same time a mast was again observed, but the smoke from the ship prevented the Germans from identifying whether it was a warship or a merchant ship. While the Germans raised steam pressure, the mysterious ship disappeared. The searching had not resulted in anything on this day either. Lütjens gave orders to sail towards another rendezvous point, called Blau, where the tankers *Schlettstadt* and *Esso Hamburg* waited. Maybe it was better to stay away from the main shipping routes for a while and hope that the *Admiral Hipper* would attract British attention, then resume operations with the *Gneisenau* and *Scharnhorst* after they had replenished their fuel.[72]

Lütjens' hopes were soon fulfilled. The *Admiral Hipper* lost contact with the convoy HG35 and failed to intercept it on the route to Gibraltar. She did find and sink the straggler *Iceland*. Even better luck was to follow. After taking the bearing of radio transmissions from the convoy SLS64, destined for Freetown, the *Admiral Hipper* intercepted the unescorted convoy, sank seven merchant ships and damaged another three, before the convoy scattered. After this success, Captain Meisel again set course for Brest, where he arrived on 14 February.

So far Lütjens had been fortunate, but the weather soon took a turn for the worse. Barometer pressure fell rapidly and a storm seemed to be brewing. Early in the morning on 11 February the wind got much stronger and the sea became very rough, while the radar showed an echo south of the German ships. Lütjens decided not to inquire into it; rather, he increased speed to 27 knots and sailed away. The echo disappeared, but four hours later, as dawn broke, another object appeared on the radar screens. Lütjens again chose to remain hidden. In both cases the vessels had moved slowly, probably not more than 7 or 8 knots, on a south-westerly course, which suggested that they were merchant ships. At this stage the German ships were in the northern part of the stretch of ocean where the convoys headed towards their destinations. The mere fact that merchant ships seemed to be in the area was some consolation to Lütjens. Had the British known that two

German battleships were present, they would probably have diverted the convoy traffic.[73]

The storm gathered during 11 February and Lütjens' ships proceeded slowly towards Blau. Not until 09.00 hours on 14 February did the *Gneisenau's* radar pick up the *Schlettstadt*. Shortly afterwards the *Esso Hamburg* was also found, but much time had elapsed since Lütjens decided to bunker. He and his staff did not have much to do except receive intelligence reports from Marinegruppe West and analyze them. It was reported that a British battlecruiser and a light cruiser, with escort, had been sighted in the area between Iceland and the Shetland Islands. Lütjens was also informed that Force H had left Gibraltar on the evening of 12 February. Marinegruppe West also reported the success achieved by the *Admiral Hipper*. The Germans believed that the 3rd Canadian Division was being shipped to the British Isles, which probably motivated the Royal Navy to send strong forces to the North Atlantic. Thus, Lütjens assumed that the HX-convoys would have powerful escorts for a few days more. As long as the weather precluded the German ships from using their reconnaissance aircraft, Lütjens' would continue to use caution in his decision-making.[74]

On the morning of 16 February, both battleships had completed bunkering and turned onto a southerly course, taking them to the area where Lütjens planned to begin looking for convoys. Lack of intelligence remained a problem. Since no successful air reconnaissance had been conducted over Scapa Flow, Lütjens did not know where the Home Fleet was and Force H had not yet returned to Gibraltar. However, the German naval attaché in Washington provided highly relevant information. A special convoy, consisting of ships from American ports, had assembled off Halifax on 15 February. It had most likely already begun its voyage east and Lütjens decided to try to find it. He chose to use the same search pattern as had been adopted more than a week previously. After all, it had worked well enough to find a convoy, although the convoy had been too heavily protected.[75]

On 17 February the German efforts to find merchant ships were all in vain, but the following day a masthead was observed. The Germans increased speed to 23 knots and the mast became gradually easier to see. Its shape resembled a warship. On the other hand, the copious smoke contradicted that conclusion. In any case, Lütjens decided to reduce speed to 17 knots and refrain from attacking the ship. At noon the same day another ship appeared from within a rainsquall. The distance was 19 kilometres, just at the effective range limit to the German radar. Again the *Gneisenau* and *Scharnhorst* increased speed to 23 knots and this time it seemed clear that they had found a merchant ship. However, as it appeared to be a lone ship, Lütjens decided to leave it unmolested. He preferred to find a convoy. To attack a single ship might reveal the existence and whereabouts of his squadron and prevent him from finding a convoy. The remainder of 18 February went by uneventfully. The following day also passed without any notable events.[76]

Lütjens believed that the special convoy had slipped away, forcing him to wait for yet another convoy to leave Halifax. The members of the German naval staff were despondent at the lack of success. Four weeks had elapsed since the *Gneisenau* and *Scharnhorst* left Kiel and thus far not a single ship had been sunk by them. Lütjens kept radio traffic at an absolute minimum, so that the British could not intercept his radio signals, from which they might be able to take bearings and locate his squadron. He sent few, very short messages. The German naval staffs on land were uncertain about Lütjens' activities and on 19 February he received a radio message: 'It remains unclear if the enemy expects enemy warships in the northern Atlantic. If you wait to commit the squadron owing to enemy situation, we consent.'[77]

However, the primary problem for Lütjens was not the Home Fleet, but rather the fact that he did not find any convoys. It had been a fundamental assumption in the German planning that convoys would be fairly easy to find. But the sea was vast and with only two ships at his disposal, Lütjens had to recognize that it could be difficult to locate British convoys. He contemplated using the aircraft carried by his ships, but they were floatplanes, to be launched from catapults. When returning to the ships, the aircraft would have to land on the sea and be hoisted on board the battleships. As the sea on the Atlantic was seldom calm, particularly during the winter months, it was often impossible to use the aircraft. Lütjens had already noted that further ships were urgently needed for searching. Even destroyers would have been useful, despite their limited sea-going capabilities.[78]

Despite all his concerns, Lütjens' hunting luck soon improved. On 20 February, his ships were on a southwesterly course, heading for a suitable position for beginning yet another search sweep. The weather deteriorated and air reconnaissance was precluded. In the evening, visibility was down to 1,500 metres, which hardly suggested that Lütjens' efforts would be successful. The following day searching continued, while Lütjens became more and more frustrated. His ships had burned substantial amounts of precious fuel oil, and had not achieved anything. At noon the *Scharnhorst* approached to send a report by signal lamp. Captain Hoffmann informed Lütjens that an unloaded merchant ship had briefly loomed when it came out from a rainsquall. Hoffmann believed that the two battleships were so far to the west that they had reached an area where convoys had broken up, to allow the ships to reach the various ports they were bound for in America.[79] This was grave news. If the ships sailed singly, the German ships were more likely to be discovered, while chances of finding a convoy were marginal. However, Lütjens hoped that the ship observed by the *Scharnhorst* was an advance observer from a larger convoy.

This time, luck was with the Germans. During the night, an echo appeared on the *Gneisenau's* radar and at dawn the situation became clear. First, smoke was observed and eleven minutes later, in another direction, mastheads could be discerned at a distance of 36 kilometres. Half an hour later two more ships could be seen. With so many ships around, it seemed unlikely that they should all be sailing singly. Finally Lütjens had found the convoy he wanted and he issued orders to attack. The two battleships parted, to catch as many merchant ships as possible before they scattered.[80] The German radio operators attentively listened for any message from *Kantara*, the first victim. It was vital to prevent the merchant ship from sending any warning. Just before 10.00 hours the radio on board the merchant ship began to transmit. Immediately, the powerful German transmitters countered by jamming the frequency, while the signal-light on board the *Gneisenau* requested the crew of the *Kantara* to abandon their ship. The warning was not obeyed. Rather, the merchant ship shifted the helm and tried to escape. Lütjens ordered a warning shot to be fired, but the only reaction from *Kantara* came from her radio. The *Gneisenau* replied by firing with her 28cm guns. After four swift salvos the *Kantara's* radio was silenced. The *Gneisenau* increased speed to close the range and sheered to assume a course parallel to the *Kantara*. The intention was to damage the *Kantara*, continue to chase the other merchant ships and then return and finish the *Kantara*. However, as the range had closed to 10,000 metres, the *Kantara's* radio began transmitting for the third time. Again the

Germans opened fire, this time with the 15cm guns. Four salvos sufficed. The *Kantara* was on fire and had ceased sending any radio messages. Amazingly, the British wireless operators had not yet given in. When the range was down to 2,000 metres, the *Kantara's* radio signals were again being transmitted through the air. This time the Germans showed no mercy. The *Gneisenau's* anti-aircraft artillery opened fire, with orders to sink the merchant. Within minutes, the *Kantara* began to sink. Her crew of 39 men, including one who had died in the engagement, was picked up by the *Gneisenau*. [81]

The *Gneisenau* sank another two ships. The *Scharnhorst* had also been successful and sank the tanker *Lustrous*. Thus far everything seemed fine, but while the *Gneisenau* chased her last victim, she had sent her floatplane to reconnoitre another ship, which could barely be discerned on the horizon. The pilot had been ordered to locate and shadow the ship. The wireless operators on the *Gneisenau* intercepted a message from the merchant ship, in which it reported being under air attack. When the floatplane returned to the *Gneisenau*, the pilot reported that he had requested the merchant ship to approach the *Gneisenau* and heave to. As the ship did not show any sign of complying, the pilot attacked it with bombs and machine guns. With his action, the pilot had revealed the presence of enemies and it seemed unlikely that the Germans would catch the ship before darkness. [82]

Lütjens was fortunate to have his radar. Immediately after 21.00 hours, it found the merchant ship at long range. The *Gneisenau* quickly closed the range and when it was down to 2,200 metres, she lit a searchlight and sank the ship. Of its crew of 41 men, 32 were saved. [83]

Despite this recent success, Operation Berlin had achieved little thus far. After a month at sea, only five ships had been sunk, a poor result that was hardly likely to trouble an opponent possessing almost 4,000 merchant ships. The only glimmer of hope was the inability of the British to form a clear picture of the German actions, rendering them unable to take effective countermeasures. The Germans had also been very lucky when a British merchant ship had observed one of the German battleships on 22 February. She gave a report, intercepted by the Germans, in which the position of the battleship was completely erroneous, which might be better for the Germans than no report at all. [84]

While still chasing the last of the five merchant ships, Lütjens decided to set course for a rendezvous point Lolo, as soon as the ship had been sunk. Lolo was located in the middle of the Sargasso Sea, an area in the Atlantic where few ships travelled. Two exceptions were the German ships *Ermland* and *Breme*, from which Lütjens intended to replenish his two battleships. Furthermore, about 150 men from the sunken merchant ships were on board the *Gneisenau*, while the *Scharnhorst* carried 37. As the battleships had little excess space to accommodate prisoners, it was preferable to transfer them to the supply ships, where better accommodation was available.[85]

The limited successes so far in the operation meant that the morale of the men serving on board the *Gneisenau* and *Scharnhorst* was low, a problem aggravated by the hardships endured at sea. A few days of rest was greatly needed after the weeks at sea. The crews' stations were often cramped and did not allow much room for physical movement, while the roll and pitch of the ships caused unwanted body movement. Often the seamen had to sleep fully dressed, as battle could be imminent. On average, the crew only had four to five hours of sleep per night. Admittedly, the seamen could sometimes snatch an hour of sleep at daytime, but eventually the effects of insufficient sleep took their toll.[86]

Another factor straining the crew was the high waves. When they washed over the ships, it was necessary to keep many hatches, doors, valves and other openings closed, leading to poor ventilation of many compartments. In this poorly ventilated atmosphere, even breathing and sweating created moisture problems. Otherwise there were few problems with the climate on board. As long as the ships operated at northerly latitudes, temperatures inside the ships did not rise above pleasant levels, but outside it was of course different. For example, the lookouts were exposed to the fury of the elements. However, if operations led the ships to the area of the Azores or the Canaries, temperatures might rise considerably.[87]

The sailors enjoyed good food. When Lütjens' two ships left Kiel, they carried fresh fruit and vegetables. As these victuals could not be stored for long periods, they were among the first to be eaten. Potatoes lasted much longer and formed a basis for the food during the second month at sea. As a precaution, vitamin pills were issued from the fourth week at sea. As merchant ships were sunk, more mouths had to be fed, but it was a minor problem; the stores of food on board the battleships were sufficient. Water supplies were however more limited. Each man in the crew could take a bath or a shower once a week. Despite these limitations, hygiene does not seem to have suffered markedly. As long as the ships remained on northern latitudes, there were cases of bad colds, but when the ships reached the Sargasso Sea, these problems disappeared. A few cases of appendicitis occurred, but they could hardly be connected to poor food, bad hygiene or other circumstances. Otherwise the hygiene and medical problems during Operation Berlin must be regarded as very slight.[88]

The German battleships reached Lolo in the afternoon on 26 February and quickly found the two tankers. Just before the rendezvous, the German wireless operators intercepted radio traffic from Spanish and Portuguese merchant ships, suggesting that they might be travelling nearby. Lütjens was concerned to remain undetected and ordered his battleships and the supply ships to move east. On 27 February, the ships began to bunker, but the rough sea made the process more arduous and time-consuming than anticipated.[89]

Originally, Lütjens had intended to allow the crews a few days of rest and to resume operations after 1 March. However, events outside his control forced other decisions. First, the *Admiral Hipper* remained longer than anticipated in Brest; she was still there when the *Gneisenau* and *Scharnhorst* began bunkering. If Lütjens' two battleships converged with Meisel's cruiser, it would be possible to attack the Allied convoy route between Africa and the British Isles with three warships. Considering how difficult it had been to find convoys, it seemed preferable to have three ships capable of searching for them. Furthermore, Marinegruppe West reported that the British seemed to have changed the schedule on the route from Freetown and northwards. It was expected that a northbound convoy would reach the area near the Canaries soon after 3 March. The *Scharnhorst* and *Gneisenau* completed bunkering and transfer of prisoners on 28 February, whereupon Lütjens ordered the ships to set course for the Canaries.[90]

On 3 February the two German battleships reached a point just west of the Canaries, The warmer temperature brought its own difficulties. In the ammunition stowage compartments, temperatures exceeded 30 ° Celsius before noon. At noon the two battleships began searching. This time Lütjens wanted to make better use of the aircraft. Unfortunately, one was already missing. Only three remained, two of them on board the *Scharnhorst*. [91] Over the next few days, while any convoys remained elusive, the seaplane belonging to the *Gneisenau* was damaged during landing, while one of *Scharnhorst's* aircraft got lost on its way back to the battleship. Hoffmann had to look for his lost aircraft rather than for convoys.[92]

The technicians on board the *Gneisenau* worked hard to repair the damaged aircraft and before noon on 4 March it was again serviceable. It made three search flights in quick succession, but when landing the third time, it again became damaged. This time, the plane was seriously damaged and could not be repaired at sea. It was exchanged with one of the *Scharnhorst's* aircraft, in order to give each battleship one fully serviceable aircraft.[93]

While these discouraging events continued, Lütjens was informed that Force H had again anchored at Gibraltar. The information suggested that no convoys were heading north along the west coast of Africa. Rather, it seemed that such a convoy had recently passed. Furthermore, from the report on Force H, it could be inferred that the German perception of British convoy schedules along the African route was faulty. The disagreement between various branches of German intelligence strengthened Lütjens' doubts as to the accuracy of the intelligence he received. Another cause for anxiety appeared soon afterwards. Little more than an hour before midnight, the wireless operators on board the *Gneisenau* intercepted a report from a German submarine. It had sighted two battleships. The worry caused by the message soon turned into indignation, when the reported position was checked. It was almost exactly the position of Lütjens' squadron,[94] but as the submarine had not identified the reported ships as German, there was a great danger that further submarines would gather and perhaps torpedo the battleships. Lütjens faced a quandary. Should he send a message to Marinegruppe West, to clarify the situation? Or should he keep radio silence, to prevent the British from taking bearings on his ships, but accept the risk of being attacked by friendly submarines? Lütjens cursed his inability to communicate directly with the submarines. After some agonising he decided to send a message to the naval staffs in Europe, while temporarily moving away from the area.[95]

Somewhat later the German battleships made contact with *U-124* and received confirmation that all submarines within the area had been informed about the presence of the two battleships. Still, the situation was deplorable. Lütjens only had fuel oil for a few days more, and then he would have to give up searching for convoys and instead focus on finding German tankers.[96]

Before noon on 7 March, a lookout on the *Scharnhorst* sighted a battleship. Lütjens concluded that it was part of the escort for a convoy heading north. No merchant ships had yet been seen, but the battleship was presumed to be moving ahead of the convoy. One hour later, Lütjens' assumption proved correct, when the lookout in *Gneisenau's* foretop discerned mastheads from approximately five merchant ships. As the enemy battleship sailed westwards, Lütjens ordered that the *Scharnhorst* and *Gneisenau* should converge at a point further east. He increased speed, but gradually so that the smoke would not betray his battleships.[97]

Fate did not seem to cooperate with Lütjens. Now a convoy had been found, but according to his own instructions, he could not attack it, as it was protected by a battleship. Only two convoys had been found during six weeks at sea, both of them protected by battleships. How many heavy ships could the British divert to convoy escort? What was he to do? One alternative was to hope that a slower convoy followed the one recently discovered. But there was an important element that differed from the convoy found off Halifax: the presence of German submarines. Perhaps they could be directed to attack the convoy, perhaps even torpedo the battleship. The problem was communications. Again he cursed the fact that he had no means to communicate directly with the submarines. He had to take the risk that sending a wireless message to the naval staff in Germany would reveal the *Gneisenau's* position. He minimized the risk by keeping his message as brief as possible: 'Very strongly protected convoy in quadrant DT9919.' It was sent at 11.25 hours.[98]

An hour later, Lütjens had still not received confirmation that the message had been received. What had happened? Had it not been received? At 13.00 hours he sent the message again, and after a further 20 minutes he finally got confirmation as well as the news that instructions had been issued to the submarines. Still, Lütjens was indignant. Of course he should have been informed immediately that his message had been received. Meanwhile, the *Scharnhorst* and *Gneisenau* continued to shadow the convoy. The enemy battleship was identified as the *Malaya*, another World War I veteran, but nevertheless armed with 38cm guns. It seemed that a few other warships also escorted the convoy.[99]

Lütjens had not nenvisaged that his battleships should shadow, leading submarines to attack a convoy. Nevertheless, the exercise worked fairly well. During the night before 8 March, two submarines attacked and sank five ships from the convoy. Afterwards, contact was lost.[100]

Fuel oil was a matter of critical importance to the German battleships. They could spend yet another day searching for convoys, but thereafter they had to refuel. Lütjens was tempted to attack the convoy he had already found. During the afternoon he approached it, but the *Malaya* soon appeared. Unknown to them, the *Malaya*'s floatplane had sighted the German ships, so the British were well informed as to their presence. The range was 16 miles and it fell to 14 miles before the *Gneisenau* turned away. The British ship tried to follow, but it was far too slow and the distance increased rapidly. Still, Lütjens' attempts to approach the convoy were futile and at 18.03 hours he ordered his ships to converge with the supply ships at the point agreed upon.[101]

While Lütjens vainly tried to attack British shipping on the Freetown route, the German naval staff considered future operations. The *Admiral Scheer* as well as the *Admiral Hipper* was supposed to return to Germany. The *Gneisenau* and *Scharnhorst* would sail for Brest, where they would be overhauled before resuming operations as soon as possible, this time together with the *Bismarck* and *Prinz Eugen*. Lütjens was expected to assume command of the forthcoming operation. But first of all he was supposed to conduct a diversion between the Azores and the Canaries, to facilitate an undetected return of the *Admiral Hipper* and the *Admiral Scheer* to Germany.[102]

Lütjens received his instructions with mixed feelings. The primary problem, as he saw it, was the condition of his two battleships. They were worn by the long period at sea. On board the *Gneisenau*, several important systems were husbanded, to save them for an emergency. Even worse was the situation for the *Scharnhorst*, where several pipes and ducts in the machinery had been damaged. She could not generate her maximum speed. Lütjens estimated that ten weeks would be needed to correct the problems afflicting the *Scharnhorst*, while four weeks would be needed to bring the *Gneisenau* into full serviceability. Thus, it was impossible to include the *Scharnhorst* in the proposed operation with the *Bismarck* and *Prinz Eugen*. The *Gneisenau* could participate, a piece of information sent by Lütjens to the naval staff.[103]

The proposed diversion manoeuvre was complicated. Lütjens regarded it as necessary to achieve some sort of success before Operation Berlin ended. Obviously, sinking British freighters was a concern for him, but he also believed the crews on board the battleships needed a success, to boost their morale. Probably such a success would be beneficial to the men serving on other ships in the German Navy too. If possible, it would be preferable to combine the diversion with a successful attack on British shipping. For these reasons, Lütjens regarded the area between the Azores and the Canaries as unsuitable. The chances of encountering single ships appeared slim, but near the American east coast prospects seemed brighter. Thus, Lütjens chose another solution than that envisaged by the naval staff, which he informed them about on 8 March. As soon as his battleships had bunkered fuel oil and taken on provisions, they would set a north-northwesterly course.[104]

On the evening of 12 March, Lütjens' battleships had completed bunkering. This time, he ordered the two tankers, *Uckermark* and *Ermland*, to follow the *Scharnhorst* and *Gneisenau*. He intended to use the tankers as an extra set of eyes to search for merchant ships, allowing the squadron to search over a wider area. In the following days, the four ships headed towards a point at the latitude of New York, about 2,500 kilometres from the American east coast. They reached it on the morning of 15 March and began to look for merchant ships.[105]

The *Admiral Hipper* sailed from Brest on the same day, heading for a point southwest of Greenland, where she was to bunker fuel oil. Thereafter she should pass through the Denmark Strait and sail to a German port. If Lütjens could attract British attention, it would be difficult for the Royal Navy to prevent the *Admiral Hipper* from reaching her destination.[106]

On the morning of 15 March two ships, probably tankers, were sighted by the *Uckermarck*. The *Gneisenau* immediately hastened towards the suspected tankers and forced them to stop, whereupon German prize crews went on board to sail the ships to German-controlled ports. The search for merchant ships continued during the day. The *Uckermark* cooperated with the *Gneisenau*, while the *Ermland* and *Scharnhorst* worked as a team. As soon as the tankers had sighted something, they reported to the battleships, which hastened to chase the victims, either sinking or capturing them.[107]

The scenes were repeated the following day. Lütjens' ships enjoyed far more success than they had previously. During one and a half days, they sank or captured 15 ships. However, time was running short. It was time for Lütjens to set course for Brest and he thanked the crew on board the *Uckermark* for their contribution during the recent days. At this moment another ship appeared on the horizon and Lütjens decided to add it to his tally. The *Gneisenau* quickly closed the range and fired a warning shot. The merchant ship, which turned out to be the *Chilean Reefer*, returned fire, laid smoke and tried to escape. The Germans replied with heavy artillery and soon the merchant ship was ablaze. Obviously it was an armed merchant ship which had escorted a convoy.[108]

The crew of *Chilean Reefer* abandoned their ship and the *Gneisenau* began to rescue the seamen. At this moment, the *Gneisenau's* radar picked up several echoes, from ships at a distance of about 20 kilometres. Within a minute, mastheads appeared on the horizon. One of them was suspiciously reminiscent of a major warship, probably a battleship of *Nelson* class. The range had closed somewhat, to 10 miles, and the British battleship required identification. Lütjens tried a trick and responded that his ship was the British cruiser *Emerald*, whereupon he turned around, ordered the highest possible speed and warned the other German ships. The distance quickly grew, while the sun set. At 21.00 hours, the silhouette of the enemy ship disappeared. Lütjens could continue on his east-southeasterly course to bunker fuel oil for the final time.[109]

The British found the situation difficult to interpret. Not until the evening of 15 March did they clearly understand that at least one German ship was in the area. Only when the *Rodney* had picked up survivors from the *Chilean Reefer* late on 16 March did the British learn that the *Gneisenau* was not far away. Furthermore, at about the same time, they realized that the *Admiral Hipper* was no longer in Brest. However, their countermeasures were haphazard, as the scattered pieces of information available were insufficient for them to gain a clear understanding of German intentions. The Germans could just as well be on their way to begin or finish operations, or in the midst of carrying out operations against convoy routes on the Atlantic. Furthermore, it could not be ruled out that the brand new battleship *Bismarck* might attempt to break out on the Atlantic, a circumstance that forced the Home Fleet to keep resources available to counter such a threat.[110]

Just as the British Admiralty began to grasp the situation, which caused some tension and anxiety, the German operations were coming to an end. After bunkering fuel oil, Lütjens set course for Brest early in the afternoon on 19 March. Soon his ships would be able to count on air cover from the Luftwaffe and early on 22 March the *Gneisenau* and *Scharnhorst* moored at Brest.[111] The following day the *Admiral Hipper* passed through the Denmark Strait, and five days later she reached Germany. Soon the *Admiral Scheer* followed, also without being sighted.[112] Operation Berlin was over.

CHAPTER 8

Operation Rheinübung

When all the German warships had returned to their bases, the Germans as well as the British used the respite to evaluate the lessons from Operation Berlin. Both sides were well informed about the activities of their own ships, but knowledge about the enemy, his means and his measures, was fragmentary. Nevertheless, a few conclusions seemed clear enough. One example was the passage of German ships back and forth from the bases on the continent to the Atlantic. The *Admiral Hipper* as well as the *Admiral Scheer* had been able to pass through the Denmark Strait fairly easily on their way from Germany and back to Germany. Admittedly, the *Scharnhorst* and *Gneisenau* had run into trouble south of Iceland, but they had subsequently passed through the Denmark Strait without trouble. Thus, it seemed that the Denmark Strait was favourable for break-out attempts. Also from the German perspective, the bases on the French Atlantic coast seemed suitable for cruiser warfare. The *Admiral Hipper* had twice put into Brest, and subsequently left the port, without being found or harassed by British forces. The *Gneisenau* and *Scharnhorst* had also been able to reach Brest, although they had been sighted by British reconnaissance aircraft. It should be remembered that all these operations had taken place during the winter, with longer nights and more periods of weather with limited visibility. During the summer months it might prove more difficult to avoid detection.

But if the Germans had met with few difficulties when attempting to reach the vast expanses of the Atlantic, they had been markedly less successful in their attempts to find convoys to attack. It seems reasonable to assume that these two observations were in response to the simple fact that the oceans were vast, while the ships available were quite few. With this in mind, the advantages of the convoy system practised by the British also become clear. Since it was almost as easy to find a single ship as a convoy, it was better to gather a large number of ships before sailing. If the Allies had chosen to let the merchant ships sail singly, the likelihood of their detection would have been greater.

However, the main advantage with the convoy system was that the warships available for protection could be concentrated in one area, allowing them to act more effectively. The Germans could not concentrate their submarines and surface ships correspondingly, because they needed to disperse their available vessels in order to find a convoy in the first place. On all three occasions when Lütjens had found convoys, a British battleship had been in the vicinity. What the Germans could not know was if it was a regular British procedure to let a battleship escort convoys, or if they did so only when intelligence suggested that German battleships were at sea. As both the *Admiral Hipper* and *Admiral Scheer* had encountered convoys not protected by battleships, the Royal Navy probably did not allocate a battleship for each convoy. The German naval staff concuded that it was of the utmost importance to continue to maintain secrecy with regard to both future break outs and ensuing operations.

Lütjens lamented the shortage of reconnaissance aircraft available to him during Operation Berlin. He wanted a hangar, similar to *Scharnhorst's*, to be fitted on the *Gneisenau*, enabling her to bring more aircraft during operations on the Atlantic. Between them, the *Scharnhorst* and *Gneisenau* could carry only four aircraft of the type Arado Ar 196, so the loss of even a single machine meant a serious reduction in their capacity to reconnoitre effectively from the air. [113]

A problem as grave as the limited number of reconnaissance aircraft was the lack of direct communication between surface forces and submarines, caused by different radio frequencies, code systems, call signs and the dependance upon on-shore commanders to forward messages. Although the submarines were often submerged and unable to intercept any wireless signals, most of the time they were at the surface. With effective communications, the surface forces and the submarines would have been able to coordinate their efforts much better. If the fleet commander could take command over a number of submarines when a battle situation arose, it would be possible to coordinate combat efforts as well as reconnaissance.[114]

One of Lütjens' basic operating principles during Operation Berlin had been to minimize risks to his squadron. He followed this principle in forthcoming operations too. Although additional ships were expected to participate, including more powerful vessels than the *Gneisenau* and *Scharnhorst*, it would be wrong to allow the ships to face unnecessary dangers. The main goal of cruiser warfare was to disrupt British trade, which was best accomplished by attacking and sinking British merchant ships. Besides the decimation of the British merchant fleet, the Germans hoped that the cruiser warfare would have collateral effects. For example, if the British were compelled to provide stronger escort for their convoys, more time would be lost while the merchant ships waited before all involved vessels had assembled, thus reducing the transport capacity of the overall system. For these reasons it remained necessary for the Germans to retain their ships as serviceable units, to be able to spend as much time as possible threatening the British shipping lanes on the Atlantic. Since the war began, only the *Admiral Graf Spee* had been lost in the cruiser warfare on the Atlantic.

An open question was the consequence of including the *Bismarck* in the projected operation. Her size and firepower increased the range of options available to naval planners. On 2 April, 1941, the German naval staff issued a directive that discussed various ideas with regard to future operations. When both the *Bismarck* and *Tirpitz* were committed, it woul be feasible for them to engage the convoy escort, sink it and then deal with the convoy.[115] However, while waiting for both these ships to become fully operational, ambitions had to be scaled down. The alternative chosen was to let the *Bismarck* tie down the escort while lighter ships attacked the merchant ships. Already at this stage it was clear that the heavy cruiser *Prinz Eugen* would accompany the *Bismarck*. The *Gnesienau* would also take part in the operation. She would put to sea from Brest and join the other two ships on the Atlantic. The *Scharnhorst* could not participate this time because the work on her machines would not be completed in time. It was decided to launch the operation, which was code named *Rheinübung*, on 26 April, at the time of the new moon.[116]

Although the directive of 2 April clearly stated that the *Bismarck* was to attract and tie down the escort, no specific instructions were given as to how she would achieve this end. It was not easy for any ship to tie down an opponent at sea, and to do so without taking risks seemed impossible. It might be possible for the *Bismarck* to depend on her superior firing range, but this was questionable. To score hits at ranges above 25 kilometres was very rare and only the oldest British battleships had a range of less than 25 kilometres. If the *Bismarck* had a range advantage, it was rather a matter of probability: she was more likely to score hits at long range, around 20 kilometres or more, but she was far from guaranteed to score the first hit. Another possibility was that the *Bismarck* could approach the convoy from one direction, while lighter German warships, such as the cruiser *Prinz Eugen*, remained hidden. If the *Bismarck* could induce a British battleship to position itself between the convoy and herself, an opportunity might be created for the *Prinz Eugen* or the *Gneisenau* to attack the convoy from another direction. This option was also discussed by Lütjens in his directives for the forthcoming operation.[117] A close reading of the directive of 2 April reveals that, as with Operation Berlin, the main objective was to sink British merchant ships. Enemy warships should only be engaged if needed to accomplish the main goal and only if it did not involve considerable risk.[118]

There were no heated discussions about the choice of commander for Operation, Lütjens was chosen without much hesitation, since the instructions he received during the final phase of Operation Berlin had clearly appointed him as commander of Operation Rheinübung too. Lütjens was probably pleased to be confirmed as commander but he soon realized that in one respect it would be a more complicated operation. Unlike the *Scharnhorst* and *Gneisenau*, which were virtually identical, the *Bismarck* and the *Prinz Eugen* were a rather ill-matched pair. Their battle capabilities were quite different, but assigning different roles to each ship should minimise the disparity. The moderate endurance of the *Prinz Eugen* was a greater concern, as she would have to bunker fuel much more often than either the *Bismarck* or the *Gneisenau*.[119] Since it remained vital for the German warships to be able to bunker oil and replenish stores at sea, eight ships were detailed for this important task.[120] Still the *Prinz Eugen* would not be able to sail as far from the supply ships as the other members of the squadron, therefore limiting the range of Lütjens' actions.

A few days after the directive was issued, events occurred that threatened to upset the plans. On 4 April, the German naval staff had emphasized the need for protecting the warships in Brest from torpedo attacks. For the moment, three battleships could be given adequate torpedo protection and another two could be placed in dock. From June onwards, another battleship could be harboured safely.[121] This was deemed sufficient to counter the threat from British torpedo aircraft, but during the night of 4 April, the Royal Air Force directed a bomber force against Brest. No significant damage was caused, but a dud fell in the dock where the *Gneisenau* was located. To remove the unexploded bomb, the battleship was moved out of the dock and the rough sea thwarted German attempts to place torpedo nets around her. At dawn on 6 April, the Royal Air Force took advantage of the opportunity and launched a surprise attack. It was a tough enterprise, but the British were favoured by haze, which made it difficult for the German Flak gunners to observe the approaching aircraft. The Canadian pilot Kenneth Campbell acted with unusual personal courage. The German fire was very intense and numerous shells exploded around his Beaufort aircraft, but he steadily held his course, a mere 15 metres above the sea. The *Gneisenau* loomed ever larger in front of him and at extremely short distance, he released the torpedo. Just as his plane felt lighter after losing the weight of the torpedo, it was hit and crashed on the surface of the sea. Campbell never saw how the torpedo hit the stern of the *Gneisenau*. For his sacrifice, Campbell was posthumously awarded the Victoria Cross.[122]

The damage caused to the *Gneisenau* was by no means critical, but it was sufficient to require at least ten weeks of work before she was fully operational, a major setback to German plans for Operation Rheinübung.[123]

As the spring of 1941 unfolded, more issues arose to delay the planned operation, and even to raise questions with regard to the whole concept of cruiser warfare. One of the most important was the suspicion that the British might have developed radar equipment for use on warships. In April 1941, the German naval staff asked Captain Kranke, who had commanded the *Admiral Scheer* during its long voyage if he had seen any evidence suggesting that British ships were fitted with radar. Kranke had seen nothing to justify the suspicion, but still it was suspected that the British cruiser *Naiad* might have used radar when the *Gneisenau* and *Scharnhorst* tried to pass between the Faeroes and Iceland on 28 February.[124]

However, lacking direct evidence to the contrary, for the time being the Germans assumed that British ships were not fitted with radar. As a precaution, a radar warning device was fitted to the *Bismarck*, perhaps the first ever to be mounted on a warship. However, it only operated within a rather narrow wavelength band and could not detect all types of radar.[125]

The radar equipment available in the early 1940s was at an early stage of development. It was not capable of precise fire direction and as long as visibility remained good, the human eye was still the most effective way of locking in on a target, since it could more accurately determine ship type, course, range and so on. On the other hand, radar was very useful as a detecting device when visibility was poor, although poor weather such as snow squalls could interfere with its efficiency. Radar could also provide fairly good information on the range and bearing of enemy ships, at least sufficient to inform tactical decisions, although not to direct fire as well as the optical instruments could do.

Nevertheless, it was clear that it was only a matter of time before radar had reached such a maturity that it could 'see' ships at long ranges, and any breakthrough in this field would have serious consequences for naval operations that depended to a large extent on the enemy remaining unaware of hostile forces in their area. German naval planners were understandably nervous at the thought that the British were employing a technology that would severely limit, if not entirely preclude, their cruiser warfare operations.

A further factor that gave rise to misgivings about the ongoing viability of cruiser warfare was the condition of the German ships when they returned from operations. As we have seen, after two months at sea, at least ten weeks were required to put the *Scharnhorst* back into serviceable order. This was not the end of the problems. On 9 April, it was reported that the *Admiral Scheer* would not be operational until mid-June. Admittedly, she had spent more than five months on operations, but it must also be considered that she had been in the shipyard for repairs during the first year of the war. The *Admiral Hipper* had put to sea at the end of November 1940, but after a mere four weeks she arrived at Brest for repairs. She would again arrive at Brest, before returning to Germany.[126] As the German ships spent so much time in shipyards while mechanical defects were repaired, the time available for operations on the Atlantic was seriously reduced. The German Navy had a very limited number of ships, so to have two or three in the shipyard at a time rendered continued operations impossible.

Furthermore, as shown by Campbell's attack on the *Gneisenau*, the German ships were not only menaced at sea, they could also be attacked while in the harbour or shipyard. The Royal Air Force did not hesitate to intensify its attacks on Brest, once the German battleships had arrived. The western French port became a primary target for Bomber Command. On the night of 6 April, a major attack was made, but no damage to the German military installations occurred. The British did not give in. A major attack was again launched on the night of 10 April. This time the *Gneisenau* was hit by four more bombs, causing fires and casualties. The damage to the battleship was limited, but the event nevertheless caused consternation among the Germans.[127]

When the German army occupied the French Atlantic coast, the German Navy rejoiced. At last suitable naval bases were available. The distance from the French ports to the convoy routes on the Atlantic was much shorter than the distance from ports in Germany. Furthermore, British countermeasures had been developed on the premise that German ships would pass through the North Sea on their way to the Atlantic. It had been an advantage for the German Navy to occupy bases in Norway, but the French ports were even better situated. The *Admiral Hipper* had twice used Brest unopposed and the *Gneisenau* and *Scharnhorst* had been able to put into Brest without being troubled, although an aircraft from a British carrier had in fact observed them shortly before reaching Brest. Unlike the Norwegian ports, there were ample shipyard and docking facilities in Brest and St. Nazaire. Maintenance and repairs could be performed to an extent not possible in Norway. Unfortunately, in April 1941 it became clear that British air power posed a threat to these plans.

Within the German Navy, opinions on how to handle the threat from the Royal Air Force were far from unanimous. There were several alternatives. The most drastic was to cease using the French ports as bases for major surface warships.[128] Instead the big ships would be withdrawn to German ports and would only use the French ports briefly. Rear-Admiral Fricke argued in favour of this alternative.[129] He emphasized the short distance between Brest and British air fields. It enabled aircraft to carry larger payloads and even allowed the use of single-engine aircraft. Also, enemy aircraft could make more frequent attacks. Another aspect was the prevalence of agents in French ports, as the resistance movement in occupied areas was a useful source of information to the British. Finally, it was easier for the Royal Air Force to reach Brest undetected. Thus, Fricke argued that the German ships should be transferred to Germany as soon as possible.[130]

However, it was Admiral Raeder who settled the issue and he wanted to keep the *Gneisenau* and *Scharnhorst* in Brest. For the moment, neither battleship was serviceable enough to put to sea. However, Raeder did not want the *Bismarck* or *Prinz Eugen* to be stationed in Brest. They would only put into Brest if no major repairs were needed, or to bunker fuel oil or take on provisions and put to sea again. In further support of the continued use of the harbour at Brest, some officers argued that the British attacks on the *Gneisenau* had been accompanied by a good deal of luck and similar random hits could occur in German harbours, like Kiel or Wilhelmshaven, too.[131]

One underlying problem was the fact that the Royal Air Force had begun to challenge German air superiority. British aircraft production had increased since 1939 and the effects were beginning to tell. In fact, as the Luftwaffe was beginning to prepare for operations in Eastern Europe, it seemed quite likely that the threat from British air power would become even more serious in the future.

The Germans made efforts to improve the safety of their ships in Brest. Unsurprisingly, the Flak defences were strengthened and barrage balloons were added. The ships were kept at higher alert, to enable their anti-aircraft artillery to participate in the defence of the harbour. Also, the Germans installed devices that could create artificial fog over the area and the fire prevention was improved. There was a suggestion that the decks and vital parts of the harbour, such as locks, should be reinforced with extra armour plates. To limit the effectiveness of a potential attack, the ships themselves were dispersed, with some destroyers sent to other ports.[132]

No more damage was inflicted on the warships during the following months so it appears that these countermeasures were effective. However, Bomber Command also directed attacks on the German ports. On the night of 9 April, the RAF attacked Emden, on the German North Sea coast. The bombers mainly carried incendiary bombs and no damage to military facilities occurred. Kiel was also attacked the same night, but again no militarily significant damage was caused. The city itself was more badly hit.[133]

In any case, the Germans were becoming more reluctant to use harbours close to British airfields. Already on 10 April, they decided that the *Bismarck* and *Prinz Eugen* should only put into Brest if moorings well protected from torpedo attacks could be arranged. If not, it would be better for them to set course for Trondheim when the operation on the Atlantic came to an end, despite the disadvantage of once more being forced to break out through the waters around Iceland.[134]

Unfortunately, Trondheim lacked the facilities needed to carry out substantial repairs. Hitler wanted a large dry dock to be constructed at Trondheim and ordered an investigation into the idea. If possible, it was to be built by *Organisation Todt*, an organization employing forced labour. Another plan he entertained was to use the Spanish naval base El Ferrol. He intended to occupy it during the autumn of 1941. As usual, Hitler had plenty of ideas, but they were not always easy to carry out. Neither of these projects ever came to fruition.[135]

The events of early April 1941 called for some reassessment of the plans for Operation Rheinübung. In retrospect, it might have been wiser to postpone the operation until more ships could participate, or even to shelve it entirely. Both the *Scharnhorst* and *Gneisenau* were expected to be fully operational by the summer of 1941, and the *Bismarck's* sister ship, the *Tirpitz*, was in the process of shaping up and training her crew. She too would become fully operational during the summer. An operation that employed these three battleships, plus the *Bismarck* and the *Prinz Eugen*, could offer a far more serious threat to the British, compared with that of the curtailed version of Operation Rheinübung that remained on the German naval staff's agenda.

However, there were also factors in favour of continuing with Operation Rheinübung, even without its ideal complement of ships. The British Navy continued to grow, as newly produced ships were commissioned and damaged vessels returned from repairs at shipyards. It was also crucial to consider the role America played. The German Naval Staff was convinced that the United States regarded Germany as a future enemy and that the American position would only become more and more hostile as time passed. If Germany became embroiled in a war with the United States, without Japan declaring war in the Far East, the Allied dominance at sea would become overwhelming. These arguments strongly suggested a prompt staging of Operation Rheinübung.

Hitler's plans to attack the Soviet Union in Operation Barbarossa also pushed Raeder towards launching Operation Rheinübung as soon as possible. In Germany, the army had traditionally been the dominating branch of the armed forces, while the Navy played the role of the younger brother. When the Luftwaffe was created, the Navy was pushed down one step further on the ladder.

With the onset of World War II, matters changed, as Raeder saw it. Except for the conquest of Norway, the German victories were mainly won by the army, However, according to the German Naval Staff, by 1941 Germany had already defeated its main land adversaries. The remaining enemy, Great Britain, was a sea power and not assailable by the German army. A maritime strategy was required to defeat her. Accordingly, Raeder demanded that the Army and the Air Force should adapt, to allow as forceful as possible a conduct of cruiser warfare against Britain's maritime trade.

Reichsmarschall Hermann Göring, head of the Luftwaffe, was strongly opposed to Raeder's suggestions. He believed the Luftwaffe alone could subdue the British and did not want to divert resources to targets deemed appropriate by Raeder, such as harbours and shipping. Göring pursued his own ambitions, which resulted in the Battle of Britain during the summer and autumn of 1940. However, as the Luftwaffe failed, British resistance increased.

By the autumn of 1940, when it became clear that the Luftwaffe had lost the Battle of Britain, Raeder argued more strongly for an expanded cruiser war over the next few months. The Luftwaffe obviously could not defeat Britain alone and the failed attempt had spoiled any chances of reaching a political solution. Great Britain, with Churchill at the helm, was prepared to fight until Germany was defeated. According to Raeder, further bombing would only serve to stiffen the British determination to continue the war. Attacking her maritime trade remained one of very few methods to defeat Britain. However, Raeder realized that once the attack on the Soviet Union was launched, his plans would take second place. He needed a significant success before Operation Barbarossa started, to reinforce his arguments for more resources for his Navy, or to convince the Luftwaffe to direct efforts against British maritime trade.

A basic tenet of the cruiser war concept held that German warships could operate either singly or in small groups. From this perspective,

the combination of the *Bismarck* and *Prinz Eugen* was equivalent to
that of the *Scharnhorst* and *Gneisenau* had been. The hypothetical con-
stellation of the *Bismarck*, *Prinz Eugen* and several more ships was
regarded as being exceptionally strong but since Lütjens policy of
avoiding confrontation with British warships had so far allowed the
Germans to avoid taking losses in their Atlantic operations, there
seemed to be no reason why the risks involved in Operation
Rheinübung would be greater. Thus, the ships would be ready to sail
from Gdynia on 28 April.[136]

If Raeder was convinced that the plan should go ahead, Lütjens still
had misgivings. Perhaps they were reinforced when Operation
Rheinübung suffered yet another setback on 23 April. A magnetic mine
detonated about 30 metres from the *Prinz Eugen*, when she sailed
through the strait between Puttgarden and Rödby. The damage caused
was slight, but would nevertheless require 12 days to repair. Still,
Raeder did not dismiss the idea of sending the *Bismarck* on Operation
Rheinübung alone.

On 26 April, Lütjens again discussed Operation Rheinübung with
Raeder and emphasized the need to wait at least for the *Prinz Eugen* to
become serviceable. He also considered it more prudent to wait until
the *Tirpitz* was ready for action, or until at least one of the battleships
in Brest could participate. If he only had the *Bismarck* and the *Prinz
Eugen* at his disposal, he would not be able to use his ships in a way
that differed significantly from Operation Berlin. If the enemy offered
dogged resistance, and the *Bismarck* destroyed the escort to allow the
Prinz Eugen to have a free hand with the convoy, some kind of damage
was almost bound to occur to his battleship. Further operations would
then be prevented until the damage was repaired.[137]

By and large, Raeder agreed with Lütjens. But still, there was the
issue of Operation Barbarossa and the possible future involvement of
the United States.[138] Nevertheless, he agreed to postpone Operation
Rheinübung at least until the *Prinz Eugen* was again combat ready.[139]

While waiting for new orders from Raeder, Lütjens continued to
work out more detailed plans for Operation Rheinübung. The most
important issues were the break-out and guidelines for combat.
Compared to Operation Berlin, the forthcoming operation suffered
from a serious disadvantage. The more the spring progressed, the
shorter the nights grew, and Iceland was so far north that the nights

would not become dark in June at all. This factor may well have weighed heavily for Raeder when he pushed for an early staging of Operation Rheinübung.[140]

In addition to the light, weather also prominently affected the chances of a successful break-out. During the autumn of 1940 and afterwards, the Germans strived to take advantage of the new moon when passing through straits like the Great Belt and the Denmark Strait at night. As spring nights became progressively shorter and lighter so that much of the ship movement would take place in daylight anyway, the weather began to play a more prominent role in the choice of time for the operation. This factor also suggested an early launching of Operation Rheinübung, as the kind of weather propitious to a successful break-out was less likely to occur during the summer months. [141]

It is understandable that the Germans studied the break-out with considerable thoroughness. The gravest threat to Operation Rheinübung was early discovery by the enemy. There were several occasions when the risks of discovery would be heightened. The first was the departure from Gdynia, where the British might become informed when the ships sailed. Once in the Baltic, there was hardly any risk of being detected, but when entering and passing through the Danish belts, the risk increased. On the Kattegat, Swedish ships might observe the German squadron. Furthermore, British submarines and aircraft patrolled the Kattegat and the Skagerrak. Along the Norwegian coast, local people, many of them members of the resistance, might catch sight of the ships. Not until the squadron had reached the Norwegian Sea did the dangers of discovery decrease again.

In the main, the dangers to the secrecy of Operation Rheinübung could be divided into three main categories: British military forces, other ships at sea and observers ashore. Of these, the first category was considered the most serious, as military units could be expected to make a more correct observation and to transmit it immediately. Neutral ships too could be expected to report by wireless that German ships had been observed, but that was not certain. Agents ashore and resistance members could not be expected to report immediately, as they often had to move their wireless equipment somewhere where they felt safe. In the latter case, the Germans estimated that there would be a delay of about 24 hours.[142]

They were hardly likely to completely avoid detection. Some of the sources used by the British would probably provide them with some kind of information. The Germans relied on two circumstances: that the information might reach the British after some delay and that it might be mixed with other information, true or false, which reached them. Thus it would be difficult for them to judge the German intentions. In fact, the German assumption was fully justified. The British had numerous times falsely believed the Germans were on their way towards the Atlantic. Furthermore, many reasons, other than a break-out, could motivate German ships to sail from Gdynia or pass through the Danish Belts.

An alternative discussed by the Germans was to use the Kiel-canal, rather than the Danish Belts. If the canal was chosen, Lütjens' squadron could subsequently sail on the North Sea, rather than the Belts, Kattegat and Skagerrak. However, there was a distinct disadvantage with the alternative, as the *Bismarck* could not pass the canal fully loaded. If she went through the canal, she would have to bunker in some North Sea port before embarking on Operation Rheinübung. The battleship would be forced to spend considerable time in port, subjecting her to the risk of being detected by British aerial reconnaissance. If so, the British would intensify their efforts to discover when she left harbour. At worst, the *Bismarck* might even be damaged by air attack.[143] Compared to these risks, the passage through the Danish Belts appeared to be the lesser of two evils. As the ice had also melted, the Great Belt could be passed in darkness, which would improve chances of avoiding detection.

According to the orders Lütjens issued for Operation Rheinübung, the ships would enter the Korsfiord near Bergen on the fourth day of the operation. Fuel oil would be bunkered. It was especially important to the *Prinz Eugen*, whose radius of action was much smaller than the *Bismarck's*. So far Lütjens' plans were quite clear. How the next phase was to be conducted was left open. He had almost the same general alternatives as during Operation Berlin. His squadron could set course for the tanker *Weissenburg* in the Arctic Ocean and bunker fuel oil before break-out. Also, the ships might try to break out immediately, either north or south of Iceland. Lütjens chose to wait before the final decision. However, in his operations order, he declared his intention to bunker from the *Weissenburg*, after the short pause in Bergen, although he remained open to other alternatives if the situation demanded a change in the plans.[144]

CHAPTER 9

The Home Fleet

When war broke out in 1939, British naval strategy rested on two pillars. The first aim was to secure Britain's transoceanic imports; and the second was to blockade Germany, which it was hoped would cause Hitler's downfall. The availability of raw materials again dictated British naval strategy, which was very much a repeat of that of World War I. However, despite the basic similarities between the wars, there were also substantial differences. The German Navy was much weaker in 1939 than it had been in 1914, so it appeared easier for the British to secure their shipping and maintain a steady flow of essential imports. The focus could switch to depriving Germany of the raw materials needed to keep up the war effort. Attention soon fell on Swedish iron ore, which was vital to the German arms industry. Plans for depriving the Germans of access to the Swedish iron ore took a long time to develop and meanwhile the Royal Navy focussed on controlling the Atlantic.

Although Italy had not yet joined the war in 1939, it was important to keep the Italian Navy in check in case she did. The role of patrolling the western Mediterranean fell to the French Navy, and French warships also helped chase away German pocket battleships during the autumn of 1939. [145]

Tacit support from the United States was also a vital factor. The strong US Pacific Navy tied down the Japanese Navy, enabling the British to commit only scant resources to the defence of their possessions in the Far East. Most of the Royal Navy was therefore available to control the seas nearer England, in areas through which the

95

German warships would have to pass, should they attempt to strike at Allied shipping on the Atlantic.

The successful German campaign in Norway in 1940 struck a harsh blow at British naval superiority. With bases in Norway now open to the German Navy, the British Navy was forced to cover larger areas to prevent the Kriegsmarine from reaching the Atlantic. Furthermore, by making use of Norwegian air bases, the Luftwaffe could pose a threat to British ships. As a consequence, the British could no longer blockade the Germans along the short line from Scotland to southwest Norway. It became necessary to cover the entire area from the Orkneys to Greenland.

The situation worsened when the German army defeated France in May–June 1940, and the support from the French Navy vanished. Mussolini declared war on 10 June 1940 and in the Far East, Japan began to act more ominously. In a short span of time, the Royal Navy was stretched to the utmost in her attempt to cover two additional theatres of war. The British Mediterranean fleet, based in Alexandria, had to be reinforced. Force H, based in Gibraltar, was created to take the place of the French Navy in the western Mediterranean.[146]

The increased demands made it impossible to provide the Home Fleet with the resources it desired in the short term, and the likely ongoing effect of losses due to battles in the Mediterranean meant that the Home Fleet could expect to be further stripped as the war went on. A respite was provided by the damage to German warships from the Norway Campaign. Three cruisers and many destroyers were lost and several other damaged ships were undergoing prolonged repairs. However, within a few months, they would be ready for service and British shipping on the Atlantic would again be endangered.

Still, there were some positive developments suggesting that the hard pressed British could allow themselves a little confidence. Several warships neared completion. Britain had been rather late in resuming production of battleships, but in the autumn of 1940 the first in a series of five was completed. Her name was *King George V* and she would soon become the flagship of the Home Fleet.[147] The British lagged behind the Germans in battleship production. The *Scharnhorst* and *Gneisenau* had been in service more than a year when the *King George V* was commissioned and the *Bismarck* and *Tirpitz* were clearly more powerful than the contemporary battleships of the *King George V* class. Admittedly, the British possessed several older battleships, but few of them served with the Home Fleet, as they were too slow.

At least the British did maintain superiority with regard to aircraft carriers. Britain had been leading the development of this new type of weapon, while the Germans, like the Italians, completely lacked carriers. When the Washington Naval Treaty (aka the Five-Power Treaty) was signed, numerous battleship projects had to be cancelled. In many cases, the already-initiated projects ended up as carriers, which were not limited by the Washington Treaty. During the decade preceding World War II, Britain also embarked on building several warships, designed as carriers from the very beginning, and some of them were already in service at the end of 1940. But the carriers too had been spread out. Of the four fully modern carriers Britain possessed, one was undergoing repairs, one was based on Alexandria and one was in Gibraltar. The brand new *Victorious* could not yet be described as fully operational. Also, the Royal Navy had two older carriers in the Indian Ocean and another two, even older, were used to transport aircraft to exposed or desolate positions like Gibraltar, Malta and bases in Africa. Consequently, Admiral Tovey had no fully combat-ready carrier when he replaced Admiral Charles Forbes as commander of the Home Fleet.[148]

Admiral John Cronyn Tovey was 56 years old, short in stature, and had served with the Royal Navy since the age of 15. During World War I he had commanded a destroyer and fought in the Battle of Jutland. When World War II began, Tovey commanded a destroyer flotilla, but soon he was appointed to command the 7th Cruiser Division and in July 1940 he fought against the Italian Navy at Punta Stilo. He was an esteemed and competent commander who inspired respect. He was also deeply religious. He always prayed, morning and evening.

When Tovey assumed command of the Home Fleet, it was stronger than it had been since the beginning of the war. As already mentioned, the *King George V* had just entered service and flew Tovey's flag. Also, he had at his disposal the battleships *Nelson* and *Rodney*, the battlecruisers *Hood* and *Repulse*, 11 cruisers and 17 destroyers.[149] It was a respectable force, in fact larger than the entire German Navy. He could also count on receiving the battleship *Prince of Wales* as soon as it was completed.

During the initial months of his tenure, Tovey's Home Fleet did not fight any major battles. He had been engaged in intensive searching activity when Lütjens' two battleships raided the Atlantic, and the activity of *Admiral Hipper* and *Admiral Scheer* also caused him to send his forces to sea. Nevertheless, these hide-and-seek games did not result in any combat.

As the German warships returned to their bases, a quieter period followed. However, it was well-known by the British that the *Bismarck* and *Prinz Eugen* had been commissioned by the Kriegsmarine and their crews had almost completed training. These two ships could be expected to participate in offensive operations at short notice, which would require Tovey's full attention. The *Gneisenau* and *Scharnhorst* still remained in Brest. It seemed clear that British attacks had caused damage to them, but it was more difficult to judge when the two battleships might again be considered battle-worthy.

Tovey's main task was clear. He had to prevent the Germans from reaching the British trade routes in the Atlantic. The *Bismarck* and *Prinz Eugen* were in the Baltic and they would have to pass the area north of the British Isles, should they undertake to reach the transatlantic trade routes. On the other hand, the *Scharnhorst* and *Gneisenau* threatened to break out south of the British Isles, so Tovey would have to cope with this threat too. If he had to act to prevent the German battleships in Brest from reaching trade routes, he could cooperate with the Force H at Gibraltar. The area north of Britain was his sole responsibility.

Reliable intelligence was a prerequisite for Tovey's attempts to prevent a German break-out, but the wear on both ships and men if they were kept constantly on patrol, as well as the consumption of valuable fuel oil was too high a price. Tovey preferred to rely on intelligence gathered from several sources, such as aerial reconnaissance, wireless interceptions and agents. Once the Germans had reached open sea, sources like agents of course had little to provide, but if the German ships sailed close to a coastline, they might still give useful information. Another important source was called ULTRA, which we will discuss later. The British decision-makers complemented this sort of information with their own observations on the weather, the phases of the moon and light conditions.

It was necessary to have fairly strong indications that the Germans were indeed staging a break-out, because if the heavy ships they sailed too early, they might consume too much fuel oil and be forced to return to port to bunker, perhaps at the most crucial moment. Thus the importance of solid intelligence was thus clear.

To make matters more difficult for Tovey, he not only had to predict when the Germans would try to break out, he also had to cover several alternative break-out routes they might follow. There were three main alternatives: (1) The southern route between the Orkneys and the Faeroes; (2) the middle between the Faeroes and Iceland; and (3) the northern route, the so-called Denmark Strait between Iceland and Greenland, which Lütjens successfully used during Operation Berlin.

Only one circumstance suggested that the Germans might be tempted to use the southern alternative: the short distance to the convoy routes. It would save fuel oil and time, but would be prone to detection, especially by British aerial reconnaissance, as the area was well within reach of British airfields.

The middle and northern alternatives were the most likely and the ones Tovey focussed on. The passage between the Faeroes and Iceland was also fairly short. Furthermore, its width would provide the Germans with plenty of room for manoeuvre, which might become vital if British naval forces appeared. On the other hand, British forces from the main base at Scapa Flow might more easily intercept German warships in this area, compared to the more distant Denmark Strait, and aircraft based on the British Isles as well as Iceland could provide effective reconnaissance of the area.

From the German point of view, the advantages of the Denmark Strait were the frequent bad weather and the distance from Scapa Flow. It would make it more difficult to find German ships and it would require more time to intercept the German ships, were they detected, unless of course heavy British units were already in the vicinity. On the other hand, the Denmark Strait was narrow, on one side the pack ice was a barrier and on the other side there were British minefields. At its narrowest, the Denmark Strait was only 130 kilometres wide, and half of that distance was covered by mines. The Germans would also have to cover a much longer distance, were they to settle for the Denmark Strait alternative, which of course meant that more fuel oil would be consumed. Finally, as the summer drew closer, the nights would be very short, or even disappear completely, at such northerly latitudes. With the long periods of sunshine, it would be more difficult for the Germans to avoid detection or shake off pursuers.

Another problem for Tovey was the disparity of the ships he controlled. In mid-May 1941, the two most modern British battleships, the *King George V* and *Prince of Wales*, were under his command. The former was his flagship, while the latter was brand new and not yet fully tested. Technicians from the manufacturer remained on board the *Prince of Wales* to solve deficiencies. The most serious defects occurred in her main armament.

Tovey also had at his disposal two battlecruisers, the *Hood* and the smaller battlecruiser *Repulse*. Finally, the carrier *Victorious* was at Scapa Flow. Like the *Prince of Wales*, she was brand new. It was intended that her first mission would be to transport fighter aircraft to Malta. Thus, she carried partly disassembled Hurricanes. They were to be reassembled when the carrier approached Malta, whereupon the Hurricanes were to be flown to the beleaguered island. They could not land on the *Victorious* and were therefore useless in the Atlantic. Besides the Hurricanes, the *Victorious* carried Swordfish and Fulmar aircraft, which could reconnoitre and carry torpedoes. Furthermore, they were fitted with a radar system which could detect ships on the surface of the sea. The disadvantage was the lack of training of the aircrew, which made the carrier an entity whose combat capabilities were difficult to assess. Finally, Tovey also had two heavy cruisers, eight light cruisers, 12 destroyers and numerous other ships.[150]

There was no obvious way in which to make best use of this disparate force. Not least, the differences in speed and endurance complicated matters. Some of the ships were earmarked for special tasks, so Tovey could not have a free hand when deciding how to use them. As mentioned, the *Victorious* was transporting aircraft to Malta, although Tovey could request permission to alter her mission if circumstances warrantd such a change. Similarly, the *Repulse* was in Clyde, to escort a troop convoy to the Middle East. As was the case with the *Victorious*, the Admiralty could change the mission for the battlecruiser if demanded by the situation.[151] There were two more battleships that might prove useful to Tovey, the *Nelson* and *Rodney*. However, the *Rodney* was destined for a complete overhaul in the United States and the *Nelson* was sailing to cover convoys between Cape Town and Britain. It seemed doubtful that these two battleships would be available if the Germans attempted to break out into the Atlantic in the second half of May.[152]

All Tovey knew for sure about the disposition of German ships was that the *Bismarck* and *Prinz Eugen* were at Gdynia in the middle of May.[153] He had to reckon that they could begin an attempt to break out into the Atlantic on any day.

CHAPTER 10

The Visit

As the date for initiating Operation Rheinübung drew nearer, the crew on board the *Bismarck* made the best use they could of the days that remained. Gdynia offered little entertainment, so Müllenheim-Rechberg usually went to nearby Sopot, where he could enjoy swimming in the sea and visit bars. Often his good friend, Lieutenant Jahreis, accompanied him on this short trip. Jahreis was Bavarian, a kind man and full of vitality, but his previous appointment as turbine engineer had just been taken over by Lieutenant Gerhard Junack. Jahreis had been transferred to command damage control, a change that had been a hard blow for him, as he was well acquainted with the turbines and had created a good relationship with his men.

During one of the trips to Sopot, Jahreis and Müllenheim-Rechberg stay far too long at the local bars and returned very late to their hotel. For some reason, neither of them woke up until the sun had already climbed high up in the sky. They realized that it was too late for them to reach Gdynia before the *Bismarck* weighed anchor for the daily exercise. After a swift journey to Gdynia their fears were confirmed: the last longboat to the *Bismarck* had already left the quay. Müllenheim-Rechberg and Jahreis persuaded the captain of a tug to take them to the battleship. When they reached the *Bismarck*, the first man they saw was Commander Hans Oels, the ship's First Officer, waiting at the gunwale. Oels was responsible for all disciplinary matters on board and with his distance and reserved manners, he was not a popular person. The men called him 'the loneliest man on board'.

Müllenheim-Rechberg and Jahreis had expected a dressing-down from Oels. However, he just looked at them in his reserved way and said: 'The captain awaits you on the bridge.'

Expecting the worst, the two culprits reported to Lindemann, but he only smiled at them. 'Well,' he said. 'Now you return to your duties.' [154]

While Lindemann, Lütjens and the naval staff thought through all the details pertaining to Operation Rheinübung, the *Bismarck* and her crew trained to become ready for action. On 28 April, the *Bismarck* was reported to be fully combat-ready and she had taken on stores sufficient for three months. The squadron still had to wait for the *Prinz Eugen* to be repaired following the damage caused by the mine detonation. On 13 May it was reported that the cruiser would be repaired and completed with stores on 16 May. Thus, the squadron tasked with Operation Rheinübung would be ready to sail on 17 May, or at the latest on 18 May. [155]

On 5 May, Hitler visited Gdynia. His intention was to study the *Bismarck* and *Tirpitz*, which were both anchored at Gdynia. Hitler was deeply interested in military technology and the two battleships had much to interest him. In the morning he boarded the tender *Hela*. The small vessel brought him to the *Bismarck*, which was moored further out in the harbour. Lütjens hosted the visitors and had commanded the crew on deck. A slightly pale Hitler paraded by, followed by Lütjens, Lindemann and the head of the armed forces staff, Field Marshal Keitel. A full tour of the battleship would take too long, so Hitler concentrated on what he found most interesting, in particular, the artillery. In the aft gunnery computer room, Lieutenant Cardinal demonstrated how the fire control system worked. Hitler as well as Keitel, who was a former artillery officer, seemed impressed by what they saw. [156] The *Bismarck* was expected to be able to fire at targets about 30km away while travelling at a speed of 30 knots. The firing control systems on the German ships had improved even on those available during World War I, which had surprised the British with their speed and accuracy.

After Hitler had inspected this technology, he listened to a presentation by Lütjens, in which the experiences from Operation Berlin were reviewed. Lütjens looked forward to using the *Bismarck* in a similar way. With such a powerful warship, it was no longer imperative to avoid strongly escorted convoys. The main problem was to reach the Atlantic undetected.

'Do not the superior numbers of the British Navy present a grave risk?' Hitler asked.

'The *Bismarck* is superior to any British battleship,' Lütjens retorted. 'Her firepower and protection is so outstanding that there is no need for fear.' After a brief pause, he added that even after a successful break-out, there were disquieting factors, in particular British torpedo aircraft operating from carriers.[157]

Hitler was not familiar with naval warfare and was anxious about the loss of prestige suffered if a major German warship were sunk. The high-ranking German naval officers were well aware of this and it may have been the reason why Lütjens gave a rosy presentation of the forthcoming operation—despite the fact that he had misgivings. Lütjens carefully avoided giving any starting date for Operation Rheinübung, possibly because he wanted to avoid objections from Hitler. Perhaps Raeder's absence was motivated by a fear that Hitler would ask him about forthcoming operations.

Lunch was served on board the *Bismarck*. It was well known that Hitler preferred vegetarian food and a vegetable stew was served. The meal was enjoyed without much conversation, but afterwards Hitler spoke about the German minority in Romania, which he considered to be persecuted by the government. If the persecution was not stopped, he intended to bring these people home to the German Reich. The issue was not the most urgent one for the German naval officers around Hitler in the mess, but when the Führer shifted topic to the role played by the United States, his audience grew more interested. Hitler did not believe the Americans would enter the war, but Lindemann disagreed. The conversation was ended with a short speech by Lütjens. [158]

After five hours on board the *Bismarck*, Hitler and his entourage left the battleship on the tender *Hela*, which brought them to the *Tirpitz*, where Captain Topp greeted them. He used the opportunity to express his wish that the *Tirpitz* might accompany the *Bismarck* during the forthcoming operation. Hitler let Lütjens and Raeder settle the issue. Neither of them agreed with Topp, as they regarded the crew of the *Tirpitz* as being insufficiently trained. As Hitler had already seen so much of the almost identical *Bismarck*, his visit on board the *Tirpitz* was briefer.[159]

The crew of the *Bismarck* used the remaining days to make everything ready for a long voyage on the Atlantic. The crew of the ship usually numbered 2,065 men but for the forthcoming operation, more officers, seamen and other officials were on board. Lütjens brought his staff, who were not included in the crew of the battleship.[160] Beside Captain Harald Netzbandt, Lütjens' chief of staff, there were many officers specialising in fields such as meteorology, communications, artillery, operations, surgery and personnel matters. In addition, there were liaison officers from the Air Force and submarine forces.[161]

Several war correspondents and photographers accompanied the *Bismarck*. They were supposed to film and write about the operations for propaganda purposes. Several prize crews had also arrived. Their task was to sail captured ships to German-controlled harbours.

The men in the so-called *Beobachtungs-Dienstgruppen* (hereafter B-Dienst), were experts in radio interception and deciphering. It was their task to monitor British wireless communications and break the codes. The British used a fairly simple code system, in which a combination of letters represented a phrase or a word. It was assumed that the receiver had a proper code book with which to decipher the message. Without the code book, the content of the message was incomprehensible.

The reality was a little different. The British had used the same system before the war and in a few instances, carelessness had resulted in messages being sent both coded and in plain language. By identifying these messages and comparing the deciphered version with the non-deciphered, the Germans gradually began to understand the British code. Then, by further comparing recently intercepted messages with those that had already been deciphered, the Germans could often work out their content.

Towards the end of 1940, the Germans could easily interpret at least half the messages sent by the Royal Navy.[162] On 11 November the German surface raider *Atlantis* had captured the British merchantman *Automedon*, on which they found a code book used by the British merchant fleet. It provided the Germans with further clues on how to decode British wireless messages. This was especially useful after the British introduced changes to their codes during the autumn of 1940. Although the B-Dienst was not quite as successful at the beginning of 1941, their service might provide vital support when decisions were to be made by the German commanders during Operation Rheinübung.

It required substantial stores to feed the more than 2,000 men on board the *Bismarck*. The meat from 300 cattle and 500 pigs was taken on board and properly stored.[163] Also, large amounts of potatoes, flour and vegetables were needed. Significant quantities of articles of consumption were loaded, such as cigarettes, which were rationed. It took several days of intense activity to make the ship ready to sail, and it was more or less impossible that this activity might go unnoticed by anyone who might want to pass that information on to the Allies. The most that could be hoped for was that unexpected delays would make it more difficult to guess when the ship was actually departing.

The squadron was finally ready to commence operations on 18 May. Although the *Bismarck* and *Prinz Eugen* attracted most of the attention, they were not the only ships that participated in Operation Rheinübung. As in previous operations, the Germans stationed several tankers and supply ships on the Atlantic. They were to sail from France or Germany in time to take up positions where few or no ships sailed regularly, from where they could provide the *Bismarck* and *Prinz Eugen* with fuel oil, but also ammunition and provisions. The tankers *Heide* and *Weissenburg* left Germany to take up positions in the Arctic Ocean and the tankers *Belchen* and *Lothringen* left ports in France to sail to predetermined positions south of Greenland. The tankers *Esso Hamburg* and *Breme* left France for positions north and south of the Azores. In addition, the supply ship *Ermland* set course for the area north of the Azores. Finally there were four weather observation ships and the tanker *Wollin*. The latter sailed for Bergen in Norway, where she would await Lütjens' squadron if he decided to refuel at Bergen.[164]

Unlike previous operations, the Germans had decided to use special reconnaissance ships to assist Lütjens during Operation Rheinübung. They used fairly fast merchant ships which would take part in the search for convoys. This was as a result of Lütjens' awareness of the valuable contribution that the tankers *Uckermark* and *Ermland* had made to Operation Berlin. They had ably assisted in searching for ships off the American coast during the final part of the operation. This time the Germans specially selected ships were detached from the very beginning, which reduced the risk of losing the valuable tankers. On 17 May the first ship, the *Gonzenheim*, left La Pallice near La Rochelle. The following day the *Kota Penang* left the same port. Both were instructed to await Lütjens' squadron south of Greenland.[165]

While Lütjens' squadron was making final preparations for sail, events were taking place elsewhere that were to have significant consequences for the war in the Atlantic. On 7 May, two days after Hitler's visit to the *Bismarck*, the German submarine *U-110* took part in attacks on a British convoy south of Greenland. The convoy was repeatedly attacked on several nights and five merchant ships were sunk. But on 9 May, depth charges from the corvette *Aubrietia* severely damaged *U-110*. The submarine was forced to the surface. In great haste, the submarine commander made a grave mistake. He ensured that the scuttling charges were properly primed before the last crewmen entered the life boats, but he forgot to throw the code books and the war diary over board. It turned out that the damage to the submarine was not as extensive as was originally believed and the charges never detonated. British seamen boarded *U-110*, where they found the code books for the German Hydra code, which was in widespread use by the Kriegsmarine in northern Europe.[166]

The Germans used a cryptography machine called Enigma. Without delving too deeply into its construction, it can nevertheless be said that it was advanced enough to lead the Germans to believe that their ciphers could not be broken. However, a branch of British intelligence, known as Ultra and located at Bletchley Park in Oxfordshire, had obtained an Enigma machine from the Polish in July 1939. Early on, the Polish intelligence had copied the Enigma machine and by 1933 they had already deciphered German radio traffic. When Poland fell to the German invasion in 1939, much of the valuable work performed by Polish intelligence had already been made available to the French and British.

The first code broken by Ultra was the so-called 'red code,' used by the Luftwaffe. Somewhat later, in April 1940, this was followed by the 'yellow code,' used by the German army. At the end of the month, the trawler *Polaris* was captured along with a copy of the German naval codes. For a few months the British were able to interpret German messages, until the German army changed its procedures and the code keys taken from the *Polaris* expired. The deciphering work became much more difficult, but in December 1940 the system used by the *Abwehr* (German military intelligence) was broken and towards the end of February 1941, the 'light blue code,' used by the Luftwaffe in the Mediterranean, was also broken.[167]

By spring 1941, Ultra could decipher Luftwaffe messages almost as quickly as the Germans, and although messages from German army units could still require weeks to break, many troop movements in the Mediterranean could be monitored, because the transportation services still used the older procedures. But there was a very important category of German signals that could not be broken by Ultra: the Hydra system used by the German Navy. At the time of Operation Rheinübung another system was about to be introduced in the Kriegsmarine, called Neptun, for use with the heavy warships. Messages coded with Hydra or Neptun could not be deciphered by Ultra. However, with the successful capture of *U-110* this all changed.

The German code keys, call signals and the Enigma machine were transferred to the British destroyer *Bulldog,* and the submarine was taken in tow towards Iceland. However, the following day the *U-110* sank and the disappointed British had to cut the rope and watch the submarine disappear. With hindsight, the British did not regret the loss of the German submarine, as they believed the Germans had agents in Iceland who would alert them to the news that one of their submarines had been captured. It might have provoked them to change at least the code keys. As it was, the Germans did not receive any information about the fate of *U-110*. Three days later, Lieutenant Allan Bacon, liaison between the Royal Navy and the British intelligence service, arrived in Iceland and examined the papers. He clearly realized the importance of the *Bulldog's* haul and sent a brief telegram: 'This is exactly what we have been looking for.' As a precaution, the documents were photographed before being flown to London.[168]

The British were also fortunate in making another fine haul. On 7 May, they captured the weather ship *München*, complete with code keys for the entire month of June. As these ships remained at sea for long periods, the British realized that the code keys must remain valid for long periods. The capture of *München* was the result of a deliberate operation to catch one of the weather ships. These two events were a breakthrough for the British intelligence services. The *U-110* was especially important, as the haul included a complete *Enigma* machine of the most recent type. With the Hydra code keys it was possible to follow the reports from German submarines, tankers, supply ships and weather ships during the forthcoming months. Furthermore, during this period, knowledge was gained which would improve the chances of breaking German codes once the current code keys had expired. Also, by studying how decrypted Hydra messages were structured, chances of breaking Neptun messages improved, although it could take between three and seven days to decipher a message from the big warships.

Still, from the German perspective the concept of waging successful cruiser warfare rested first and foremost on their ability to surprise the enemy. British acquisition of the codes meant that the required secrecy could no longer be depended upon, although for the moment the German Navy had no idea that their codes could be broken. When Lütjens attended to the final details for the planning of Operation Rheinübung, he had no inkling of how close the enemy was to gaining the initiative.

PART 2

CHAPTER 11

Departure

At dawn on Sunday, 18 May, the increasing light revealed thick cloud cover over Gdynia. The wind was calm and the weather was well suited for leaving the Baltic port and commencing Operation Rheinübung. In the morning Lütjens gathered the two commanders, Lindemann and Brinkmann, on board the *Bismarck*. He wanted to make his intentions for the forthcoming operation clear. The plans that had been prepared previously were to be followed. The squadron would pass the Great Belt in Denmark and continue through the Kattegat and Skagerrak. Then, Lütjens would set course for the Korsfjord, near Bergen, where fuel oil would be topped up, to replace the quantity burned during the voyage from Gdynia. However, there was an alternative. If the weather proved favourable, Lütjens would choose to go for the tanker *Weissenburg* in the Arctic Ocean. Thereafter, the break-out attempt would be directed through the Denmark Strait, where the fog prevalent along the edge of pack ice could be used to advantage.[169]

The purpose of the operation would still be kept secret from the crews. They were to be informed that the squadron sailed for the North Sea. Not until Lütjens gave his final order for the break-out would his real intentions be revealed. Furthermore, Lütjens elaborated on the use that should be made of the sea planes carried by the *Bismarck* and *Prinz Eugen*. His instructions were obviously influenced by the experiences from Operation Berlin. He made it clear that the aircraft were not allowed to attack enemy ships and they were only allowed to start upon receipt of written orders.[170]

After about an hour the meeting closed. The weather cleared, but since they were a long way from British bases, it was more important that the weather made the task difficult for British reconnaissance aircraft during the following days. The decision to sail was abided by, and at noon the two German ships left Gdynia.

'I wish you good hunting,' Lütjens announced to the crew on board the *Bismarck* and the seamen unable to attend on deck heard him on the many loudspeakers within the battleship. Her orchestra played '*Muß i denn ...,*' a tune often performed when ships of the German Navy departed on long voyages.[171] With hindsight, the music selection has been identified as a lapse in secrecy. To what extent the information may have affected subsequent events is unclear, but by itself it was not enough to justify British action. In any case the first part of the voyage was very short. The German ships just moved further out in the harbour. Still within sight of land, they took on more fuel oil. A mishap occurred when a hose broke. The consequence was that the *Bismarck* lacked about 200 tons of fuel oil when she and the *Prinz Eugen* weighed anchor later in the evening, under cover of darkness. Operation Rheinübung had begun, even though the two ships initially sailed separately.[172]

During the night, the ships ploughed forward on the Baltic to a point north of Cape Arkona, on the northern shore of the island of Rügen, where they converged and were joined by several destroyers, led by Commander Alfred Schulze-Hinrichs. At a speed of 17 knots the warships proceeded westward, until they reached a point northwest of the Island of Fehmarn, where the helm was shifted to continue north, towards the mouth of the Great Belt. The German naval staff had closed the strait for all civilian shipping during the night between 19 and 20 May, to allow the warships an unobserved passage.[173]

While the *Bismarck* and *Prinz Eugen* enjoyed the calm sea, other German units were busy gathering information. A Focke-Wulf Fw 200 had been sent to investigate the ice north of Iceland, but bad weather hampered the mission. Nevertheless, it seemed clear that there was no drifting ice within 130 kilometres of Iceland, a promising circumstance for Operation Rheinübung. A less comforting observation concerned eight Swedish fishing-boats in Skagerrak. If they remained there when Lütjens' squadron sailed by, there was a serious risk of detection.[174]

At dusk on 19 May, Lütjens' squadron approached the Great Belt and two hours after midnight they passed into the narrow strait, unfortunately slightly later than planned. As dawn broke on 20 May, the seamen on deck could see Fyn to the west and Sjælland to the east. The grey sky was at least some help to the Germans, as it reduced the morning light. It was a consolation for Lütjens and his staff, but also a grave disadvantage, as the same cloud cover extended all the way to Scapa Flow and prevented German aerial reconnaissance. Thus the Germans received no information on the Home Fleet and its whereabouts.[175]

As the *Bismarck* and *Prinz Eugen* continued northward, the cloud coverage gradually disappeared and the seamen on deck could see the small island of Anholt on the starboard. Lütjens and his staff had every reason to be worried. Everything that might increase the risk of discovery was disadvantageous.[176] Müllenheim-Rechberg clearly recalled this part of the voyage: 'If only we hadn't had to steam in such clear view of the Swedish coast and among innumerable Danish and Swedish fishing boats. They seemed to be everywhere, these little white craft with their

chugging motors, some of them bobbing up and down beside us.'[177]

German fears were soon justified. The Swedish aeroplane cruiser *Gotland* was conducting firing exercises off Vinga. At 13.00 hours Lütjens reported to Marinegruppe Nord that the *Gotland* had been sighted. But what really mattered was that the *Gotland* had reported the observation of two battleships of *Bismarck*-class, and three destroyers. The erroneous identification of the *Prinz Eugen* is understandable, as the silhouettes of two ships differed little. At a distance, the *Gotland* followed the German squadron, until 15.45 hours, when the Germans set a northwesterly course.[178] However, the *Gotland* had not been the first to report the German squadron to the Swedes. Just before her report, a Swedish aircraft had reported that three destroyers, one cruiser and a larger warship presumed to be the *Bismarck* sailed on a northerly course 35 kilometres from Vinga.[179]

Before long, it became apparent that Operation Rheinübung was no longer a secret. The question was what neutral Sweden would do with the information obtained? It was by no means certain that the knowledge about the two heavy German warships would be passed on. The Germans regarded Swedish neutrality as fairly benevolent and Admiral Carls, commander of Marinegruppe Nord, did not believe the information would leave Sweden.[180] But even if there were no intention to inform the British, there was always a risk that leaks would provide the British with information.

We do not know Lütjens' opinion on the issue. From a military ship secrecy could be expected, but the civilians did not have such limitations. Perhaps the *Gotland* was regarded as a lesser risk than the small fishing-boats. On the other hand, the Swedish military of course had much better means of distributing the information rapidly. In any case, the British would need the information quickly if they were to prevent the German break-out, which was the critical consideration. Lütjens' experiences from Operation Berlin suggested that it was very difficult to find his squadron once it had reached the expanses of the Atlantic. Thus, the Swedish observers need not be much of a problem.

While Lütjens' squadron continued on its course towards the southern coast of Norway, another drama took place south of Cape Farewell, the southernmost point of Greenland. Here the British convoy HX126 from Nova Scotia was attacked by several submarines and suffered serious losses. Its worst day was 20 May, when no less than

seven ships fell prey to the German U-boats. Of these, three fell victim
to Herbert Wohlfahrt and *U-556*. He had already torpedoed the *British
Security* and *Cockaponset*, when he found a straggler, the freighter
Darlington Court.[181] Wohlfahrt only had one torpedo left, but he
decided to attack. The navigation officer objected and suggested that it
might be better to save the remaining torpedo for a better target on the
way home, but Wohlfahrt replied: 'Better a sparrow today than a
possible pigeon tomorrow.'[182] He fired the last torpedo and the
Darlington Court gradually capsized and sank in the Atlantic. A week
later he was to bitterly regret this action.

On board Lütjens' ships, the tension mounted. The time for the
break-out came nearer and nearer. Had the British any inkling of the
German actions? A German reconnaissance aircraft flew over Scapa
Flow and this time weather was more favourable. The air crew reported
it had seen one carrier, three battleships and four cruisers in the main
base of the Home Fleet. Thus, Lütjens concluded that the main strength
of the Home Fleet remained in port. Had these ships weighed anchor, it
would have been a strong indication that the British had become aware
of the German plans.[183]

Towards the evening of 20 May the German squadron approached
the south coast of Norway, not far from Kristiansand and as the sun set,
the German lookouts could see land on the starboard side: magnificent
scenery with the beautiful Norwegian coastline glowing beneath a red
sky. Few seamen had the time to look at the view. The area was known
to be dangerous, as it was patrolled by British submarines. The German
ships zigzagged at 17 knots. During the night, the hydrophone operators
on board the *Prinz Eugen* registered propeller noise that might originate
from a submarine. Otherwise, the night passed uneventfully.

On the morning of 21 May, the B-Dienst on the *Prinz Eugen*
intercepted a British wireless signal instructing an air unit to search for
two battleships and three destroyers on a northerly course.[184] Except
for the mistaken identification of the *Prinz Eugen*, this was a correct
description of Lütjens' squadron.

Soon thereafter another ominous observation was made. 'Shortly
after 07.00,' Müllenheim-Rechberg remembered, 'four aircraft came
into view—mere specks against the sun. Were they British or our own?
So quickly did they vanish that we wondered if we had imagined them.'
The aeroplanes were so distant that their type or nationality could not

be determined, but nevertheless the observation was troublesome. The B-Dienst was of the opinion that the aircraft did not transmit any radio signal, but when the German squadron approached the Korsfjord south of Bergen, there were strong indications that it had been discovered.[185]

When Lütjens' ships weighed anchor in Gdynia, the British had their eyes rivetted on the events in the Mediterranean and on the submarine warfare in the Atlantic. A few weeks earlier, German army units had pushed an Allied expeditionary force off mainland Greece, forcing the British to yet another seaborne evacuation. The Commonwealth troops were shipped to Egypt and Crete and Churchill decided that Crete should be defended. Crete's geographical position was almost as strategically important as Malta and there still remained time to strengthen her defences.

In North Africa, Rommel had recaptured the areas taken by General Richard O'Connor during his offensive against the Italians in December 1940. Three days before Lütjens' squadron sailed from Gdynia, British forces in North Africa, commanded by General Archibald Wavell, launched Operation Brevity. The offensive was stopped dead in its tracks by Rommel. No useful results were produced by the British attack and the overall situation in the desert remained precarious. In addition to the problems in Africa, the British had strong indications that the Germans intended to attack the Soviet Union.

To all these worries, the situation on the Atlantic was added, where the German submarines continued their ravaging and further attacks from German cruisers and battleships were expected. No German surface ships had been in action in the Atlantic since the end of March, but evidently the *Bismarck* and *Prinz Eugen* were combat-ready by mid-May. On the other hand, available British intelligence suggested that the *Scharnhorst* and *Gneisenau* were not ready for action yet, as they probably were not fully repaired. For the Home Fleet, the major threat came from the *Bismarck*, the *Prinz Eugen* and possibly from the *Tirpitz*.

Admiral Tovey strived to keep as good a surveillance as possible over the most critical areas, without taxing the endurance of his ships and men. In particular, he had to be foresighted about the Denmark Strait, as it lay a considerable distance from the British bases, making it difficult to send reinforcements to the area without ample forewarning. For the time being, the first cruiser division, comprising the heavy cruisers *Norfolk* and *Suffolk* commanded by Rear-Admiral

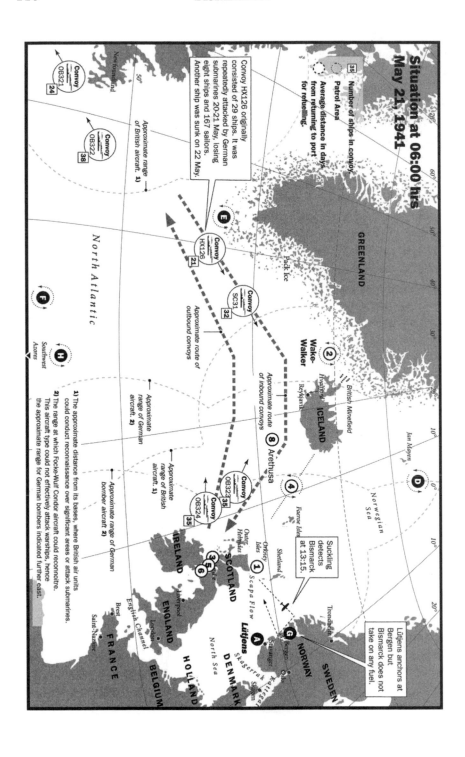

Situation at 06:00 hrs
May 21, 1941

35 Number of ships in convoy.

Patrol Area

Average distance in days,
from returning to port
for refuelling.

Convoy HX126 originally
consisted of 29 ships. It was
repeatedly attacked by German
submarines 20-21 May, losing
eight ships and 167 sailors.
Another ship was sunk on 22 May.

Approximate route of
outbound convoys

Approximate route
of inbound convoys

GREENLAND

Pack ice

New Foundland

50°

North Atlantic

60°

50°

40°

30°

Approximate range
of British aircraft. 1)

Convoy
OB321   24

Convoy
OB322   38

Convoy
HX126   21

E

Convoy
SC31   32

Wake-
Walker   2

British Minefield

Hvalfjord
Reykjavik

ICELAND

Jan Mayen

Norwegian
Sea

F

Southwest
Azores

H

20°

10°

0°

10°

Approximate
range of German
aircraft. 2)

Approximate
range of British
aircraft. 1)

Approximate range of German
bomber aircraft 2)

8 Arethusa

Convoy
OB323   35

Convoy
OB324   35

4

D

Faeroe Isles

Outer
Hebrides

Orkney
Isles

Shetland

Suckling
detects
Bismarck
at 13:15.

20°

IRELAND

SCOTLAND

ENGLAND

Liverpool

London

Brest

Saint-Nazaire

FRANCE

BELGIUM

HOLLAND

English Channel

North Sea

DENMARK

Lütjens   A

Scapa Flow

3
5
6

Trondheim

Bergen

Stavanger

Oslo

G

Skagerrak

Kattegat

NORWAY

SWEDEN

Lütjens anchors at
Bergen but
Bismarck does not
take on any fuel.

1) The approximate distance from its bases, where British air units
could conduct reconnaissance over significant areas or attack submarines.

2) The range at which Focke-Wulf Condor aircraft could reconnoitre.
This aircraft type could not effectively attack warships, hence
the approximate range for German bombers indicated further east.

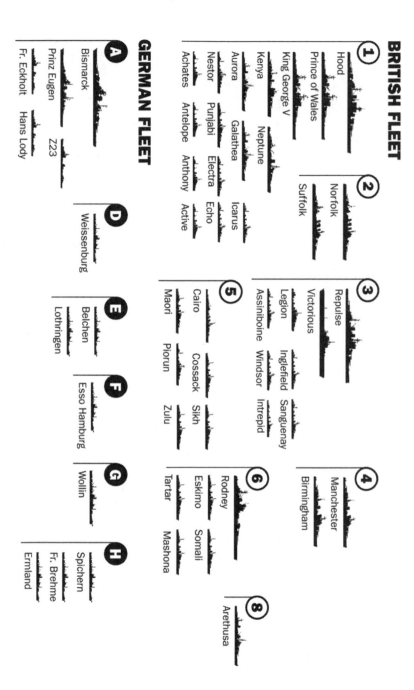

BRITISH FLEET

1
Hood
Prince of Wales
King George V
Kenya Neptune
Aurora Galathea
Nestor Punjabi Electra
Achates Antelope Anthony Echo
Icarus Active

2
Norfolk
Suffolk

3
Repulse
Victorious
Legion Inglefield Sanguenay
Assiniboine Windsor Intrepid

4
Manchester
Birmingham

5
Cairo
Maori Cossack Sikh
Piorun Zulu

6
Rodney
Tartar Eskimo Somali
Mashona

8
Arethusa

GERMAN FLEET

A
Bismarck
Prinz Eugen Z23
Fr. Eckholt Hans Lody

D
Weissenburg

E
Belchen
Lothringen

F
Esso Hamburg

G
Wollin

H
Spichern
Fr. Brehme
Ermland

Frederick Wake-Walker was guarding the Denmark Strait.

On 18 May, Tovey explicitly ordered the *Suffolk*, then patrolling the Denmark Strait, to keep vigilant supervision of the strait. In particular, Tovey emphasized the need to ensure that the area close to the pack ice was well covered. At the same time he instructed Wake-Walker to be on constant alert to reinforce the *Suffolk* with the flagship *Norfolk*, if necessary. For the moment, *Norfolk* was moored at Hvalfjord, just north of Reykjavik on Iceland. On 19 May she weighed anchor with Wake-Walker on board. She was to relieve the *Suffolk*, to allow the latter ship to bunker fuel oil at Hvalfjord. It was essential that the cruisers had sufficient fuel on board if the Germans were attempting a break-out. In addition to the first cruiser division, Tovey also dispatched a few light cruisers, to patrol the area between Iceland and the Faeroes. The remaining ships of the Home Fleet remained in their bases while Tovey waited for more information about the German activities. [186]

Soon Tovey would receive the information he hoped for. Roscher Lund was in Stockholm, as military attaché of the Norwegian government in exile. He was well acquainted with the British naval attaché in Sweden. Lund had also made good contacts with important people in the Swedish intelligence service and on 20 May they leaked the information on the German squadron to Lund.[187] He quickly contacted the British naval attaché, captain Henry Denham, who was dining at a restaurant. Denham rapidly paid the bill and went to the British mission, where they transmitted the important information to the Admiralty in London.

Further confirmation was to follow. In Kristiansand, on the southern coast of Norway, Viggo Axelsson went for an evening walk together with a few friends before having dinner at a club. When they reached a place called Runningen, they halted and looked out upon the sea in front of them. Visibility was excellent and almost immediately they discerned a group of ships at high speed. One man in the party had a small binoculars and Viggo Axelsson asked to borrow it. He could clearly see two major warships escorted by several smaller as well as planes providing air cover. Axelsson returned the binoculars and said it was time to go to the club.[188]

In fact, Viggo Axelsson was a member of the Norwegian resistance and had sent information to London several times before. Usually he gave the messages to Arne Moen, a bus driver who took them to

Gunvald Tomstad. The latter lived in Flekkefjord, half way to Stavanger, where he had a radio transmitter.[189]

As most of the party was unaware of Axelsson's work for the resistance, he had to create a cover story. He excused himself and said that he had to go back to his office, where he had forgotten something. Once at the office, he wrote an encoded message which he gave to Arne Moen, just before the bus was to depart for Flekkefjord. Late in the evening, Tomstad got the message. He realized it was urgent and transmitted it immediately, without taking his transmitter to some desolate place. Thus, the Admiralty received confirmation of the information sent by Denham and Lund.[190]

Tovey was, of course, informed. He was on board his flagship, the *King George V*, where he had a direct cable to the Admiralty in London. Tovey raised the readiness on his ships, but did not yet make the decision to sail. If the ships sailed too early, they might consume valuable fuel oil unnecessarily and perhaps lack it when urgently needed. Rather, Tovey intnded to direct air reconnaissance as soon as daylight and weather allowed.[191]

The German intentions were by no means obvious, but the available information suggested that the German squadron would reach Bergen early on 21 May. At least it allowed for a fairly useful direction of the reconnaissance. Lieutenant Michael Suckling took off with his Spitfire from the Scottish air field at Wick and steered towards the southwest coast of Norway. At first he found nothing remarkable. He could see the sea, fjords, bays and Norwegian fishing boats, but no German warships. Still he had fuel for a run over Bergen and nearby fjords. While remaining at high altitude, Suckling steered his Spitfire over Bergen and saw two warships at sea. His aircraft was equipped with special cameras and they performed as expected. On the ground, nobody seemed to notice the small aircraft high up in the sky. When Suckling had taken his photographs, he turned west, towards the open sea. Fifteen minutes later, the air raid alarm was heard in Bergen, but by that time, the British pilot had already covered a significant part of the distance to Wick.[192] As soon as Suckling had landed, the films were taken to the darkroom and developed. They clearly showed a battleship of *Bismarck*-class, a cruiser of *Admiral Hipper*-class and several smaller vessels.

The commander of the Home Fleet was promptly informed, as was the Admiralty. Tovey's quandary over whether or not he should sail was not alleviated by the confirmation that the *Bismarck* was in Bergen. The weather over Norway and the North Sea rapidly deteriorated and he received no further intelligence. He could not know if the enemy ships remained at Bergen, or if they had already put to sea. If they were heading for the Atlantic, a disaster might follow, as no less than 11 Allied convoys were plodding on the Atlantic.[193] Tovey decided that Vice-Admiral Lancelot Holland should immediately sail with the *Hood,* *Prince of Wales* and six destroyers, to reinforce Wake-Walker's cruisers in the Denmark Strait. If reports received suggested that the Germans intended to break out between Iceland and the Faeroes, Holland could turn back and within 24 hours he could assume a central position between Iceland and the British Isles. Most of the remaining Home Fleet warships were ordered to remain in Scapa Flow, but at high alert. The light cruisers *Manchester* and *Birmingham*, on patrol between Iceland and the Faeroes, were ordered to bunker fuel oil immediately and then resume patrolling. The light cruiser *Arethusa*, on its way to Reykjavik, was ordered to stay in Hvalfjord after bunkering and be placed at Wake-Walker's disposal. [194]

The Admiralty wanted to mount an air attack on the German ships in Bergen. The Air Ministry concurred. The commander of Coastal Command, Frederick Bowhill, however, wanted to let his staff examine the photographs taken by Suckling, before staging an air attack. Suckling was the only available pilot on the air base at Wick. Again, he had to get behind the controls of his Spitfire, this time to fly to London. When he approached Nottingham at dusk, his fuel was almost consumed. Fortunately, he was close to his home district. He landed outside Nottingham, borrowed a car from a friend and drove in darkness to London, where he delivered the photos. Both the Air Ministry and the Admiralty confirmed the conclusions drawn in Wick.[195]

The delay caused by Bowhill's desire to examine the photographs in person proved disadvantageous. In the darkness navigation became difficult and when the 18 dispatched bombers reached the Norwegian coast, they found it covered by fog. Only two bombers reached the Korsfjord and they saw nothing. The weather deteriorated further during the night. At dawn on 22 May, the clouds were very low, in some cases only 60 metres above sea level. These were poor conditions for a successful air attack or reconnaissance in the Bergen area. [196] Still, it remained vital to establish the whereabouts of the German ships.

CHAPTER 12

Bunkering in Norway?

Lütjens' decision to enter the Korsfjord had negative consequences. During his meeting with Lindemann and Brinkmann before the squadron left Gdynia, he had communicated his intention not to enter Bergen, but rather to set course for the tanker *Weissenburg* in the Arctic Ocean and bunker fuel oil from her. Before entering Bergen, Lütjens had already received information suggesting that the British had become aware of the impending operation. Thus it would have been wiser to set course for the *Weissenburg*, as he had initially intended. Bergen was well within reach of British air power. To make matters worse, Lütjens' squadron arrived at Bergen when visibility was at its best and the risks greatest. The two ships would be easy to find and attack.

If Lütjens had chosen to continue towards the *Weissenburg*, the British would not have had the opportunity to attack him. The delay caused by the repeated analysis of Suckling's photographs was an advantage Lütjens could not have counted on. There was another, perhaps even more important, advantage with the *Weissenburg* alternative—it would be very difficult for the British to estimate when the Germans attempted to break out. They would have to act on very sketchy information. Was a German break-out attempt already in progress, or were the Germans just loitering in the Arctic for a good opportunity to break out, or had the Germans already passed south of Iceland? Perhaps they had even turned back, towards Germany. Had Lütjens opted to go for the *Weissenburg*, genuine insecurity would have afflicted Tovey. However, when the German squadron entered Bergen, Suckling was given the opportunity to reveal it, thereby sparing Tovey many uncertainties.

Why did Lütjens make for Bergen rather than for the Arctic? One possible explanation is that he may have received weather forecasts telling him to expect favourable weather in the days that were to follow. As the *Prinz Eugen* needed to replenish her fuel oil, Lütjens may have chosen the quickest way to do it. If he had chosen to go for the *Weissenburg*, much time would have been lost.

The amount of fuel oil on board the ships was a very significant factor to consider. When the *Prinz Eugen* arrived at Bergen, she had 2,547 cubic metres of fuel oil, about three quarters of her full complement. It is more difficult to judge the amount remaining on the *Bismarck*. The voyage from Gdynia to Bergen amounted to about 850 nautical miles. The available information on the squadron speed suggests about 17 knots. Hence, it seems reasonable that the *Bismarck* had burnt approximately 800 cubic metres during the voyage to Bergen. Thus she would be about 1,000 cubic metres short of her maximum capacity of fuel oil. [197]

Lütjens decided to top the *Prinz Eugen* up with fuel oil. She took on 764 cubic metres from the tanker *Wollin*, a procedure requiring three hours. However, the *Bismarck* did not take on any fuel oil. Again we do not know why Lütjens made his decision. Perhaps he took it for granted that the endurance of the *Prinz Eugen* was the limiting factor. Thus, it would not matter much if the *Bismarck* was topped up or not.[198]

The *Bismarck* possessed an impressive radius of action. At a speed of 19 knots, she could travel 8,525 nautical miles (15,800 kilometres) if she began the voyage with full tanks. As a comparison, the British battleships *King George V* and *Prince of Wales* could only manage 4,750 nautical miles (8,800 kilometres) at 18 knots. At higher speeds, the radius of action decreased, but even at a speed of 28 knots, the *Bismarck* could cover 4,500 nautical miles (8,300 kilometres)—about as much as the British battleships managed at 18 knots. Obviously, the *Bismarck* had a substantial advantage over her opponents in the Royal Navy. With this background, perhaps it did not seem to matter much if the *Bismarck* had only 90% of her maximum fuel-oil load. On the other hand, we do not know how well informed Lütjens was about the performance of the brand new British battleships.

Perhaps Lütjens believed it was most important to quickly reach the Denmark Strait, as he had reason to believe his squadron was discovered. If so, it may have appeared preferable to bunker in Bergen and refrain from going to the *Weissenburg*. A mere three hours were required to refuel the *Prinz Eugen* and four hours ought to have been sufficient to top up the *Bismarck*. Certainly, Lütjens must have calculated with the *Belchen* and *Lothringen* that were waiting south of Greenland.[199] Nevertheless, his decision not to let the *Bismarck* bunker any fuel oil remains puzzling. The riddle will probably never be explained.

During the brief sojourn in Bergen, an unexpected visitor boarded the *Bismarck*. Lt. Commander Adalbert Schneider's brother, the army doctor Otto Schneider, who was stationed with the occupation forces in Bergen, happened to be notified about the unexpected arrival of the battleship. In a borrowed motorboat, Schneider and two comrades went to the *Bismarck*. 'After a short trip we were out in the bay,' he recalled, 'and caught sight of something bewitching. In front of us lay the *Bismarck*, almost like a silver grey dream from the Arabian Nights.'

Permission to come on board was granted and the visitors met a delighted Adalbert. A long time had passed since the two brothers had met and their reunion was a happy one. Otto Schneider, who certainly was not a sailor, was deeply impressed by the fast boat trip to the battleship. 'The motorboat made over 30 knots,' he enthusiastically explained to his brother.

'Well, we can do that with the *Bismarck* too,' Adalbert said with a smile, 'and a little more in fact.'

Adalbert took his visitors to the gun-room, where they discussed the battleship and naval warfare in general. Afterwards, a meal was served. Later, Otto followed Adalbert to his cabin, where the first artillery officer showed photographs of his three daughters. Adalbert seized the opportunity to write a few postcards, which Otto offered to put in the mailbox. It was the last private mail ever to leave the battleship.

By 17.00 hours, the *Prinz Eugen* had completed bunkering. The German ships weighed anchor and Otto Schneider had to leave the battleship. As he climbed down the ladder, a sense of uneasiness overtook him. Despite Adelbert's assurance that 'the *Bismarck* is faster than anything stronger and stronger than anything faster,' he left the battleship with a feeling of foreboding. The morale of the crew was high, but the German doctor had found the discussions in the gun-room ominous.

Under cover of darkness, the German squadron left Norway by negotiating the narrow fjords north of Bergen. At this moment,

Müllenheim-Rechberg became aware that the British had probably discovered the operation. Together with a group of officers, he was on the quarter-deck when Lieutenant Commander Kurt-Werner Reichard, head of the B-Dienst of the squadron, hastened by with a message to Lütjens. They asked him what it was about and he confidentially told them about the signal intercepted by the *Prinz Eugen* earlier during the day, which had said that British air units were to search for two German battleships and three destroyers. 'I can't deny that the information was slightly depressing,' wrote Müllenheim-Rechberg, 'as we had not had an inkling that the British had got notice about Operation Rheinübung. Now it felt as if we had been discovered and it was somewhat of a shock.' [200]

At midnight, when the two ships had reached open sea, a northerly course was set. Four hours after the squadron left Bergen, the destroyers, which had thus far escorted the battleship and the cruiser, veered off to the east, heading for Trondheim. From this moment the *Bismarck* and the *Prinz Eugen* were on their own.[201]

Lütjens had scant knowledge on the British whereabouts. Not long after the three destroyers left the squadron, the lookouts had reported the glimmer of searchlights reflected in the clouds above Bergen. Just before 11.00 hours on 22 May, a signal from Marinegruppe Nord reached Lütjens. It confirmed that British bombers had bombed the moorings near Bergen where the *Bismarck* and *Prinz Eugen* had been berthed. If any doubts that the British had discovered Operation Rheinübung had still lingered, they must definitely have been dispelled with this message. Unfortunately, more than 30 hours had passed since Lütjens last received any information about the British ships at Scapa Flow. Much could happen during such a long period of time. By travelling at 21 knots, British ships could easily cover the distance from Scapa Flow to Iceland in 30 hours. Neither did British wireless traffic reveal anything about the activities of the Home Fleet, but whether this was caused by inactivity or strict radio silence was impossible to know.[202]

One factor did favour the Germans. The weather deteriorated rapidly. Visibility was reduced and prospects of an undetected passage through the Denmark Strait appeared favourable. At noon on 22 May, Lütjens decided to set course immediately for the Denmark Strait.[203] At the same time Raeder attended a meeting with Keitel, Ribbentrop and

Hitler in Berchtesgaden, where he revealed that the *Bismarck* had been at sea for a few days. Hitler's reaction was not surprising. He was anxious about the impact the activities of the *Bismarck* could have upon American neutrality, or how it could affect the forthcoming attack on the Soviet Union. And what were the odds in an encounter with the Royal Navy? He talked about the risks imposed by British carriers and torpedo planes, fears expressed by Lütjens more than two weeks ago. Hitler wanted to recall the ships, but Raeder managed to persuade him that cancelling entailed greater dangers than continuing with the operation.[204]

Finally Hitler acquiesced. Operation Rheinübung would continue. Off the Norwegian coast, Lütjens had already veered off on the first leg of the route towards and through the Denmark Strait. His decision was not irrevocable. If the weather cleared, the German ships might still turn northeast and bunker from the *Weissenburg*.[205]

CHAPTER 13

Holland and Tovey Put to Sea

On the afternoon of Wednesday, 21 May 1941, an unusually large number of longboats travelled between the *Hood* and the *King George V*. To those who could interpret the events, it soon became clear that several heavy units of the Home Fleet would soon put to sea. The smoke from the funnels of the *Hood* and the *Prince of Wales* became denser and darker. Six destroyers left their berths and set course for the Switha sound, where a gate had to be negotiated. They continued towards the open area south of the Orkneys, the Pentland Firth. Just before midnight, the *Hood* and the *Prince of Wales* also weighed anchor. The barrier at Hoxa opened its gates and the nets protecting the area from submarines were temporarily removed. A drizzle fell over Scapa Flow and shrouded the two massive ships as they proceeded in the dark night. Outside the system of protection devices at the entrance to the harbour area at Scapa Flow, the two warships converged with the destroyers, whose hydrophones had already searched for German submarines before the heavy ships arrived. Despite it being rather late in May, the night was chilly.

With the *Hood* and the *Prince of Wales* heading towards Iceland, Tovey had taken the first step towards catching the *Bismarck*, but like Lütjens, the British admiral had only incomplete information on his enemy's whereabouts. He tried to use the available information to guess Lütjens' intentions. There were several plausible alternatives that could explain the presence of the German squadron at Bergen. The photographs taken by Suckling also showed several transport ships. It was conceivable that the German warships had protected vulnerable

126

transports loaded with equipment or troops destined for northern Norway. Such shipments had been observed during the preceding weeks. Considering the information indicating German intentions to attack the Soviet Union, these ship movements could also be part of preparations for an operation against Murmansk.[206]

It was also possible that the Germans were preparing an attack on Iceland. Another option was that the German warships had escorted the transport ships to Bergen, whereupon they would simply return to Germany.[207]

The most threatening scenario was a German break-out onto the Atlantic, in order to attack British convoys. If this was their intent, Tovey believed the Germans would probably use the Denmark Strait. His available information suggested that the Germans had used this narrow passage during all their previous break-outs. Still, he could not exclude the area between the Faeroes and Iceland, especially as the German ships had paused at Bergen this time. Also, it was conceivable that the Germans could attempt to pass between the Faeroes and the Shetlands, but this seemed unlikely due to the short distance from Scapa Flow and British airfields. For the moment Tovey did not make any changes. The miserable weather on the morning of 22 May showed no signs of abating, and in fact deteriorated even further. The bombers and torpedo aircraft standing by to attack the German warships would have had little chance of finding their targets and the attack was considered impossible.[208] The reconnaissance flights were all in vain, despite many attempts. A gale blew over the North Sea and the clouds were hanging extremely low. The reconnaissance aircraft made it to the Korsfjord, but the clouds were so low that the aeroplanes were likely to hit mountain slopes if the pilots attempted to go low enough to fly beneath them. After returning, one of the airmen was asked why he believed the German ships had left. He sarcastically answered: 'Well, I didn't crash into anything when flying at sea level in the fiord, so they have probably sailed.'[209]

Suppositiion was not enough, however; Tovey needed more solid proof. At the Hatston airfield, the main naval air base on the Orkneys, Captain Henry St. John Fancourt was in command. The Fleet Air Arm trained from this base and among Fancourt's officers, there was an old fox, Commander G. A. Rotherham, who mainly had desk-work to do in May 1941. Still, Fancourt believed that if anyone could manage to find Bergen in the prevailing weather, it had to be Rotherham. Fancourt contacted the Coastal Command, which Rotherham served with, and asked if there were any objections. As none was raised, Fancourt phoned Tovey's staff, which approved the mission. Rotherham's hastily scrambled crew, Lieutenant Noel Goddard and the wireless operator Willie Armstrong, were permitted to use one of Halston's two Maryland aircraft for the surveillance.[210]

At 16.30 hours on 22 May, the Maryland aircraft started. In the weather conditions, it was highly unlikely that Rotherham and his crew would manage to find his target by setting course towards it. In fact, they were quite likely to hit a mountain if they tried. Rotherham found it more prudent to aim for a goal located some distance from Bergen. When the Maryland swept over the Firth, he set course towards an island about 25 kilometres south of Bergen. From there, it would be easier to find the mouth of the Korsfjord and follow it.

The reconnaissance aircraft was soon shrouded in fog and the pilot took it to an altitude of 1,000 metres. Soon Rotherham decided to go down to sea level again. It was dangerous to fly close to the surface, but Rotherham quickly got an indication of the wind conditions and the aeroplane returned to a higher, and safer altitude. After another brief sweep just over the sea, Rotherham calculated that the coast of Norway would be reached within ten minutes. They had to descend once more to sea level. Just as they began to worry about crashing into a cliff, the small island Rotherham wanted to find appeared before their eyes.[211]

When the island had been found, the most difficult part was over, at least as far as navigation concerned. Fairly good weather met them once they neared the Norwegian coast. As the Maryland steered towards the Korsfjord, the men in the aircraft strained their eyes to find the German warships. Nothing was seen of them, but as a precaution they made a sweep over Bergen too. At this moment German Flak opened fire. Rotherham and his men winced as splinters hit the fuselage and tracers painted lines ahead of the aircraft. However, the pilot dived away from the fire and continued towards the open sea. Luck accompanied Rotherham and his crew and the wireless operator could send the message: 'The battleship and the cruiser have sailed.'[212] Unfortunately no confirmation of the message was received.

'We had been instructed to use a frequency and codes utilized by the

Coastal Command,' Armstrong said, 'but I kept calling without receiving any reply.'

This was a serious problem. German single-engine fighters were known to operate in the area and there was a significant risk that the Maryland would be shot down before the information reached Tovey. As the rest of the crew anxiously searched the sky for German fighters, the wireless operator tried a frequency used for target practice at Scapa Flow. 'We tried and immediately a reply was received. It was pure luck that somebody listened at Scapa Flow.'[213]

The Maryland successfully reached the Shetlands and as soon as Rotherham had climbed down from the aircraft, he was called to the telephone, where Tovey's chief of staff waited at the other end of the line. Tovey had actually received the radio message, but nevertheless decided to wait half an hour to issue confirmation.[214]

As a German break-out to the Atlantic was the gravest threat, Tovey chose to assume that this was indeed the reason for the departure from Bergen. Consequently, he ordered the *Suffolk*, which had bunkered fuel oil at Hvalfjord, to resume coverage of the Denmark Strait, together with the *Norfolk*. Similarly, the *Arethusa* was ordered to search the passage between Iceland and the Faeroes, where *Birmingham* and *Manchester* already patrolled. Tovey also demanded air reconnaissance between Greenland and the Orkneys, although there was little chance that the air crew would see much, as dusk was imminent and the weather poor. Less than an hour before midnight, anchor chains clattered as Tovey weighed anchor with the battleship *King George V*, the carrier *Victorious*, four cruisers and seven destroyers. He probably wished that the battleship *Nelson* had been in Scapa Flow too, but presently she was in the southern Atlantic. Soon Tovey's ships had passed the gates at Hoxa sound, almost 24 hours after Holland's squadron left Scapa Flow, and the seamen on deck saw the silhouette of the rocky Orkney Islands fade away in the darkness behind the ships. Tovey intended to assume a central position that would enable him to intervene against a German break-out, either south or north of Iceland.[215]

While all this took place, Holland's squadron continued towards the Denmark Strait. One of the seamen serving on the *Hood* was signalman Ted Briggs. The 18 year old youth regarded service on board

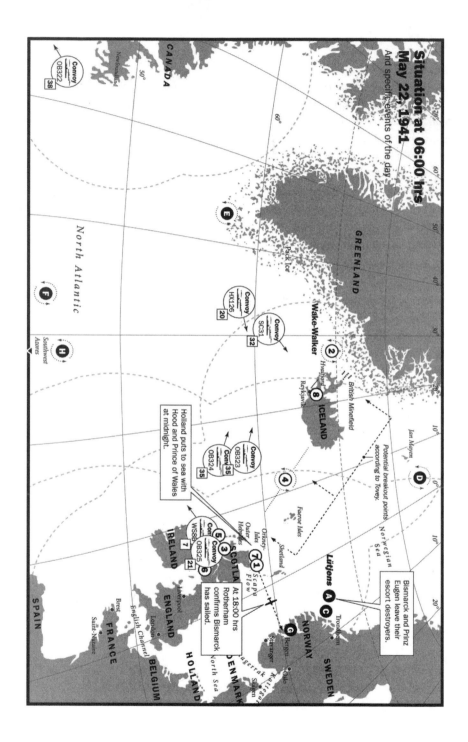

Situation at 06:00 hrs
May 22, 1941
And specific events of the day

Bismarck and Prinz Eugen leave their escort destroyers.

At 18:00 hrs Rotherham confirms Bismarck has sailed.

Holland puts to sea with Hood and Prince of Wales at midnight.

Potential breakout points according to Tovey.

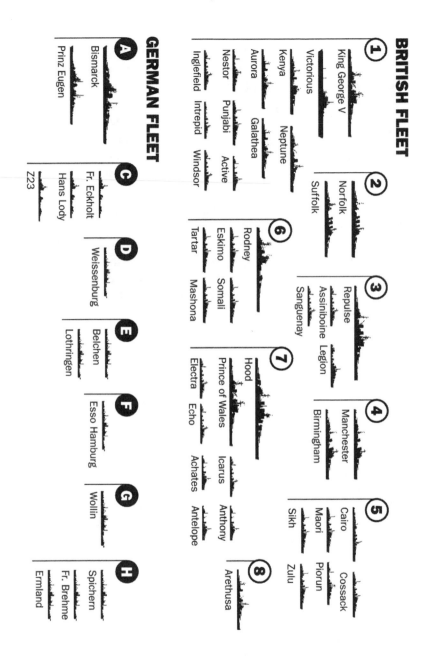

BRITISH FLEET

1
King George V
Victorious
Kenya
Aurora
Nestor
Inglefield
Neptune
Punjabi
Galathea
Intrepid
Active
Windsor

2
Norfolk
Suffolk

3
Repulse
Assiniboine
Sanguenay
Legion

4
Manchester
Birmingham

5
Cairo
Maori
Sikh
Piorun
Cossack
Zulu

6
Rodney
Eskimo
Tartar
Somali
Mashona

7
Hood
Prince of Wales
Electra
Echo
Icarus
Anthony
Achates
Antelope

8
Arethusa

GERMAN FLEET

A
Bismarck
Prinz Eugen

C
Fr. Eckholt
Hans Lody
Z23

D
Weissenburg

E
Belchen
Lothringen

F
Esso Hamburg

G
Wollin

H
Spichern
Fr. Brehme
Ermland

the battlecruiser as a boyish dream that had come true. He had dreamt of it since the age of 12, when he had seen the ship at anchor outside the town of Redcar. Local boat-owners made a bit of cash by taking passengers on a sightseeing tour to the battlecruiser, but Briggs' parents could not afford it. One day, the young boy sneaked away to the local enlistment office, where he tried to persuade the staff to enlist him. He was told to come back in three years. Briggs followed their advice and one week after his fifteenth birthday he signed up for service with the Royal Navy. To his immense joy, 16 months later he was stationed on the ship that had first attracted his curiosity. He could hardly expect that his name would forever be connected with her.

When the *Hood* was commissioned in 1920, she was the largest warship in the world. Many found her to be an unusually beautiful warship. As World War I had ended when she was ready, her first missions could perhaps best be described as British gunboat diplomacy. In 1923 she commenced a circumnavigation to confirm the ties between Britain and the Commonwealth. After leaving Plymouth in November, she appeared at Sierra Leone and Cape Town and continued to Zanzibar in East Africa. Thereafter she crossed the Indian Ocean for a goodwill visit at Ceylon and Singapore. Every stop was characterised by lavish parties and sports events, where the *Hood's* cricket and football teams played against local teams. After the visit to Singapore, where she raised a warning finger at Japanese imperialist aspirations, the battle-cruiser set course for Australia. She moored at Fremantle, Adelaide, Melbourne, Hobart and Sidney. Wellington and Auckland in New Zealand followed, whereupon the Australian and New Zealand governments were so impressed that Australia placed orders for two cruisers and New Zealand bought one of the cruisers that accompanied the *Hood*. The battlecruiser continued over the Pacific, visiting Fiji, Samoa, Hawaii and San Francisco, before negotiating the Panama Canal. Once she had reached the Atlantic again, she set course for Jamaica and Canada. Finally, she crossed the Atlantic and arrived in Britain on 9 September 1924, completing a voyage lasting almost a year.[216]

Most of the time the *Hood* was in commission was characterized by peace, there were still troubling episodes. In 1931 she was involved in a mutiny at Invergordon, when her crew refused to work after being told that their wages would be cut. These reductions in pay were far-reaching, but so ill-conceived that they were soon reconsidered. The episode tarnished the otherwise immaculate reputation of the battle-cruiser. Two years after the events at Invergordon, Commander Rory O'Connor assumed command of the *Hood* and he worked hard to remove the lingering effects of the mutiny. O'Connor made considerable efforts to reduce the gulf between officers and seamen and introduced regulations promoting mutual work towards a common objective. The results were encouraging. 'She became a so-called happy ship,' recalled seaman Ron Paterson, who served with the battlecruiser at that time. 'Everybody made their best, everybody assumed responsibility. The officers were excellent and were there to help.'[217]

In 1935, one of the first steps towards large scale war was taken, as the Italian dictator Benito Mussolini launched an attack on Ethiopia. The *Hood* was employed to deter Italian aggression, but to no avail. Her next mission came after the civil war in Spain had begun. The *Hood* was used to escort British merchant ships defying Franco's blockade of the Loyalist ports. During this period, it became increasingly clear that the *Hood*, after almost two decades of service, needed extensive rebuilding and modernizing, requiring quite some time in a shipyard. In particular, her armour protection was called into question. The *Hood* had been designed before the Battle of Jutland and not all of the lessons learned from that battle had been applied to her. In particular, a significant portion of the Battle of Jutland had been fought at such ranges that shells might hit the deck armour at very steep angles. Much thicker deck armour was needed to prevent them from reaching vital parts of the ship. Up to the mid-1930s, the weak deck armour was of little import, as no action against enemy battleships was likely in the foreseeable future. However, as war in Europe loomed, the *Hood's* deck armour became a much more serious problem. However, she was needed in commission, and the modernization of other Royal Navy ships took priority.

The first year at war gave the *Hood* little chance to fire her guns at German warships. Most of her time was spent patrolling or on escort duty. When France was defeated by Germany in June 1940, the *Hood* was dispatched to Admiral Somerville's Force H, based on Gibraltar. As the admiral's flagship, the *Hood* was given the unenviable task of attacking French naval units in Oran, where more then 1,000 former allies were killed. This was the *Hood's* first battle, initiated under very favourable circumstances. Engaging the *Bismarck* would be something quite different.

From January to March 1941, the *Hood* received some attention. Her machinery was overhauled and gunnery radar was fitted. Captain Glennie relinquished command of the battlecruiser, to receive a new assignment in the Mediterranean. He was replaced by Captain Ralph Kerr. After the refit, the *Hood* was again sent out to search and patrol, in particular during the last stage of Operation Berlin.[218]

While several capital ships of the Royal Navy had participated in major naval battles, it seemed that the *Hood* would never get the chance to do what she had been designed for. When the loudspeakers announced that the *Hood* was about to weigh anchor and sail from Scapa Flow, Briggs and his comrades had wondered, tempered by previous experiences, if they were finally to see 'the real action,' or if it was yet another of all these endless, cold and wet patrols?

The first part of the voyage seemed to confirm their fears. But on the evening of 22 May, a message arrived that changed everything. It was Briggs himself who had to run to the bridge with it. He gave it to Holland's signal officer, who quickly read it and then loudly said: 'The *Bismarck* and *Prinz Eugen* have put to sea. Continue to, and watch the area southwest of Iceland.' Ted Briggs returned to his comrades. He felt hungry, yet did not want to eat. [219] The chase was on.

CHAPTER 14

Break-out

Lütjens' squadron quickly increased distance between them and the Norwegian coast. Initially, his ships had been within reach of German aircraft operating from Norway, and thus could count on support from the Luftwaffe. However, as the distance to the coast increased, this possibility vanished. Only a few German reconnaissance aircraft possessed the range required to reach as far as the present position of the *Bismarck* and *Prinz Eugen*. Overall, the two German warships were on their own. As there was no longer any chance of air support, there was also no risk of being mistakenly attacked by German bombers. To facilitate the identification of the warships, large swastikas had been painted on the deck fore and aft. Lütjens ordered them to be painted over, just as the side camouflage had been painted over during the pause in Bergen. With some luck, British aircraft could be fooled about the identity of the German warships.[220]

When contemplating the interaction between Lütjens, as Fleet Commander at sea, and the naval staffs ashore, it becomes strikingly clear that Marinegruppe Nord had little influence upon the operation and that its direction depended very much upon Lütjens himself. Nobody ashore even knew whether he would choose to go south or north of Iceland. For example, Admiral Dönitz, commander of the German submarines, could only instruct his forces that the *Bismarck* and *Prinz Eugen* were going to break out onto the Atlantic. Either Lütjens would go south of Iceland, probably during the night between 22 and 23 May, or through the Denmark Strait the following night. Lütjens' choice would be strongly influenced by local weather conditions.[221]

At least three factors lay behind this situation. The first was the need to make decisions according to local circumstances, like weather. Conceiving a plan and strictly adhering to it was not a recipe for success, as circumstances could rapidly begin to differ from the assumptions underlying the plan. The weather was the most striking example, especially at these latitudes. A brilliant day, when ships could be seen at very long distances, could quickly change into rain storm with virtually no visibility, and vice versa. Of course the commander on the spot was best placed to judge the local conditions, not somebody hundreds of miles away ashore.

Another important reason was secrecy. If the final decisions were made at sea, they were far less likely to become known by the enemy. The third reason was tradition. In the German armed forces, there was a long tradition that the commander on the spot would make the important decisions. In the army, it was called *Auftragstaktik*, mission-oriented orders. During the ground operations in World War II, this practice was to serve the German army well and contribute to many successes. In the French and British armies, there was a stronger tendency for commands to be issued by leaders who were not on the ground, which often allowed the Germans to take the initiative. The German concept was also applied within the navy. It is worth noting that the Royal Navy also allowed its commanders at sea a fairly wide latitude.

Marinegruppe Nord did not make any decisions with significant impact on Operation Rheinübung after 22 May. However, although Admiral Carls, commander of Marinegruppe Nord, was disconnected from the decision making, he could ensure that information was transmitted to Lütjens. In particular, weather forecasts and reconnaissance reports could provide information vital to Lütjens' decision-making. Also, intelligence gleaned from intercepted wireless transmissions could be of significant importance. Furthermore, information from German agents keeping an eye on the ships departing from Gibraltar, Canada and Africa could be forwarded to Lütjens. It was less common that information travelled in the opposite direction, from the squadron at sea to Marinegruppe Nord. The German ships usually maintained radio silence at sea. However, if British forces had already established contact with the German warships, they could of course use their radio equipment without restrictions. Still, most of the time, the

German naval commanders ashore had a rather vague perception of the actions performed by the ships at sea.

Radio silence was particularly important during a break-out, but the importance was by no means confined to the Germans. The Royal Navy also practised radio silence at this stage, as they too valued secrecy. Tovey did not want the Germans to know the location of either his force or of Holland's squadron. Consequently, the British commanders faced a similar situation to that of their German counterparts, and the Admiralty did not have a clear understanding on what transpired at sea. Even at sea, neither Tovey nor Holland knew exactly what the other was doing. They had to make guesses, based on what they had discussed before Holland put to sea. If either of the admirals changed his plans as a result of new information, he could only communicate it by radio, thus running the risk of informing the enemy too. Lütjens did not have this difficulty to contend with, as his squadron was the only German surface force at sea for the moment.

At dawn on 23 May, the weather seemed to confirm Lütjens' decision to attempt a break-out through the Denmark Strait. The sky was covered by thick clouds. Fog and rain reduced visibility further. Lütjens' two ships made between 24 and 27 knots and quickly approached the area north of Iceland. At noon they had reached a point due north of Iceland and approached the most difficult part, the narrow passage between the northwestern tip of Iceland and Greenland. Here, the Denmark Strait was narrowest and the Germans knew there were British minefields close to Iceland.[222]

Perhaps Lütjens felt confident. The evening before, he had received a report stating that air reconnaissance had found that four major ships, one of them probably a carrier, were still at Scapa Flow. This information suggested that his decision to stage a quick break-out through the Denmark Strait was the right one If Tovey's battleships were still in Scapa Flow, they would not be able to intercept the German squadron before the latter had already reached the vast expanses of the Atlantic. Once there, Lütjens' ships would be very difficult to find. Late in the evening, Lütjens also received reports on the battle at Crete, telling him that the Luftwaffe had sunk several Royal Navy ships near the strategically valuable island. Perhaps it would make it more difficult for the British to detail ships against his squadron.[223]

Unfortunately for Lütjens' plans, the report telling him that the

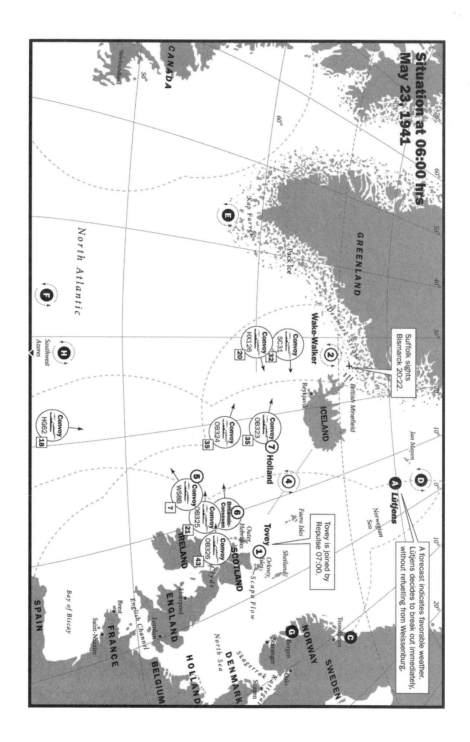

Situation at 06:00 hrs
May 23, 1941

CANADA

Newfoundland

50°

60°

North Atlantic

Azores

Southwest

GREENLAND

Kap Farvel

Pack Ice

Denmark Strait

British Minefield

Suffolk sights
Bismarck 20:22.

Wake-Walker

Convoy
HX126

SC31

20

Convoy

32

ICELAND

Reykjavik

Convoy
OB324

OB323

35

Convoy

Convoy (7) Holland

H

Convoy
HG62

18

Convoy
OB325

W88B

7

Britannic
Convoy

Convoy
OB326

Convoy

21

IRELAND

43

Clyde

SCOTLAND

Outer
Hebrides

Tovey

Orkney
Islands

Scapa Flow

Faeroe Isles

Shetland

Tovey is joined by
Repulse 07:00.

Jan Mayen

Norwegian
Sea

Lütjens

A forecast indicates favorable weather.
Lütjens decides to break out immediately,
without refueling from Weissenburg.

G

NORWAY

Trondheim

Stavanger

Bergen

Oslo

SWEDEN

Skagerrak

Kattegat

Slagen

North Sea

DENMARK

HOLLAND

BELGIUM

ENGLAND

Liverpool

London

FRANCE

Saint-Nazaire

Brest

English Channel

Bay of Biscay

SPAIN

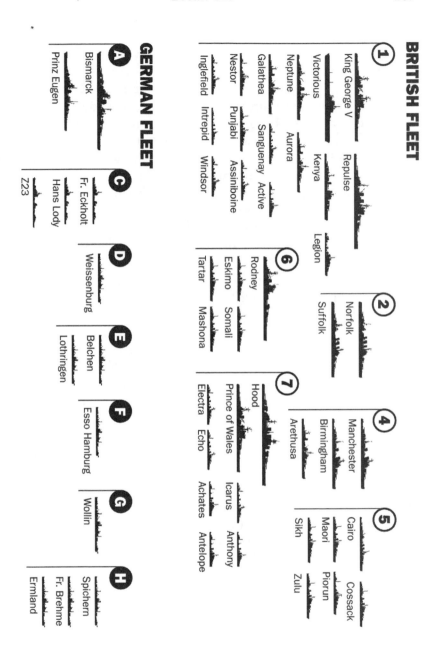

BRITISH FLEET

(1)
King George V
Victorious
Neptune
Galathea
Nestor
Inglefield Intrepid
Punjabi
Sanguenay Active
Assiniboine
Windsor
Aurora
Kenya
Repulse
Legion

(2)
Norfolk
Suffolk

(4)
Manchester
Birmingham
Arethusa

(5)
Cairo
Maori
Sikh
Cossack
Piorun
Zulu

(6)
Rodney
Eskimo
Tartar
Somali
Mashona

(7)
Hood
Prince of Wales
Electra Echo
Arethusa
Icarus Anthony
Achates Antelope

GERMAN FLEET

A
Bismarck
Prinz Eugen

C
Fr. Eckholt
Hans Lody
Z23

D
Weissenburg

E
Belchen
Lothringen

F
Esso Hamburg

G
Wollin

H
Spichern
Fr. Brehme
Ermland

Home Fleet was at Scapa Flow on 22 May was erroneous. The *King George V* still remained at Scapa Flow when the German reconnaissance aircraft passed over the naval base, but she left after dusk. Holland's squadron was already at sea. The reasons for the mistake are unclear, but at least some explanations appear plausible. The old battleship *Iron Duke* remained at Scapa Flow. It was a vessel built before World War I and no longer operational, but still in use as depot ship. Furthermore, there were two dummy battleships, constructed of wood and fabric. During 1941, the British began to doubt that they would be of any use, but perhaps they played a decisive role at this stage of Operation Rheinübung. Had Lütjens known that significant parts of the Home Fleet were already at sea, he might have made quite different decisions.[224]

Early on 23 May, Lütjens received a weather forecast promising well. Overcast weather, as well as rain, was predicted in the Denmark Strait. Visibility was expected to vary from slight to poor. Conditions seemed favourable for a break-out. Lütjens stayed with his previous decision, but he realized the importance of the accuracy of the forecast. The squadron would pass the narrowest part of the Denmark Strait at night, but at this time of the year, the night was not particularly dark at these northern latitudes. Favourable weather was an indispensable cover, since he could not capitalize on the long, dark nights that had aided Operation Berlin.[225]

Had Lütjens known that four British convoys passed south of Iceland at the same time, he may have made different decisions. The convoys OB323 and OB324 with 70 ships altogether had left Britain and headed west. The SC31 approached from the opposite direction, as did the decimated HX126, in all more than 50 ships carrying equipment and supplies to Britain. If Lütjens had chosen to pass south of Iceland, he might very well have run into at least one of these convoys. The story of Operation Rheinübung would then have taken a very different turn. However, Lütjens would have had to sneak past the British cruisers patrolling between Iceland and the Faeroes, something that had eluded him during Operation Berlin. The risk of early detection would have been aggravated by the reconnaissance aircraft of Coastal Command, which had been forced to cancel all flights over Norway due to the weather, but still could patrol the area between Iceland and Scotland. The Home

Fleet was also within shorter distance, had Lütjens chosen the passage south of Iceland. He might very well have ended up squeezed by Holland's squadron to the west of him and Tovey's ships to the east.

The passage through the Denmark Strait was not without its risks either. On their way to the Denmark Strait the Germans suffered a setback. At about 16.00 hours visibility, which had so far been very poor, suddenly improved. Except for brief periods of snow squalls, the visibility became quite good. It was a serious disadvantage, as Lütjens' squadron now approached the British minefields. The distance between the mines and the pack ice was hardly more than 60 kilometres. If two British ships patrolled the passage, a visibility of only a quarter of that range would be sufficient to ensure the discovery of Lütjens' squadron. To make matters worse, there was little or no room for evasive manoeuvres in the area.[226]

Action stations had been ordered on the German ships and as mines were an obvious threat, the electrical protection system against magnetic mines had been activated. Although visibility was far better than the Germans had wished, nature still played tricks. At 19.11 the alarm sounded in the ships, as a ship had been observed to starboard. Eleven minutes later, it had become apparent that the 'ship' was in fact an iceberg and the previous alert level was resumed.

Such mistaken observations were not unusual in the area. The proximity to the huge ice mass on Greenland, which extended far onto the sea, caused warm and cold air to form different layers. In the boundary between such layers, light could be reflected, much like mirages in the desert. The nervous lookouts could easily mistake such images for an enemy. Apart from a few of the higher-ranking officers, few of the Germans who served on the two warships had ever before been in such northerly waters.

Lütjens wanted to sail as close to the pack ice as possible, so that he could hide in the fog created by the humid air being cooled by the ice. However, this time luck deserted him. Indeed there was fog, but close to Iceland, where the risk of encountering the British minefields was unacceptably high. The dangers of drifting ice could not be ignored. If the ships were forced to steer away from drifting ice, they ran the risk of inadvertently straying into the nearby minefields. Thus, despite the greater risk of discovery, Lütjens had to follow the pack ice where visibility was unusually good.[227] Many of the officers were deeply concerned about the unfortunate change in visibility.[228] Müllenheim-Rechberg was one of them:

> *In the direction of Iceland, heavy haze hung over the ice-free water; on our bow, in the direction of Greenland, there were shimmering, bluish-white fields of pack ice and the atmosphere was clear. The high glaciers of Greenland stood out clearly in the background, and I had to resist the temptation to let myself be bewitched by this icy landscape longer than was compatible with the watchfulness required of us all as we steamed at high speed through the narrowest part of the strait, with our radar ceaselessly searching the horizon.*[229]

It was still quite light when the alarm again sounded in the German ships. It was 20.22 and a shadow could be discerned on the port bow. Was it another iceberg? It did not seem likely, as both hydrophones and radar had picked up something in that direction. The range was 13 kilometres, which was no match for the German guns.

'I stared through my director,' Müllenheim-Rechberg remembered, 'but could not see anything. Perhaps the contact was hidden from me by the ship's superstructure. Our guns were ready to fire, awaiting only the gunfire-control information. It never came.'

For a brief moment the enemy ship could be seen through the haze and she was quickly identified as a cruiser of *County*-class. Moments later she had again turned into a vague shadow again, quickly disappearing into the bank of fog towards Iceland.

The question was: Had the British cruiser observed the *Bismarck* and *Prinz Eugen*?

In the meantime, Admiral Tovey had considered many different questions. When it became known that the *Bismarck* had left Bergen, the Admiralty had subordinated the *Repulse* and *Victorious* to the commander of the Home Fleet. As mentioned previously, these ships had been earmarked for convoy escort, to the Middle East and Malta, respectively. Now they were at Tovey's disposal, but the *Victorious* first had to unload her partly disassembled Hurricane aircraft.[230] On paper, the addition of a carrier and a battlecruiser was a significant contribution to Tovey's forces, but the combat capabilities of the two was questionable. The *Victorious* was brand new and perhaps not yet fully trimmed, but most problematic was the incomplete training of her aircrew. A few hours after being informed about Suckling's discovery, Tovey sent for Captain Henry Bovell, commander of the *Victorious*, and asked him if his aircrew could conduct an attack on the *Bismarck* in Bergen. Bovell's answer was negative, but he added that his carrier could accompany the Home Fleet if the *Bismarck* were to try to break out into the Atlantic.[231] The carrier could not be regarded as anything but a joker in the pack.

Tovey also had reservations with regard to the *Repulse*, stemming from his concern as to what speed the fleet should sail at. The *Repulse* was already sailing north and would attach to Tovey's forces north of the Outer Hebrides, on the Scottish west coast. Her endurance was limited and if Tovey chose to go at too high a speed, the *Repulse* might be forced into a port, to bunker fuel oil. If Tovey on the other hand settled for a low speed, the German warships might slip away into the Atlantic before he had engaged them. Finally, he settled for 15 knots as a compromise, as soon as the *Repulse* had joined the Home Fleet, which she did at 07.00 hours on 23 May.[232] But in addition to the limited endurance, the *Repulse* was also quite old and weakly armoured.[233]

At the same time, Holland had reached a position about 200 kilometres south of Iceland and continued westward at high speed. As Tovey was still far to the east, Holland realized it was only his ships that could force the Germans to battle, if they had decided to sail through the Denmark Strait. He did not know exactly when the Germans had left Bergen, but he had to reckon with the fact that they could have departed almost immediately after Suckling took his photographs. If so, Holland could not possibly reach the narrow part of the Denmark Strait before the Germans. However, he still had a good chance to intercept them about 200 to 300 kilometres southwest of the narrow passage. It meant that he could only expect to force the Germans to battle in a large area, where he would have scant chances of finding them by his own means. Thus, he was unlikely to engage the Germans unless Wake-Walker's cruisers found them in the Denmark Strait and managed to shadow the German warships, while constantly informing on their positions.[234]

Wake-Walker had the unenviable task of sailing back and forth over the same area, searching for an enemy that might never appear. Very little happened and the alarms always proved to be false. In these northern waters, the climate was very demanding. The sea was usually rough and the cold was palpable. Rain, snow and fog added to the misery for the seamen. The view towards the Greenland ice could indeed be enchanting, but often nothing was seen of it, due to the poor weather. The *Norfolk* and *Suffolk* had patrolled the Denmark Strait for a long time and the charm of novelty had faded away. Before the *Suffolk* was ordered to Hvalfjord to bunker fuel oil, she had already patrolled the Denmark Strait for ten consecutive days.[235]

Unlike the *Norfolk*, the *Suffolk* had recently been modified to better cope with the demands associated with patrolling the Denmark Strait. First of all, she had been fitted with more modern and sophisticated radar, compared to the old set installed on the *Norfolk*. Second, her bridge had been reconstructed to be better protected from wind and sea and also provided with a heating system. On the open bridge of the *Norfolk*, very warm clothes were required to endure prolonged stay. One of the officers on the bridge of the *Norfolk* was Admiral Wake-Walker.

William Frederick Wake-Walker had joined the Royal Navy as a midshipman in 1904 and had become a torpedo specialist. He was a practical man, technically gifted and had played a prominent role in the efforts to organize the evacuation from Dunkirk the year before. He was not known for humour or imagination, but such qualities were not needed in the present situation. He knew the *Bismarck* and *Prinz Eugen* had left Bergen and understood that they could appear in the Denmark Strait at short notice. As he was well aware of the fact that fog often reduced visibility near the ice edge, Wake-Walker gave the *Suffolk*, with her modern radar, the task of covering the area near the pack ice. The *Norfolk* would patrol further south, closer to Iceland.[236]

His task might seem simple to accomplish, but it had its share of complications. The British ships had to travel back and forth along a line that roughly stretched from northeast to southwest. As the German warships were expected to approach from the northeast, it meant that Wake-Walker's cruisers might very well meet the German squadron on collision course. In that case, the Germans might get a good chance to open fire before the British ships could veer off. That was a bleak prospect for Wake-Walker and his seamen. The armour carried by the British cruisers was wholly insufficient to withstand the shells fired from the *Bismarck's* 38cm guns. If any of her shells were to hit the British cruisers, luck was the only kind of protection the British seamen could count on. Compared to the *Prinz Eugen* too, the British cruisers were at a disadvantage. The German cruiser was ultramodern, while the *Norfolk* and *Suffolk* were almost 15 years old. The *Suffolk* did not even carry torpedoes. Had Wake-Walker been fully informed about the performance of the German ships he might have been even more concerned. The *Prinz Eugen* was better protected, had more effective artillery and was also slightly faster than the British cruisers. The latter only had a marginal speed advantage over the *Bismarck,* and in terms of firepower and protection, the battleship was of course overwhelmingly superior.[237]

To avoid battle, it was necessary to detect the Germans before they could open fire. This was not easy. At first glance, it might seem as if the *Suffolk's* radar would give her that chance, but despite being among the best available to the British, her radar had a range of 23 kilometres at most, considerably less than the range of the German guns. Although the accuracy decreased with increasing range, the fire from German guns still posed a serious threat. The *Norfolk*, with her old radar, was at even greater peril.

The limited range of the radar was not the only disadvantage. As the British cruisers had been constructed at a time when radar still lay in the future, it had not been possible to mount it in an optimum position. Certain sectors were blocked by superstructures. On the *Suffolk*, there was a blind sector aft. It meant that each time she was on a southwest leg, the Germans might approach her from a direction where the radar could not give any warning at all.[238] Furthermore, radar at this time was still in an early phase of its development and was not fully reliable. For example, snow squalls could often create false echoes. Thus, the task at hand for the men of the 1st Cruiser Division was not easy. It was almost always boring, but it was a boredom that could suddenly turn into deadly peril.

Captain Robert Ellis commanded the *Suffolk*. According to the orders he had received from Wake-Walker he had set course to assume his patrol line. He soon realized that visibility was quite good close to Greenland, while dense fog prevailed near Iceland. Just like Lütjens, he noted that the visibility conditions were quite opposite to what was common in the Denmark Strait. As the eye could see further under the prevailing conditions, he mainly relied on his lookouts. However, he was well aware that the Germans could see far too and decided to remain as close as possible to the fog. In case of contact with the enemy, he could quickly steam for cover into the fog. The radar would enable him to follow the Germans even if the *Suffolk* remained concealed by the fog.[239]

Just after 20.00 hours, the *Suffolk* was on a south-westerly course, just the situation when the radar coverage was limited. The lookouts had to be on full alert. Captain Ellis was very careful to remain close to the fog and ordered the lookouts to be reinforced.

At 20.22 a yell was heard from petty officer Newell. Bored to death, he had searched with the help of fixed binoculars on the starboard side aft of the bridge, when suddenly all weariness disappeared, as a dark shadow appeared.

'Ship, bearing 140 degrees,' he cried, which was immediately corrected to 'Two ships, same bearing.'

Ellis dashed to the starboard side and in his binoculars he could see the *Bismarck*, followed by a cruiser. 'Steer hard aport! Full speed ahead!' he said to the officer on duty, who immediately forwarded the order to the engine control room and wheelhouse.

It was precisely the situation Ellis had feared, and the *Suffolk* was in grave peril. 'Range to the enemy ships?' he demanded and was told that it was 13 kilometres. He glanced at the fog in the east. It was close and seemed to turn towards the cruiser as it sheered.

Why did the enemy not open fire? Did they not want to reveal themselves, hoping that they had not been detected? Or was the lightly painted *Suffolk* difficult to see against the background provided by the dense fog? The *Suffolk* quickly came closer to the fog.

'Report to the Admiralty that we have seen them,' Ellis said to the signal officer, as the grey fog veiled the *Suffolk* and the two enemy ships gradually disappeared. They made between 28 and 30 knots. Ellis let his ship remain in the fog while the radar kept contact with the enemy.

Now there was one obvious task that overshadowed all else: to enable the heavy British units to engage the *Bismarck* and *Prinz Eugen*.[240]

CHAPTER 15

Pursued

On board the *Bismarck* and *Prinz Eugen* the movements of the British cruiser were anxiously followed with radar and hydrophones. She was invisible to the naked eye, but the instruments all told the same story – the enemy ship first disappeared astern, but soon joined the same course as the German squadron. Soon the signal intelligence on board the *Prinz Eugen* intercepted a message from the *Suffolk*. It was coded, but the communications officer, Lieutenant Commander von Schultz, urged his crypto experts to decode it. They did not require much time to break the code. One of them wrote the text of the message on a form and handed it to von Schultz.

The troubled von Schultz hastened to the bridge, where he gave the paper to Brinkmann. A few minutes later a signal lamp flashed on the German cruiser. The message was recorded by a signalman who handed it to Lütjens. A quick glance told the admiral that all hopes of an unnoticed break-out into the Atlantic were dashed. 'One battleship and one cruiser observed, bearing 20 degrees, distance 13 kilometres, course 240 degrees' read the intercepted message and everything the German commander knew suggested that the British cruiser was following his squadron at a safe distance.[241]

Since the ships had been spotted, there was nothing for Lütjens to risk by breaking radio silence. 'Notify Marinegruppe Nord,' he said, 'that we have sighted a British cruiser in this quadrant.' It was possible that the British message had been intercepted by the German staffs on land too, but as a safeguard Lütjens could just as well confirm it.[242] He also instructed his captains that they were allowed to open fire if the

147

enemy cruiser came close enough, or if other enemy vessels appeared.

On board the British cruiser *Norfolk*, Captain Alfred Phillips had been interrupted in the midst of his supper by the signal received from the *Suffolk*. Phillips immediately ordered that his cruisers should set course towards the position where the German squadron could be expected, a measure that caused the *Norfolk* to head more or less directly towards the *Bismarck*. Phillips and Wake-Walker briefly deliberated on the bridge, but could only conclude that they were in a very dangerous situation. Visibility was poor and *Norfolk's* obsolete radar provided scant assistance. It had several wide sectors without any coverage. Hence, the element of surprise might fully favour the Germans.

At 20.30 hours the alarm was again heard on board the *Bismarck*; her radar had discovered a ship ahead. The dense fog made it impossible to see anything at long range. The radar on the German battleship could give a position accurate enough to open fire, but still accuracy would be less than that allowed by data from the optical instruments. Captain Lindemann decided to hold fire, but ordered his artillery to be ready to fire immediately upon receiving the order to do so.[243]

As the *Bismarck* and the *Norfolk* sailed head to head, the range between them was quickly reduced. 'Enemy sighted on port side,' Lindemann informed his crew via the loudspeakers. 'Battle imminent.'[244]

Suddenly the fog lifted and the silhouette of the *Norfolk* was clearly visible from *Bismarck's* bridge. The range was only 6,400 metres and Adalbert Schneider did not await instructions. He immediately ordered fire. A violent crash indicated that the *Bismarck* had for the first time fired her guns in battle.

The crew of the *Norfolk* had misjudged the position of the enemy ships, and from the bridge Philips and Wake-Walker saw the huge battleship suddenly appear from out of the fog. The *Bismarck* cut through the waves, creating large cascades of spray and with her guns pointing straight towards the *Norfolk*. The sight had scarcely sunk in, when an orange blaze flashed through the haze and a huge dark cloud of smoke rose from the *Bismarck*.

'Steer hard starboard!' Phillips ordered. 'Make smoke!'

The *Norfolk* had just begun to turn, when columns of water thrown up by the large calibre shells appeared unpleasantly close on the starboard side. A few splinters hit the British cruiser; one of them darted by the bridge, right in front of Wake-Walker and Phillips. A moment later the thunder from the explosions rolled over the ship.

Bismarck fired five salvos at *Norfolk*, but despite three of them straddling the cruiser, miraculously no shell hit it. Except for insignificant damage from splinters she was unharmed. Subsequently she was protected by the fog.[245]

With their hearts in their mouths, the crew on board the *Norfolk* waited until the German ships turned southwest, before beginning to pursue them together with the *Suffolk*. Meanwhile Wake-Walker reported that the *Bismarck* and *Prinz Eugen* had been sighted. The initial report by *Suffolk* had not been received on board Tovey's flagship, but Wake-Walker's message was heard. Tovey finally became aware of the *Bismarck's* position. Even though the *Bismarck* obviously had almost reached the Atlantic, Tovey found consolation in his previous decision to dispatch Holland's squadron in advance. His estimates had proved correct and there was still time to halt Lütjens. Tovey himself would not intercept the Germans if they continued southwest, but if they turned south or even southeast matters would look decidedly different. Then he would certainly be in a position to intercept them. As a precaution he decided to increase speed to 27 knots, which was almost the best *King George V* could do.[246] However, if the German ships continued on their present course, only Vice-Admiral Holland had any chance of catching them before they had left the Denmark Strait behind. Tovey's main hope was that Holland too had heard the signal from *Norfolk*.

Meanwhile 1st Cruiser Division shadowed the German squadron, while repeatedly reporting on the situation. The weather was fickle. At one moment visibility could be fairly good and the two enemy ships could be discerned as two great towers at the horizon, then they could suddenly disappear in fog, rain or even snow. British chances of bringing the German squadron to battle depended on Wake-Walker's cruisers and their ability to keep contact with the enemy. Without *Suffolk's* radar it would probably have been an impossible task.

With the sudden appearance of the British cruisers, Lütjens had to consider what to do next. The cruisers themselves were hardly a menace to his squadron, which was vastly superior in firepower. The real danger was what British actions would follow on receipt of the information from the cruisers. It is likely that the intelligence Lütjens had received from Marinegruppe Nord played a prominent role in his considerations. In particular the air reconnaissance report from 22 May, which stated that the British battleships were still in Scapa Flow, must have been important. It meant that he should have a great lead if he maintained the present course. He would have plenty of time to shake off the cruisers. When the German ships had reached further south, and the land mass of Greenland no longer restricted manoeuvre, it would be very difficult for the British to force him to battle. Unfortunately Lütjens did not know that he was basing his decisions on an inaccurate reconnaissance report.

Had Lütjens known how close Holland's force really was, he may have decided upon a completely different course of action. His response to the circumstances as he knew them was to focus on breaking contact with the British cruisers, in order to give the *Prinz Eugen* a chance to refuel within a few days. He had several options for refuelling and there was no immediate hurry. When the two British cruisers appeared, the *Prinz Eugen* still had almost two thirds of the oil she had taken on at Bergen.[247]

Lütjens had three options to choose from. The first was to turn back and steer towards Norway. Since his intelligence suggested that the Home Fleet was still in Scapa Flow, this seemed unsuitable. The distance from Lütjens' present position to Trondheim was twice as great as the distance between Scapa Flow and Trondheim. An encounter with heavy British ships was very likely if he returned.

A second alternative was to sink the British cruisers. However, they probably had enough of a speed advantage over the *Bismarck* to escape. The third alternative was to continue according to plan. *Prinz Eugen* still had enough fuel oil to proceed for another 40 hours if she matched her speed to that of the slightly slower *Bismarck*. The British ships would probably have to refuel during that period. Lutjens did not know if the British had bunker ships in the Atlantic, but even if they did, they would be forced to break off their pursuit in order to refuel.[248]

Lütjens' more immediate concern was the bow radar on the *Bismarck*, which had been disabled when her 38cm guns fired. The construction had not been able to withstand the violent vibration caused by the heavy guns. Lütjens decided that the *Prinz Eugen* should move into first place in the squadron, so that full 360 degrees of radar coverage would be restored. The fact that *Bismarck* was placed closest to the pursuing enemy cruisers was another advantage to the manoeuvre.[249]

The *Prinz Eugen* increased speed while *Bismarck* slowed down and made a slight starboard turn. The two ships were so close that Lütjens could wave to the crew on the cruiser, while he let a message be sent: 'Admiral to captain: You have a wonderful ship.'

Brinkmann replied and during the brief exchange he sent a sentence that puzzled Lütjens. 'What do you think about the latest information from Marinegruppe West?'

No messages from Marinegruppe West had been received on board the *Bismarck*. As the squadron moved through the Denmark Strait it passed from the area of Marinegruppe Nord to the sector for which Marinegruppe West was responsible. It was not surprising that the latter sent reports. Lütjens himself had made a report after the encounter with the *Suffolk*. The shore staffs ought to be aware that his squadron was about to enter the Atlantic. None of the weather and reconnaissance reports Brinkmann had received gave any notable information. What really worried Lütjens was the fact that the radio messages had not been intercepted by the radio receivers on the battleship, which suggested that some technical deficiency might rob him of vital information. This problem was to recur several times during the days that followed.

While the ships were in the midst of changing position, the *Bismarck's* rudder unexpectedly jammed at a very inconvenient angle and the battleship began to veer off towards the *Prinz Eugen*. Brinkmann quickly realized what was about to happen, but while the cruiser travelled at full speed, as she did for the moment, regulations did not allow for radical shifts of the helm, for safety reasons. In the sudden emergency Brinkmann disregarded the regulations and ordered the helm to be shifted as far as possible so that *Prinz Eugen* turned away from the *Bismarck*.[250]

Soon the cruiser was in the lead. The *Bismarck* had moved behind and was keeping an eye on the two British cruisers, assisted by her stern radar. The two British ships could be discerned only sporadically by the Germans. The *Suffolk* sailed westward and was usually visible; the *Norfolk* could only occasionally be glimpsed behind the increasingly frequent snow squalls. Sometime before midnight, Lütjens decided to try attacking the shadowing cruisers and began a 180 degree turn, to meet them head on. The manoeuvre did not meet with success. The bow radar was inoperable, so the battleship could not track the enemy ships during the turn and as she broke through the squalls where Lütjens expected to find the cruisers, the sea was empty. He ordered another 180 degrees turn, to bring the battleship back to its previous course. Soon the echoes on her aft radar appeared again, showing that the British cruisers remained behind him, but kept a healthy distance. The behaviour of the British ships during this incident provided some confirmation to the suspicions held by the German Navy that not only were the British ships equipped with radar, but that it was a very sophisticated system. If this suspicion were true, the strategy of cruiser warfare against British shipping had to be completely reassessed.

All information available to Lütjens suggested he should continue on the southwesterly course. Forecasts and general knowledge about the climate in the region indicated that poor weather could be expected and as the squadron reached further south, the nights would be longer. The *Bismarck* was capable of such high speed that the pursuing cruisers could ill afford any mistakes. If they lost contact even for a brief moment they would have to set an accurate course almost immediately. With a speed advantage of one or two knots, they would only have to set a course that was just a few degrees off, and the distance to the German squadron would increase. As long as pursued as well as pursuer were confined to the narrow Denmark Strait, there was little room for manoeuvre. But further to the south, Lütjens would get more freedom of action.

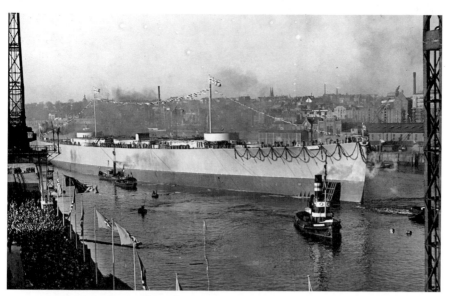

The *Bismarck* afloat just after launching at the Blohm & Voss shipyard, Hamburg, Germany, 14 February 1939. (Photo courtesy of the U.S. Naval Historical Center)

Adolf Hitler making his only visit to the *Bismarck*, on 5 May 1941, along with Field Marshal Wilhelm Keitel. Ship's Captain Ernst Lindemann is second from left and Admiral Lütjens is behind Hitler's left. (Photo courtesy of Michael W. Pocock and MaritimeQuest.com)

The German battleship *Bismarck*. (Photo courtesy of the U.S. Naval Historical Center)

The *Bismarck* as spotted by RAF reconnaissance aircraft near Bergen, Norway, on 21 May 1941, just prior to her sortie into the Atlantic. Two merchant-type ships are also present. (Photo courtesy of the U.S. Naval Historical Center)

German Admiral Günther Lütjens, shown here wearing a Knight's Cross of the Iron Cross and the uniform of a General-admiral. (Photo courtesy of Michael W. Pocock and www.MaritimeQuest.com)

The *Bismarck* in a refueling drill with the cruiser *Prinz Eugen*, 1941. (Photo courtesy of the U.S. Naval Historical Center)

Battle of the Denmark Strait, 24 May 1941. Fifteen-inch shells from HMS *Hood* hit near the German cruiser *Prinz Eugen*, early in the action.

Bismarck engaging HMS *Hood* and HMS *Prince of Wales*. Shells from the latter are falling short of the *Bismarck*, which had been hit previously and is slightly down by the bow.

HMS *Prince of Wales* (smoke column to left) under fire from *Bismarck* and *Prinz Eugen*, with smoke from the sunken HMS *Hood* at right.

Two views of *Bismarck* firing on HMS *Prince of Wales* during the Battle
of the Denmark Strait, as seen from the heavy cruiser *Prinz Eugen*.
Copied from the report of officers of *Prinz Eugen*, with identification by
her Gunnery Officer, Paul S. Schmalenbach, 1970.
(All photos on this and facing page courtesy of the U.S. Naval Historical Center)

HMS *King George V*, seen here in 1942 after suffering bow damage in a collision with the destroyer HMS *Punjabi*.
(Photo courtesy of Michael W. Pocock and www.MaritimeQuest.com)

The next to last photo of the *Bismarck*, as seen from *Prinz Eugen*,
24 May 1941, after the Battle of the Denmark Strait.

This is the last photograph of *Bismarck* taken by the Germans, just
before she and the heavy cruiser *Prinz Eugen* separated.

The *Bismarck* in a Norwegian fjord, 21 May 1941, shortly before departing for her Atlantic sortie. Location is probably Grimstadfjord, just south of Bergen. *Bismarck*'s camouflage was painted over before she departed the area. (Photo courtesy of the U.S. Naval Historical Center)

CHAPTER 16

Collision Course

The sudden encounter in the Denmark Strait caused no real changes in Tovey's or Lütjens' plans. The British Admiral ordered a significant increase of speed, while Lütjens only increased his speed slightly. At this time, both Tovey and Lütjens remained on their original courses. However, on the bridge of the *Hood*, it was obvious that the reports from the British cruisers mandated a new decision. When the Germans were observed by Wake-Walker's force, Holland and his warships were south of the German squadron. With these positions a successful interception seemed quite likely.[251]

Holland's most important concern was to choose a precise course. From the British viewpoint it would be preferable to engage the German squadron as far north as possible, with Holland attacking from east or southeast. Lütjens would then find little room for manoeuvre, squeezed between Holland's squadron and the pack ice. But could Holland achieve this favourable position? By maintaining his present course and speed the two British capital ships would take him west of Lütjens' position. That was unacceptable, since it would enable the enemy to turn east and avoid the trap. It would therefore be more prudent to alter course to the north and then turn west immediately before engaging the German warships. If everything went according to plan, Lütjens' squadron would be intercepted where the strait was narrow. But there was also a risk inherent in this option—that Holland steamed too far north and thereby allowed the German warships to evade him in the poor weather. Holland had to choose a course that did not present the enemy with undue opportunities to escape.

The interception was only the first step in the sequence of events Holland had to consider. Next came the actual battle. As Holland was continuously informed by Wake-Walker about the whereabouts of the German warships, while probably nobody knew about Holland's presence, there was every possibility of an engagement on favourable terms. For example, he knew that the Germans were following a south-westerly course, while the wind blew from southeast. Spray caused by the wind would hit the lenses on the German range finders, while *Hood* and *Prince of Wales* could use their leeward instruments. Another opportunity would be to approach the German warships in such a way that the silhouettes of Holland's ships would be harder to see, so that it was more difficult for the Germans to identify them and to judge the distance.

Another alternative of Holland's would be to choose such a course that all the heavy British guns could be used while only the fore guns of the *Bismarck* could target the British warships. The latter would constitute a classic 'T-position,' a kind of schoolbook solution. The merits of such a solution were perhaps not as clear in a situation where only a handful of ships were engaged, but during the initial phase of the battle it could nevertheless be an advantage.

At first glance it looked as if Holland was in full swing towards a decidedly advantageous battle, with two capital ships against only one. Unfortunately, as he was well aware, his ships had a number of short-comings that diminished his prospects of success. One of these was the *Hood's* thin deck armour. Another was the teething-troubles suffered by the *Prince of Wales*. The brand new battleship had defects that had still not been fixed. Particularly serious were the problems with her main guns. Technicians from the manufacturer, Vickers-Armstrong, had been on board to solve the problems when the Admiralty was alerted about *Bismarck's* departure. They remained on the battleship when it weighed anchor and were deeply concerned that their innocuous occupation suddenly seemed to bring them to an expected naval battle.[252]

Holland knew that the *Bismarck* as well as *Prinz Eugen* were brand new, but that unlike the *Prince of Wales* they had had ample time to conduct testing and training, thus bringing the warships to full war readiness. They could both be expected to be formidable opponents.

Ever since the Battle of Jutland in 1916 the British had had great respect for the German ability to build well-protected warships. Like the *Hood*, *Bismarck* carried eight 38cm guns, but as the German battleship had been launched almost 20 years later than her opponent, her armament might, for all Holland knew, be superior to that of *Hood*. Previous experience suggested that the German gunners quickly found their mark, even at long range. Holland had good reason to believe that the German battleship held the upper hand against each of his. His own advantage was mainly in the number of ships.

There was no question as to whether Holland should attack or not. According to Royal Navy practice, her ships only avoided battle when there was a compelling reason to do so. What he had to consider was how to do it. *Hood's* weak deck armour remained a crucial circumstance to consider. At ranges of 25,000 metres and above, the trajectories would be high, with shells striking the deck armour at a steep angle, thus enabling them to penetrate the battlecruiser's deck armour and reach critical parts of the ship, like the magazines or machinery. Conversely, shorter ranges meant reduced risk. Thus Holland had to reduce the range quickly, preferably to 15,000 metres. Judging from his available information, Holland probably concluded that he could enter the battle in such a way as to reduce his own risks while placing the enemy in an unfavourable position.

After weighing the pros and cons of the various alternatives Holland decided to set a northwesterly course after midnight. He estimated that the new course would bring the German squadron before his guns just after sunset. Behind his ships would be the dark night, whereas the silhouettes of the German warships would stand out against the brighter evening sky.

Holland increased speed to 27 knots, but in the rough weather the destroyers could barely follow the big ships. He had already sent two of his six destroyers to Hvalfjord to refuel. Now the remaining four pitched feverishly in the dreadful sea. On board the *Electra*, Lieutenant T. J. Cain anxiously observed how the ship heaved when its stem cut through the waves and the huge cascades of pale green water that surrounded the destroyer:

Sheets of spray shot up and over the ship like heavy rain. Our sisters, the rest of the destroyers, were often quite invisible beneath the water they displaced, and the battlewagons rose and fell with the sound of thunder as they pressed majestically on, jettisoning great streams of water from around their cable

*chains, and streaming around their 'nostrils'—the gaping
hawse-holes that flanked their bows—like a pair of angry
dragons.*[253]

Holland had no intention of reducing speed. A message was conveyed
to the commanders of the destroyers that they would have to try to do
their best, even if that meant lagging behind. By reducing speed just a
little, the destroyers managed to ride on the waves, rather than breaking
through them. Because the destroyers had been able to keep pace, at
midnight Holland could order them to form a screen ahead of the
capital ships.[254]

Meanwhile, Wake-Walker's cruisers struggled to shadow the
German squadron. Even with the invaluable aid provided by *Suffolk's*
modern radar, it was a difficult task, so much more so as the weather
deteriorated further during the night. The fog banks became even
denser and the snow squalls multiplied. These demanding conditions,
combined with the tension of the lookouts, created illusions. Just as the
German lookouts had seen British warships, which later turned out to
be icebergs, the British crews mistakenly made observations and
sounded the alarm. After following the Germans for two and a half
hours, the men on *Suffolk's* bridge noted that *Bismarck* altered course
slightly while in a heavy rain squall. The German warship disappeared.
About a minute later the dumbfounded British saw the battleship
heading straight towards them. Immediately the helm was shifted and
the British cruiser veered northeast. As the minutes passed, doubts
began to surface. Not a trace was seen of the *Bismarck* and finally it
dawned upon Ellis and the other officers that the Germans had not
reversed course after all. It was just a delusion, and it had now allowed
the Germans to increase their distance from the pursuing cruisers to an
alarming extent. Ellis ordered full speed southwest, hoping to find the
German warships again. [255]

If Lütjens had known what transpired on *Suffolk's* bridge, he would
most certainly have ordered full speed and also altered course, since his
warships had by this time passed the narrowest part of the Denmark
Strait and his squadron had more room for manoeuvre. Lütjens did not
have this knowledge, however, and *Suffolk* was able to regain contact.

While the men on board the warships in the Denmark Strait
strained their eyes and nerves, less colourful, but nevertheless vital

events took place in an ugly concrete building not far from Downing Street and the Houses of Parliament in London. The building was called the citadel and contained the Admiralty, the hub of the Royal Navy and its actions all over the world. Here vast amounts of information on the war at sea, originating from warships, wireless interceptions, agents and all other sources, civilian as well as military, were collected, filtered and analysed. On two huge maps, Wrens fastened pins to mark the positions of warships, submarines, transport ships and convoys. At this very moment, several British convoys were sailing on the Atlantic. Six of these were heading towards Britain and five were on their way to transatlantic ports. Two of the inbound convoys—SC31 and the already decimated HX126—were south of the Denmark Strait, and in danger of converging with the German squadron, should Lütjens shake off his pursuers and turn south. The other convoys were too far south to be in imminent danger.

As previously mentioned, the westbound convoys OB323 and OB324, each with 35 merchant ships, were south of Iceland, while OB325 plodded on a few days behind the other two. A fourth convoy, OB326, was just about to leave Liverpool. The most important outbound convoy was WS8B, one of the monthly troop transports to the Middle East. WS8B should have been escorted by the *Repulse* and the *Victorious*, but as these warships had been transferred to Tovey, the protection of the convoy was limited to the cruiser *Cairo* and five destroyers. The latter belonged to the 4th Destroyer Division and was commanded by Commander Philip Vian, who had already gained fame in Britain after boarding the German supply ship *Altmark* in 1940.

In addition to these convoys, the battleship *Rodney* was at sea. She was commanded by Captain Frederick Dalrymple-Hamilton and had left Clyde the previous day with four destroyers and the troop carrier *Britannic*. As the *Rodney* was heading towards Boston for a major overhaul, it was not surprising that these ships sailed together. An American naval officer, Lieutenant Commander Joseph Wellings, also climbed on board *Rodney* before leaving Britain. He had been assistant naval attaché in London for almost a year. In May 1941 he was appointed to a new assignment in the United States and it seemed sensible for him to accompany the British battleship on its journey over the Atlantic. He could not have predicted the story he would bring home.[256]

With all these convoys at sea, Vice Admiral Somerville, the commander of Force H in Gibraltar, received orders to put his ships on full alert. His force included the battlecruiser *Renown*, the cruiser *Sheffield* and the carrier *Ark Royal*. Its mission was to meet convoy WS8B and assume responsibility for the protection of the transport ships. In order to gather sailors on leave in Gibraltar, patrols were dispatched to search bars, pubs and other places of entertainment. Meantime, on board the warships, boilers were fired to raise steam pressure, and two hours after midnight Somerville's Force H, escorted by five destroyers, left Gibraltar.[257]

In the Denmark Strait visibility deteriorated further. Shortly before midnight it was so bad that at times little could be seen beyond a few hundred metres, boding ill for the British hopes of keeping contact with the German squadron. Lütjens decided to use the weather to his advantage. He ordered smoke and altered to a southerly course. Simultaneously the German warships increased speed to 30 knots. German radio-interceptors attentively monitored British radio traffic and soon noted a change in the reports. It seemed that the new course ordered by Lütjens had been detected by the British ships, since they also followed a southerly course. On the other hand, the Germans noted that the British reports only contained their own positions; the information on the German ships that had been included previously was now lacking.[258]

Had Lütjens managed to shake off his pursuers?

In fact, since *Bismarck* had disappeared into one of the numerous snow squalls, she had not been observed from the British warships. Then suddenly she was simply gone. Even the radar operators on the *Suffolk* lost contact. No matter how hard they tried, the blips on the radar screens did not reappear. Just after midnight Ellis sent a new report about his position, but it contained no information about the German warships.[259]

While Lütjens interpreted the paucity of information in *Suffolk's* report as a sign that the British might have lost contact with him, Holland took it as confirmation of the fact. He had almost reached the position where he intended to make his turn north, when his signal officer handed over a series of disquieting reports. The first said that *Bismarck* had altered course to 20° port. The next read: 'Enemy hidden by fog near the ice. Estimated course 200°.' It was followed by a message confirming the course, but stating that the enemy was completely covered by a snow squall.[260] Holland immediately understood how the situation had changed. If the cruisers were to lose contact, a successful interception was unlikely. Soon a message from *Norfolk* established that *Bismarck* had indeed slipped away.

What would Holland do? While the crews on board *Hood* and the *Prince of Wales* checked their guns and optical instruments, or in other ways prepared for the coming battle, Holland considered the new situation. One thing was clear. He would still be positioned south of the Germans for a few hours, but after that he could very well pass Lütjens' squadron without sighting it. If that happened, he would find himself behind the Germans, in a race very likely to be won by the enemy. After weighing the alternatives he settled for a compromise. He set a northerly course, and intended to follow it for a few hours. Then, if no contact with the German ships had been achieved, he would turn south.

Ted Briggs was about to begin his shift, heading for the bridge, when he met his friend Frank Tuxworth, another signalman. Like Briggs, he was equipped with a gas mask hanging in its case on his chest, a life jacket and the flat helmet hated by British sailors as it was reputed to catch the pressure waves from explosions and break the neck of the wearer. 'Do you remember, Briggo,' Tuxworth asked, 'that when the *Exeter* went into action with the *Graf Spee* there was only one signalman saved?'

Ted Briggs remembered. 'Well, if that happens to us,' he laughed, 'it will be me they save.'[261]

He reported at the bridge, just in time to hear the orders to shift the helm. The British warships altered course to bear towards north, with a darkening horizon behind them, steering straight towards the blizzard and the supposed enemy. Apart from the lamps above the charts and the binnacle, the lighting on the bridge was as sparse as the conversation was unobtrusive. Holland rested in the captain's chair, with the captain of the *Hood*, Commander Kerr, standing to the right of him. They all wore thick duffel coats, flameproof equipment and helmets. Briggs suddenly became aware that he, the lowest in rank of all present, was the only person on the bridge who wore shoes. All the others wore thick boots.

At 01.30 hours, when the sun was just about to set and there were no signs that the gale would abate, *Suffolk* and *Norfolk* still reported nothing but their own positions, course and speed. Holland sent a brief signal to the *Prince of Wales*: if the Germans had not been sighted before 03.10 hours, he would probably turn south.[262]

On board the *Prince of Wales* preparations were made to launch a Walrus aircraft. Air reconnaissance could be useful in relocating the German warships. Unfortunately, visibility deteriorated while preparations were still going on, and it was decided to drain the aircraft of its fuel and put it in cover. Launching the aircraft would have been risky for other reasons. If the Germans saw the reconnaissance aircraft they might realise that the Home Fleet was in the Atlantic, not safely at Scapa Flow. While the British squadron headed north, Holland sent a message to the *Prince of Wales*, in which he outlined his intentions for the forthcoming battle. He wanted both ships to concentrate their fire on the *Bismarck*, while *Suffolk* and *Norfolk* should engage *Prinz Eugen*.[263] It was hardly an order that surprised Captain Leach, the commander of *Prince of Wales*. The disparity in armour and armament between a cruiser and a battleship was of such magnitude that the cruiser was an almost insignificant danger for the heavy ship, unless range had closed to such an extent that torpedoes could be used. In the manuals of the German Navy too, it was clearly stated that cruisers should not engage battleships. Accordingly, the part of the drama Holland wanted to unfold was the duel between the two British capital ships and the *Bismarck*.

Since Holland wanted *Norfolk* and *Suffolk* to engage *Prinz Eugen*, it may appear surprising that he did not inform Wake-Walker about his intentions. It was an 'omission' for which he was later to be criticized. However, by transmitting a signal to Wake-Walker, he would have risked disclosing his presence to the Germans, possibly alerting them to his presence and course. Furthermore, as Wake-Walker's cruisers were lagging behind the German squadron, they were not in a position to enter combat quickly. Thus Holland's decision not to break radio silence seems sensible enough.[264]

Unfortunately, the cruisers did not manage to regain contact with the German squadron. Holland's self-imposed time limit inexorably drew nearer without any heartening news reaching him. Still, at 03.00 hours, nothing suggesting that *Suffolk* or *Norfolk* had found *Bismarck* had reached the commander of the British force. He had no choice but to signal Captain Leach on board *Prince of Wales* that the two big ships should set a new course, to south-southwest. Holland surmised that the Germans still remained further north, and ordered his remaining four destroyers to search in that direction. In fact, the course held by the British force had been more or less perfect, and would almost certainly have led to an encounter, had not Lütjens made a slight adjustment to his own course in order to stay closer to the pack ice. As events unfolded, Holland's destroyers missed the German ships by a close margin and continued north, away from the anticipated battle. The alert level on the *Hood* and the *Prince of Wales* was slightly lowered. Thus far the warships had been at full combat readiness, but battle no longer seemed imminent. The crews could be allowed some rest. Some of them actually managed to catch a nap at their stations, but in the tense atmosphere most of them simply could not settle down.[265]

On board the German warships, everything suggested that Lütjens had achieved his first aim, to shake off Wake-Walker's cruisers, but the elation caused by this fact did not last long. At 03.20 hours, approximately two hours after *Suffolk's* report on the lost contact, one of the British cruisers was again observed from the German warships. It was the *Suffolk*. She had found the German battleship, thanks to her radar, and soon the lookouts confirmed that the demanding search during the last few hours had not been in vain.

The *Bismarck's* stern radar had not provided any warning about the approaching *Suffolk*, which was a serious concern. When he realized this, Lütjens ordered the *Prinz Eugen* to assume coverage of the sector behind the two German ships. About 20 minutes later, the B-Dienst intercepted a radio message from the British cruisers containing all the relevant data regarding the course, speed and position of the German squadron.[266]

While Lütjens believed that the *Suffolk's* success in finding the German squadron again was indicative of British possession of superior radar technology, such sentiments were not held on the *Prinz Eugen*. Brinkmann believed that the British tracked the German ships simply by using their hydrophones. According to him, the large gap between the British cruisers supported this conclusion. By comparing the direction of the sound from the German propellers, the British could pretty well estimate the position of the German ships. Brinkmann also suspected that the British had found means of taking the bearing of the shortwave transmissions used for communication between the two German ships, when visibility prevented optical transmission.[267] Whatever the reason, Lütjens' squadron had failed to shake off the pursuers.

On the *Hood*, the signal from *Suffolk* was received with delight. This elation, however, subsided once the situation had been properly assessed. The message was received at 03.47 hours. After studying the reports and the bearings taken, it was concluded that the German squadron was close, about 13 miles away, but not north of Holland's position, as hoped, but rather to the northwest. Instead of being south of the Germans, Holland's force was more or less on a parallel course, on the enemy's port side. Unless the Germans made some kind of manoeuvre that placed them in a tactically unsuitable position, there was no longer any possibility for Holland to enter battle as he had intended.[268]

Holland ordered a speed of 28 knots and altered course 40° to starboard. The *Prince of Wales* could not make higher speed, but the present course and speed would bring Holland's force in contact with the German squadron. Visibility remained poor, but nothing suggested that the Germans were aware of the presence of two heavy British warships. The bad weather might also enable Holland to close the range before the guns could fire accurately. Still, it remained crucial that Wake-Walker's cruisers maintained contact. If they once again failed to keep Holland informed about the course, speed and position of the German warships, he might never again come close to engaging Lütjens' squadron, as the enemy got more and more room for manoeuvre as it raced south.[269]

Many men on board *Hood* had finally fallen asleep, when the loudspeaker abruptly told them to prepare for imminent battle. The men made themselves ready at their battle stations. The noise from boots running on ladders and slams from doors and hatches echoed inside the battlecruiser. Corporal Bob Tilburn, who had his station at a 10.2cm gun on the port side, pondered over the unknown that lay ahead of him. 'We were as well prepared as we could be,' he recalled. 'We knew there would be casualties—but others would suffer, not me.'[270]

On board the *Prince of Wales* Captain Leach addressed his men and told them he expected to engage the enemy imminently. He was followed by the priest, who took the microphone: 'Dear God, you know how busy I will be today,' he prayed. 'But if I should forget you, I ask you not to forget me.'

The weather cleared somewhat. In the east the first rays of daylight gave the low clouds a pink tint and the sky turned from black to blue. But still it was a morning of harsh weather. The sea was very rough, with waves rolling from northeast. In the west the dense clouds promised further rain, possibly even snow.

No discussions were heard on the bridge of the *Hood*. Everyone's eyes were rivetted on the horizon to the west. At 05.30 hours, the lookout in the fore-top shouted: 'Alarm! Starboard, green 40!'

A suspicious shadow had been discovered at a distance of approximately 27,000 metres, 40° starboard compared to *Hood's* course. The observation was soon confirmed. It was the *Bismarck*. 'Report on the enemy,' Kerr said with a low voice to the navigation officer, almost as if the Germans could hear him if speaking too loudly. 'Urgent message to the Admiralty and to the commander of Home Fleet.'

The Navigation Officer dictated the report to the Yeoman of Signals, gave him the enemy course, distance and position, and added the course and speed of Holland's force. The Yeoman of Signals wrote the message on his signal-pad and repeated it through the voice pipe to the radio room. Confirmation of the transmission was soon received.

Ted Briggs, who could barely stand the tension on the bridge, could no longer keep silent. 'How long do you think it will last, sir?' he whispered to one of the non-commissioned officers next to him. The NCO briefly glanced at Briggs, then he replied with a friendly tone, 'I think it will be over in a few hours, Ted.'[271]

CHAPTER 17

Battle in the Denmark Strait

Lütjens had absolutely no knowledge about Holland's presence until the British squadron was so close that battle was imminent. The first indication of the enemy was received at 05.25 hours, only five minutes before the British lookouts sighted the German ships, when the hydrophones on the *Prinz Eugen* picked up propeller noise on the port side. Twelve minutes later a masthead was sighted, believed to be part of a British cruiser, and a few minutes later another masthead was seen, close to the first. The two ships seemed to travel at about the same speed as the *Bismarck* and *Prinz Eugen* and while Lütjens' ships held a 220 degrees course, the enemy ships were estimated to travel at 240 degrees. Were these newcomers cruisers or perhaps heavier ships?

On board the *Hood* the lookouts strained their eyes to make out details of the German ships. More and more of their masts and super-structures became visible as the range gradually decreased. However, unlike Lütjens, the British commanders did not have any doubts about the identity of the ships they approached. Holland had originally intended to advance towards the German ships on their port bow, where he might remain unobserved until the last moment, but the confusion of the previous night meant that he closed on her port aft.

Furthermore, instead of being able to fire with all 18 of his heavy guns against only the four heavy guns on *Bismarck's* bow, he could now only use the ten bow guns of the *Hood* and *Prince of Wales*, while the *Bismarck* would be able to fire with all her eight guns. He had to adjust to the altered situation and his first priority was to close the range as quickly as possible, to reduce the German advantages of better deck armour and accuracy at longer range.

As soon as the German squadron was sighted, Holland had ordered a change of course, from 240 degrees to 280 degrees and his ships now steamed directly towards the enemy ships. The British ships presented as small a silhouette as possible, so that they were a difficult target. When the range had been reduced sufficiently, Holland would turn his ships to allow all heavy guns to fire. At that point, the British ships would present larger targets, but on the other hand, the disadvantage of the *Hood's* weak deck armour would be greatly reduced at the shorter range. Lütjens initially tried to avoid battle and changed course from 220 to 265 degrees.

At this stage, mistakes were made on both sides. As *Bismarck* and *Prinz Eugen* had changed positions, after the breakdown of the flagship's radar, Holland believed that the first ship in the German squadron was the most dangerous enemy. On board the *Prince of Wales*, a correct identification of the German ships had been made, but Holland continued into the battle aiming at the *Prinz Eugen*.

For their part, the Germans were struggling to identify the enemy ships, whose steep angle of approach made their silhouettes difficult to recognise. In the fire control centre of the *Prinz Eugen*, Commander Jasper was of the opinion that the two enemy ships were cruisers. Lieutenant Commander Schmalenbach, the second artillery officer, was more pessimistic. He studied the huge surge from the bow of the ships and said that one of them was a modern battleship and the other a battlecruiser.

'Nonsense!' Jasper seemed certain. 'It's either a cruiser or a destroyer.'

'I'll bet you a bottle of champagne,' Schmalenbach offered, 'that it's the *Hood*.'

'Taken!' replied Jasper, thinking he was sure to win this bet. 'Load with high explosive shell and impact fuses!'[272]

The officers on board the *Bismarck* were also unsure about the identity of the ships. Schneider believed they were cruisers and issued orders accordingly. Commander Albrecht, who was in the fore fire direction turret, protested over the telephone and said they were battleships or battlecruisers.

The moment when the heavy guns would open fire approached quickly. Members of Holland's staff watched the German ships in their binoculars. They felt neither enthusiasm nor despair, because they were not certain whether the advantage lay with the British squadron or the German. On paper, the British were superior in firepower, because the *Prinz Eugen* was a much lighter vessel, but the circumstances of the British approach reduced their advantages. As Holland's ships were on a bearing towards the wind, spray from their bows spattered the lenses of the range finders at the fore turrets, just the situation Holland had probably intended to place Lütjens in. All fire had to be directed from the inferior range finder at the main director. It was an aggravating circumstance, especially worrisome as the enemy could be expected to fire very accurately. The known problems with the *Prince of Wales's* guns were also cause for uncertainty. The civilian technicians from Vickers-Armstrong were nearby to attend to any technical problems that might occur during battle.

The course and formation of their approach was a further disadvantage for the British ships, since Holland's push to gain on the enemy as quickly as possible meant they were bunched closer together when viewed through German target sights.Thus it would be easier for the Germans to shift target, without wasting much time on finding the range and direction. The battle promised to be uncomfortably even, much more so than Holland had initially believed.

Ted Briggs, who had remained on the bridge, was firmly focussed on his own tasks. He had been at Oran the year before. That time the battle had been more of a slaughter than anything else. Now the *Hood* faced the kind of task she had been designed for. Briggs was fully confident in the battlecruiser, even more so than the knowledgeable officers around him on the bridge. 'My emotions were a mixture of expectation, wild excitement and fear,' he recalled. 'I don't believe there was anybody on board who did not consider our mighty *Hood* to be too much for the *Bismarck* and *Prinz Eugen* to handle.'

The time was 05.53 hours and the *Hood* made 28 knots.[273] The seaman down at the admiral's bridge reported that the range at which Holland had intended to initiate the battle had been reached. The admiral looked in his binoculars at the German ships one more time and then said: 'Execute!'

'Open fire,' commanded Captain Kerr.

A second later the voice of the first artillery officer was heard: 'Fire!'

The fore guns of the *Hood* woke with a tremendous thunder, the wind swept a huge cloud of black cordite smoke over the bridge and four shells, each weighing more than 800 kilograms, began the 23,000 metre-long journey towards the intended target.

All German doubts disappeared as the *Hood*'s guns fired, almost immediately followed by the main guns of the *Prince of Wales*. The huge muzzle flashes and the long firing range were signs clear enough. 'Blast!' exclaimed Jasper, on board the *Prinz Eugen*, realizing his mistake. 'Those guns are not mounted on any cruiser. They are battleships.'

Schmalenbach, cursed silently. He had just won a bottle of champagne. Whether he would ever be able to drink it or not was a completely different question.

'Request permission to open fire,' crackled Schneider's voice in the loudspeaker on the bridge of the *Bismarck*, but Lütjens hesitated and the *Bismarck*'s guns remained silent. The seconds ticked by in what seemed an eternity. All was silent, except for the rushing when the bow split the waves and the wind that whistled and whined in the masts and bracing-wires. 'As the shells passed over our heads,' remembered the engine-man Josef Statz, who was stationed in the damage-control centre and heard the howling shells through an air intake, 'They literally whipped the noise through my body. A noise that can not be described.'

Pillars of water thrown up by the shells landing around the *Prinz Eugen* made it clear that the *Hood*'s fire was not far off the mark. Soon the shells from the *Prince of Wales* followed, also falling near the *Bismarck*. As the fountains of water fell, the crack of the explosions reached the ears of the German seamen. 'The enemy has opened fire.' Schneider's voice was again heard from the loudspeaker, this time much more impatiently. 'Their fire is accurate. Request permission to open fire.'

At this moment, the thunder from the firing British ships caught up with the shells and passed over the German ships. On the horizon, new muzzle flashes from the British guns could be seen. Lütjens still hesitated. His orders were to avoid all contact with major enemy ships. Now he suddenly found himself in a battle with two British battleships or battlecruisers. Should he fight or flee?

'It is the *Hood*!' Albrecht shouted through the loudspeaker. 'It is the *Hood*!'

Holland had now turned 20 degrees to port, to allow the aft turrets to fire too, and the Germans could more easily make out the silhouettes of the British ships. Funnels and superstructures could be distinguished and any remaining uncertainty was dispelled. The Germans no longer hesitated; it was the *Hood*. Soon the other battleship had been studied well enough to determine her identity. The Germans believed her to be the *King George V*, the virtually identical sister ship of *Prince of Wales*. As the British shells fell around his ships, Lütjens struggled with his decision. His ships were faster than the *Prince of Wales*, but it would be more difficult to outpace the *Hood*. If he fled, only four heavy guns of the *Bismarck* would be able to fire, while the enemy would be able to use ten, at least until the *Prince of Wales* was out of range. Flight was not particularly tempting. But was the alternative better? Did Lütjens dare to fight against the two most powerful ships of the Royal Navy?

'I will not let my ship be shot away beneath my butt,' muttered Captain Lindemann, who wanted to engage the enemy immediately.

The fore guns of the *Hood* flashed out their sixth salvo and suddenly Lütjens made his decision. 'Open fire,' he said to Lindemann and subsequently ordered a change of course, from 265 degrees to 200.

On board the *Hood*, Corporal Tilburn watched as orange flashes left the *Bismarck*'s fore guns. His own gun was on the port side, but he could still see the dark silhouette of the German battleship, as a huge black cloud of smoke was swept away from it by the wind. The battle between the largest British and German warships was now being fought on both sides. Müllenheim-Rechberg, who had been ordered to watch the British cruisers while Schneider directed all the guns from the main fire control centre, monitored how the orders were issued over the headset. The first salvo was short. The second was fired as a 400-metre bracket and was classified as 'over' and 'on target.'

'Straddling!' Schneider yelled. 'Full salvos good rapid!'

There was no longer any need to wait for the fall of shot to adjust the fire.[274] The turrets could fire as soon as the breechblocks had been closed behind the propelling charges. The flagship as well as the cruiser fired at the *Hood* and soon the battlecruiser was engulfed by white fountains from the shells striking the water unpleasantly close to her.

'I remember watching with a mixture of dread and fascination how the guns of the *Bismarck* spitted out four glowing stars,' Ted Briggs wrote, 'and realized they were shells aimed at us.'

He heard how someone from the spotting-top shouted: 'We're shooting at the wrong ship. The *Bismarck* is to the right not to the left!'

Holland did not allow himself to be excited by this news. 'Shift the fire to the target on the right,' he said with a calm voice.[275] But due to the long order chain between commander and gun crews, and the fact that the ship was soon hit, the order was not executed in time. On board the *Prince of Wales*, the misunderstanding had already been corrected and she was firing at the *Bismarck*. The sixth salvo covered her and it was judged that the enemy battleship received at least one hit. However, the first significant damage was incurred by the *Hood*.

'The ship shuddered,' Briggs recalled, 'and Commander Gregson, the torpedo officer, ran out on the starboard wing to investigate. He returned and reported a fire at the base of the mainmast.'

On the shelter deck Corporal Tilburn and a few other gunners had just been ordered to extinguish the fire, when some of the ammunition began to explode and the gunners had to take shelter by throwing themselves to the deck. Almost immediately afterwards, the *Hood* was hit again, this time by a shell from the *Prinz Eugen* which struck the fore-top without exploding. The shockwaves from the hit threw many seamen off the mast and onto the deck below. Some of them were dead before they hit the surface. Tilburn, who was already lying down, felt a heavy blow on his leg and when he turned to see what had happened, he found to his horror that parts of a body had struck him.

Another body fell on the open deck outside the compass platform. Commander Kerr told midshipman Bill Dundas to check who it was. Dundas glanced through the window, grew pale and shook his head. 'I don't know, sir,' he said. 'It is a lieutenant, but I can't see who it is. He has no hands and ... he has no face.'

As the ships exchanged fire, a British Sunderland flying boat approached. It had started from Iceland and passed right over the *Suffolk*, when the commander of the aircraft, captain R. J. Vaughn, discovered the muzzle flashes from the battle below. 'As we closed in,' he later reported, 'we saw two columns of two ships, each going on a parallel course separated by approximately 20 kilometres.'

Vaughn saw that the leading ship in the left column was on fire, but it still fought back with its fore as well as aft guns. He still did not know that the burning ship was the *Hood*; in fact, he did not know which column was German and which was British. He slowly turned his big

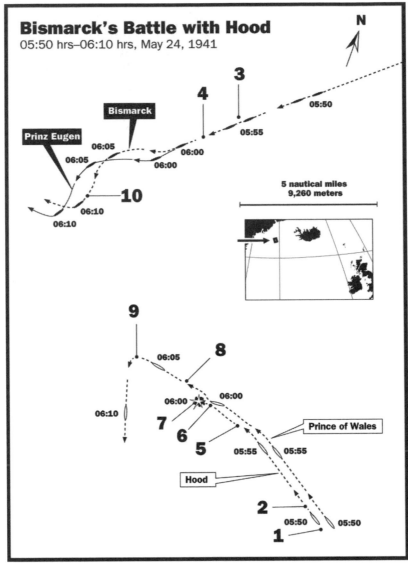

Bismarck's Battle with Hood
05:50 hrs–06:10 hrs, May 24, 1941

N

Bismarck

Prinz Eugen

05:50

05:55

06:05
06:05
06:00
06:00

06:10
06:10

10

5 nautical miles
9,260 meters

9

06:05

8

06:00
06:00
7
06:10
6
5
05:55
05:55
Prince of Wales

Hood

2
05:50
05:50
1

1 Holland gives instructions to fire on the forward enemy ship

2 Holland's squadron opens fire on Prinz Eugen.

3 Bismarck and Prinz Eugen open fire.

4 Salvo from Prince of Wales hits Bismarck

5 Hood is hit by a salvo from Prinz Eugen.

6 Hood begins making a turn to port

7 Hood blows up.

8 Prince of Wales is hit by a salvo from Bismarck.

9 Leach breaks off the action.

10 The last salvo fired by Bismarck.

sea plane to take a closer look at the column on the right.[276]

The time was now 06.00 hours. On board the *Hood*, Holland ordered: 'Turn twenty degrees to port together.' The distance was down to about 16,000 metres.[277] The *Hood* had to assume a course more parallel to the German ships, in order to prevent the rear turrets from being obstructed from firing by superstructures. On board the *Prince of Wales*, the Yeoman of Signals observed how the flagship hoisted two blue flags in the yardarm, indicating that Holland had ordered a 20 degree turn to port. Captain Leach and his staff welcomed it. One of the guns in the forward turret was malfunctioning, but with the turn, the aft turret would be able to fire, thus adding four guns to Leach's broadsides.[278]

When the *Hood* began to sheer, the shells from the *Bismarck's* fifth salvo were probably already in the air. It is possible that one of them would have hit the battlecruiser anyway, but as she turned, a shell penetrated the *Hood's* side armour.[279]

'I did not hear any explosion,' Briggs recalled, but he was thrown to the deck by the impact. A fantastic flame of fire with the intensity of a welding torch, shot up on both sides of the bridge, right before his eyes.

Exactly where the fatal shell hit the *Hood* may never be known, but the ensuing detonation seems to have set alight the cordite in the magazine for the aft 10.2cm guns. As the cordite began to burn, it almost immediately created such high pressure that nearby bulkheads collapsed and opened the way to the adjoining compartments. The flame moved ahead to the engine rooms, where it turned up through the ventilation system and caused a huge flame to shoot up in the air. The same flame also moved astern and reached the magazine under the X-turret, which contained almost 50 tons of cordite. When this detonated, a 15-metre hole was blown in the side armour and coxswain French, who stood near one of the AA guns on board the *Prince of Wales*, saw how *Hood's* X-turret was blown off.[280] In a fraction of a second, the flame had also reached the Y-turret and a section 70 metres long, from the two aft turrets to the forward machine room, had been destroyed to such an extent that the ship was broken apart.[281]

Despite the fact that many thousand men fought in the battle, only a few of them actually saw the explosion and all of them experienced it differently. It was described as being 'like an enormous blowtorch' by

Captain Leach. Other observers regarded it as a 'red white glow, shaped like a funnel,' 'like a bunch of red rhubarb' or 'as a long pale red tongue of fire.' From the *Norfolk*, about 24,000 metres northwest of the dying *Hood*, it was described as 'a sea of fire shaped like a fan or an inverted cone.' On board the *Suffolk*, almost 30,000 metres from the explosion, it had not been possible to see much except the muzzle flashes from the duelling ships. Suddenly Commander Porter observed 'a very thin column of fire, reaching between 200 and 300 metres up in the air.'[282] All observers were unanimous in one respect, that they did not hear any remarkable sound. Most of them considered the explosion to be completely silent; a few believed they heard a low hissing sound.

From the air, Captain Vaughn had approached the right column. He noted that the rearmost ship produced an unusual amount of smoke and oil traced behind it. He moved closer to it as the first ship in the left column suddenly disappeared behind an eruption of smoke and fire.[283]

Despite the explosion that ate its way along the hull of the ship and immediately killed every man in its way, a few seconds elapsed before the officers on the admiral's bridge realized that the battle was over. 'The compass is out of order,' the officer of the watch said calmly.

'Steering's gone, sir,' reported the helmsman through the voice pipe.

'Change over to emergency steering,' the captain ordered.

At this very moment, the ship began to list to port, at first by 10 degrees, then 20, 30, and everybody on the bridge realized she would never again regain trim. The *Hood* was capsizing.

'There was never any panic,' Briggs recalled. 'And nobody ordered us to abandon the ship. It simply was not needed.'

He made his way towards the door leading to the open bridge on the starboard side and saw that Commander John Warrand, the navigation officer, blocked his way. Warrand took a step aside, smiled kindly towards Briggs and let him pass by. It was a smile that etched itself on Briggs memory.

On the shelter deck, Corporal Tilburn felt how the ship shuddered powerfully and saw a tremendous flame between the bridge and the B-turret.[284] He saw one of his comrades fall down on his back, dead. As Tilburn let his eyes sweep over the deck, he saw another seaman, whose stomach had been ripped open by a splinter and incredulously watched his intestines fall out onto the deck. The sight was so disgusting that

Tilburn staggered towards the gunwale to vomit. Once there, he realized that the sea was not where previous experience would suggest it ought to be. The dark waves were rapidly coming nearer. He managed to throw off his steel helmet before the waves washed the deck.[285] Then he was below the surface of the water. He tried to swim upwards, but discovered that a cord from an antenna had caught one of his feet and dragged him down. With a presence of mind that would later surprise him, he grasped his knife and cut off the cord but in the time taken to do so he had been dragged down quite deep into the water.

For a moment, Briggs hesitated in the door to the bridge. He took a glance into the bridge and saw Holland sitting huddled up on his seat, resigned about the fate engulfing them all. The defeated admiral was the last person seen by Briggs, before ice cold water surrounded him and pulled him down into the bubbling depths of the ocean. At the same time Bill Dundas had struggled to overcome the list and reached a window on the port side. He managed to break the glass and was half way out when the water rushed in and covered him.

On board the *Prince of Wales* orders were quickly issued to avoid colliding with the sinking flagship. A turn to port had previously been initiated, but the helm had to be shifted sharply to starboard.

To the Germans watching the *Hood's* destruction, the sight was as fantastic as it was terrifying. In the charthouse, Lieutenant Commander Neuendorff had heard Schneider shouting 'Straddling!' and dashed to the eye-slits on the port side. Somebody yelled that the *Hood* was ablaze and moments later there was a blinding explosion. Neuendorf's assistant stood next to him:

> *At first we could see nothing but what we saw moments later could not have been conjured up by even the wildest imagination. Suddenly, the* Hood *split in two, and thousands of tons of steel were hurled into the air. More than a thousand men died. Although the range was still about 18,000 metres, the fireball that developed where the* Hood *still was seemed near enough to touch. It was so close that I shut my eyes but curiosity made me open them again a second or two later. It was like being in a hurricane. Every nerve in my body felt the pressure of the explosion. If I have one wish, it is that my children may be spared such an experience.[286]*

The cry 'The *Hood* is ablaze!' was followed by 'She is blowing up!' and the men on board the *Bismarck* looked at each other with incredulity in their faces. Moments later they realized that they had won the brief duel with the enemy warship, thus dramatically increasing their chances of surviving the battle. They began to shout and cheer and slap each other's backs. In the damage-control centre the shouting was heard through the intercom and Commander Oels was beset by an exuberant joy artificer Statz had never seen before. Just like the astonished Statz, Lieutenant Jahreis and the others gazed at Oels, 'the loneliest man on board,' as he ecstatically urged them to 'three 'Sieg Heil' for the *Bismarck*.'[287]

Far below, in one of the *Bismarck*'s boiler rooms, Leading Seaman Johannes Zimmermann found it difficult to accept what was going on. When the loudspeakers at first announced that the *Bismarck* was about to enter battle with the *Hood*, he briefly believed that the message concerned an exercise or a war game. Hardly had he brought himself to accept that the battle was raging, when the loud cries about the destruction of the *Hood* penetrated into the lower parts of the German battleship. 'It was like a shock,' he said. 'At first we were all smiling, but gradually we realized what it meant. I got a strange feeling in the stomach – tomorrow it could be us.'[288]

In his director, Müllenheim-Rechberg heard in his headset the voices multiply, until it was impossible to make out the words. Something remarkable had happened. He left the task of watching the *Norfolk* and *Suffolk* to a subordinate and moved to the port sight.

> *While I was still turning [the director] towards the Hood, I heard a shout, 'She's blowing up!' 'She' – that could only be the Hood! The sight I then saw is something I shall never forget. At first the Hood was nowhere to be seen; in her place was a colossal pillar of black smoke reaching into the sky. Gradually, at the foot of the pillar, I made out the bow of the battle cruiser projecting upwards at an angle, a sure sign that she had broken in two. Then I saw something I could hardly believe: a flash of orange coming from her forward gun! Although her fighting days had ended, the Hood was firing a last salvo. I felt great respect for those men over there.*[289]

This final salvo from the *Hood* was probably not a conscious act. It seems more likely that some kind of shortcut in the electrical firing system may have fired the guns one last time. Another plausible explanation is that Müllenheim-Rechberg did not see gun flashes at all, but a flash caused by an explosion in the fore magazines of the *Hood*. The explosion had made its way horizontally towards the bow. Confined by the armour deck it moved forward compartment by compartment as the bulkheads gave way, being delayed a fraction of a second each time. This delay in turn caused a slight pause between the explosions in the aft and fore magazines. It was sufficient for the German lieutenant to move to the port sight to observe the event. From the *Prince of Wales*, Coxswain French had seen flames shooting up from the water along most of the *Hood's* hull and he believed he saw how the ship was broken just ahead of the A-turret.

Coxswain Westlake on the *Prince of Wales* also got the impression that the battlecruiser's hull was broken in the fore part.[290] When the *Hood* rolled over and sank, Lieutenant Commander A. H. Terry, who was situated very high up on the *Prince of Wales*, briefly saw the damage wrought to the battlecruiser's hull and keel. He could see into the interior of the ship and the exposed frames where plating had disappeared.[291]

With the tormented noise of broken metal, bubbles of air rushing to the surface of the sea and the beating of his heart echoing in his ears, Briggs struggled desperately for his life in the dark water. He tried to swim, but the suction created by the sinking *Hood* dragged him down.

Panic had gone. This was it, I realized. But I wasn't going to give in easily. I knew that the deckhead of the compass platform was above me and that I must try to swim away from it. I managed to avoid being knocked out by the steel stanchions, but I was not making any progress. The suction was dragging me down. The pressure on my ears was increasing each second, and panic returned in its worse intensity. I was going to die. I struggled madly to try to heave myself up to the surface. I got nowhere. Although it seemed an eternity, I was under water for barely a minute. My lungs were bursting. I knew that I just had to breathe. I opened my lips and gulped in a mouthful of water. My tongue was forced to the back of my throat. I was not going to reach the surface. I was going to die. I was going to die. As I weakened, my resolve left me. What was the use of struggling? Panic subsided. I had heard it was nice to drown. I stopped trying to swim upwards. The water was a peaceful cradle. I was being rocked off to sleep. There was nothing I could do about it -goodnight, mum. Now I lay me down ...I was ready to meet God. My blissful acceptance of death ended in a sudden surge beneath me, which shot me to the surface like a decanted cork in a champagne bottle. I wasn't going to die. I wasn't going to die. I trod water as I panted in great gulps of air. I was alive. I was alive.[292]

Corporal Tilburn and Midshipman Dundas also shot to the surface, saved by a mysterious force that was later presumed to have originated from an exploding boiler. As they struggled on the surface, they saw the forecastle of the battlecruiser disappear as if it had been a toy in a pond. The other two parts of the ship, the mid and aft sections, had already begun their decent to the bottom of the ocean. The rumbling and hissing sounds from the sinking ship died out; the blazes disappeared as if by a stroke of magic. Soon only a dark cloud, already beginning to dissolve, and a large patch of dark oil, mixed up with wreckage, remained where the *Hood* had once been.

But the battle had not ended. When the sixth salvo from the *Prince of Wales* straddled the German battleship, Captain Leach noted that the *Bismarck* was hit. There might still exist a chance to turn the battle in British favour. Then the *Bismarck's* first salvo aimed at the *Prince of Wales* found its mark. One of the shells crashed into the bridge, but fortunately for Leach, it was a dud which continued straight through the bridge and out on the other side of the battleship, before tumbling into the water. Still, even a non-exploding 38cm shell wrought havoc. A moment earlier, Leach had had a properly working staff around him. A fraction of a second later he was in a slaughterhouse of smoke, screams, blood and cut off body parts. As the dazed Captain struggled to get back on his feet, he saw that only the Yeoman of Signals was standing. Everybody else was on the floor, all but one of them were dead.

It was just the beginning. Shell after shell hit the British battleship. Radar systems and sights were knocked out, boats and cabins were destroyed. A Walrus-plane, just about to be launched to direct fire, was riddled by splinters and the aircrew hastily abandoned it. The *Prince of Wales* returned fire, but several of her guns malfunctioned. Despite the efforts of the civilian technicians, problems with the guns occurred more rapidly than they were repaired. Finally Leach gave orders for retreat. If the uneven duel had continued, the outcome was clearly not going to be favourable. It was better to save the ship.

The range between the combatants rapidly opened up, until only wreckage, oil and three men remained in the area. Two of these men were Tilburn and Dundas. The third was Ted Briggs. His boyish dream to serve with the *Hood* had become a nightmare that would haunt him for the rest of his life.

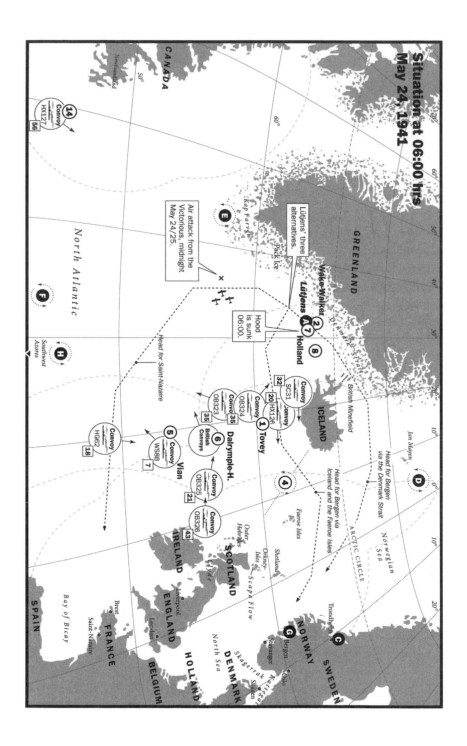

Situation at 06:00 hrs
May 24, 1941

Lütjens' three
alternatives.

Air attack from the
Victorious, midnight
May 24/25.

Hood
is sunk
06:00.

Head for Bergen via
Iceland and the Faeroe
Isles

Head for Bergen
via the Denmark Strait

Head for Saint-Nazaire

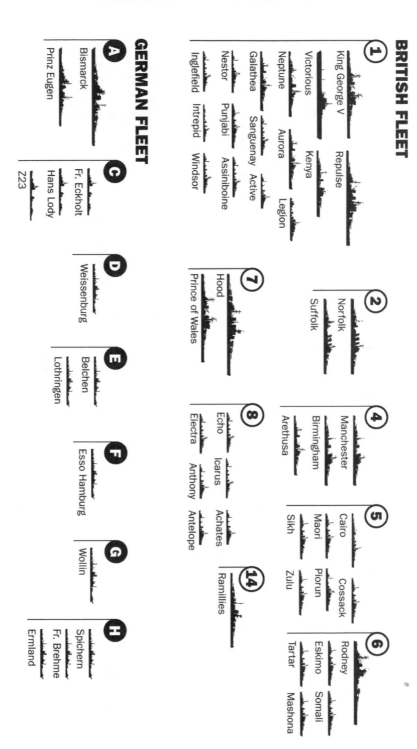

BRITISH FLEET

1
King George V
Victorious
Neptune
Galathea
Nestor
Inglefield
Repulse
Kenya
Aurora
Sanguenay
Punjabi
Intrepid
Active
Legion
Assiniboine
Windsor

2
Norfolk
Suffolk

7
Hood
Prince of Wales

4
Manchester
Birmingham
Arethusa

8
Echo
Electra
Icarus
Anthony
Achates
Antelope

5
Cairo
Maori
Sikh
Cossack
Piorun
Zulu

14
Ramillies

6
Rodney
Eskimo
Tartar
Somali
Mashona

GERMAN FLEET

A
Bismarck
Prinz Eugen

C
Fr. Eckholt
Hans Lody
Z23

D
Weissenburg

E
Belchen
Lothringen

F
Esso Hamburg

G
Wollin

H
Spichern
Fr. Brehme
Ermland

CHAPTER 18

'Roll out the barrel'

The battle in the Denmark Strait was over and the *Hood* was gone. It seemed beyond belief to the Germans on the *Bismarck* and *Prinz Eugen*, terrifying to Captain Leach on board the *Prince of Wales*, and an enormous shock to Wake-Walker, Phillips and Ellis on the *Norfolk* and *Suffolk*. When the flagship had been destroyed and Vice Admiral Holland had perished, Rear Admiral Wake-Walker assumed command of the remaining ships.

While the two cruisers continued to shadow the German squadron, and the *Prince of Wales* attached, Wake-Walker sent a message stating that the battlecruiser had blown up and then asked for a damage report from Captain Leach on board the *Prince of Wales*. The priority was still to retain contact with the Germans, so there was no time to rescue survivors from the *Hood*. Holland's four destroyers would have to do that. An hour later, Captain Leach reported that his ship was again combat ready and could make 27 knots. Wake-Walker ordered him to assume position on the *Norfolk's* port side.[293]

Where the *Hood* had blown up, three men struggled to stay afloat on their small Carley floats. The hours passed and the mood of the men vacillated between a burning desire to survive and an ever increasing fatigue as well as the conviction that they would never see land again. Tilburn felt closer and closer to unconsciousness. He had heard that the best way to freeze to death in the water was to fall asleep first. Then he would pass away from this world serenely. But if he fell asleep, he might slip off the Carley float and drown, which he believed was far worse. The instinct of self-preservation made him struggle on each time he tended to close his eyes and disappear.

It was Midshipman Dundas who kept them going. He spoke to them and encouraged them to sing 'Roll out the barrel,' to prevent the coldness and exhaustion from overcoming the three desperate men. For a long time, they managed to keep their rafts close together, but eventually they became separated.[294]

On board the destroyer *Electra*, one of Holland's escort ships, the signal officer received Wake-Walker's message and turned in shock towards the commander, Lieutenant Commander Cain. 'From the *Norfolk*, sir,' he said. 'The *Hood* has blown up!'

Cain, who believed the signal officer had gone mad and tried some kind of weird joke, began to scold him, until he saw the tears in the face of the signal officer and finally the truth dawned upon him.

'For God's sake, sir,' the signal officer said. 'It is true...'

On the *Bulldog*, another of Holland's escorting destroyers and the very ship that had captured the *U-110* a few weeks earlier, the commander refused to believe the message just received and was convinced that there must have been some kind of mix-up of ship names. On board Somerville's *Renown*, Dalrymple-Hamilton's *Rodney*, on board British ships patrolling in the Far East or Royal Navy ships hunkering under air attacks by the Luftwaffe, the effect and the reactions were the same: distrust, shock and grief. To the British, the loss of the *Hood* was more than the loss of a warship, it was the loss of a symbol for the nation. She had been bigger, faster and better armed than most warships. Suddenly she no longer existed and from her crew of more than 1,400 men, only three men survived to bear witness about the final moments on board the battlecruiser. Just as most Englishmen remembered what they were doing on the day Britain declared war on Germany, so many remembered what they were doing when they were told that the *Hood* had blown up.[295]

At Chequers, Churchill was woken up with the news that the *Hood* had been destroyed. He got up, walked to the room where Averell Harriman had his accommodation for the night and spoke briefly with the American envoy. 'The *Hood* has been sunk,' Churchill said, dejected.

However, further disappointments awaited the Prime Minister. Churchill went to bed again, but had hardly fallen asleep when Martin, his private secretary, came with further information

'Have we sunk her?' Churchill asked hopefully.

The secretary shook his head. 'No,' he said, 'and the *Prince of Wales* has disengaged.'

When Tovey's signal officer arrived at the bridge on board the *King George V* with Wake-Walker's message, he read the text with an unusually loud and excited voice. Although Tovey must have been perplexed by the message, he remained outwardly composed as he received it. 'It is fine, Jacobs,' he calmly answered. 'There is no need to shout.'

But the situation had deteriorated considerably. A few hours earlier, Tovey had had three fairly powerful and fast ships, the *Hood*, *Prince of Wales* and *King George V*. Now one of them was gone and the other damaged. While the lookouts on the flagship sighted the ravaged remnants of convoy HX126 heading east, Tovey assembled his staff to reconsider the situation. They did not appreciate the picture that emerged and their despondence was shared by the Admiralty in London. Now it was important to scramble as large a force as possible to sink the *Bismarck*. Admiral Somerville's Force H had already been ordered to meet convoy WS8B, which was heading for the Middle East, but it now appeared imperative that Somerville's ships be committed to chasing the *Bismarck*. Further reinforcements were sent into the operation. The two battleships *Revenge* and *Ramillies*, old vessels mainly used for convoy escort, were ordered to assume suitable positions. The *Revenge* was in Halifax and would have to sail immediately to have any chance of engaging the *Bismarck*. The *Ramillies* escorted convoy HX127 and was presently about 1,700 kilometres south of the German squadron. She was ordered to leave the convoy and position herself west of the line the *Bismarck* would follow if she continued on her present course.[296]

To send these aged battleships into combat against the *Bismarck* shows the Admiralty's determination to sink the German battleship. The range of the main guns carried by the *Revenge* and *Ramillies* did not exceed 22 kilometres, approximately 15 kilometres less than those of the *Bismarck*. Considering that the German battleship was also roughly 10 knots faster, it would require very favourable circumstances for these old ships even to get the chance to fire a shot at the *Bismarck*. The German ship could either sail away, or choose to fight at ranges beyond the reach of the old guns of the *Ramillies* and *Revenge*.

The *Rodney* was a more useful ship. Although her maximum speed was limited to 23 knots, her armament and protection was of a much more modern standard than that of the *Ramillies* and *Revenge*. When the battle in the Denmark Strait was fought, the *Rodney* was on her way towards Halifax. Before noon, Captain Dalrymple-Hamilton received the order to try to engage the *Bismarck*. If necessary, the *Rodney* was to leave the *Britannic*, which she soon did.[297]

Further ships became involved in the operation in various ways. The Royal Navy needed to monitor the *Bismarck*, in order to bring her to battle. For the moment the *Norfolk*, *Suffolk* and *Prince of Wales* shadowed Lütjens' two ships, but there was always a risk that contact would be lost, or the pursuers might be forced to break off, for example due to lack of fuel. Three cruisers, *London*, *Edinburgh* and *Dorsetshire*, were in the area east and northeast of the Azores. They received orders to move in a northwesterly direction, to reach a suitable position in case contact with the German squadron was lost.[298]

None of these measures would have any immediate effect and Tovey would have to cope with the present forces for another day. If he could bring the *King George V* and *Repulse* into gun range with the German squadron, while the *Prince of Wales* maintained contact, he would have three capital ships against one German. However, such a scenario was indeed difficult. The initial reports on the battle in the Denmark Strait gave Tovey no reason to assume that the *Bismarck* had suffered any significant damage. On the contrary, she steamed on at 27 to 28 knots, which was equal to the maximum speed of the *King George V* and *Prince of Wales*. As Tovey's force was still almost 700 kilometres from the German squadron, prospects of a battle appeared gloomy.[299]

Even if Tovey could manage to engage the *Bismarck* with all three capital ships, the outcome of such a battle need not be favourable to him. The *Prince of Wales* had been damaged in the battle in the Denmark Strait and her guns had repeatedly suffered from various problems, preventing them from firing. The *Repulse* was weakly protected, even in comparison with the *Hood*. To make matters worse, nothing suggested that the *Bismarck's* combat capabilities had been impaired. However, such risks seem not to have deterred the British. On the contrary, they displayed a remarkable willingness to stake everything on one card. An example of the determination was a request made by the Admiralty to Wake-Walker, where he was instructed to describe his intentions to bring the *Prince of Wales* into battle again.

In fact, the message came from Churchill. The Prime Minister had been preoccupied with the disastrous events at Crete and North Africa, when he received the news about the destruction of the *Hood*. While he was torn between the catastrophes, he was deeply concerned about what would happen if the *Bismarck* found a British convoy on the Atlantic. In particular, the safety of convoy WS8B, which was bearing vital reinforcements for the Middle East, worried him profoundly. He asked the First Sea Lord, Admiral Dudley Pound, to inquire whether the *Prince of Wales* could re-engage the German battleship.

Wake-Walker did not know that the inquiry originated from Churchill, he assumed that it had been sent due to some kind of general impression within the Admiralty. He was familiar with the inner workings of the Admiralty and interpreted the message as an indication that he *ought* to engage the *Bismarck* as soon as possible. If this was the unspoken order, Wake-Walker, who was on the spot and had a clearer insight into the situation, disagreed. He had himself witnessed the remarkable accuracy of the German fire. The second salvo had straddled the target; a very impressive feat considering the range. The *Prince of Wales*, on the other hand, had exhibited grave problems with her guns, which had malfunctioned frequently in the battle. Finally, the British battleship was damaged and it was doubtful if she could generate the speed needed to force the Germans to battle. After carefully considering the alternatives, Wake-Walker informed the Admiralty that he did not intend to engage the *Bismarck* until further heavy British units had arrived, or if all other options had failed.[300] However, a suspicion that the Admiralty was dissatisfied with his unwillingness to engage the German squadron had taken root in him.

One point of the utmost importance to both sides was whether the *Bismarck* had been damaged and, if so, to what extent. Of course, the British were hard put to get any knowledge on the matter, but it was not easy for the Germans either to form an accurate picture. The German flagship had in fact been hit by three shells, all of them fired from the *Prince of Wales*. One of the shells had passed through a boat and continued into the ocean without exploding. Another shell had passed through the forecastle, in section XXI, and ruptured oil tanks. Finally, one shell had struck the water, hit the battleship below the side armour in section XIV and detonated against a torpedo bulkhead. The sections were numbered from stern to bow, thus section XIV was located slightly aft of the two forward main turrets.[301]

The long-term effects of these hits could not be established at this stage, but Lütjens, Lindemann and the staff officers formed a fairly accurate impression quite soon after the battle. The hit in section XIV was not particularly serious. In general, the hull had absorbed it very well, but a leak caused water to enter a generator room and a boiler room. The *Bismarck* had been constructed with redundant capacities so that her generators could produce more than twice the electricity needed, for example. The loss of the generator room just meant that her safety margins had been reduced. If no other damage was sustained, it was inconsequential.

The hit in the bow caused more concern. It meant not only that the oil in this section was lost, but also that oil from the section ahead could not be pumped astern. A significant portion of *Bismarck*'s fuel was either lost or unavailable, severely curtailing her radius of action. In addition, the flow of water rushing in through the hole resulting from the hit could be a significant concern. As long as the ship did not sail at very high speed, it was not much more than a nuisance, but at speeds close to 30 knots, the pressure caused by the water on the bulkhead between section XX and XXI became alarmingly strong. Lütjens ordered the speed not to exceed 28 knots. It was still rather impressive, and equal to the speed of the *King George V* and *Prince of Wales*, but the loss of two or three knots meant that the *Bismarck* no longer had a speed advantage over the fastest British battleships.[302]

As neither Lütjens, nor Lindemann or any other of the senior officers survived Operation Rheinübung, we can only surmise as to how they reached their decisions. In addition to the condition of the flagship after the battle in the Denmark Strait, there were several other factors that are likely to have influenced Lütjens and the other officers. The first and most obvious one was that the Royal Navy had been able to send a task force into battle against the German squadron so soon after it had left Bergen. The inescapable conclusion was that the British must have been informed that the *Bismarck* and *Prinz Eugen* had left port almost as soon as it happened, or they would not have been able to reach the Denmark Strait in time to catch up with the German battleships. It was just wishful thinking to hope that the British capital ships had happened to be near Iceland for some other reason. The evidence suggested that Operation Rheinübung had been disclosed, which meant that more strong units of the Royal Navy were perhaps not far away.

Lütjens also seems to have been convinced that the enemy had a new and very effective radar, a further factor to take into consideration. The officers on the two German ships expressed somewhat different interpretations about the means by which the British had shadowed them so successfully, but the message Lütjens sent to the naval staff sent in the morning put forward his conclusions.

Operation Rheinübung, if not the entire concept of cruiser warfare, now had to be called into question. The *Bismarck* was damaged and any secrecy surrounding the operation had been breached. If the British also had radar that would enable them to track down their enemy, then a new plan was urgently required.

If Lütjens broke off Operation Rheinübung, he had two main alternatives. The *Bismarck* ought to set course for a harbour so that she could make some repairs. Thus either he had to detach the *Prinz Eugen*, to allow the cruiser to continue operations against British shipping alone, or else both ships should break off the operation and put into port. Irrespective of the alternative settled for, there were a number of ports to choose from, on the French Atlantic coast, in Germany or in Norway. Lutjens choice was limited because not all harbours had a dry dock big enough to hold the *Bismarck*. In France there was a very large dry dock at St. Nazaire; in Germany there were a number of dry docks large enough. However, in Norway there was no dock large enough, although provisional repairs could be made in Norway, before continuing towards Germany where she could be laid in a dry dock.

The choice of harbour of course determined the course to be set by Lütjens. If he chose to head for St. Nazaire, he would initially have to follow a southerly course and later turn southeast and finally east. If he opted to set course for Germany or Norway, he would have to turn east quite soon. The southerly route to St. Nazaire would bring Lütjens' ships into larger areas of open sea, where the nights were longer and darker, which would make it easier to shake off his pursuers. Lütjens' knowledge of the dispositions of the Home Fleet was scant, but the fact that most of its heavy ships were based at Scapa Flow suggested that he was less likely to encounter them on a southerly course. Another advantage with the southerly alternative was the possibility of disengaging the *Prinz Eugen*, to allow her to continue to fight on her own. The damage suffered by the *Bismarck* could probably be repaired quickly and a sojourn in St. Nazaire would be little more than a brief pause in the operation. It would be easier to reach the Atlantic unnoticed from St. Nazaire than from the German ports.

However, St. Nazaire did have its disadvantages,. From Lütjens' present position, the distance to St. Nazaire was 1,700 nautical miles, compared to about 1,150 to Bergen. Even if Lütjens should decide to double back through the Denmark Strait, the distance would be at most 1,400 nautical miles. Those differences could prove critical as part of the *Bismarck's* fuel oil had been lost. It was probably assumed that the oil in section XXII could eventually be pumped astern of the damaged section XXI, in which case the differences in distance may not have influenced Lütjens' decisions heavily. Finally, he had to consider that the southern route might allow him to shake off the pursuers and rendezvous with a German tanker.[303]

Little more than an hour after the destruction of the *Hood*, Lütjens informed the naval staff that the *Bismarck* was heading for St. Nazaire. The *Prinz Eugen* would conduct cruiser warfare on her own.

In the Denmark Strait, hope had almost deserted the three distressed men from the *Hood*. Gradually they became more and more separated and numb with cold, drowsiness overcame them. Briggs could faintly hear that Dundas still sang '*Roll out the barrel*,' but his voice became more and more distant and finally Briggs began to wish the midshipman could shut his mouth so that they all could die serenely. As Briggs sank into some kind of haze, he noted that the song ceased and was followed by a wild scream from Dundas: 'A destroyer! It is coming towards us!'

Briggs suddenly regained energy and saw that Dundas was correct. Heaving through the large waves, a British destroyer approached, heading straight towards the three distressed men. With eyes stinging from the sea water, Briggs could discern the designation H27 on the ships hull and he realized that it was one of their destroyers. 'It is the *Electra*!' he cried ecstatically. '*Electra*! *Electra*!'

Tilburn too saw the ship. The three men in the water shrieked and gesticulated as if they had gone crazy. The *Electra* had steamed south since she received the order to search for survivors. Two hours elapsed before they reached the location where the *Hood* had blown up, but they found precious few to save. Jack Taylor manned one of the machine guns on the *Electra*. Like many other seamen on the destroyer, he was preparing to rescue hundreds of survivors. The gale that had raged during the night had destroyed most of the boats. Instead, hand-lines were lowered alongside the hull, while measures were taken to accommodate the survivors. Blankets were made available, as well as medical equipment. Food and warm beverages were prepared. The men were gathered on the deck, ready to throw out ropes. Taylor stared at the grey water below:

> *It was only what seemed like a matter of minutes when we broke out of a mist patch into the clear. And there it was. The place where the* Hood *had sunk. Wreckage of all descriptions was floating on the surface. Hammocks, broken rafts, boots, clothes, caps. Of the hundreds of men we expected to see there was no sign. An awestruck moment and a shipmate next to me exclaimed 'Good Lord, she's gone with all hands.'*[304]

The sailor was almost right. A few large oil patches were seen on the water, then a desk drawer surrounded by white sheets of paper. The rest were wrecked goods and dress equipment. That was all.

Except three men yelling and waving in the water.

'A shout went up as a man appeared clinging to a piece of flotsam a little further away,' Taylor remembered. 'Two more were seen – one swimming, the other appeared to be on a small float.'

'But there *must* be more of them,' exclaimed the Chief Engineer. 'There can't be only three! Where the hell are all the others?'[305]

But they were all that remained of the *Hood's* crew of 94 officers and 1,324 men: two seamen shouting the name of the destroyer and a midshipman singing '*Roll out the barrel*' as if his life still depended on it.

The destroyer slowed down beside the three men. Many of her crew had climbed down the ropes and hung half way down to the water, holding out their hands to grab the men in the water. A lifeline was thrown down to Briggs and despite fingers almost rigid from cold, he managed to grasp it.

'Don't let it go,' somebody from the destroyer shouted.

'You bet your bloody life I won't.'

When the three men tried to climb up the scrambling nets, the hours in the cold water finally overcame them. Their energy had been sapped and they would not have managed to climb on board the destroyer had not the seamen climbed down and helped them.

The search continued for another hour, but as the battle had recently been fought, any survivors could not have drifted far away. Soon it had to be accepted that there were no more survivors. The destroyers set a northerly course, towards Iceland.

In London, Churchill received his third and very painful piece of news that morning. Not only had the *Hood* been lost; virtually her entire crew had followed the battlecruiser to the bottom of the ocean.

'I don't care how you do it,' he ordered the First Sea Lord, 'but sink the *Bismarck*!'

CHAPTER 19

Farewell, Bismarck!

On board the *Bismarck*, engineers, damage control parties and others worked to establish a correct picture of the damage inflicted upon her. Then they would have to deal with it. As already mentioned, the hit in the bow was the most serious, as there was a risk that the bulkhead astern of the compartment could not withstand the pressure caused when water flowed in at high speed. A flooding-control party was ordered to construct some kind of support for the bulkhead, which would enable the ship to steam at full speed. Also, attempts at making the oil in the compartment ahead of the hit available, were made. Lieutenant Karl-Ludwig Richter led a few damage-control groups who tried to use the emergency exits to make their way to the foremost compartment. Once there, they might be able to switch on the pumps and pump the oil to other fuel oil tanks, further astern in the ship. Unfortunately, the pumps turned out to be submerged, and the attempt failed. It was proposed that the pumps in section XVII could be used, by connecting hoses to the forward section. This attempt was also unsuccessful, and it became apparent that the valves to the oil pipes in the forecastle had been damaged as well.[306]

The hits had resulted in a few thousand tons of water leaking into the hull at the bow and on the port side, so that the starboard propeller was partly above the surface of the sea. Chief engine-room artificer Wilhelm Schmidt was ordered to fill the trim tanks, to restore trim. The manoeuvre was uncomplicated and could swiftly be carried out. A more worrisome problem was the fact that oil poured out from the hit fuel tank in compartment XXI and left a visible trail after the battleship. It might help the British pursuers to find the *Bismarck*, if they were to lose contact.[307]

No one on the *Bismarck* had been killed or severely wounded during the battle. All weapons were still fully combat-ready. Ammunition expenditure comprised 93 38-centimetre shells, equal to about one tenth of the overall supply. Similarly, the armour was completely unharmed and the machinery in perfect order. The German battleship remained a formidable opponent if the British should again try to engage her and all the available evidence suggests that the crew remained confident in their ship.[308]

Regardless of the feelings of the crew, Lütjens was probably more worried. In his directive for the operation, he had emphasized the need to minimize risks, and the recent battle in the Denmark Strait had clearly shown the dangers inherent in combat with equal opponents. Even though the few hits had been relatively harmless, the operation had to be discontinued. This necessity confirmed the wisdom of the ideas underlying the directive.

In the morning, Lütjens ordered his two ships to exchange places, to allow the officers on the cruiser to study the trail of oil left behind by the *Bismarck*. The manoeuvre lasted for approximately 40 minutes, whereupon the ships resumed their positions. Immediately afterwards, Captain Brinkmann give his report, which was disquieting. The trail of oil was wide and could hardly escape the British. In daylight it would be very difficult to shake off the pursuers.

There remained one option that Lütjens had not yet tried. During Operation Berlin, he had attempted to cooperate with the submarines, but it had been difficult. This time prospects seemed better. As Dönitz's headquarters had monitored the radio transmission made by Lütjens, he knew the position of the German squadron. Submarines could be directed to the area where Lütjens and the shadowing enemies were expected to pass. Furthermore, the *Bismarck* and *Prinz Eugen* were soon to enter an area where many submarines operated.[309]

Lütjens wanted the submarine command to organize a line of submarines right across the course presently held by his squadron, at about the same longitude as the southern tip of Greenland. Hopefully the submarines would be able to attack the pursuing British ships on the morning of 25 May. From this request it can be inferred that Lütjens intended to continue on the southwesterly course, which suggests that he did not regard the fuel oil situation as critical. If he continued the present course for another 12 to 24 hours, his ships would travel far to the west, thus requiring the *Bismarck* to use the oil in the bow, or bunker from a tanker at sea.[310]

If Lütjens was not yet unduly concerned about the *Bismarck's* fuel situation, he was surely well aware of the limited endurance of the *Prinz Eugen*. It was very important that the cruiser could be detached as soon as an opportunity was given, to allow her to rendezvous with a tanker. At 15.20 hours, Lütjens sent a message to the *Prinz Eugen* by signal lamp. The message contained instructions for the detachment. During the next rain squall the *Bismarck* would turn west, while the *Prinz Eugen* continued south. The British attention was mainly directed on the *Bismarck*, which sailed behind the cruiser, and would probably follow the battleship as she sheered to starboard. Conditions seemed favourable to an unnoticed detaching of the cruiser, but success would be dependent on the effectiveness of the British radar. In any case the *Prinz Eugen* was to maintain her southerly course for another three hours. Unless she had to sheer due to some unforeseen event, she would manage to evade the pursuers. If successful, she could set course for the *Belchen* or *Lothringen* to bunker fuel oil. Thereafter, she could go after convoys on her own. The scheme was to be set in motion upon receipt of the code word 'Hood'.[311]

Lütjens' plans were facilitated by the changed weather from noon onwards. The sea became rougher. Rain squalls were succeeded by fog. An attempt to detach the *Prinz Eugen* seemed quite likely to succeed, even before dusk. However, before the plans were realized, two things happened. The first was a reduction of speed, to 24 knots, by the German squadron. The second was change of course, to south. Speed was reduced to aid the work of the damage control parties in the bow. The change of course is more difficult to explain, as it meant that Lütjens' ships would pass east of the submarine line that was forming. Perhaps Lütjens wanted to increase the distance to Greenland, to create more room for manoeuvre before trying to detach the cruiser. If so, the change of course was probably intended to be temporary.[312]

In the poor weather, Lütjens decided to attempt to detach the cruiser. The ships approached a rain squall and at 16.40 hours, the signalmen on board the *Prinz Eugen* could report that the flagship had sent the message 'Carry out Hood'. According to the plan, the *Bismarck*

sheered west and soon she could not be seen, but the enemy nevertheless maintained contact. Only a few minutes later the *Bismarck* could
again be seen from the *Prinz Eugen* and a signal lamp on the flagship
flashed 'cruiser on starboard'. Evidently, the rain squall was not heavy
enough, but further opportunities were likely to occur.

In the meantime, Admiral Tovey was troubled by the unfolding of
events. Unlike Lütjens, he did not lack vital information. In fact, his
awareness of the situation was fairly complete. Unfortunately, the facts
available to him were not encouraging. With the course and speed
maintained by the Germans, he slowly shortened the distance to the
enemy. If the Germans became aware of his position, perhaps by a
German submarine observing his ships, Lütjens would be able to
increase the distance. As if this was not bad enough, all calculations of
the distance, speed, course and the fuel consumption of the British ships
indicated that they would run out of fuel oil before catching the
Germans.[313]

There were only two things Tovey could hope for. The first was that
damage sustained in the battle would force the Germans to turn; the
second was that they would be forced to find a tanker to bunker fuel
oil from, whereupon perhaps British ships could surprise them. For the
moment nothing suggested that any of these scenarios were likely. A
Sunderland seaplane reported that the *Bismarck* left oil behind her, but
initially no conclusions were inferred from this observation. Towards
the afternoon, the British did begin to nurture hopes that there was at
least something wrong with the *Bismarck*. There was no suggestion that
she had suffered severe damage, but her trail of oil provided some
hope.[314]

Meanwhile, Force H was heading north from Gibraltar, but Admiral
Somerville's ships could only cover one of many alternatives that the
Admiralty had to consider as German options. Other ships were much
closer to the main action. The *Ramillies* had sailed at a paltry speed of
8 knots when she received the signal from the Admiralty instructing her
to leave convoy HX127 and take part in the hunt for the German ships.
If the old battleship was to reach the 18 knots ordered, she would have
to raise steam pressure rapidly, thus emitting large clouds of dark
smoke which would be clearly visible at considerable distances. Captain
Read had sharply criticized many of the merchant ships for doing

precisely this, because the smoke could easily be seen from enemy submarines. Now he had to engage in the same sort of behaviour himself and he realized than many commanders on board the freighters laughed up their sleeves. But orders were orders and the Admiralty obviously accepted the risks involved.

It was not the only risk accepted by the Admiralty. Several ships, among them Wake-Walker's cruisers, but also the cruisers *Edinburgh* and *London*, which had been redirected from other tasks to take part in the chase for the German squadron, were ordered to search for the *Bismarck* at any cost. Once contact had been made, the German battleship was to be shadowed as far as possible, even if it meant that the British ships would run out of fuel and become immobile in the midst of the Atlantic.[315]

When Lütjens decided to change course and reduce speed, the situation transformed. Wake-Walker reported the changes made by the German ships as soon as possible. Up to now, Tovey's situation had appeared hopeless, but at a stroke chances of success improved notably. If the *Bismarck* maintained her latest course, it would be possible to intercept her with the *King George V* and *Repulse*. The chances were still far from good, because the German change of course and speed might be temporary, but an opportunity had at least been revealed. The distance between Tovey and Lütjens diminished hour by hour. Also, Tovey had yet another card to play. The torpedo planes carried by the *Victorious* might damage the *Bismarck*, perhaps reducing her speed. The weather was unsuitable for air power, especially for the poorly trained air crew assigned to the *Victorious*. Also, the distance to the German battleship remained great, making the task daunting. However, the poor weather also increased the risk that during the time it would take Tovey's heavy ships to catch up with the *Bismarck*, he might lose contact with her. Without the *Suffolk's* radar, the British would hardly have been able to shadow the German squadron. Despite the risks, an air attack by the torpedo planes from the *Victorious* had to be attempted.[316]

If it were to be possible to conduct the air attack at all, the *Victorious* had to be detached and set a southwesterly course, while Tovey's main force would sail on a south-southwesterly course. The split of forces was mainly mandated by the differences in speed and endurance between ships and aircraft. The latter of course travelled much faster, but their range was limited. With a southwesterly course, the *Victorious* would pass astern of the German squadron, but close enough to enable the aircraft to reach the *Bismarck*. However, it was unthinkable to allow the *King George V* and *Repulse* to set the same course, as it would deprive them of any chances to intercept the German ships, unless the latter were severely damaged by the air attack.

There was a distinct disadvantage with this decision. The *Victorious* would probably not be close enough to launch an air attack on the German ships on 25 May. Even worse, her reconnaissance aircraft would not be within range to act as scouts in case contact with the German squadron was lost. Nevertheless, Tovey decided to accept the risks and just before 16.00 hours, the four cruisers *Galatea, Aurora, Kenya* and *Hermione* together with the *Victorious* were detached, all of them led by the commander of the 2nd Cruiser Division, Rear Admiral Curteis.[317]

At this stage, Tovey could not expect too much of the battleships and battlecruisers, except the *King George V*. He was well aware of the shortcomings of the *Revenge* and *Ramillies,* and the *Rodney* was still too far away. Force H was of course even further from the scene. If the air attack launched by the *Victorious* failed, or if Wake-Walker lost contact, virtually all hope of engaging the *Bismarck* would be lost.

Wake-Walker and his squadron still played a vital, role. He not only had to maintain contact with the Germans, he also had to ensure that his ships were not surprised by the Germans. In the poor weather, the *Norfolk,* with her inferior radar, could easily lose contact with the Germans and become vulnerable to surprise attacks. At 13.30 hours Wake-Walker ordered the *Norfolk* to turn around 360 degrees, positioning her three to four nautical miles astern of the other two British ships. The decision was justified about 40 minutes later, when Lütjens attempted to detach the *Prinz Eugen* and suddenly the *Bismarck* appeared eight nautical miles from the *Norfolk.* As we have seen, the *Bismarck* turned east immediately, whereupon the *Norfolk* lost contact, but this time she was informed of the change by the *Suffolk,* whose radar still provided admirable assistance. Thus the *Norfolk* escaped further unpleasant surprises.[318]

In addition to radar and lookouts on Wake-Walker's ships, reconnaissance aircraft provided surveillance. The advantage with the aircraft was that they could keep an eye on the Germans at a distance from which the latter could not strike back. Wake-Walker, on the other hand, had to manoeuvre his ships in such a way that he balanced two risks, the risk of being hit and the risk of losing contact, against each other. The fickle weather made the task even more difficult, as visibility changed dramatically from minute to minute.[319] Early in the afternoon the Hudson that had thus far watched over the Germans returned and was replaced by a Catalina that had started from Iceland. Unfortunately the Catalina suffered engine problems and had to break off the mission after two hours.

While all this took place, Wake-Walker found some time to ruminate on the Admiralty's inquiry after his intentions to re-engage the Germans with the *Prince of Wales*. He was fairly certain that Tovey would prefer it if there were no actions before the *King George V* and *Repulse* arrived, with the *Victorious'* torpedo planes as backup. Nevertheless, it appeared that the Admiralty held a different opinion to that of Tovey. Wake-Walker must have asked himself numerous times if he was being too cautious and defensive. His available information suggested that the Admiralty thought along those lines, or else the signal would not have been sent.

Wake-Walker decided upon a compromise. To stage a naval battle against the *Bismarck* and *Prinz Eugen*, with the ships he commanded, appeared ill-conceived, but perhaps he could 'tease' the enemy to chase the British ships and thereby lure Lütjens closer to Tovey. He ordered the *Suffolk* to leave her position on the right flank and move closer to the *Norfolk*, while the *Prince of Wales* increased speed and assumed a position ahead of the cruisers. Wake-Walker's navigation officer objected and emphasized that the arrangement would render it more difficult to shadow the enemy, but the admiral overruled these objections. He wanted to manoeuvre his unit as a close formation.[320] No one should accuse him of lacking offensive spirit.

In that way, the inquiry from the Admiralty unintentionally played into Lütjens' hands, because at 19.14 hours he decided to make another attempt to detach the *Prinz Eugen*. On board the German cruiser, Captain Brinkmann was dictating a message to his signals officer. He intended to suggest to Lütjens that the squadron should first attract the British pursuers to the trap formed by the German submarines and then, provided the enemy ships had lost contact, rendezvous with the *Belchen* and *Lothringen* and bunker fuel oil. If the scheme did not bring the intended results, he suggested a change of course, to south, while the tankers *Esso Hamburg* and *Spichern* would be instructed to sail north, to meet the German warships.

However, Brinkmann's message was never transmitted. Suddenly the signal officer reported: 'To the *Prinz Eugen* from the Fleet Commander...'

Without hearing the rest of the message, Brinkmann nevertheless understood the content. The *Bismarck* had already begun to turn to starboard, while her fore gun turrets traversed to enable them to fire on the enemy.

'...carry out Hood!' the signal officer finished.

The *Prinz Eugen* increased speed to 31 knots while the *Bismarck* turned sharply. On board the *Suffolk*, the radar screen suddenly indicated that the range to the German battleship rapidly fell. Ellis quickly ordered the helmsman to turn sharply to port, while the engine control room was ordered to increase to full speed. It was at the very last moment. Shells from the *Bismarck*'s 38cm guns splashed into the water unpleasantly close to the British cruiser, and as the *Suffolk* replied with her own guns, trained abaft of the beam, pressure from the blast of the B-turret shattered the bridge windows. Fortunately, the poor visibility limited the accuracy of the *Bismarck*'s fire. The *Prince of Wales* hastened to support the cruiser, but only a brief exchange of fire between the two battleships ensued, without either of them being hit.[321]

On board the *Prinz Eugen*, which managed to evade detection in the tumult, the crew could hear the thunder from the *Bismarck*'s guns, soon followed by the more distant noise when the enemy fired back. Many of the men who were not busy gathered at the gunwales to get a glimpse of the fighting. Briefly they were rewarded with the dark silhouette of the battleship on the horizon; they saw a few gun flashes and the brown clouds of smoke that rose towards the thick grey clouds above. Then she disappeared behind a rain squall.

'There our big brother disappears,' Jasper said at the bridge. 'We're going to miss him very, very much.'[322] They would never see the *Bismarck* again.

CHAPTER 20

Air Attack

The brief battle between Lütjens and Wake-Walker did not result in any casualties or damage, but it altered the scenario. One of the changes was the successful detachment of the *Prinz Eugen*, of which the British lost track. With only one ship to manoeuvre, Lütjens' chances of shaking off his pursuers improved. The most fundamental change, however, pertained to Wake-Walker's dispositions. He had received reports telling him that German submarines infested the area he was sailing into. Consequently, he ordered his ships to assume a zigzagging course, to minimize the risk of torpedo hits. Furthermore, Wake-Walker neglected to send the *Suffolk* back to her previous position on the right flank. Rather he kept the *Suffolk* close to his flagship, in case the *Bismarck* attacked again. Thus, the sector on the *Bismarck's* starboard aft was left empty.

At 20.30 hours on 24 May, Wake-Walker received a signal from the Admiralty telling him to expect an air attack launched from the *Victorious* any time after 22.00 hours. This signal coincided with a period when contact with the *Bismarck* was lost, and at the time when the air attack could be expected, contact had still not been regained. Tension mounted aboard the British ships as minute after minute passed without seeing the German ships, but fortunately the air attack had been delayed. At 23.30 hours, the *Bismarck* was again observed and the *Norfolk* could report that the German battleship sailed approximately 11 nautical miles ahead of her.[323]

Meanwhile, the *Victorious* prepared for an attack that bordered on the desperate. She was going to launch her Swordfish aircraft, a type often described as relics of bygone days, as their biplane construction suggested, an impression reinforced by the fuselage consisting of canvas, wires and struts. The perception is, however, precipitate, because the Swordfish aircraft in fact had many advantages. They were employed as a combination of torpedo, reconnaissance and fire-direction aircraft. The Swordfish could negotiate very difficult weather conditions and their aero-dynamic qualities were indispensable to the forthcoming attack.

The attack force consisted of nine Swordfish and was led by the division commander, Lieutenant Commander Eugene Esmonde. He had joined the Royal Air Force as a fighter pilot in 1928, but after five years of service, he began to fly mail and passenger aeroplanes to Australia. At the outbreak of World War II, he was offered the command of the 825th Swordfish Division. Esmonde was known as a daring and determined commander and he was well suited for a mission like the one he was just to embark on.

The attack force was divided into three groups. Esmonde commanded one, while the other two were led by Lieutenant Percy Gick, a former instructor at the Navy Torpedo School, and Lieutenant 'Speed' Pollard, who according to the traditions of the Navy received his nickname because he was known as a notorious idler. These three men were the only pilots who had any experience of missions like the one to be conducted. The other participants were hardly experienced or trained enough for the task. Many of them had conducted their first landing on a carrier a mere five days before and except for the three group commanders, none had even practised a torpedo attack in division formation before.

Nevertheless, the airmen tried to appear cocky when orders were received. They would start from a carrier deck swept by heavy squalls, fly 160 kilometres and attack enemy warships in the declining light. Then, if they survived the enemy anti-aircraft fire, they would fly back to the *Victorious* and take their aircraft down on the deck in darkness. But beneath the plucky façade, they knew this might very well be a mission they would not return alive from.

The nine Swordfish were moved onto the flight deck. The Swordfish were capable of generating much lift at low speeds, and the strong wind almost made them take off and veer off on their own. The maintenance crews had to keep them down while the air crews entered their machines. The engines coughed and fired up. The dark smoke from the exhausts was immediately dispersed and swept away by the strong wind. Soon Esmonde indicated that he was ready to start. The torpedo plane raced ahead over the flight deck and quickly climbed up in the air. The other machines followed. All made a successful start. Esmonde could assemble his force and set a southwesterly course. Soon the planes disappeared into a rainsquall. The clock showed that only an hour remained of 24 May, while the noise from the vanishing Swordfish was drowned as three Fulmars started from the *Victorious*. They would follow Esmonde's force and report what they saw.

Further west, the American coast guard ship *Modoc* worked her way through the large waves, searching for survivors from the convoy HX126. She had not found any sailors, only deserted lifeboats and rafts. It was a monotonous voyage and the crew was bored to death, but soon their hope for a change was to be fulfilled. The news that the *Hood* had blown up had already reached the American ship. Intercepted radio messages as well as a brief exchange with the British corvette *Arabis* had provided the information. The crew of the *Modoc* also realized that the *Bismarck* and *Prinz Eugen* were not far away. Despite this knowledge, the mighty silhouette of the *Bismarck* caused a great stir on the *Modoc*, as it suddenly became visible through the showers of rain pouring down from the thick clouds. Sailors who were not tied to a specific task hurried up on the deck. As they looked at Germany's largest warship, they spotted a number of tiny dots above the horizon. With a mixture of dismay and rapture they saw how Esmonde's slow biplanes broke through the clouds and approached the American ship with an unpleasant purposefulness.

Despite the poor visibility, Esmonde had managed to navigate with such precision that the enemy ships appeared as blips on the radar equipped aircraft, almost exactly when expected. For a brief moment, the *Bismarck* could even be seen in a gap between the clouds. However, the contact was lost soon afterwards. Esmonde had to bring his Swordfish formation below the clouds, to seek assistance from the British cruisers shadowing the German battleship. He found Wake-Walker's flagship, which signalled that the *Bismarck* was 12 nautical miles ahead, on the starboard bow. The Swordfish steered in the direction indicated, while they climbed into the covering clouds. Soon an echo appeared on the radar screens and Esmonde gave attack orders.

The squadron descended through the clouds and manoeuvred into attack positions, but there was something wrong. The British aeroplanes headed towards a ship that appeared too small. Furthermore, it seemed remarkably peaceful. Indeed, it was so small and quiet that it could hardly be the *Bismarck* or *Prinz Eugen*. In the last moment Esmonde realized that a mistake was about to be made and gave new orders to the other planes.

Unlike the Germans, who had been aware of the *Modoc's* presence before the ship was sighted, the British pilots had no knowledge about her. The British pilots broke off the attack on the innocent American ship in time, but their mistake nevertheless had negative consequences. When the British aircraft dived towards the *Modoc*, they were seen from the *Bismarck*, whose anti-aircraft gunners were alerted.

As Friday gave way to Saturday, Esmonde's group began the approach towards the *Bismarck*. It was still not dark, but twilight was quickly coming nearer from the east. Müllenheim-Rechberg was in the aft fire control tower on the *Bismarck*:

> *Several pairs of aircraft were seen approaching on the port bow. They were beneath a layer of clouds and we could see them clearly, getting into formation to attack us. [...] Aircraft alarm! In seconds every anti-aircraft gun on the Bismarck was ready for action. One after the other, the planes came towards us, nine Swordfish, torpedoes under their fuselages.*[324]

Esmonde's original intension had been to pass the battleship's bow and turn to enable an attack from starboard with his group, but the *Bismarck* opened effective fire and a rudder was hit. The machine was still manoeuvrable, but Esmonde realized it might be prudent to launch the attack while his aircraft could still fly.[325]

As the three aeroplanes reduced the distance, the *Bismarck* fired with almost every gun barrel she had. Tracer belched out from her lighter anti-aircraft guns and converged towards the biplanes. Heavy 38cm shells splashed into the sea, raising huge pillars of water, enough to shatter any aircraft that flew into them. Salvo after salvo left the heavy guns, but every time the water receded, the three Swordsfish remained, now closer to the battleship.

It appeared unfathomable that none of the three aircraft was shot down, but several factors made the task complicated for the gunners and rendered the aircraft difficult targets. One of them was the fact that the high explosive shells were set to detonate after a certain time of flight. Shells were prepared in such a way that the time set would diminish as the aircraft flew closer and closer during the attack. The procedure meant that shells with gradually shorter time before detonation were fired as range from the battleship to the aircraft diminished. The Germans did not realize how slow the Swordfish planes flew and most shells burst at too short range. Thus, the slow speed of the Swordfish was in fact an advantage in this situation. Another factor aiding the British was the rough sea, making it difficult for the AA crews, and when the *Bismarck* began to zigzag to avoid the awaited torpedoes, the aiming of the guns was further complicated.

At the open bridge aboard the *Bismarck*, Lindemann supervised the engagement. He gave orders directly to Corporal Hans Hansen, the helmsman. Lindemann did not need his binoculars to see how the torpedoes were jettisoned from Esmonde's group. He ordered Hansen to steer hard to starboard and all the torpedoes from the first group passed aport of the battleship's bow.

Immediately behind Esmonde's group, the second group followed. 'We approached just above sea level,' recalled Sub-lieutenant Les Sayer, who was an observer in Lieutenant Gick's plane. 'They fired at us, but fortunately we were not hit as we closed in.'

When Hansen turned to starboard, the ship twisted in such a way that Gick's group suddenly found itself approaching the battleship on her starboard quarter. Gick's comrades pressed the attack home, but Gick himself decided that the angle of attack was too unfavourable and turned away to make another attempt. 'At that moment I thought: To hell!' Sayer remembered. 'We've been through it once, now we had to do it all over again.'

While Gick turned away, the other two aeroplanes in his group continued and jettisoned their torpedoes. Hansen saw them, but at this stage all the noise from the firing weapons had deafened him to such an extent that he no longer heard what Lindemann said. He steered the ship on his own initiative.[326]

The German attention was now shifted to the third group, which had been reduced to two aircraft, as one had got lost in the clouds.

They made a wide tack in front of the German battleship. One plane turned and attacked from port bow. The other passed ahead of the *Bismarck*, before turning as sharply as the Swordfish was capable of and approached from starboard.

Hansen managed to avoid this attack too, but the Germans did not see that Gick had made a semicircle after the failed initial attack and now came in again. He flew at an extremely low altitude. The landing gear almost hit the waves and the setting sun was behind him. This time he felt certain of hitting his target. 'We approached at a speed of 170 kilometres per hour, just above the sea,' Sayer remembered. 'No one saw us and no fire was directed at us.'[327]

After releasing the torpedo, the Swordfish turned away. As Gick and Sayer strived to get out of range of the German guns, they were rewarded with the sight of a high column of water on the starboard side of the battleship. 'I saw what we regarded as a hit,' Sayer recalled, 'as a huge cascade of water rose from the hull. That was we, I thought. That was *our* hit.' [328]

The shock wave that went through the battleship when the torpedo exploded threw Petty Officer Kurt Kirchberg onto a bulkhead with such force that he was killed. Five other seamen had to be taken to the hospital with broken bones. 'The torpedo hit us on the starboard side,' Corporal Zimmermann recalled, 'and in the boiler room it caused bolts and nuts to ricochet around with such violence that they threatened to kill somebody.'[329]

A seaman on one of the lower decks was hurled several metres by the shock wave. Dazed, he got up and could hear his Chief engine room artificer ask calmly: 'But Budich, where were you going in such a hurry?'[330]

When the British planes hastened east, to return to the *Victorious*, a few final salvos were fired by the *Bismarck's* main guns. One of the shells struck the water beneath Gick's machine and the impact was so powerful that it ripped open a gaping hole in the bottom of the fuselage. 'We must have been in the outskirt of one such cascade,' Sayer told, 'that ripped away part of the canvas. The plane hadn't suffered any significant damage. It was just that suddenly you could see the sea between your feet.'[331]

The British airmen were not yet safe. Although they were beyond the range of the *Bismarck's* guns, they still had to survive a perilous flight in the darkness before they safely landed aboard the carrier. At these longitudes dusk occurred after midnight, with the clocks set as they were on the British and German ships and aircraft. The radio beacon on the *Victorious* was out of order and despite the dangers posed by German submarines, Captain Bovell decided to switch on searchlights and direct them on the clouds, to help the air crews to find the carrier. When Admiral Curteis ordered him to switch the lights off, Bovell pretended he had not understood the signal. Curteis had to send another signal, in sharper words, before Bovell complied. Still, he periodically flashed with the most powerful signal lamp on the carrier.

Esmonde never saw any beams from the *Victorious*. His division missed the task force. It soon became apparent that they had flown too far. Esmonde and the other pilots had to make a 180° turn and flew towards the area where they expected to find the carrier. They struggled on in the darkness and were finally rewarded a light, which turned out to originate from Curteis' cruisers. Despite their lack of experience, the pilots successfully landed on the flight deck in the dark night. All machines made it safely. Bovell and his officers felt relieved, as did the British airmen, in particular Gick with his damaged Swordfish. During most of the return flight he had heard the increasingly desperate words from the chilled Sayer in the intercom system: 'It's getting really cold back here!'[332]

Far less luck accompanied two Fulmar aircraft, which had started at 01.00 hours to relieve the aircraft reporting on the attack. Both lost their way and disappeared. Thirty-six hours later two of the airmen were found by the freighter *Braverhill*. The other two were lost.[333]

CHAPTER 21

'Have lost contact with the enemy'

Although the torpedo hit did not cause any damage to the *Bismarck*, the air attack nevertheless had repercussions. To avoid the torpedoes, she had increased speed and manoeuvred violently. The stresses induced, combined with the vibrations resulting from the recoiling heavy guns, damaged the flooding control arrangements made near the bow. Water again poured in. It was necessary to reduce speed to 16 knots, to allow the repair teams to take care of the problems.[334]

Beyond this, the death of Kirchberg and the seamen with broken bones, the results of the British air attack were meagre. The *Bismarck*'s main armour belt had withstood the impact of the torpedo. However, morale may have suffered. The sinking of the *Hood* surely boosted the confidence of the *Bismarck*'s crew considerably, but the air attack clearly showed them that further enemies were on their trail. This time, the ship's capabilities were not impaired, but what would happen next time? Obviously a carrier, perhaps accompanied by further heavy units, could not be far away from the *Bismarck*. To make matters worse, Petty Officer Kirchberg had been a very popular man aboard and his death did not pass unnoticed. Although morale remained high, rumours spread rapidly. 'It was reported that eight of the torpedo planes had been shot down,' recalled Engine Room Artificer Statz, 'which was incorrect. The mere fact that the planes had attacked us made me think. Perhaps we were not unsinkable, after all.'[335]

The *Bismarck* was concealed by the dark night, but at dawn renewed air attacks could be expected. At 20.50 hours the *Bismarck* was reached by a signal from the naval staff, which had not received the

Bismarck's morning report until noon, in which Lütjens was recommended to shake off the pursuers first and then refuel at sea. Not until then was he to set course for a port.

Lütjens decided to disregard the suggestion. The *Bismarck* was heading toward St. Nazaire. Two hours later, at 22.32 hours, he informed Marinegruppe West that he had stuck to his previous decision. The fuel shortage forced his decision. After the air attack, the problems in the bow had become worse, suggesting that the ship should not remain at sea longer than necessary. Perhaps it was the final circumstance convincing Lütjens to break off the operation. But what course should he set? If he were to reach St. Nazaire with the fuel available, he would have to abandon the southerly course quite soon.[336] Such a decision would render the planned submarine line irrelevant and when Lütjens informed Marinegruppe West that he intended to take the shortest route to St. Nazaire, the intended trap became useless. Dönitz would have to try to create a new trap along the route to St. Nazaire.[337]

Further issues forced the members of the German naval staff thoroughly to reconsider the situation. Lütjens had been reticent in his report, in particular concerning the damage suffered in the battle and the fuel situation. The officers at the naval staff made an estimate of the amount of fuel remaining on board the *Bismarck*. Their calculation was based on the distance sailed since she left Gdynia, her speed and the amount of fuel she had taken on before departure. After weighing all available information, it was concluded that the German flagship ought to have approximately 5,000 tons of fuel oil. This was a respectable amount, probably more than the British battleships carried, although the Germans could not be certain. Bearing this in mind, the message received from Lütjens at 22.32 hours must have appeared surprising. He had just announced his intention to sail almost along the shortest route to St. Nazaire. He made some attempt to justify his decision by referring to a shortage of fuel, but gave no details. Also, he stated that it was impossible to shake off the pursuers due to their radar. He had not mentioned that the fuel oil in the bow was inaccessible.[338]

Lütjens' message, sent before the air attack, suggests that he no longer had much hope of outrunning the British and therefore hoped to arrive within range of German airpower before the British could attack with overwhelming forces. The only sensible solution was to set the shortest course towards the Bay of Biscay, a route that also coincided with his need to economize on fuel. For this reason Lütjens decided to disregard the naval staff's advice. No German surface warships could assist and it was not easy to direct the submarines in a useful way, as their speed was too low. For the moment, the *Bismarck* was so far from German air bases that any air support was out of the question. The battleship would have to sail at least 24 hours before she came within range of German aircraft. Bearing these circumstances in mind, it is not surprising that Lütjens based his decisions on information available to him. The naval staff was in agreement with this and refrained from doing anything other than providing some prudent advice.[339]

Admiral Tovey had received the reports from the *Victorious* with increasing interest. A torpedo had hit, and after the attack the *Bismarck* had reduced speed to 22 knots. Suddenly a chance of attacking simultaneously with the *King George V*, *Prince of Wales* and *Repulse* seemed to be within his grasp. Tovey had as much reason to worry about fuel as Lütjens. Both the *Repulse* and the *Prince of Wales* would soon be unable to continue the operation. The *King George V* had more fuel oil, but her margins were not great. The destroyers escorting Tovey had been forced to abandon the operation at midnight, as their fuel would only suffice to take them back to port. Gradually, it dawned upon Tovey that the *Bismarck* had increased speed again and that she had lost little – if any – speed on account of the torpedo hit. However, there remained one chance. If the *Bismarck* continued with her present course and speed, Tovey could intercept her at approximately 09.30 hours on 25 May. If that happened, the *Repulse* could participate in the battle, but otherwise she would have to sail to Newfoundland to bunker.[340]

The Admiralty clearly understood the effect of the fuel shortages, both for the British ships and the *Bismarck*. For some time, it had been clear that the Germans had tankers on the Atlantic, allowing them to bunker fuel oil at sea. It is somewhat surprising that the Royal Navy had not prepared for such a contingency by sending British tankers to prearranged positions, allowing the Royal Navy to bunker on the Atlantic. Now it was too late to remedy the neglect, but it was still possible to search for the German tankers. The cruiser *London*, which had originally been directed to search for the *Bismarck*, was given another task. She was instructed to search for German supply ships southwest of the Azores.[341]

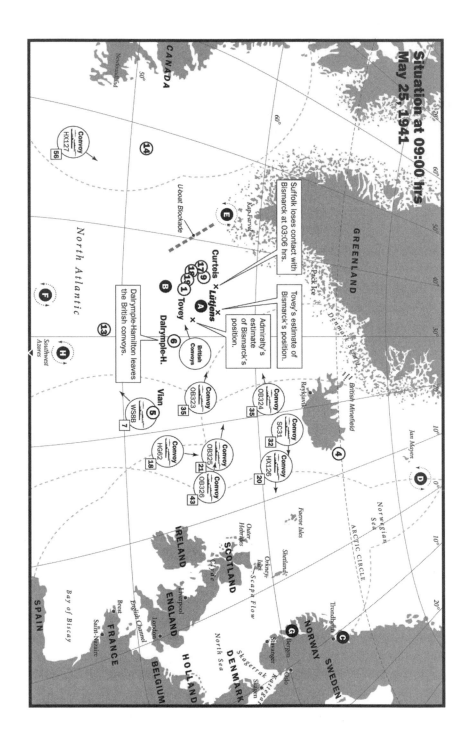

Situation at 09:00 hrs
May 25, 1941

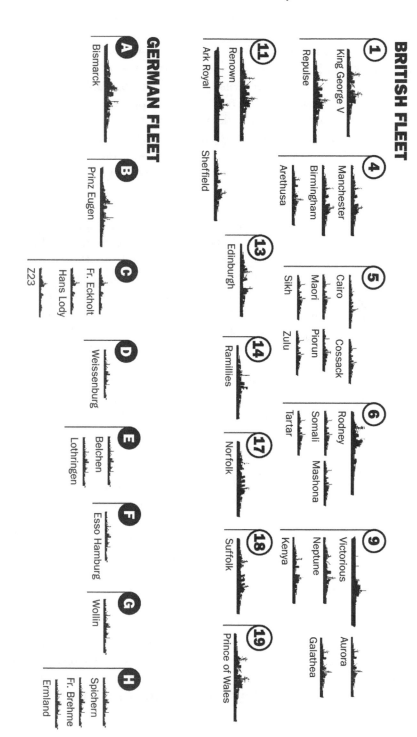

BRITISH FLEET

1. King George V
   Repulse

11. Renown
    Ark Royal
    Sheffield

4. Manchester
   Birmingham
   Arethusa

13. Edinburgh

5. Cairo
   Maori
   Sikh
   Cossack
   Piorun
   Zulu

14. Ramillies

6. Rodney
   Somali
   Tartar
   Mashona

17. Norfolk

9. Victorious
   Neptune
   Kenya
   Aurora
   Galathea

18. Suffolk

19. Prince of Wales

GERMAN FLEET

A. Bismarck

B. Prinz Eugen

C. Fr. Eckholt
   Hans Lody
   Z23

D. Weissenburg

E. Belchen
   Lothringen

F. Esso Hamburg

G. Wollin

H. Spichern
   Fr. Brehme
   Ermland

The critical fuel situation did not allow for any mishaps. Wake-Walker's ships had to retain contact with the *Bismarck*. As we have seen, he had concentrated his ships to try to entice Lütjens to set a northeasterly course. The attempt failed, but after the brief gun duel when the *Prinz Eugen* was detached, he continued to keep his ships closely together. The *Prince of Wales* was abaft the *Norfolk*, while the *Suffolk* – ahead of the *Norfolk* – was responsible for keeping contact with the German battleship. Thus, Wake-Walker's force was no longer able to search on a wide front and in the darkness they depended on the *Suffolk* and her radar.[342]

The danger posed by the German submarines made the task even more difficult, as it forced Wake-Walker's ships to zigzag. In addition, it was necessary to keep sufficient distance from the *Bismarck*. Her guns outranged the *Suffolk's* radar, but as long as the visibility was poor, Captain Ellis dared keep his ship within range. In the present weather conditions, accurate fire was almost impossible to attain, especially at ranges exceeding 20 kilometres. Mainly the *Suffolk* stayed behind the *Bismarck* on the port side. The zigzagging meant that the British cruiser alternately shortened and increased the range from the German battleship, depending on whether she was on a southwesterly or southeasterly leg. When she was far to the east, the *Bismarck* was beyond the range of her radar, but on a south-westerly leg, the radar again picked up the echo.[343]

By now, the operation had continued for so long that both officers and men began to suffer from fatigue. While enemy ships were close, the alert level remained high, on German as well as British ships. On the *Suffolk's* bridge, Captain Ellis had remained awake since the shadowing began on 23 May. He had been on the bridge for 30 hours without a break, aided not only by a constant supply of steaming hot coffee, but also pills furnished by the ship's doctor. The men on the *Suffolk* were also suffering, since the sheltering windows had been shattered by the blast from her own guns and they had no protection from the harsh weather of the North Atlantic.[344]

At 03.06 hours on 25 May, the *Suffolk* turned port to begin a south-easterly leg in her zigzagging, thus opening the distance to the German battleship. Shortly afterwards, Lütjens ordered a sharp starboard turn, bringing her on a westerly course, while the British continued their southeasterly course, beyond radar contact. As the *Suffolk* had moved so far away from the *Bismarck* that she had lost radar contact on many prior occasions, it was not regarded as remarkable. After about half an hour, the *Suffolk* made a starboard turn, entering a southwesterly leg. Ellis listened to the monotonous reports from the radar operators, expecting contact with the *Bismarck* to be regained soon. However, the minutes ticked away and no echo appeared on the radar screen. After another 20 minutes he began to suspect trouble. At about 05.00 hours, it was evident that something serious had happened.[345]

Ellis signalled to Wake-Walker: 'Have lost contact with the enemy.'

It is unclear if the turn made by the *Bismarck* was a shrewd tactical manoeuvre by Lütjens, or if it was just a coincidence that it occurred just as the *Suffolk* had began the southeasterly leg. Maybe he was not aware of the enemy's zigzagging, but his hydrophone operators ought to have been able to report that the sea on the starboard side was empty. In any case, the manoeuvre perfectly fitted the situation. After turning west, the *Bismarck* held a steady course for half an hour, whereupon she increased speed to 27 knots and sheered north. After 10 minutes she began slowly turning starboard and after a while she had assumed an easterly course. Thus the German battleship passed behind the pursuers and continued in an easterly direction. This very day was Lütjens' fifty-second birthday and to shake off the obstinate pursuers ought to have been a welcome birthday present. However, he was unaware that the British had lost contact.[346]

On the *Suffolk's* windswept bridge, Ellis had to make a quick decision. He believed that either the *Bismarck* had made a long starboard turn and passed behind the British ships, or else she had increased speed and set a southerly course. Considering that she had only sailed at 16 knots before losing contact, the latter alternative was very alarming. In an hour, the German battleship could have increased the distance by as much as 10 nautical miles, very serious as the British had followed her at long range already before losing contact. As the *Bismarck's* course was unknown, her lead might be impossible to reduce.[347]

It is probable that Ellis' first signal did not reach Wake-Walker. Not until 18.00 hours did he realize what had happened. His orders then led his ships westward, away from the *Bismarck's* true position. Thereafter Wake-Walker took a nap on a bunk, while Phillips remained on the bridge. 'It was a disappointment, yes – of course it was,' Phillips

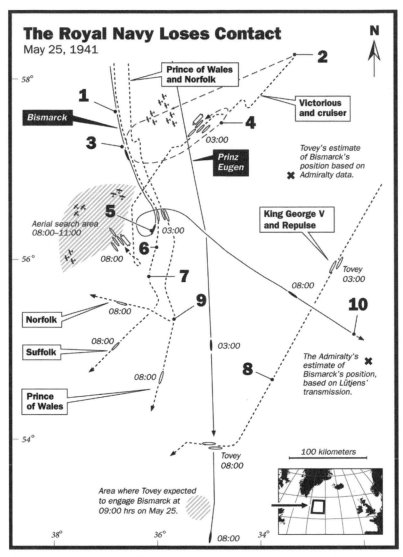

The Royal Navy Loses Contact
May 25, 1941

N

1

2

Prince of Wales and Norfolk

Bismarck

Victorious and cruiser

3

4

03:00

Prinz Eugen

Tovey's estimate of Bismarck's position based on Admiralty data.
✗

King George V and Repulse

Aerial search area 08:00–11:00

5

03:00

6

08:00

Tovey 03:00

— 56°

7

08:00

Norfolk

08:00

9

10

Suffolk

08:00

03:00

The Admiralty's estimate of Bismarck's position, based on Lütjens' transmission.
✗

Prince of Wales

08:00

8

— 54°

Tovey 08:00

100 kilometers

Area where Tovey expected to engage Bismarck at 09:00 hrs on May 25.

38°   36°   34°
08:00

1 Lütjens informs Marinegruppe West that he intends to set sail for Saint-Nazaire.

2 Esmonde's topedo bombers launched from Victorious.

3 Esmonde's topedo attack on Bismarck.

4 Esmonde's aircraft return to Victorious.

5 Lütjens begins his attempt to shake off Wake-Walker at 03:06.

6 Suffolk returns to her southwesterly course but the German Battleship does not appear on the radar screen.

7 Ellis reports that contact with Bismarck has been lost.

8 Tovey is informed that contact with Bismarck has been lost.

9 Prince of Wales is detached to join Tovey.

10 Lütjens begins a lengthy transmission to Marinegruppe West.

remembered. 'But it wasn't the end of the world. I passed the news on to John Tovey in case he hadn't heard and set about finding her again.'[348]

Tovey was first informed at about 06.00 hours that the *Bismarck* had eluded her pursuers. Of course it was a major reversal and all his planning was overthrown. Unfortunately, Lütjens had several options to choose from, either sailing towards a port or going for a tanker somewhere on the Atlantic. In the latter case, Tovey believed it was most likely that the *Bismarck* would rendezvous with a tanker west of Greenland. If Lütjens had chosen to set course for a port, he might well encounter a convoy en route. In the east, the OB323 headed west. Somewhat further to the south, the important troop convoy WS8B sailed and from southwest, the large convoy HX127 approached, consisting of 56 ships from Newfoundland heading towards Britain. Tovey decided to concentrate his search efforts west of the latest known position of the German battleship.[349] It is not difficult to imagine how much Tovey would have given for the information that the *Bismarck* in fact was almost due north of the *King George V* and that Lütjens was about to sail through an area recently passed by Tovey. The distance between them was less than 100 nautical miles and if Tovey had made a 180 degree turn he would have intercepted the *Bismarck* within a few hours.

However, the British admiral lacked this vital information and neither could he direct considerable reconnaissance to the area where he believed the *Bismarck* might be found. The only ships near enough were Wake-Walker's. But Tovey still had a strong card to play – the aircraft on board the *Victorious*. Before noon they were sent to search in a semicircle, north and east of the latest known position of the enemy. The cruisers that had lost contact were also directed to the same area, but all efforts were in vain. Tovey himself set a southwesterly course and ordered the *Prince of Wales* to join him. The *Repulse* had to break off the operation and proceed to Newfoundland, as she was running out of fuel oil.[350]

As the *Bismarck* had made a 300 degree turn, she had in fact assumed a southeasterly course during the morning of 25 May. Thus she passed astern of Tovey's ships, which had continued on a southwesterly course. The distance was great enough to preclude any lookouts from seeing the enemy ships. Tovey's prospects of finding the enemy were very gloomy. The searching was conducted in the wrong area, his ships sailed on a completely inappropriate course, which brought them further and further away from the *Bismarck* and allowed her to gain a healthy lead in the direction of the French ports. To make matters worse, Tovey's force was reduced as the the ships were forced to refuel. *Repulse* had already set course for Newfoundland. Soon the *Prince of Wales* would also have to break off the operation as she had very little fuel oil left. Tovey wanted to keep her as long as possible, but eventually he had to detach her. She set course for Iceland, and made her way slowly to Hvalfjord, which she reached at noon on 27 May with only 50 tons of fuel oil remaining in her tanks.[351] It was not much for a ship whose fuel oil capacity amounted to thousands of tons.

Thus, within a few hours, Tovey first faced the loss of contact with the *Bismarck*, then he had to detach two of his capital ships. Even if the *Bismarck* was found, he could not engage her with the *King George V* alone and have any hope of success. Admittedly he could place some reliance on the *Ramillies*, but this old battleship would not have bothered the brand new German battleship much. The *Revenge* had left Halifax in the afternoon on 24 May, but she was too far away, unless the *Bismarck* really had turned west. Few other ships remained. The *Rodney* was at a position suitable if the German battleship sailed towards Brest, but she hardly had the necessary speed to force the *Bismarck* to battle. Perhaps slightly greater hopes could be placed on Force H. Admiral Somerville had at his disposal the battlecruiser *Renown*, which was hardly equal to the *Bismarck*, and the carrier *Ark Royal*. Also a few smaller ships were available to Somerville. Mainly it was on the carrier that hopes rested. She might search successfully and perhaps slow the *Bismarck* down if she could achieve torpedo hits. Nevertheless, all circumstances suggested that Tovey had lost the first round.

CHAPTER 22

A Mysterious Signal

A few hours before noon on 25 May, the radio silence was broken repeatedly. An encrypted message with the following content travelled through the air over the northern Atlantic:

> *Enemy radar equipment, possessing a range of at least 35 kilometres, strongly affects operations on the Atlantic adversely. Our ships were detected in the Denmark Strait, despite thick fog, and the enemy did not lose contact thereafter. All attempts to shake off the enemy failed, despite favourable weather. Bunkering at sea no longer feasible, unless it is possible to sail away from the enemy due to superior speed.*
>
> *Running battle between 20800 metres and 18000 metres. The* Hood *destroyed by explosion after five minutes, thereafter change of target to the* King George V, *which turned away, under black smoke, after being hit and was not seen for several hours. Own expenditure of ammunition: 93 rounds. Thereafter,* King George V *only accepted battle at extreme ranges. The* Bismarck *was hit twice by* King George V, *one hit beneath side armour belt in section 13 to 14. Hit in section 20 to 21 reduced speed and caused the bow to lay one degree deeper and loss of fuel oil. The* Prinz Eugen *was detached in fog, when the battleship attacked the enemy ships. Own radar prone to breakdown, in particular when firing.*[352]

215

The message, divided into several parts sent separately, originated from the *Bismarck*.[353] It has been the source of many questions and the most fundamental is why it was sent at all. It hardly contained much new information for the intended recipients, Marinegruppe West and the naval staff. Even if the content had been new, it was not of such a character that the receivers could make much of it. The fact that Lütjens at all sent it strongly suggest that he still believed the British shadowed him, despite the fact that they had actually lost contact six hours earlier. On the *Prinz Eugen*, the signal provoked amazement. Her radio operators had intercepted most British signals and the B-Dienst had been able to interpret them. To Brinkmann and the other officers on the cruiser it seemed quite clear that the British had lost contact with the German battleship. They realized that Lütjens had not understood that he had managed to shake off the pursuers, but why was he unaware that the British had lost track of him?

One possible explanation is that the British radar signals were picked up on the German battleship. The radar worked by transmitting short radio pulses, which were reflected when they hit an object like a ship. Some of the reflected radio energy was picked up by the ship that had sent the pulses. Thus, bearing and range could be calculated. However, it also meant that the pulses transmitted had to be quite strong, as only a miniscule fraction of the radiated energy would actually form an echo to be detected. Hence, it was possible to detect transmitting radar at greater distances than the radar itself could 'see' something. Consequently, it could be possible that radar pulses from the British ships were picked up on the *Bismarck*, despite the fact that the echo was too weak to be caught on the British ships. Wake-Walker's ships were at least 200 kilometres away from the *Bismarck* when the message was sent but Tovey's ships were closer. If the Germans detected any radar pulses, they must have originated from Tovey's ships.[354]

It will probably never be possible to establish the reasons behind Lütjens' belief that the British still maintained contact, but it seems clear that Marinegruppe West was surprised by his signal. A few hours before sending the long message, Lütjens had sent a few messages with short-signal technique, which was very difficult to obtain bearings from. One of them stated that one British battleship and two cruisers still maintained contact. It caused Marinegruppe West to send a report, with date-time group 08.46. According to this message, the latest

British report showing the position of the *Bismarck* was dated 03.13. Subsequently none of the reports contained the position of the German battleship. Marinegruppe West concluded that the British pursuers had lost track of the *Bismarck*, which has emphasized in the report to Lütjens. However, Lütjens does not seem to have received the report, which was sent more than an hour before his own long messag.[355]

The danger with Lütjens' message was not the risk that the content could be understood by the enemy, but the fact that the bearings could be taken when such a long transmission filled the air. At the time the British could not break the codes used by the heavy German ships, at least not quickly enough to have any operational effect. However, the British wireless operators, like their German counterparts, could learn the 'fingerprint' of wireless operators. It was not a foolproof method, but it suggested to the British that the long signal that had been transmitted through the air originated from the *Bismarck*.

When the British had become convinced that the long message might originate from the battleship they had lost contact with, they plotted the bearings. Unfortunately, only two radio stations, not far apart, had taken any bearings. Both of them were located in Britain. To establish the position of the transmitter, a line was drawn from the stations that had intercepted the signal, towards the direction it had come from. Ideally, several lines could be drawn from different stations and where the lines crossed, this marked where the *Bismarck* was located when she transmitted. Thus, if two receivers close to each other picked up the signal, the lines drawn became almost parallel, causing a small error in the process to have significant effect on the overall precision. Ideally, bearings would be taken by receivers positioned in such a way that the lines drawn formed an angle close to 90 degrees, and preferably many receiving stations could be used to obtain greater reliability. In this particular case, no radio stations on Iceland or in Gibraltar had received Lütjens' message.

As each receiver only had its own basic data, consisting of its own position and the direction from which the wireless signal had originated, they passed this data on to the Admiralty. Usually, the data was analysed at the Admiralty, whereupon the resulting position was sent to the units at sea. However, before this operation, Tovey had requested that only the basic data be sent to him, not the position estimate made by the Admiralty. The reason was that the Home Fleet had been provided with two destroyers equipped to take bearings. Thus, it seemed likely that Tovey and his staff at sea might be better able to correctly estimate the position, because the Home Fleet could combine the Admiralty's data with data from the destroyers. The advantages with several, widely separated receivers, would clearly be with Tovey. However, at this time, Tovey had in fact been robbed of his two specially equipped destroyers. One had suffered engine trouble soon after leaving Scapa Flow and had to return and the other was on its way to Iceland, to bunker fuel oil. To make matters worse, its equipment for taking bearings had broken down.[356]

Thus, Tovey and the Admiralty had the same data to work with, but they analysed it separately. The result was two widely separated position estimates. With hindsight, we know that the estimate made by the Admiralty was close to correct and showed that the signal had been sent from a position southeast of the point where the *Suffolk* had lost contact. However, on the *King George V*, it was concluded that the *Bismarck* had reached a position east of the point where the *Suffolk* had last seen the German battleship. Thus, it seemed quite clear to Tovey that Lütjens was heading towards southern Norway or a port in Germany; a course north of the British Isles. The divergent estimates on the position of the enemy would soon have serious repercussions, but at least they allowed Tovey to cease searching far to the west.

Tovey relayed his version of the *Bismarck's* position and ordered the ships of the Home Fleet to search in the area he inferred from the estimated position of the enemy. Unfortunately, relatively few ships of the Home Fleet had sufficient fuel to carry out the order. The *King George V* still had at least 50 per cent of her fuel oil, but most other ships had less than half their capacity. The most important ship was the *Victorious*, thanks to the search capacity provided by her aircraft. She was ordered to cease searching in the westerly direction, where she had been looking since dawn. Her aircraft were recalled, but one of them did not return. Bovell decided to search for it. Thus, the *Victorious* did not immediately set course for the new area designated by Tovey.[357]

As stated above, the Admiralty had reached different conclusions. Lieutenant Commander Peter Kemp at the operations department at the Admiralty plotted the position and arrived at a point further south than Tovey. The difference between the positions was so great that very different conclusions were drawn. While Tovey's estimate clearly suggested that Lütjens was heading back towards Norway or Germany, Kemp's calculations undoubtedly indicated that the *Bismarck* was heading for France. Between the two routes lay the British Isles. Kemp informed his superior, Rear Admiral Clayton, and suggested that his results should be transmitted to Tovey immediately. Clayton turned down Kemp's proposition, as Tovey, aided by the specially equipped destroyers, probably was better helped with the basic data from the radio stations that had taken the bearings. However, within the Admiralty, Kemp's calculation was used. Two new bearings were taken at 09.48 hours and 10.54 hours, which reinforced Kemp's previous conclusion that the *Bismarck* was heading towards France.[358]

Force H was instructed according to Kemp's estimates and less than an hour later the *Rodney* was also give similar instructions. Early on the morning of 25 May, the commander of the battleship, Captain Dalrymple-Hamilton, assembled a provisional 'operations committee,' in which the American assistant naval attaché also participated. Dalrymple-Hamilton's decision was prompted by the information that Wake-Walker's ships had lost contact with the *Bismarck*. A day earlier, he had left the *Britannic*, which proceeded west escorted by the destroyer *Eskimo*, and since then Dalrymple-Hamilton had focused solely on chasing the German battleship. The committee assumed that the *Bismarck* had been damaged during the battle in the Denmark Strait, as she left the oil trail and was presumed to have reduced speed. Also, the air attack from the *Victorious* might have aggravated the damage incurred. The conclusion was that she was heading towards a French port, probably St. Nazaire or Brest. This conclusion was based mainly on the assumption that the passage between Greenland and Scotland was too risky and also German airpower and submarines were believed to be better placed to support the *Bismarck* along the southern route. Furthermore, the *Scharnhorst* and *Gneisenau* were probably almost ready for operations, again suggesting that Lütjens headed towards a French port.[359]

The committee was not unanimous and it presented various alternatives to Dalrymple-Hamilton. However, at about 20.00 hours the commander decided to remain at the present position for the moment. If no new information was received within two or three hours, the *Rodney* would set course according to the assumption that the

Bismarck was sailing towards a French port. The bearings taken from the *Bismarck's* wireless signal thus came at the right moment and as soon as the Admiralty's data reached the *Rodney*, the staff began to plot the position of the German battleship. The result suggested that the *Bismarck* was heading towards France, so the officers on board the *Rodney* were surprised to receive Tovey's signal to search further north. The staff checked the plotting again, but reached the same conclusions as previously. The *Bismarck* headed towards France and it was considered that the Admiralty ought to correct Tovey's signal.[360]

After careful consideration, Dalrymple-Hamilton decided to ignore Tovey's instructions. The shortest route from the *Bismarck's* latest known position to Bretagne was plotted. Presently, the *Rodney* was south of that line and Dalrymple-Hamilton set a north-northeasterly course and increased speed to 21 knots. Hopefully this would bring her to a position ahead of the German battleship. Another circumstance affected Dalrymple-Hamilton's decision. Considering the present situation, his battleship was probably too far away if the *Bismarck* sailed towards Norway. However, if the German battleship was steaming for France, the *Rodney* could contribute in a meaningful way. Soon afterwards, at 11.58 hours, Dalrymple-Hamilton received an order from the Admiralty, instructing him to act according to the assumption that the enemy was sailing towards a port in the Bay of Biscay.[361]

The reasons for the plotting mistake made by Tovey's staff are unclear.[362] With hindsight it is easy to see that some mistake was made on board the *King George V*, but it is much more difficult to establish which mistake. Maybe strain, exertion and pressure against the clock contributed. Whatever caused the mistake, it lead Tovey to set a north-easterly course with the *King George V*, as was done for those of his ships that were not prohibited from continuing the operation due to lack of fuel. Although the new direction was at least somewhat less dis-advantageous than the westerly direction searched along previously, every minute could be crucial and Tovey's new course meant that the *Bismarck* would increase her lead.

Of course the Admiralty could have sent a signal to Tovey, correcting the mistake, but as the officers in London still believed Tovey had his destroyers with equipment for taking bearings, they refrained from doing so. When Tovey reported that he intended to search in the area further north, the Admiralty presumed he had good information backing up his decision. Thus the decision makers in London waited, but they also ordered Catalina aircraft to search the most likely routes the *Bismarck* would follow if she steamed towards France, as well as those she would follow if she returned towards the North Sea.[363]

Shortly afterwards, at 13.20 hours, another signal was picked up and bearings could be taken. This signal originated from a point where the *Bismarck* could be expected if she followed the route towards St. Nazaire. Armed with this important information, the Admiralty regarded its previous conclusions confirmed. Oddly, this was actually a mistake. After the long signal, Lütjens seems to have realized that the British had lost contact; perhaps the signals from Marinegruppe West had finally convinced him. He did not make any further wireless transmission. Instead, the signal intercepted by the British in fact originated from a German submarine, which just happed to be in the area where the *Bismarck* sailed. Thus, a pure mistake actually contributed to confirming the belief that the *Bismarck* headed for France.[364]

As Wake-Walker and Tovey spent several hours searching in the wrong direction, Lütjens gained a considerable lead. In fact, at noon on 25 May, the distance between the *Bismarck* and the forces of Home Fleet was so great that Tovey would be unable to catch up with Lütjens any more, at least under his own means. Speed as well as distance and the fuel shortages spoke against him. Perhaps he did not yet realize it, but only the *Rodney* and Force H had any chance of getting in touch with the German battleship before it reached a French port. Thus, only two British capital ships remained between the *Bismarck* and her destination and none of them were modern enough to engage the German battleship on even terms. In fact, all British hopes rested on the carrier *Ark Royal*.

While the Home Fleet spent hours searching in the wrong area, Lütjens continued on a southeasterly course. Despite the precarious situation, the voyage had thus far been quite successful. The *Bismarck* had sunk the largest British warship and damaged the most modern. Thereafter she had ridden out an air attack without suffering more than minor damage and then, although the crew did not know it yet, the pursuers had been shaken off. The original mission of attacking convoys would however not be accomplished.

Müllenheim-Rechberg indulged in expectations of learning more about the situation when he proceeded to the bridge. To his disappointment, he found only one officer at the bridge, Lieutenant Commander Karl Mihatsch. He was officer on duty, but did not have much more knowledge about the overall situation than did Müllenheim-Rechberg. Nevertheless, they held a small-scale council of war and agreed that the *Bismarck* probably would make it to a port before British forces could draw her into battle again. Their ship had gained a considerable lead and as long as she could make at least 28 knots, the enemies more to the west were hard put not to lag even further behind. The Gibraltar based Force H, believed to be heading north, was a more serious threat, but it would not be easy for Admiral Somerville to find the *Bismarck*. Both officers thought that the greatest menace was British aircraft. If the British had a carrier nearby, further torpedo attacks could be expected. It was imperative that the *Bismarck* was not damaged in such a way that her speed or manoeuvrability was impaired. If so, the British forces to the west might catch up with her and if several British warships converged on the *Bismarck*, chances to win were slim.[365] But did the Royal Navy have a carrier close enough?

Müllenheim-Rechberg left the bridge with a stronger sense of optimism, which was soon reinforced as good news quickly circulated on the battleship: the pursuers had lost contact! The encouraging effect it had was soon taken away by the speech made by Lütjens at noon. A few minutes before noon he received a message from Raeder, in which the Grand Admiral congratulated Lütjens on his birthday and wished him further victories during the to come. Soon afterwards, the loudspeakers on the *Bismarck* announced that Lütjens would address the crew. Within a few minutes his voice could be heard on the shelter deck and in the compartments where loudspeakers had been fitted:

> *Seamen on the battleship* Bismarck! *You have covered yourselves with glory! The sinking of the battlecruiser* Hood *has not only military, but also psychological value, for she was the pride of England. Henceforth, the enemy will try to concentrate his forces and bring them into action against us. I therefore released the Prinz Eugen at noon yesterday so that she could conduct commerce warfare on her own. She has managed to evade the enemy.*

> *We, on the other hand, because of the hits we have*
> *received, have been ordered to proceed to a French port.*
> *On our way there, the enemy will gather and give us battle.*
> *The German people are with you, and we will fight until*
> *our gun barrels glow red-hot and the last shell has left the*
> *barrels. For us seamen, the question now is victory or*
> *death!*[366]

Perhaps it was Lütjens' intention to raise morale, but the speech had the opposite effect. Most of the crew, in particular the young and inexperienced, had believed that the battle was already won. Just like Müllenheim-Rechberg and Mihatsch they believed that a quick sail towards a French port was all that was needed. The loudspeakers had continuously informed about the enemy activities and lately it had been clear that they were far behind, virtually without any chance of closing the distance. So why did Lütjens speak of a life and death struggle?

In fact the British had virtually no chance to halt the *Bismarck* before she reached a French port. Müllenheim-Rechberg had remained in the after director where he had recently assumed responsibility as duty officer, allowing the seamen to attend Lütjens' address. Müllenheim-Rechberg did not hear the speech, but when his men returned, it instantly became clear to him that the address had had a detrimental effect on the audience. Lindemann too understood the effects of Lütjens' speech and decided to address the crew, which he did an hour later. His speech was concise and said nothing about the British forces gathering to sink the *Bismarck*. Rather Lindemann alleged that the British could hardly catch up with the *Bismarck*, which was expected to reach a French port in a short time.

The crew's anxiety was relieved somewhat by Lindemann's speech and afterwards another project was initiated, whose purpose at least partly must have been to encourage the men. It was decided to build a dummy funnel, which would hopefully fool British aircrews into identifying the *Bismarck* as a British battleship. A second funnel would be created on the flight deck, ahead of the hangar. Also the top surface of the main gun turrets was painted yellow. By utilizing metal plates and canvas, a foldable 'funnel' was created and painted in the same colour as most other surfaces of the ship. For various reasons, the ruse was never used, but during the process of creating it, the Chief Engineer,

Commander Walter 'Papa' Lehmann, repeatedly went out on the deck to see how the work proceeded. He was impressed, but nevertheless worried about how it would look when the funnel was in place. 'We must ensure that it smokes as much as the real funnel,' he joked.

On the bridge, the joke soon became known and it was decided to take it one step further. On the loudspeakers it was ordered: 'The off-duty watch is to report at the second-in-command's cabin to receive cigars. They are to be smoked in the second funnel.'[367]

The joke amused the crew. If the responsible officers could joke like that, the situation could not be too bad. But while the activity connected to the dummy funnel caused amusement on the deck, Lehmann had a far more worrisome problem to attend to in the machinery. The hit in section XIV had finally begun to affect the battleship's mobility. As a consequence of the flooding, the feed water to one of the turbo-generators had been polluted by salt water, a complication that might also afflict the power plants. If salt water leaked into the feed water, there was a risk that drops of water would follow the steam into the main turbines, which would have destroyed the turbine blades quickly. The feed water had to be exchanged, but as the high-pressure boilers contained large amounts of feed water, the procedure required time. After considerable exertion, Lehmann and his men succeeded in produceing sufficient feed water from the ship's four condensers and an auxiliary boiler, so that by the evening of 25 May the situation was well in hand.[368]

In France, Marinegruppe West prepared to receive the *Bismarck*. The situation appeared brighter with every hour that passed. She had shaken off her pursuers and decrypted British wireless messages showed that several ships had returned to escorting convoys. It had not yet been confirmed that Force H was searching for the *Bismarck*. Somerville's ships could just as well be at sea to protect a convoy. Comfort was also provided by a weather forecast, which indicated that a gale in the eastern Atlantic was under way. It would render British air operations, in particular from carriers, more difficult. Orders were issued to Luftwaffe reconnaissance and bomber units to stand by in support of the *Bismarck* as soon as she came within range of German air power. Five submarines were also instructed to take up positions along the route followed by the *Bismarck*. Hopefully they would be able to attack any pursuers. In St. Nazaire, the dry dock was prepared to receive the battleship and torpedo nets were placed in the harbour, to allow her to moor safely.[369]

After dusk, Lütjens could delight after a day without any signs that the enemy had seen the *Bismarck*. In stark contrast to 24 May, with the battle against the *Hood* and *Prince of Wales*, followed by the exchange of fire with the cruisers and the air attack, the daylight hours had passed as quietly as if it had been a peacetime cruise. In the afternoon, a message from Hitler had been received: 'Congratulations on your birthday.'

Lütjens' birthday and the ensuing night passed in tranquillity on the *Bismarck*, but it would come to an end. All around them, the British searched frantically to find the *Bismarck* and avenge the *Hood*. The morning of 26 May broke with a rough sea swiftly sweeping along beneath a dark greyish cloud cover. At 10.30 hours, warnings were heard on the loudspeakers: 'Aircraft on port!' Then the air alarm echoed in the battleship.

CHAPTER 23

'Battleship sighted'

The British efforts to find the *Bismarck* continued, despite the fact that prospects of success diminished with every hour she proceeded towards St. Nazaire. To return to 25 May, just after the Admiralty erroneously but fortunately interpreted the signal from a German submarine as originating from the *Bismarck*. Although the bearings taken suggested that the German battleship headed towards France, the situation remained ambiguous, as Tovey persisted in searching further north. Another circumstance complicating the situation was the delays caused when messages were sent. A signal first had to be encrypted, then transmitted, received and decrypted before the content could be of value to the recipient. Thus much time could be lost while information, reports and orders crawled through the system. Furthermore, the delays were not consistent, which meant that one signal could in some cases be received before another, even if the latter had been sent earlier. This could cause serious confusion.

At about 14.30 hours, the Admiralty ordered the *Rodney* to disregard the previous conclusion that the German battleship headed towards France and instead act according to Tovey's instructions.[370] The origins of this signal have not been established and it is quite surprising, considering that the Admiralty clearly regarded the southern route as the most likely to be followed by the *Bismarck*. Possibly the Admiralty wanted to reduce the distance between the *Rodney* and Tovey. However, as Dalrymple-Hamilton had already ordered a north-northeasterly course, the Admiralty's signal did not induce him to make any alterations, but it did affect Tovey.

While Tovey acted according to the erroneous calculation, further bearings had been taken, which were gradually forwarded to the ships. Aboard the *King George V*, the staff made new calculations from the original bearings and gradually it appeared that a mistake might have been made. Soon afterwards, at 15.30 hours, the bearings from the German submarine reached the flagship. This information, added to the suspicion that a mistake might previously have been made, prompted Tovey to assume that the *Bismarck* was in fact heading towards France and he set a course leading to Brest. However, shortly afterwards, he received the signal to the *Rodney*, instructing her to act according to Tovey's previous assumption that the German battleship was heading towards the area north of the Faeroes. Thus Tovey abandoned his recently ordered course towards France and turned east, as a kind of compromise between the Faeroes and France. Once more he set a course distancing him from the *Bismarck*. Ironically, it was the effect of his own orders, which had been delayed, which now struck back against him.

At 16.21 hours, Tovey signalled the Admiralty asking whether it was believed that the *Bismarck* was making for the Faeroes. This signal indicated that Tovey was no more certain than the Admiralty, and after some consideration the previous order to the *Rodney* was counter-manded. She was again to act according to the assumption that the *Bismarck* was sailing for France. Unfortunately Tovey lost valuable time while waiting for the reply.[371]

While Tovey and the Admiralty worked feverishly to bring clarity to the confused situation, the cryptographers worked hard at Bletchley Park to break the *Hydra* and *Neptun* codes. Their efforts did not meet with any success and none of the messages sent by the German navy were deciphered in time to affect the operation. However, a few important observations were made. The first was the increased volume of radio traffic from the German naval staffs in France when Lütjens' squadron had passed through the Denmark Strait. In fact this was due to the simple fact that Lütjens' squadron had passed the boundary line between Marinegruppe Nord and Marinegruppe West, although the British interpreted it as an indication that the *Bismarck* was sailing towards France. During the afternoon of 25 May, another observation seemed to confirm that the German battleship had set course for France. Although the Ultra machine was unable to break the code used by the German Navy, it could easily decipher Luftwaffe messages.

General Hans Jeschonnek, chief of staff of the Luftwaffe, was in Athens to monitor the German airborne attack on Crete. One of his relatives served as a cadet on board the *Bismarck* and as Jeschonnek wanted to know if he was expected to arrive in France or Scandinavia, he sent an inquiry encrypted in the 'red code'. [372] Bletchley Park quickly deciphered this message, as well as the reply: that the *Bismarck* was sailing for a French port, probably Brest.[373] This vital piece of information was reinforced by further ULTRA deciphering. A number of Luftwaffe messages showed that air units in France were reinforced, in particular in the area of the Bay of Biscay.[374] The Admiralty was informed that intelligence had acquired clear evidence that the destination was a French port, although the circumstances showing how the information had been obtained remained top secret. This was done during the early evening and at 19.34 hours the Admiralty sent a signal to all units that the *Bismarck* was sailing towards France.

Valuable as this information was, it did not have much impact on the outcome. Tovey waited several hours for the reply from the Admiralty, while still maintaining the eastern course that constituted a compromise between the two alternatives. However, at 18.10 hours, without having received the reply from the Admiralty, he decided that the *Bismarck* was on her way towards France and set an east-southeast course. When he received the final report from the Admiralty it confirmed his decision and no further mistakes held him back. Unfortunately, the errors made so far had ruined his chances of intercepting the *Bismarck*, which by now had a lead of at least 80 nautical miles.

At dawn on 26 May most of the British ships that had not yet been forced to break off the operation for lack of fuel, sailed on converging courses towards France. At the same time one of Coastal Command's new Catalina seaplanes set a southwesterly course to the Atlantic. It had taken off from Lake Erne in Northern Ireland an hour earlier and the first rays of morning light had done little to reassure the crew about their mission. The weather above western Ireland was miserable, with a cloud base varying in altitude from 30 to 300 metres and visibility of 7,000 metres at best, but often down to zero. Conditions hardly improved as the aircraft left the land behind and flew over the open sea, with the crew anticipating yet another boring patrol. The most excitement that they expected was derived from the meals cooked on a small spirit heater, usually consisting of beans and bacon, or the hour long nap on the bunk every fourth hour. None of them believed they would catch sight of a battleship.

In fact, this particular reconnaissance flight was a result of a special request from the commander of Coastal Command, Frederick Bowhill, the same man who had ordered Suckling to London and thus contributed to a delay that allowed the *Bismarck* to get a head start. Now he had given orders for a mission that was to prove far more profitable than his previous mistake had been detrimental. While most officers within the Admiralty believed Lütjens had decided to follow the shortest route to France, probably Brest, Bowhill found it more plausible that the German admiral would make a more southerly tack, to avoid passing too close to the British Isles. For this reason, he demanded that one of the Catalinas should search south of the shortest route to Brest. The Admiralty accepted.[375]

Lieutenant Dennis Briggs was captain on the Catalina, but he was not the only pilot on board. A Catalina could remain airborne for 28 hours, so at least two men were needed to pilot the aeroplane in order to make best use of its impressive endurance. Briggs could rely upon Lieutenant Tuck Smith to assist him. Smith was an American pilot who had been detailed to help the British with the new aircraft model. As the United States was not a belligerent nation, Smith's involvement was quite a sensitive issue, not least in America, where only a few people knew that American airmen participated in missions such as this. 'If Congress finds out,' Roosevelt told the Navy airmen, 'I will be impeached.'[376]

On numerous occasions, Briggs and Smith had to alter course to avoid flying into zones with very bad weather. Off and on, visibility improved, but above 300 metres it was never good enough. The chances of finding the *Bismarck* were slight in conditions like these.[377]

However, Smith was to be lucky during the mission; in fact he may very well have made the most important combat effort by an American officer since the war began. He had been at the controls for about 15 minutes after they reached the search area, when he spotted something through a gap in the clouds. 'What's that?' he asked Briggs, who was sitting next to him.

Briggs straightened himself up in the seat. Before them, perhaps seven nautical miles away, a dark grey shadow could be made out in the haze. Gradually it took on the shape of a major warship. It could very well be the *Bismarck*.

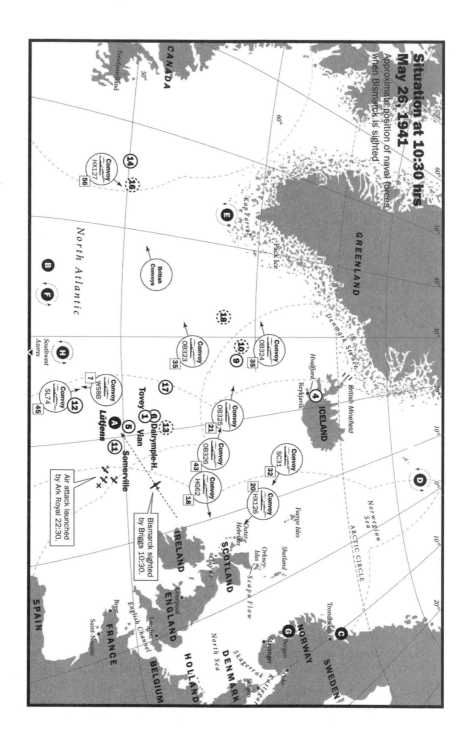

Situation at 10:30 hrs
May 26, 1941
Approximate position of naval forces
when Bismarck is sighted.

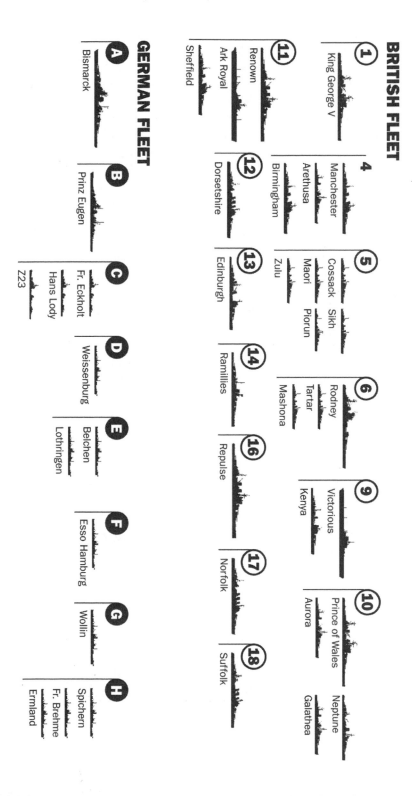

BRITISH FLEET

(1) King George V

4
Manchester
Arethusa
Birmingham

(5)
Cossack
Maori
Sikh
Zulu
Piorun

(6)
Rodney
Tartar
Mashona

(9)
Victorious
Kenya

(10)
Prince of Wales
Aurora
Neptune
Galathea

(11)
Renown
Ark Royal
Sheffield

(12)
Dorsetshire

(13)
Edinburgh

(14)
Ramillies

(16)
Repulse

(17)
Norfolk

(18)
Suffolk

GERMAN FLEET

A
Bismarck

B
Prinz Eugen

C
Fr. Eckholt
Hans Lody
Z23

D
Weissenburg

E
Belchen
Lothringen

F
Esso Hamburg

G
Wollin

H
Spichern
Fr. Brehme
Ermland

'It looks like a battleship,' Smith said.

Briggs believed it was an enemy warship. 'We will have to take a closer look,' he said. 'A British battleship would be surrounded by escorting destroyers.'

'Definite recognition was impossible at the time due to visibility,' Smith wrote later in his report. 'I immediately took control from 'George' (automatic pilot); started slow climbing turn to starboard, keeping ship sited to Port, while the British officer went aft to prepare contact report.'

Smith intended to approach the ship by taking advantage of the cover provided by the clouds, allowing observation at short range. Hopefully it would permit as firm an identification as possible. If it was the *Bismarck*, the Catalina would shadow it at a safer distance. However, he misjudged the distance and turned up too close. Suddenly he realized that his aeroplane was right above the ship, in an opening between the clouds.

'Upon reaching 2000 ft' Smith wrote, 'we broke out of a cloud formation and were met by a terrific anti-aircraft barrage from our starboard quarter.'[378]

Briggs quickly finished the message and handed it to the wireless operator. When the Catalina took off from Lake Erne, it had as a matter of routine been armed with depth charges. In haste, Smith released them and tried violent evasive actions to avoid the enemy anti-aircraft fire. The Catalina was almost shot down. One crew member had been asleep, when the blast from an exploding shell abruptly threw him off the bunk.

Briggs quickly returned to the cockpit. He had just reached his seat when a splinter smashed through the floor and continued through the roof. Another crewmember, the flight engineer, appeared and reported, needlessly, that the plane had been hit by several splinters. Smith turned back and forth to present a more difficult target to the enemy gunners and during one of the turns he could clearly see the ship below. 'I saw it was a battleship and that it was the *Bismarck*,' he wrote. 'She had made a 90 degree turn to starboard and fired broadsides at us. The fire continued until we were out of range and concealed by the clouds.'[379]

Shortly afterwards, the signalman sent Briggs' famed message: 'A battleship sighted, bearing 240 degrees.' It was followed by range to the enemy, his course and Briggs' own position. It ended with date and time, 10.30 hours on 26 May. After eluding the British for more than 30 hours, the *Bismarck* had again been discovered.

CHAPTER 24

The Second Air Attack

Briggs' report sent waves of hope as well as disappointment through the Royal Navy, from the Admiralty, which soon sent an orientation on the *Bismarck's* position, to every officer, NCO and seaman on board the British warships that were in pursuit. To many, it became perfectly clear that they would play no further part in the action. The *Repulse* had been forced to break off the operation long ago. The *Victorious*, *Prince of Wales* and *Suffolk* had set course towards Iceland to bunker fuel oil. On board the *King George V*, Tovey received the message with mixed feelings. The fact that the *Bismarck* had been located was of course advantageous, but he realized that his own forces were too far away if she remained on her course and at the same speed towards France. Dalrymple-Hamilton on the *Rodney* and Wake-Walker on the *Norfolk* were as ill positioned as Tovey.

Captain Vian, whose destroyer flotilla had escorted WS8B when he was ordered to leave the convoy and join Tovey, could have intercepted the *Bismarck* a few hours earlier, had he set a more easterly course. At about 08.00 hours, his destroyers had crossed the line that Lütjens had passed merely 30 minutes earlier. For the moment, Vian's flotilla was in the wake of the German battleship, when he received the information that the *Bismarck* had been sighted. He must have realized how close the *Bismarck* had been to WS8B. Had the *Bismarck* sailed a few knots faster, the freighters would have appeared ahead of the *Bismarck's* guns. Vian realized that his destroyers had a fair chance of intercepting the enemy battleship before it reached France. However, to set course directly towards the *Bismarck* would mean disregarding the orders

233

received from Tovey, because the commander-in-chief was currently located north of Vian's present position:

> *If we disregarded this order, the two battleships,* King George V *and* Rodney, *which alone could force a decision, would be left entirely unescorted against attacks by U-boats as they closed the enemy. If either were to be torpedoed,* Bismarck, *unless stopped by air attack, seemed sure to make port. It was clear that the course to take was the one most likely to suit the Commander-in-Chief; interpreting him, we hoped, aright, we plumbed for heading straight towards* Bismarck. *Strict wireless silence was being maintained; we did not, therefore, inform Admiral Tovey, or anybody else, of this decision.*[380]

Vian altered course to south-southeast, but still he remained several hours behind the *Bismarck*.

Only Admiral Somerville's Force H had a reasonable chance of intercepting the *Bismarck*. Vice Admiral Somerville was a tall man with a cheerful temperament. He had an irrepressible tendency to see amusing details in everything surrounding him and he gladly took any opportunity to tell dirty jokes. In 1940 he had been given the unenviable task of sinking French navy vessels in Oran, an experience that left an indelible scar on his soul, but did not affect his ability to command Force H.

His present task required all his skills as sailor and commander. His ships had proceeded northward in extremely bad weather ever since leaving Gibraltar behind them. On the morning of 25 May, Somerville had to order his destroyers to turn back to Gibraltar, but the *Ark Royal* and *Sheffield* still accompanied his flagship, the battlecruiser *Renown*. For the moment, the admiral's primary concern was not the *Bismarck*, but the *Gneisenau* and *Scharnhorst*, since he feared that they would put to sea to support Lütjens. Somerville had instructed one of his destroyers to wait until it had reached a position 130 nautical miles south of his own, before transmitting a question to the Admiralty: were the German battleships in Brest still at their moorings? While waiting for the reply, he sent a reconnaissance aircraft towards Brest. Additionally, he directed a more comprehensive search effort in the area northwest of his task force, hoping to find the *Bismarck*.[381]

When the Admiralty's signal on the *Bismarck's* position was received, excitement instantly grew. Somerville and the other officers realized that the German battleship currently was located further west, and was in fact headed into the area where the reconnaissance aircraft from the *Ark Royal* intended to search. For a while, the Admiral contemplated redirecting his aircraft to support the Catalina, but he refrained. There was always a risk of mistakes and incorrect interpretations when orders were countermanded. However, soon afterwards, Briggs' report that the Catalina had lost contact with the *Bismarck* was intercepted. Again, Somerville considered redirecting his aircraft, but he was interrupted by a report originating from one of his searching aeroplanes and contained the encouraging news that a large warship had been sighted slightly east of the position Briggs had given. For some reason, the crew on the aircraft identified the ship as *Prinz Eugen*, but soon another Swordfish reported, correctly identifying the ship as the *Bismarck*. As the positions given by the two reports were identical, they obviously shadowed the same ship, regardless of its identity. Furthermore, the enemy was closer than expected, not more than about 60 nautical miles away.

Somerville ordered Captain Loben Maund, the commander of the *Ark Royal*, to stage an attack as soon as the reconnoitring aircraft had landed and been armed with torpedoes. Thereafter he set a course that would place the *Renown* and *Sheffield* between the *Bismarck* and France. However, at 11.45 hours an order from the Admiralty was received. It instructed Somerville to engage with the *Renown* only if the *King George V* or *Rodney* were already in battle with the *Bismarck*. The protection of the aging battlecruiser was not sufficient to withstand direct hits from the *Bismarck's* guns. The Admiralty wished to avoid a repetition of the outcome in the Denmark Strait. Somerville changed his plans, but detached the *Sheffield* to shadow the German battleship, while Tovey struggled to close in. In the meantime, Somerville staked everything on an air attack. The *Sheffield* had been informed by signal lamp, but the instruction had not been forwarded to the *Ark Royal*. An encrypted message was sent from the *Renown*, reporting the activities of Force H, to both Tovey and the Admiralty. The same information was also sent to the *Ark Royal*, not as an urgent message but as general information. For this reason, the wireless operators did not hurry to decrypt the message. Maund therefore did not know that the *Sheffield* might appear not far from the *Bismarck*.

Meanwhile, Maund's aircraft had managed to land on the *Ark Royal*, despite the rough sea. The flight deck rose and fell down as the ship heaved in the large waves. All except one of the pilots had succeeded in taking his aircraft down, but one misjudged the seaway. Instead of touching the flight deck when it was moving downwards, the pilot suddenly saw the flight deck heaving up towards him. The contact was violent enough to break the landing gear and the aircraft collapsed as it slid along the deck. All crewmembers survived and the remains of the aircraft were pushed overboard.

The preparations for the attack were soon in full swing. Lieutenant Commander Stewart-Moore was entrusted with the dangerous mission. The take-off would be even more difficult than it had been during the reconnaissance mission, as the aircraft would carry the heavy burden of a torpedo and the weather showed no sign of improving. Furthermore, they would have to attack through intense fire, from heavy guns as well as the lighter anti-aircraft guns. The airmen at least found some consolation in the fact that none of Esmonde's aeroplanes had been shot down. They had no fear of attacking friendly ships, as they had been instructed that the only warships in the area were either the *Bismarck* or the *Prinz Eugen*. Furthermore, the men serving with the 820th Division were veterans from the war in the Mediterranean. As uncertainty about the identity of the ship still lingered, it was decided to reduce the depth setting of the torpedoes from ten to eight metres, to enable the magnetic detonators to operate irrespective of the two possible targets. [382]

The attack force took off from the *Ark Royal* just before 15.00 hours. All aircraft made it without mishaps, despite the bad weather. Maund saw them disappear in the clouds. Once airborne, the radar-equipped machines switched their sets on and scanned the sea ahead. Within 30 minutes, they got an echo from a ship. It was about 30km closer to Somerville's force than expected, but as no British ships were supposed to be in the area, Stewart-Moore decided to initiate the attack. Twenty minutes later the 15 Swordfish planes dived towards the sea, to make a coordinated attack from several directions.[383] Soon the pilots could make out a large shadow behind veils created by the weather and a warship loomed large in the rain.

It was a textbook attack. Altitude and speed were correct; the angle of attack was suitable. The surprise must have been complete, as the ship had not yet opened fire. The pilot in the lead watched the target through his goggles. The ship grew larger as the range closed quickly. Its grey shape gradually revealed details; guns, masts, gunwales and ladders, men moving on decks. He released his torpedo and felt how the aircraft was pulled upwards when the weight of the torpedo disappeared.

But there was something wrong. The target suddenly seemed so familiar. Immediately before the nose of the Swordfish raised and the ship disappeared below him, he clearly saw the crews standing by their anti-aircraft guns. Why did they not fire back?

The ship had *two* funnels!

On board the *Sheffield* Captain Larcom saw Stewart-Moore's unit appear below the cloud cover. He knew the attack force had started and was not surprised to see the Swordfish aircraft. But instead of just flying past the *Sheffield*, the unit split and began to fly towards the *Sheffield* from many directions. A few seconds later, Larcom understood what was about to happen. 'Good Heavens – they are attacking *us*!' he exclaimed. 'Full speed ahead. Steer hard aport!'

In a second, the bridge seemed to explode in activity. Rapid orders were issued by voice pipes and intercom systems; the loudspeakers announced that the aircraft were British and it was forbidden to open fire on them. The seamen on deck saw how the first aircraft released its torpedo. It disappeared in the water and began its journey towards the British cruiser. Another two followed the first aircraft, but their torpedoes exploded when they hit the water. The *Sheffield* arduously began to turn away from the first torpedo.

While Larcom skilfully manoeuvred his ship between the approaching torpedoes, the remaining Swordfish attacked, except three whose crews realized they were about to make a grave mistake, but none of the torpedoes hit. However, three of them exploded after passing the *Sheffield*, indicating that something was seriously wrong with the weapons. At this stage, it was also clear to the crews of 820th Division what had happened and they returned distressed towards the *Ark Royal*.

'Sorry for the kipper,' one of them signalled to the *Sheffield* before the Swordfish disappeared into the clouds. When Stewart-Moore landed at the *Ark Royal* and reported, he was sorry about the mistake. 'It was a perfect attack,' he reported. 'Right height, right range, right cloud cover, right speed, and the wrong f——ng ship!'[384]

While Stewart-Moore conducted his failed attack, Tovey continued eastwards with the *King George V*. It was clear to him that, under the prevailing conditions, he had lost the race. He had already reduced speed to husband scarce fuel oil and the *Bismarck* would have reached France long before he could catch her. Tovey and his staff waited eagerly for the report on the air attack, when one of the lookouts on the port side shouted: 'Ship, bearing red seven-oh!'

For a moment it was feared that the distant object might be the *Prinz Eugen* and the crew quickly assumed battle stations. But when the superstructure of the unknown ship was revealed, her identity became clear. The *Rodney* had attached to the commander-in-chief. Numerous signals were exchanged between the ships. One of them concerned the maximum speed the *Rodney* could attain. Tovey received the reply: 22 knots, which happened to be the speed the *King George V* was making for the moment. Tovey decided to continue at 22 knots, but the *Rodney* slowly but inexorably lagged further and further behind. Finally Dalrymple-Hamilton had to signal: 'Am afraid your 22 knots are faster than ours.'

It was gratifying for Tovey to have two battleships again, but still the prospects remained dim, and when he received the report on the air attack, it seemed even worse. Somerville had chosen not to report any details of the attack on the *Sheffield*, he confined himself to reporting that no hits on the *Bismarck* had been observed. However, Somerville reported that he intended to launch another attack as soon as conditions permitted, probably at about 18.00 hours. Tovey acknowledged Somerville's report and added that it was probably the last chance to halt the *Bismarck* before she reached a French port. Tovey could not sail fast enough to reduce the distance to the enemy, but would have to be content to avoid lagging further behind. Unless the *Ark Royal's* aviators managed to score a hit that reduced the enemy's speed, the pursuit was definitely over.

To Lütjens and the *Bismarck's* crew, the sight of Briggs' Catalina made it obvious that they had been discovered again. A few hours earlier they had seen the masts of Vian's destroyers, as the latter passed in their wake on their way to join Tovey, but nothing suggested that the British seamen had seen them.[385] The seaplane was very different. Anti-aircraft guns had opened up, but it managed to evade the bursting shells and was soon out of gun range. Soon afterwards, the German wireless operators intercepted Briggs' message, which was promptly handed over to the B-Dienst. The code was quickly broken and Lütjens was given the same information as the Admiralty received. At the same time, it was observed that the Catalina was following at a safe distance.

The knowledge that the *Bismarck* was being followed again caused some anxiety, which soon turned into discouragement when another aircraft was observed. This time it was not a seaplane but a biplane with a fixed undercarriage. At this stage the Catalina had disappeared, but the new aircraft was much more ominous than the seaplane. Müllenheim-Rechberg immediately knew the implications:

> *A wheeled aircraft! So there must be an aircraft carrier quite nearby. And other, probably heavy, ships would be near her. Would cruisers and destroyers pick up contact before we ran into them? And were we now to experience a new version of our happily ended pursuit by the* Suffolk *and* Norfolk?
>
> *We in the* Bismarck *had the realization forced upon us that another page had been turned. After thirty-one hours of almost unbroken contact, thirty-one hours of broken contact had now, perhaps for good, come to an end – an exactly equal number of hours, how remarkable! Did the carrier plane really signify a decisive turn of events? Morale sagged a little among those who could read the signs.*[386]

But the expected attack did not occur, although the shadowing Swordfish aircraft was joined by second. The *Bismarck* continued east. The weather deteriorated further. Brief showers washed the decks and visibility alternated between poor and virtually zero. Was the weather too poor for air operations? Quite possibly it was. Or did the shadowing Swordfish aircraft, which were soon joined by a new Catalina, have longer range than their armed sisters? In that case, the carrier might be too far away. The Germans were completely unaware that the respite was caused by Stewart-Moore's mistaken attack on the *Sheffield*. When the afternoon was relieved by the evening, the Germans hoped to be spared the trial of yet another air attack.

Shortly after 18.00 hours, a shadow was sighted in their wake and for a brief moment, it was possible to identify it as a cruiser of *Southampton*-class. Lütjens presumed that it must be the *Sheffield* and that Force H could not be far away. The pursuit was again in full swing.

CHAPTER 25

One in a Hundred Thousand

At 19.00 hours Maund was ready to let his 15 Swordfish machines make yet another attempt on the *Bismarck*. The strong wind from the northwest persisted and the cloud base was very low, about 200 metres above the heeling *Ark Royal*. Violent rainsqualls swept over the area when the carrier turned against the wind to allow the torpedo aircraft to start. Intermittently, she seemed almost out of control, but eventually the 15 aeroplanes got away safely.

This time, Lieutenant Commander Tim Coode, who was determined not to repeat the *faux pas* with the *Sheffield*, led the aircraft. In one respect the attack on the British cruiser had brought advantages. It had showed that the magnetic detonators suffered from some kind of defect. Without that mistake, the aircraft would have attacked the *Bismarck* with virtually useless torpedoes, but instead another type of detonator had been used. In addition, rather than relying on radar, the *Sheffield*, which was in the wake of the enemy, was to send a homing signal for the unit to use to help them find the cruiser. When the latter had been located, Larcom would instruct the aviators to their target.

Coode remained at low altitude, carefully avoiding the dark grey clouds above, while he navigated towards the *Sheffield*, aided by her homing signal. Behind him the other aeroplanes formed up, until they had assembled in six groups of two or three machines each. About an hour later, the *Sheffield* was sighted by Coode's observer, Lieutenant Carver, who signalled to the cruiser for the exact position of the German battleship. Carver had been detailed to fly Hurricanes between Malta and Gibraltar, when it became known that the *Bismarck* had broken out. When Force H left Gibraltar, he followed as a reserve and soon ended up in a Swordfish as Coode's observer. Now he received Larcom's reply, that the *Bismarck* was 10 nautical miles ahead.

Fully aware of the bitter comments the seamen on board the *Sheffield* must have uttered when they saw the 15 Swordfish planes, Coode ordered his groups to ascend until the clouds obscured them. The poor visibility not only concealed the aeroplanes from the *Bismarck*, it also caused them to become separated. When they had reached above the clouds, at 1,700 metres, they had to spend valuable minutes forming up again. But soon the attack force assumed a course that would bring it directly towards the *Bismarck*. However, before they saw the enemy battleship, a huge formation of cloud loomed ahead of the airmen. When Coode initiated the dive that was to develop into an attack from several directions, he realized that it would not work:

> *Visibility was limited – a matter of yards. I watched the altimeter go back. When we reached 2,000 feet I started to worry. At 1,500 feet I wondered whether to continue the dive. At 1,000 feet I felt sure something was wrong, but still we were completely enclosed by cloud. I held the formation in the dive, and at 700 feet only we broke cloud, just when I was running out of height.*[387]

Coode again signalled to his group commanders; this time instructing them to attack on their own. The clock now showed 20.54 hours.

On board the *Bismarck*, the air alarm resounded through the ship when Coode's force approached from above. The gunners hastened to ensure they were ready to fire and the damage control teams made ready. An air attack had been expected ever since the Swordfish had been observed, but as it had not occurred many had begun to hope that it would grow too dark for an attack.

The noise from the enemy aircraft increased, but then decreased and faded away. Had the thick clouds concealed the battleship so well that the British flyers had missed it? Minutes passed and when orders were given to the gun crews to stand down, a wave of relief swept through the ship. It did not last long. Suddenly the air alarm was heard again and this time the sight of the approaching torpedo planes almost immediately followed.[388]

Coode's group had descended from the clouds far ahead of the battleship, which would force him to attack against the wind. Thus he broke off the attack, to find a better angle to attack from and turned back into the thick grey clouds. Soon anti-aircraft shells were bursting around him and the crew realized that the task ahead of them was going to be difficult indeed.

Lieutenant Godfrey-Fausset and Lieutenant Pattison made the first attack from the second group. It had ascended to an altitude of 3,000 metres, where the aircraft became afflicted by the build up of ice. Despite this problem, two of the aircraft were able to manoeuvre into a suitable position for attacking the battleship. They descended on the *Bismarck*'s starboard beam and immediately began the approach to release the torpedoes. At the same time, aircraft from the third and fourth groups attacked from the opposite side.

The battleship opened fire with all her weapons and the scenes from Esmonde's attack, with almost all their features, were repeated. The only significant difference was the very rough sea on this evening. To the German seamen on deck, the aircraft appeared to hang immovable in the air, sometimes so low that their wheels seemed to disappear behind the crests of the wave. It was incredible that none of the aircraft was shot down, but the rough sea and the movements of the ship combined to make the aircraft into difficult targets. The pilot in one of the planes was wounded by shell splinters, as was his gunner, but despite the fact that 175 holes were later counted on the plane, the pilot, Lieutenant F. A. Swanton, pressed home the attack.

'The tail air gunner would later tell me I nearly shouted my head off as we ran in,' Woods remembered. 'Probably true, but what it was I have no idea. All I do know is that as we dropped our 'tinfish' A4 'Charlie' almost leapt into the air, and as we turned away aft tightly, we were suspended motionless for a split second that felt like an eternity as every gun seemed to concentrate upon us.'[389]

The *Bismarck* turned to present a smaller target area. At the same time more torpedoes splashed into the water. The ship's guns fired into the water, in the hope of disrupting the trajectories. Maybe the efforts met with success in some cases, or perhaps the torpedoes would have missed anyway. It was very difficult to release the torpedoes, as they had to fall into a down period, not a crest. If the torpedo was released into a wave crest, its course would be erratic. When the six machines turned away to avoid the intensive fire, the observers and rear gunners could not see any obvious signs of hits, although some of them would later argue that one torpedo might have found its mark.

Soon after the first wave of the attack had disappeared Coode could again be seen from the battleship, as he approached together with the other two machines in his group. Somewhat behind, a fourth aeroplane from another group followed, as it had become separated from its group. Again the thunderous noise from the battleship's anti-aircraft guns and heavy artillery filled the air. 'We came out of the cloud at 700 feet and 4,000 yards from the *Bismarck,*' one airman recalled, 'and all her anti-aircraft pieces opened up upon us immediately. It was an impressive and frightening amount of glowing balls that flashed past.'

The second aircraft in the group was hit several times, but the machine as well as the crew survived and continued to release its torpedo. In the third plane, Lieutenant John Moffatt saw the battleship grow gradually in his sight. Between him and the ship, huge cascades of water rose when the heavy shells hit the sea. They created a curtain of water spray in the strong wind. He tried to calculate altitude, speed, range and aiming-off simultaneously. It was not easy, as tracer fire of various colours darted out from the mist, while the blast from exploding shells shook the aircraft. To release the torpedo at a range of 900 metres was regarded as the optimum, but he had to avoid the high wave crests. Moffatt wondered if he would really make it, when a voice crackled in the headphones: 'I'll tell you! I'll tell you!' it said. 'I'll tell you when to let it go!'

Moffat turned his head, discovering his observer hanging halfway out of the aircraft. 'I'm not kidding,' Moffat wrote later. 'There he was leaning right out, and his head down ... and then I realized what he was trying to do.'

By watching the waves below, the observer tried to judge the correct moment to release the torpedo, 'Not yet ... not yet!'

Moffatt again concentrated on the battleship, which was rapidly becoming larger ahead of him. He had to release the torpedo before it was too late: 'He held me there far too long.'

'Not yet...Now! *Now!*'[390]

Moffatt pressed the release mechanism and turned as sharply as he dared, to avoid the projectiles aimed at his aircraft. The *Bismarck* was shrouded in smoke from all her firing guns, which continued to spew shells at the fourth plane, thereby preventing Moffatt and his crew from seeing if the torpedo had hit.

While his comrades set course back towards the *Ark Royal*, Coode returned to the area. He made a few sweeps out from the clouds, but could see nothing that suggested any damage to the *Bismarck*. Neither could he see any more Swordfish attacking the beast. With disappointment, he instructed Carver to report that the attack had failed.

On board the *King George V* Tovey and his staff waited nervously for any news of the air attack. Night approached quickly. Suddenly the signal hummed in the radio room and the signal officer communicated the content of Coode's report: 'From the attack force commander,' he said. 'Estimate: No hits.'

Tovey did not reply. While he fended off the rolling movements of the flagship with one hand, he absorbed the message. So, everything had been in vain? At dawn, the *Bismarck* would be within range of the Luftwaffe and the British ships would have to turn north, or else their fuel oil would not be sufficient to allow them to reach harbours in England. All the staff officers remained silent. All of them watched their commander, waiting for his response. When Tovey finally reacted, it was with only a forced smile. They had done all they could.[391] And they had lost.

However, the report had been premature. The observer in the fourth plane, which had been a few hundred metres behind Coode's three aircraft, had seen a column of water shoot up from the sea on the *Bismarck*'s port side, just abaft of the battleship's funnel. The gunner on the same plane was certain that he had seen smoke, but could not exclude the possibility that it originated from the firing weapons of the ship. In fact, Moffatt's torpedo had hit the *Bismarck* on the port side.

This was not the only hit. Godfrey-Faussett's and Pattison's attacks had also met with success. Corporal Georg Herzog, commander at one of the anti-aircraft guns on the starboard side, saw the two Swordfish machines approach quickly. The courage of the British aviators surprised him. Despite the hail of fire, they came closer and flew so low that they almost hit the crests of the waves. Soon the planes were so close that the guns could not be depressed sufficiently to fire effectively. Then the torpedoes were released: one aimed amidships, the other abaft. The *Bismarck* sheered to port to avoid the torpedoes, but soon an explosion resounded and Herzog saw a fountain of water shoot up astern.[392] The force of the explosion made the ship heave in the sea and then buck in such a way that seamen in the fore and aft had to hold on, or else they would have been thrown onto the deck. Hardly had the

Bismarck calmed down before Chief Engine Room Artificer Schmidt's message 'presumed torpedo hit aft' reached damage-control centre. The first inspection of the damage revealed that the torpedo had blown a hole in the plating on the bottom of the hull, through which water had rushed in and filled the compartments of the steering gear. Water splashed to and fro as the ship moved in the seaway. A man would be hard put to stay alive there, far less be able to repair anything.

Müllenheim-Rechberg was in the aft fire control tower when he felt the impact through the ship:

> *The attack must have been almost over when it came, an explosion aft. My heart sank. I glanced at the rudder indicator. It showed 'left 12 degrees.' Did that just happen to be the correct reading at that moment? No. It did not change. It stayed at 'left 12 degrees.' Our increasing list to starboard soon told us that we were in a continuous turn. [...] Our speed indicator still showed a significant loss of speed. [...] In one stroke, the world seemed to be irrevocably altered.*[393]

The attack had knocked out the ship's manoeuvrability and now she began to sheer as the rudders had jammed at an unfavourable angle. At the same time, she began to list heavily to starboard. Many seamen believed she was about to capsize, when Lindemann ordered speed to be reduced, thereby regaining trim. However, the situation for the *Bismarck* had instantly changed from one of relatively safety to near catastrophic.

Coode's initial report had been incorrect in more ways than one, because all but two of the Swordfish aircraft had launched their torpedoes against the target. Several of the pilots had been forced to return to the *Sheffield*, to get a new bearing to the target, as they had lost track of the *Bismarck* in the rainsqualls. Lieutenant Beale signalled to the cruiser, requesting a new direction. In the message, he used the term 'target' for the battleship. Larcom could not refrain from answering sarcastically: 'The *Enemy* target is ten miles ahead.'

The sixth group had also returned to the *Sheffield* after losing sight of the *Bismarck*, but when they found her again, they were met with such intensive fire that one of the aircraft released its torpedo at a range of 2,000 metres, while the second dropped its torpedo in the sea and returned to the *Ark Royal*. Lieutenant Owen-Smith approached the battleship from astern, but realized it was an impossible attack angle. He tried to manoeuvre into a better position from the starboard side, but was surprised to see the *Bismarck* gradually turning to port. Thus she exposed more and more of the port side to Owen-Smith. He too released his torpedo and returned to the carrier.

The last pilot to make a determined attack at short range was Sub-Lieutenant Beale. After receiving instructions from Larcom, he had made a wide tack to approach the *Bismarck* on her bow. He ended up in the teeth of the wind, just the situation Coode wanted to avoid, but perhaps the choice turned out to be fortunate. Whether the lookouts on the *Bismarck* did not see Beale, or the anti-aircraft gunners were engaging other targets, remains unclear. In any case, Beale and his crew did not meet with any fire on their attack approach merely 15 metres above the surface of the sea. The torpedo splashed into the water, whereupon the Swordfish turned away. At this moment the anti-aircraft gunners opened fire on Beale's plane. Beale's rear gunner fired a few salvos with the machinegun, despite the fact that it could not harm the *Bismarck*. A few seconds later, a huge fountain shot up amidships on the *Bismarck*. 'The tail air gunner was dancing a small jig,' Sub-lieutenant Friend recalled, 'as I excitedly told Beale. By turning the Swordfish quickly, he too was able to see the splash subsiding. Thus, all three of us saw our hit.'[394]

On the *Sheffield*, visual contact had been lost with the *Bismarck* during the air attack, but she could be followed on the radar. When the haze suddenly cleared, consternation beset the officers on the bridge, as the *Bismarck* did not present the narrow silhouette expected. Rather she had turned port and exposed her entire broadside. It was assumed that the German battleship had turned to manoeuvre away from the torpedoes, but suddenly this thought faded away as her main guns flashed. Had she turned to attack the *Sheffield*?

The first salvo was short by more than a kilometre but new flashes from the 38-centimetre guns were seen. Less than half a minute later, a forest of water columns surrounded the *Sheffield*, as the German salvo straddled her. Splinters from one of the bursting shells swept over the cruiser's superstructures, wounding 15 men manning the anti-aircraft guns. Larcom ordered a drastic change of course, while smoke was placed to conceal the cruiser. The last he saw in his binoculars, before the battleship was obscured by the smoke, was the *Bismarck* sailing on a north-northwesterly course, straight towards Tovey's main force.

PART 3

CHAPTER 26

The Last Night

'What do you mean with course 340 degrees?' Tovey asked the signal officer. His forehead was wrinkled as he read the message.

The *Sheffield's* report had been received not long after Coode's disappointing signal and the Admiral was not in the mood for careless reporting. 'I fear Larcom has joined the reciprocal club,' he snubbed.

Tovey concluded that Larcom had misjudged the silhouette of the *Bismarck* in the poor weather. He thought such an experienced commander ought not to make such a mistake, but it was fairly common. Some of the other officers suggested that the estimate indeed was correct, as the *Bismarck* might have altered course due to the air attack. The opinions diverged, but no one could yet guess the true facts.

Soon another signal arrived, this time from one of the two Swordfish aircraft shadowing the enemy battleship, claiming that her course was northerly, which confirmed Larcom's report. Might Coode's report be erroneous? Or was the *Bismarck* about to resume her original course after the air attack, after being forced to make some extensive evasive manoeuvre? The latter alternative seemed more plausible.

Nevertheless, the two messages gave rise to new hopes and revived energy. When the humming noise was again heard from the radio room, the tension was so great that virtually everybody winced. 'Enemy steering north-northwest,' the report of the second Swordfish aircraft read. It was soon followed by another signal from the *Sheffield*, saying that the *Bismarck* was now on a course due north.[395]

Was Lütjens attempting to shake off the pursuers by a series of evasive manoeuvres before darkness fell, or was the ship indeed

248

damaged? If the latter was true, the situation had changed dramatically.

When Coode's Swordfish returned to the *Ark Royal* (all of them had survived and managed to land on the careening flight deck) the airmen delivered an optimistic but confused report on what had transpired. Maund was cautious and did not want to jump into conclusions. Everything happened very quickly during the kind of attack they had just carried out and the psychological stress was considerable. Thus, it was difficult to form a correct picture of what had actually taken place. The clouds and rainsqualls made it difficult for the airmen to observe their comrades attacking. Finally Maund felt convinced enough to report that at least one torpedo had hit. When Somerville later asked Maund whether he intended to stage another attack, in darkness, the reply was negative, but Maund added that the *Bismarck* had probably been hit by a second torpedo, abaft on starboard. If so, this raised the possibility that the British might catch up with the *Bismarck* before she reached harbour.

If Maund, Somerville and Tovey could have seen what occurred on the German side, their assurance would have been much greater. On the *Bismarck*, Lindemann struggled to make his ship regain the proper course. He tried all conceivable speed combinations on the three propeller shafts. On a few occasions he managed to get the ship on a proper course, but the damaged rudder caused her to turn northwards against the wind, bringing her straight towards the enemy ships.

All the men on the *Bismarck*, from Lütjens to the seamen in the damage-control parties, discussed what could be done to repair the damage. The rudder was controlled electrically, but there were reserve systems, manual as well as electrical. None of these systems worked and it was impossible to reach the compartments next to the rudders, as they were water-filled. Worst of all, the rough sea caused water to move violently back and forth in the compartments, making it impossible to enter them. The waves were very high, as in a full-blown storm.[396]

In the damage-control centre, Artificer Statz saw a team of divers return after attempting to repair the damage. One of them had almost drowned when some sharp object cut off his air hose. They all appeared downhearted.

'It won't be done,' stated Commander Oels after receiving their report. 'If we only had the type of diving equipment they use in the U-boat service.'[397]

Many proposals were made. One was to simply blow away the rudders with explosives. As they had jammed at an unfavourable angle, it was impossible to steer with the propellers. However, the propellers might be damaged as well if the rudders were blown off. Nevertheless, the suggestion was seriously discussed. Finally, the rough sea precluded the proposed solution, as it would be impossible for divers to attach the explosives in the harsh weather. In fact, some seamen volunteered for pure suicide missions: to fasten explosives on their bodies, swim to the rudders and blow themselves up together with the rudders. Their offer was turned down, since in even the most perfect of conditions it would have been extremely difficult to swim with the amount of explosives that would be needed. In the current weather, the most likely outcome of such an attempt would simply be that the swimmer drowned or damaged some other part of the ship.[398]

It was also suggested that something like an old fashioned steering-oar should be fastened to the starboard side, which would counteract the jammed rudders. This might have have succeeded, but again the rough sea prevented such work.[399] Another idea was to secure a submarine at the stern and try to steer with its help. Such ideas betray a sense of desperation, which is hardly surprising considering the circumstances, and they were scarcely realistic. After the war, Captain Schulze-Hinrichs suggested that the *Bismarck* might have attempted to travel to France in reverse. It is unclear whether this idea would have worked, or what speed the battleship might have attained in the attempt.[400]

After considering the alternatives, it seems that it was not possible to save the *Bismarck*, at least not in the prevailing weather. Lütjens appears to have quickly accepted the fate awaiting him, the *Bismarck* and the crew. When Coode passed over the ship for the first time, he had already signalled Marinegruppe West: 'Attack by carrier planes.' This message was followed 11 minutes later by 'Torpedo hit aft' and then 'Ship no longer steering' and 'Torpedo hit amidships'. Less than an hour after Coode's Swordfish began the attack, Lütjens reported that it was no longer possible to control the ship, but that she would still fight to the end.

As the night rapidly approached, the Swordfish planes shadowing the *Bismarck* had to return to the carrier. This would not have been any complication to the Royal Navy while the *Sheffield* was still in a position to follow the German battleship with her radar, but unfortunately a shell splinter had knocked out the radar. If the crew on the German battleship had been able to repair the damaged rudder to such an extent that she could have continued towards France, this minor, improbable damage to the *Sheffield* would have been a significant setback. Again the British efforts were favoured by luck.

Hardly had the downheartedness settled within Larcom's staff, before a lookout yelled: 'Ships! Red one-five!' In one moment visible at the wave crests, only to disappear beneath the waves with no more than the mastheads perceptible, Vian's five destroyers of the 5th destroyer flotilla approached. He had arrived just as the *Sheffield* lost contact. A signal lamp flashed from the *Cossack*, requesting Larcom to provide the latest known position of the *Bismarck*. The destroyers then spread out, to increase the area they could search, and set course in the direction Larcom had indicated. Forty minutes later, the Polish destroyer *Piorun* reported that she had found the German battleship, at about the same time as the last shadowing Swordfish landed on the *Ark Royal*.

Vian now asked himself: would he be content to shadow the enemy, or should he attack it? He did not know the effects of the air attack and decided to try to damage the *Bismarck* sufficiently for her speed to be reduced so that Tovey could catch up with her at dawn. If he could accomplish this, without exposing his ships to unnecessary risks, it was worth making the attempt.

The *Piorun* had already engaged in an exchange of fire with the *Bismarck*, which could be seen against the approaching night in the east. Unfortunately the Polish destroyer and *Maori*, her closest sister, appeared as a clear silhouette against the setting sun in the west, allowing the Germans to open fire. Vian ordered them to fall back and manoeuvre to attack the *Bismarck* from the north, while the *Cossack*, *Sikh* and *Zulu* were to try to approach the battleship from the south. A coordinated attack would then be staged. The *Piorun* maintained her course and was soon so close to the battleship that her tiny guns could reach the enemy. Briefly the small Polish destroyer exchanged shots with the huge German battleship. The commander on board the *Maori* found the enemy salvos too close to the mark and sheered to port, in order to try to attack from the south.

While Vian struggled to get his ships into suitable positions, the true situation finally dawned upon Tovey and his staff. The crews of the

Swordfish that had been following the *Bismarck* were able to fill in many of the gaps remaining in the accounts given by the attacking crews. This allowed Maund to present more accurate reports, confirming that several torpedoes had hit the battleship. Even more importantly, she had been observed making two complete circles, at low speed. From this information it seemed clear that the torpedoes had not only hit, but at a very vulnerable point. This information reached Tovey before midnight, and confirmed the reports he gradually received from Vian. The last air attack had rendered the *Bismarck* impossible to manoeuvre.

Now, Tovey faced a difficult decision. Should he attack the *Bismarck* in the night or wait until dawn? The *Bismarck* could regard every ship as hostile, allowing her to fire on them at will. However, the British risked firing upon their own ships, especially in the confusion of darkness. Also, the weather and light conditions were unfavourable. The horizon behind him was clear, while the *Bismarck* was more likely to be concealed by rainstorms and poor visibility.[401] At dawn it would be much easier to coordinate the efforts.

On the other hand, there were risks associated with waiting. In particular, the crew on the German battleship might repair the damage. If she regained speed and manoeuvrability, while Tovey waited, the Admiralty could be expected to be very critical. Nevertheless, Tovey decided to wait. According to the plan he conceived, Force H would be positioned south of the *Bismarck*, to avoid getting harmed in the forthcoming battle. At the same time, he would set a north-northeast-erly course with the *King George V* and *Rodney*, to ensure that the enemy would be cut off from France. At dawn, he intended to make a 180 degree turn, bringing him on a course directly towards the enemy ahead. At the same time, Wake-Walker closed in from the north; he had ordered full speed ahead when notified about the air attack. If all went according to plan, the *Bismarck* would be attacked from all sides simultaneously. Furthermore, from Tovey's battleships she would appear against the gathering sunlight, making it easier for the British gunners to find the mark.

While Tovey worked to get his scattered forces into position for an attack at dawn, Vian strived to stage a coordinated attack with his five destroyers. This proved difficult in the increasing darkness. Waves 10 to 15 metres high splashed over the destroyers and tossed them violently in the heaving water. Speed had to be reduced, or else men on deck would be washed overboard. The poor visibility, which alternated between less than three hundred metres up to a few nautical miles, did not make the task any easier. The conditions did not facilitate a coordinated attack.

Another factor complicating Vian's plans were the erratic, haphazard and unpredictable movements of the German battleship. It was difficult to interpret her manoeuvres. When first observed, she had been on a southeasterly course. During the initial battle with the *Piorun*, the battleship was seen sheering to port, apparently to enable all her heavy guns to be trained on the destroyer. The *Piorun* broke off the engagement and retired behind a curtain of smoke. The commander on board the *Piorun* did not know that the enemy ship was uncontrollable and her movement was an effect of the sea and Lindemann's attempts to steer her with the propellers. When the *Piorun* had reached far away enough to be safe, her crew could catch a glimpse of the *Bismarck*, which again appeared to sail on a southeasterly course. When the *Sikh* sighted the *Bismarck* after midnight, aided by the muzzle flashes, the German ship was sailing northwest.

It was a very long night for the men on board the *Bismarck* as well as on the destroyers. The *Piorun* lost contact at midnight and did not see the battleship again, but the other destroyers had made an outflanking movement, allowing them to attack from the south. The German battleship could be made out as a faint silhouette against the last glow of the sunset in the northwest, but Vian hoped his destroyers would be invisible against the darkness to the south. He was quickly disabused of this hope when the *Bismarck*'s guns flashed and her shells landed so close to the *Cossack* that splinters tore off her radio mast. Vian quickly made a 180-degree turn. Soon the *Zulu* found herself the target. This time too, the first salvo straddled the destroyer, which had to turn away with three wounded seamen. The British concluded that the German guns must have been radar controlled, but this was not correct. The German optical instruments were of such quality that Schneider and Albrecht could accurately direct the fire with these, despite the poor visibility.

While the *Cossack* and *Zulu* regrouped, Commander Stokes in the *Sikh* assumed responsibility for shadowing the enemy and reporting on her whereabouts. He carried on for half an hour and reduced the range to less than four nautical miles, when the next salvo flashed from the *Bismarck* muzzles. Stokes had just been busy preparing for a torpedo salvo, when the enemy forestalled him. He had to retire and his torpedoes remained unused on his destroyer.

At this stage, Vian had been informed that the *Bismarck* had been damaged during the air attack. Indeed, his own observations clearly suggested that the battleship did not move in the way expected from a ship heading rapidly towards a French port. The primary reason for his attacks thus seemed to have been rendered irrelevant. He could have chosen to break off the attacks and be content with shadowing the enemy, while awaiting the arrival of Tovey's heavy ships. But if the crew on board the *Bismarck* managed to repair the rudder she would be able to evade. Vian decided to continue attacking, although he abandoned the coordinated attack and instructed his destroyer commanders to attack individually, when a propitious situation occurred.

In his fire control tower, Müllenheim-Rechberg saw how the enemy destroyers appeared and disappeared in the darkness:

> *We did not know how many destroyers there were around us. The pitch-blackness of the night and frequent rain squalls made it impossible for us to make out silhouettes, so we couldn't tell whether we were seeing a few destroyers over and over again or whether there was a great number of them. The only thing clear to us was that we could expect endless torpedo attacks. Everything was going to depend on extreme vigilance and the flawless functioning of our range finders.*[402]

Although Vian's attacks had so far not resulted in any damage to the *Bismarck*, they adversely affected the German activities. The damage control party still worked to repair the jammed rudder, but the muzzle flashes from turrets Cesar and Dora prevented the men from staying on the aft deck.[403]

Despite the abandoned ambition to launch a concerted attack, the first torpedo salvoes were fired within a short period of time. First out was the *Zulu*. Commander Graham had manoeuvred into a position northwest of the *Bismarck*, when he suddenly saw her sailing north-northwest. He closed in on her port side and began the attack. Hardly had he set course on the battleship, before its medium artillery opened fire. Again the accuracy was disturbingly good. With a very slender margin, the destroyer avoided being hit and could fire four torpedoes at a range of about 3,000 metres. At this moment, the *Bismarck* made yet another of her erratic movements and all the torpedoes missed.

At the same time, Commander Armstrong on the *Maori* had attempted to attack from almost the same position as Graham. Armstrong fired light flares, but these only revealed an empty ocean. Then, muzzle flashes betrayed the *Bismarck* and Graham fired yet more flares, this time illuminating the German battleship. He promptly attacked. At 01.37 hours, about 15 minutes after Graham had conducted his attack, two torpedoes left the *Maori* and disappeared in the dark sea. Somewhat later, when the destroyer was already in full retreat from the shells of the battleship, the crew saw a sharp flash from the *Bismarck*, which they believed resulted from one of their torpedoes hitting her. In fact, it was one of the star shells fired from the *Maori*, which had landed on the battleship's deck and caused a fire.

At the same time as the *Maori* plunged herself at the battleship's port side, Vian attacked from starboard. He launched three of his four torpedoes and then turned back. The flash from the flare was also observed from the *Cossack* and again it was concluded that a hit had been scored. As the destroyer retired, Vian visited the radar operators in their cabin and made a very unpleasant discovery. As he watched the screen, a strange echo left the battleship and rapidly moved towards the *Cossack*.

'What's that?' Vian asked.

'Shells from the *Bismarck*, sir,' one of the men told him. 'On their way towards us.'

'They induced some unpleasant moments,' Vian wrote later, 'until the shells plunged into the sea, exploding with a violent concussion and throwing up huge pillars of water which seemed to tower above us.'[404]

After these almost simultaneous attacks, a more tranquil period followed. Vian received an order from Tovey that star shells should be fired at regular intervals. The reason was not to enable the main British force to locate the *Bismarck*, but because Tovey suspected that the positions given by the destroyers might differ from his own, as it had not been possible to take any sun sightings and fix accurate positions. He wanted to avoid the risk of an unexpected encounter with the

Bismarck, or of some of his ships being hit by straying torpedoes.

The *Bismarck* enjoyed an hour of respite before the destroyers resumed their attacks. The *Sikh* had reconnoitred for several hours, after losing contact with the battleships following the exchange of fire. Not until after 02.00 hours did her lookouts again observe the enemy ship between two rainsqualls. This time Stokes was more cautious and fired his torpedoes at longer range. This attack also failed. Vian made yet another attempt an hour later, which exhausted his supply of torpedoes. Except for the *Piorun*, which was already sailing towards Britain as her fuel oil was almost consumed, only the *Maori* still had any torpedoes but, she did not manage to put in any more attacks before dawn.[405]

Within Marinegruppe West the *Bismarck* had confidently been expected to reach a French port on 27 May. The news that an aeroplane with fixed undercarriage had been seen, as well as the observation that a British cruiser had assumed position astern of the *Bismarck*, lessened the optimistic mood. Lütjens' report on the air attack, the torpedo hits and the inability to control the ship turned nervousness into despair. Admiral Saalwächter ordered all submarines in the Bay of Biscay to set course immediately towards the *Bismarck's* latest known position. Soon after 22.00 hours he informed Lütjens, and an hour later he ordered air reconnaissance to begin at 04.30 hours, followed by bombers starting at 06.30 hours. He also ensured that the tanker *Ermland* could sail from La Pallice at dawn. There was little else he could do.

At about midnight, Lütjens sent another message, addressed to Hitler: 'We will fight to the last in our faith in you, *Mein Führer*, and in our unshakable trust in Germany's victory.' Lütjens also reported to Marinegruppe West that the ship was not manoeuvrable, but he did not report any deficiencies in her armament.

The response from Marinegruppe West said that tugs had already put to sea, to assist the *Bismarck*, but also included messages suggesting that those on shore had little hope of the *Bismarck's* survival. The first originated from Saalwächter: 'Our wishes and thoughts are with you and your ship. We wish you success in your difficult fight.' It was followed by a message of a similar kind from Raeder: 'All our thoughts are with you and your ship. We wish you success in your difficult fight.'

Lütjens conveyed these messages to the crew to strengthen their morale, as well as information on the condition of the battleship. However, this information, just like his speech the day before, seems to have had the opposite effect. All the well-meant words gave the impression that it had already been accepted that the *Bismarck* and her crew belonged to the dead. Almost exactly coinciding with the beginning of the torpedo attack by *Zulu*, *Maori* and *Cossack*, two messages from Hitler reached the *Bismarck*. In the first message, Hitler thanked Lütjens in the name of Germany. The second message was addressed to the crew and was read over the loudspeakers as soon as the British destroyers had turned away and firing had ceased: 'All of Germany is with you. What can be done will be done. Your devotion to duty will strengthen our nation in its struggle for its existence. Adolf Hitler.'

During the later part of the night, a number of signals were sent between the *Bismarck* and Marinegruppe West. They dealt with the weather and cooperation with the Luftwaffe. The final message said that Commander Adalbert Schneider had been awarded the Knights Cross for the destruction of the *Hood*. This message at least generated a wave of applause and cheerful cries in the ship.

Neither the crew of the *Bismarck* nor the men on board the British destroyers knew that the nightly cat and mouse game had been watched by an unknown observer. At the moment he emerged from the depths of the ocean to transmit a wireless message, Commander Wohlfarth on *U-556* could see the flares in the clouds, while the horizon occasionally lit up with the gun flashes from the *Bismarck*. Wohlfarth was the submarine commander who had promised to protect the *Bismarck*. He had been on his way back to port when he received the general instruction to converge on the battleship's last known position. This he did, even though he had already fired his last torpedo at the *Darlington Court*, and so had no means to attack enemy vessels. On the evening of 26 May, he dearly regretted that he had not followed the advice of his navigation officer to hold back that last torpedo. The *Renown* and *Ark Royal* approached at high speed from the sea spray. He quickly dived before the British lookouts saw his submarine, but well concealed beneath the surface, he had a perfect opportunity to fire. Such a shot could hardly have missed. 'The enemy came straight towards me,' he wrote in the war diary, 'without escorting destroyers or zigzagging.'

What Wohlfarth saw was Somerville and Force H, soon after Coode had started for the decisive attack. When they had passed, he returned to the surface and tried to follow. He reported the position, hoping that some other submarine might take advantage of the opportunity. The British ships sailed at a speed too high for his submarine to follow and he soon lost contact. Nearly four hours later, *U-556* was almost caught unawares when a destroyer came towards the submarine in the darkness. Again Wohlfarth had to submerge quickly and the destroyer – probably the *Cossack*, *Zulu* or *Sikh* on their way to attack the *Bismarck* from the south – thundered past ahead of the German submarine, without showing any sign of detecting it.

Soon Wohlfarth returned to the surface. The rough sea caused the submarine to career violently and the rainsqualls made it difficult to see much except the revealing light from flares and gun flashes. Wohlfarth realized he would not be able to fulfil his commitment as guardian to the *Bismarck*. He sent repeated messages to direct other submarines to the area. 'It felt horrible,' he wrote in the war diary, 'To be so close yet unable to assist.' Finally he had to leave off, or else his fuel would not be sufficient to reach the base in France.

CHAPTER 27

The Last Battle

Tuesday May 27, 1941 dawned as a gloomy day with dark grey cloud cover and a strong westerly wind that refused to allow the sea any rest. British destroyers split the waves as white foam washed over the decks. The larger ships were better suited to the weather, but the wind that swept past the *Ark Royal's* flight deck was so strong it was feared that the Swordfish aeroplanes would be damaged.

In spite of the depressing morning, morale on board the British ships remained high. The previous day, the *Bismarck* had seemed to escape the revenge so dearly longed for by the Royal Navy. Now the situation had reversed completely and preparations were made for battle. All loose items were secured or stowed away. The seamen changed socks and underwear as a precaution against infection in case of suffering from wounds. Men serving on deck or in gun turrets and as shell handlers collected the white equipment that protected against gun flashes and burns. Lifebelts and steel helmets were put on, whereupon resolute men who tried to collect their thoughts as well as possible, to cope with the tasks they had to perform, manned battle stations. Although most of the men on the British cruisers and battleships felt anxiety as well as fear, all but a few also looked forward to avenging the destruction of the *Hood*. Fatigue was forgotten. A final exhortation, a final battle, and the men could return to the sleep, the safety and the recreation on land.

On the *Bismarck*, exactly the opposite situation prevailed. The seamen had already persuaded themselves that the dangerous part of the voyage lay behind them. Plans for home leave or adventures in

France were already being discussed. Then, suddenly came the improbable torpedo hit. The younger men perhaps did not realize quite how desperate their situation was. In their minds, they were immortal. Men died in war, but other men, not they. It would be dangerous, but somehow they would survive. The older and more experienced were more realistic. They could not know much about the forthcoming battle, but they realized the British would send sufficient forces to ensure their destruction. However, they kept their thoughts to themselves so as not to spread unnecessary panic among the younger men. The only chance of survival lay in every man performing his duties as well as possible.

The officers knew what the damaged steering system would mean to their chances in the forthcoming battle. They could afford to ignore the calls in the loudspeakers urging the crew to watch for German submarines and aircraft, as they realized it was only a measure to strengthen morale.

In the damage-control centre, Artificer Josef Statz decided to remain at his post, no matter what happened during the coming battle, and to follow the ship to the bottom of the ocean if the battle ended badly. After a long period of inactivity, Lieutenant Jahreis called for their attention. 'We have some time now,' he said. 'Let's think once more of the homeland!'

'Yes, and of wives and children most of all,' someone added.[406]

When Müllenheim-Rechberg made a final visit to the gunroom, he was met by an oppressive silence, sometimes interrupted by dispirited comments. Suddenly one of the officers made a remark that would forever engrave itself on Müllenheim-Rechberg's memory: 'Today, my wife will become a widow, but she doesn't know it yet.'

'It was depressing,' Müllenheim-Rechberg wrote later, 'too depressing to stay.'[407]

He left the gunroom and continued to the bridge, where silence met him. To his surprise, he saw that Lindemann already wore a life vest and appeared absent-minded.

He saw me coming, but he did not return my salute, which I held as I looked at him intently in the hope that he would say something. He did not say a word. He did not even glance at me. I was greatly disturbed and puzzled. After all,

I had been his personal adjutant and the situation we were
in seemed to me unusual enough to merit some remark. I
would have given a great deal for a word from him, one
that would have told me what he felt about what had
happened. But there was only silence, and I had to
interpret it for myself.[408]

It was decided that one of the floatplanes would fly to France with the
ship's war diary, the films shot on board and an account written by one
of the war correspondents. The fortunate airmen who were given a
chance to avoid the impending catastrophe dressed for the mission
while their Arado was moved from the hangar to the catapult. When
the pilots reached the deck, seamen who had written their last words to
parents, friends, wives or fiancées and wanted these greetings to be
taken home surrounded them. With a mixture of relief and disgrace for
leaving all the other men to their fate, the airmen put the papers in their
pockets and entered the aircraft. But the aircraft could not be launched.
After a while, it was discovered that a splinter originating from a shell
fired by the *Prince of Wales* had punctured the container with the
compressed air that propelled the catapult. It could not be repaired and
the two airmen were again left to share the fate of their comrades.

Meanwhile, Tovey tried to gather his forces, to coordinate the
attack. Although the *Bismarck* was damaged, she could not be
dismissed as an impotent adversary. It could not b forgotten that she
had sunk the *Hood* within a few minutes. The position reports given by
Vian's destroyers did not seem to fit with Tovey's data and he could not
see any star shells or flares. He wanted to approach the enemy head to
head, from the west-northwest. But he could not accomplish that
without knowing the position of the enemy. The latest report, from the
destroyer *Maori*, told him that the enemy sailed at a course of 300
degrees. Fifteen minutes after dawn, Tovey altered to an easterly course.
To the north, he could see the *Rodney*; not as close as the *Prince of*
Wales had been to the *Hood* but allowing Dalrymple-Hamilton
sufficient room for individual manoeuvre.

Like Tovey, Somerville had his share of problems to consider, partly
caused by the unreliable position reports. He feared that Force H would
accidentally encounter the *Bismarck*, which might hit and damage, or
even destroy, the *Ark Royal* or *Renown* before Tovey arrived on the

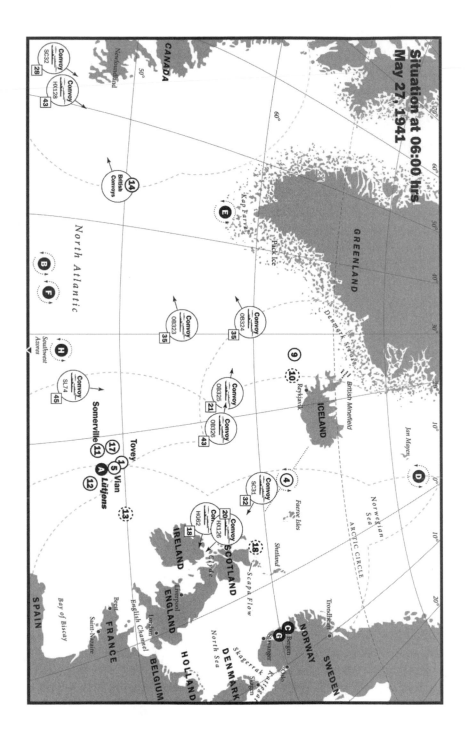

Situation at 06:00 hrs.
May 27, 1941

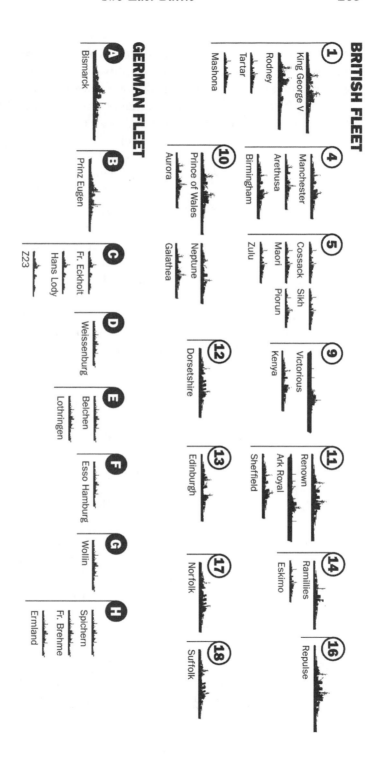

BRITISH FLEET

1. King George V
   Rodney
   Tartar
   Mashona

4. Manchester
   Arethusa
   Birmingham

5. Cossack Silk
   Maori Piorun
   Zulu

9. Victorious
   Kenya

10. Prince of Wales
    Aurora
    Neptune
    Galathea

11. Renown
    Ark Royal
    Sheffield

12. Dorsetshire

13. Edinburgh

14. Ramillies
    Eskimo

16. Repulse

17. Norfolk

18. Suffolk

GERMAN FLEET

A. Bismarck

B. Prinz Eugen

C. Fr. Eckholt
   Hans Lody
   Z23

D. Weissenburg

E. Belchen
   Lothringen

F. Esso Hamburg

G. Wollin

H. Spichern
   Fr. Brehme
   Ermland

scene. There was also a risk that the *Renown* might mistakenly be fired upon by Tovey's battleships when visibility was reduced by rainsqualls. Aerial reconnaissance had not produced any results yet.

By 03.00 hours Somerville had already inquired when Maund could launch another torpedo attack. He had been told that the aircraft were ready, but he did not want to launch them until daylight made it possible to separate friend from foe. Now, Maund asked if it would not be better to cancel the attack altogether. The incident with the *Sheffield* was still clearly remembered and the miserable weather would make it harder to avoid such mistakes, if it permited air operations at all. Somerville agreed and informed Tovey. In order to establish the position of the enemy, Somerville turned north and shortly afterwards sighted the *Maori*, which could report the enemy's exact position. Satisfied with this information, Somerville returned south. He could keep his ships outside the coming battle.

At the same time, yet another British ship moved towards the scene. The heavy cruiser *Dorsetshire* was escorting the convoy SL74 when she received the Admiralty's broadcast on the report from the Catalina. The commander, Captain Benjamin Martin, realized his cruiser was in a position to intercept the *Bismarck*. The northbound convoy was left behind as the *Dorsetshire* increased speed and set course towards the Bay of Biscay. She approached the *Bismarck* from southeast.

On 27 May it was Rear Admiral Wake-Walker on the *Norfolk* who first caught sight of the *Bismarck*. He had been sailing westwards until midnight between 25 and 26 May. Now he saw the *Bismarck* in the sea mist ahead. However, he mistakenly identified the shadow as the *Rodney* and sent a recognition signal, but immediately afterwards realized his mistake. The Germans did not bother sending any recognition signal. Instead, the *Bismarck*'s main guns flashed and a few seconds later her shells landed around the British cruiser, which turned around and soon reached safe distance. Wake-Walker waited for Tovey to arrive. He did not have to wait long; soon the masts and superstructures of the *King George V* and *Rodney* became visible on the horizon. 'We were rather tired at this point,' Phillips remembered. 'There hadn't been much sleep during the last days. But the battleships turned against the enemy.'

All the efforts finally paid off. All that remained was to defeat the crippled enemy. Rapid signals were exchanged between the British ships and at 08.43 hours the loudspeakers on the *King George V* announced that the *Bismarck* had been sighted.

When the crew on board the British battleship cheered, many officers on the bridge felt jubilant as the long pursuit was finally coming to a successful end. At last they saw her: the ship they had chased for four days. Many times they had felt despair as she seemed to evade them indefinitely. 'Veiled in distant rainfall,' Lieutenant Commander Hugh Guernsey wrote. 'A thick, squat ghost of a ship, very broad in the beam, coming straight towards us.'

'I think it was the most magnificent ship I ever saw,' recalled Ludovic Kennedy, a Lieutenant on board the destroyer *Tartar* and son of the late commander of the *Rawalpindi*. 'Massive – 50,000 tons. But despite her beauty, we realized she had to be destroyed.'[409]

On board the *Rodney*, Captain Dalrymple-Hamilton sent a thought, proud as well as worried, to his son who served with the anti-aircraft artillery on the *King George V*. Then he grasped the microphone for the internal loudspeaker system and said: 'We're going in! Good luck!'

A second later the barrels of the forward gun turrets flashed, the sea ahead of the battleship was temporarily flattened by the blast and six 40.6cm shells had begun their trajectory towards the *Bismarck*. The time was 08.47 hours, the wind northwesterly and the range 25,000 metres.

'The alarm bells were still ringing,' Müllenheim-Rechberg remembered, 'when, returning from the bridge, I entered my action station.' He grasped the receiver to the control telephone and heard that the waiting was over: 'Two battleships port bow.'[410]

> *I turned my director and saw two bulky silhouettes, unmistakably the* King George V *and* Rodney, *at a range of approximately 24,000 metres. As imperturbable as though they were on their way to an execution, they were coming directly towards us in line abreast ...*[411]

In his headset, Müllenheim-Rechberg heard Schneider calmly issuing orders: 'Main and secondary batteries ready, request permission to fire.'[412]

But it was Dalrymple-Hamilton who opened the battle. When the first

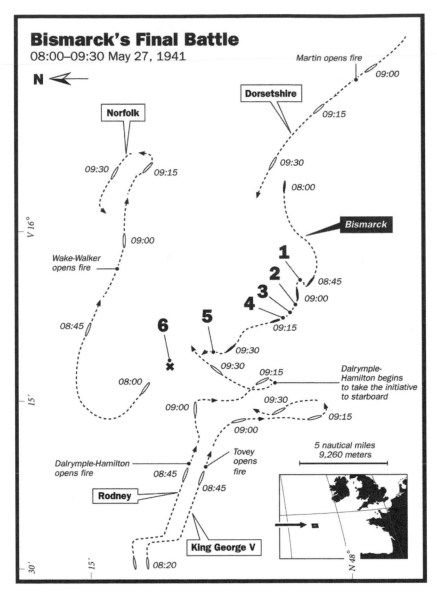

Bismarck's Final Battle
08:00–09:30 May 27, 1941

N

Martin opens fire
09:00

Dorsetshire
09:15

09:30

08:00

Norfolk

09:30   09:15

Bismarck

09:00

V 16°

1

2   08:45

3   09:00

Wake-Walker
opens fire

4

09:00

5
09:15

6   09:30
09:30

09:30

08:45

Dalrymple-
Hamilton begins
to take the initiative
to starboard

09:15

08:00

09:00

09:30   09:15

09:00

15'

5 nautical miles
9,260 meters

Tovey
opens
fire

Dalrymple-Hamilton
opens fire

08:45

Rodney

08:45

King George V

N 48°

30'   15'   08:20

1 Lütjens opens fire.

2 Bismarck's fore artillery is silenced by a salvo from Rodney.

3 Müllenheim-Rechberg assumes responsibility for directing fire on Bismarck.

4 Bismarck's aft fire control center is put out of action.

5 Oels gives instructions that Bismarck should be scuttled.

6 Bismarck sinks 10:39 hrs.

shots were fired, the British battleships were on an east-southeasterly course, with *King George V* ahead and the *Rodney* slightly abaft on the port side. The *Bismarck* approached from the south, on a north-north-westerly course, placing her more or less ahead of the bows, just slightly to the starboard of the British ships. Seen from the *Bismarck's* position, the *Norfolk* was located 30 degrees to starboard and the *Dorsetshire* 90 degrees to starboard. Both cruisers remained at a safe distance.

King George V opened fire soon after the *Rodney*. Müllenheim-Rechberg knew it would take less than a minute for the shells to reach their target, but it seemed like much longer. 'Finally,' Müllenheim-Rechberg wrote, 'white mushrooms, tons of water thrown up by heavy shells, rose seventy metres into the air. But they were still quite far from us.'[413]

Three minutes later than the *Rodney*, the *Bismarck* opened fire. On the British battleships, the huge orange flashes from the *Bismarck's* guns could easily be seen. A thick cloud of smoke, much darker than the smoke from the British guns, drifted away over the stormy sea. It would take little more than half a minute for the shells to cover the distance between the ships, and the British could not yet tell if the target was the *Rodney* or the *King George V*.

One of Tovey's officers made a quick estimate on the time needed for the German shells to reach their target. He began to count down loudly as he looked at his watch.

'For God's sake,' Tovey interrupted, 'Shut Up!' Like everyone else on the bridge, he had put on his steel helmet and placed cotton in his ears to protect them from the sharp sound when the flagship's main guns fired. He was as aware as anyone else what would happen if the enemy's salvo hit the bridge and he did not want to know exactly when this would happen.

In his binoculars, Tovey observed the shell splashes near the enemy battleship. The *Rodney* seemed to have got the range correct after a few salvos, but Tovey's gunners were far from the mark. The *Bismarck* was half concealed by rainsqualls and it was difficult to make correct observations of the shells hitting the water. But the radar operators on the flagship ought to obtain a better range estimate. Why was not the fire more accurate?

Tovey's thoughts were interrupted by a whizzing sound and the crash when the first German salvo landed. Clearly, the target was the *Rodney* and to Tovey's resentment, he could see that the *Bismarck's* fire was more accurate than his ships could accomplish. A series of water columns shot up ahead of the *Rodney*, some of them so close that the water washed over her deck as it fell back. 'I watched the *Rodney*,' Guernsey recalled, 'To see if she was hit, but she just sat there like a great slab of rock blocking the northern horizon, and then suddenly belched a full salvo.'[414]

Thomas Kelly, an officer on board the destroyer *Tartar* who had served on the *Hood* more than a decade earlier, saw how the *Bismarck's* first salvo crashed down around the *Rodney* 'We could hear the shells from the Bismarck,' he remembered, 'and the salvo straddled *Rodney*. I turned to the Captain and said 'God, sir, not again!' My thoughts were with the *Hood*.'[415]

Schneider, the artillery officer, observed his first three salvos as successively 'short, 'straddling' and 'over,' Müllenheim-Rechberg noted. 'An extremely promising start that I only knew about from what I heard on the telephone; the swinging back and forth of the *Bismarck* allowed me only intermittent glimpses of the enemy.'[416]

Dalrymple-Hamilton quickly reacted to the German fire. He had prepared a number of manoeuvres, which would make it more difficult for Schneider to aim his salvos, and they were now initiated. First he sheered to port, thus increasing the distance between the *Rodney* and *King George V*. At the same time, the fire controllers on the British battleship made a grave mistake when estimating the range to the *Bismarck*, forcing them to again begin firing spotting rounds.

Both sides fired ineffectively for a few minutes. Schneider's first salvos, which had been very close, could not be followed by further accurate fire, as the *Bismarck* moved erratically in the sea and made all gunnery calculations difficult. The machines making the ballistic computations needed data from the steering system, to compensate for the movements of the ship, but this did not work with the damaged rudder. The gunnery officers had to make improvised calculations to compensate for the ship's movements, but they could not be as accurate or as rapid as would have been the case with a properly working steering system. Also, the unpredictable movements compelled the gun turrets to traverse almost continually.

At this stage it was discovered why the gunnery radar on the *King George V* had not produced any reliable data. The radar operators had not taken account of the rapidly shrinking range. When the echo from the *Bismarck* was suddenly lost on the screen, they had continued to search at the range where she had previously been located. When six minutes had elapsed since the first shots were fired, they again saw an echo from the *Bismarck* on the screen. The range was estimated at 20,500 metres. A double salvo was fired with a 200-metre bracket. The fire was immediately on the mark and a hit in the *Bismarck's* forebody was noted.[417]

The *Rodney* too had found the range and the two battleships bombarded the enemy with four salvos per minute. The medium guns also joined in, as did the *Norfolk* with her 20.3cm guns. The German battleship disappeared amid the fountains of water. Tovey ordered a turn southward, to allow the *King George V* to fire full broadsides. The *Rodney* soon followed, but not before scoring a few hits that had a profound influence on the subsequent events.

On board the *Rodney*, Captain Donald Campbell had an excellent overview from the anti-aircraft directory. He saw how the shells rose, lingered at the top of their trajectory and then descended on the *Bismarck*. At the same time the enemy fired and for a fraction of a second, the trajectories met, allowing Campbell briefly to see them gathered slightly above the masts of the enemy ship. Soon three pillars of water rose from the sea around the *Bismarck*, which meant that two shells had found their target. One of them hit the central directory and probably killed Schneider and the men surrounding him. The other hit ahead and the turret Bruno was surrounded by fire and brown smoke.

Campbell was only partly aware of these hits, as his eyes followed the growing projectiles from the *Bismarck* as if he had been hypnotized. When they had passed the highest point of their trajectory and begun to fall, he could even see how the bronze surfaces glistened. The salvo seemed so well aimed that it could be on its way towards the tip of Campbell's nose. He could not suppress an instinctive reaction to duck, despite the fact that it would provide absolutely no protection. Pillars of water shot up on both sides of the *Rodney*; a perfectly aimed salvo, but the British battleship was lucky, none of the shells hit. A fist-sized splinter whizzed through Campbell's action station, destroyed a few vital components in the fire control system and finally came at rest on the floor. One of the seamen triumphantly lifted it up, but a second later he screamed from the pain as the white hot metal burned into his hand.[418]

This moment marked the beginning of the defeat of the *Bismarck* and her drawn out death struggle. During the following minutes, the fore fire control was also hit and both main turrets silenced. At this stage, the *Dorsetshire* had also closed the range, enabling her to open fire. Thus the *Bismarck* was pounded by two battleships and two heavy cruisers.

'It was hard work keeping those eight-inch guns roaring,' Walter Fudge recalled. He belonged to the artillery crews on the *Dorsetshire* and had a special relationship with the *Bismarck*. One morning during Fudge's earlier shore training in Plymouth, his group was ordered to draw up at the barracks square. Fudge and a few of his comrades had been late and ended up far down the line. An officer had counted off 24 men and told them to pack. They received orders to serve on the *Hood*. The others, including the late arrivals would serve on less important ships. Fudge had been number 26 and at the time he had been very disappointed. However, on the previous day, he was informed that the *Hood* had been sunk, with only three survivors. His relief of escaping such a fate was mixed with regret at the loss of his comrades. Now he was close enough for revenge. 'At one time our turret was firing twin eight-inch projectiles every eight seconds with no misfires,' he wrote. 'My own personal feelings were many and varied. The biggest thought was to do it to them or they will do it to us. Like others I was somewhat on edge waiting for the 'wipe out' to us which never came.'[419]

Shell after shell hit the *Bismarck*. Most of them hit in the forebody. In the aft fire control centre, Müllenheim-Rechberg was informed that contact with Schneider had been lost and the fore turrets had been silenced. It fell to him to direct the aft turrets. By this time the *King George V* and *Rodney* had completed their starboard turns, while the *Bismarck* had slightly turned to port. Thus, the ships passed each other on opposing courses. As the *King George V* was well ahead of the *Rodney*, and the latter ship was in a blind spot from Müllenheim-Rechberg's position, he had to shift fire to the *King George V*. His first salvo was slightly too far to the right of the British flagship. He corrected:

'Ten more left, down four, a salvo!'

'Middle over!'

'Down four, a salvo!'

'Middle short!'

'Up two, good rapid!'

The forth salvo was straddling, and Müllenheim-Rechberg had just ordered continuous fire with all guns when

> *My aft director gave a violent shudder, and my two petty officers and I had our heads bounced hard against the eyepieces. What did that? When I tried to get my target in view again, it wasn't there; all I could see was blue. I was looking at something one didn't normally see, the 'blue layer' baked on the surface of the lenses and mirrors to make the picture clearer. My director had been shattered. Damn! I had just found the range of my target and now I was out of the battle.*[420]

As his optical instrument was destroyed, there was little Müllenheim-Rechberg could do. The time was almost 09.15 hours and he ordered the aft turrets to fire individually. His men asked for permission to leave the battle station – as far as they knew orders to abandon the ship could already have been issued – but Müllenheim-Rechberg held them back. As long as British shells hit the ship they would be safer in the armoured turret than on deck.

The *King George V* had reached a position south of the *Bismarck* and the visibility was obstructed by smoke from her own weapons as well as by the cordite smoke clouds leaving the *Rodney's* guns, which formed a curtain between the *Bismarck* and the British flagship.

Dalrymple-Hamilton too had passed the enemy and even launched a torpedo salvo as he did so.[421] He clearly understood that the smoke would present a serious hindrance if he continued southward. Furthermore, the course would bring him to a position between the *King George V* and *Bismarck*. Instead of waiting for the flagship to turn 180 degrees, Dalrymple-Hamilton used the latitude given by Tovey. He turned starboard, bringing the *Rodney* away from the flagship's field of fire and onto a course parallel with the *Bismarck*. Soon the German battleship could be seen clearly from the *Rodney*. A few minutes later, the *King George V* too made a 180-degree turn, which resulted in the flagship getting into a position abaft of the *Bismarck* on her port side, while the *Rodney* was almost on her port beam.

At this stage of the battle, the thick layers of cloud began to break up. Blue patches appeared between white clouds. The colour of the sea, which had for so long reflected the thick cloud cover with its depressing grey hue, suddenly changed to dark green with the windswept wave crests glittering. The dark body of the *Bismarck*, swept in dark brown smoke, partly interrupted by yellow spots where fires raged, appeared in stark contrast to the white pillars of water indicating shells striking the water close to her.

The turret Dora struggled for another six minutes after her crew received the order to fire individually. Then there was a barrel explosion, which killed several men in the turret. At 09.25 hours the *Bismarck's* fore turrets fired another salvo, but they were to be the last shells that left the fore main guns. Turret Cesar continued firing during the following four minutes, whereupon her guns too were silenced. One of the last shells hit the water very close to the *Rodney's* forebody. The doors to the British battleship's torpedo battery were rendered inoperable and the crew manning this weapon had a severe shock. However, the British ships did not suffer any further damage. All shells that hit fell on the *Bismarck*. The barrels of turret Anton had come to rest on the gunwale and the rear part of turret Bruno was blown off. To British officers studying the *Bismarck* in their binoculars, the consequences of turret Dora's barrel explosion were clearly visible. The barrel was split open like a peeled banana. From the aircraft hangar, thick smoke belched out and the ship's list to port was obvious. In addition, it was clear that the central director was destroyed, that the fore-top had been shot into the sea and many of the fires raging inside the ship must have damaged or destroyed communications systems.[422] 'What that ship was like inside,' wrote George Whalley, a young officer on the destroyer *Tartar*, 'Did not bear thinking of; her guns smashed, the ship full of fire, her people hurt; and surely all men are much the same when hurt.'

Despite all this, some of the secondary guns still battled on and the black, white and red German naval ensign still streamed in the wind.

CHAPTER 28

The End

Despite the fact that all men on the *Bismarck* were within 250 metres of each other, their activities differed remarkably. Those who had their battle stations on or above the battery deck or in gun turrets fought for their lives. Many other men remained relatively inactive during the initial phase of the battle. Their normal duties included administrative matters, cooking, laundry and other non-combat activities. Many of them assisted as, for example, stretcher-bearers and medical orderlies, but others could shelter in safer areas of the ship. As Corporal Herzog was not needed at his anti-aircraft gun, he and a few of his comrades had been ordered to their mess at the aft battery deck. The continuous noise above was depressing, as was the knowledge of the outcome. Herzog went to his closet, where he allowed himself a few nips of liqueur. Then he lay down in his hammock and listened to the battle. It was not long before he felt drowsy. Vaguely he heard the loudspeakers announce that Lütjens and Lindemann had been killed in action. Somewhat later, it was denied that Lindemann had been killed. The message was followed by a loud crash not far away, soon accompanied by the screams of the wounded. All of this happened as Herzog was half sleeping in his hammock. The battle indeed appeared unreal.[423]

Down in the middle engine room, Lieutenant Commander Gerhard Junack heard the noises of battle diminish. He already knew what the *Bismarck's* weapons sounded like. He had heard them many times during the nine-day voyage. A new element was the distant noise and vibration of enemy projectiles hitting the ship. It soon became apparent that the battle was going badly for the *Bismarck*. Water began to trickle

273

down through ventilation shafts and through them the noise of shell splinters hitting metal could also be heard, sounding like a hailstorm hitting a tin roof.

In the damage-control centre, Commander Oels concluded that collecting information on damage and directing the damage-control parties was becoming pointless. The list, combined with the ship's rolling in the rough sea, at times placed the deck armour at an angle rendering it far less effective against the British shells. Perhaps the deck armour had been penetrated, allowing shells to reach the aft turbine room and the starboard boiler room. Explosions in that area, combined with the breakdown of communications to the bridge, may have convinced Oels to make a decision.[424] The battle was over and the *Bismarck* had lost. Two things remained: The *Bismarck* should not be allowed to fall into enemy hands and as many as possible of her crew had to be saved.

'Prepare the ship for scuttling,' he ordered, 'And ensure that the entire crew leaves her.' The order was disseminated to all compartments that could still be reached, whereupon Oels, Jahreis and the other men evacuated the damage-control centre. But when they left the cabin, Artificer Statz refused to follow them. He could hear the shells hitting the ship above them and firmly stuck to his previous decision not to leave the safety beneath the deck. That decision probably saved his life. Jahreis remained for a moments in the doorway, saluted and left Statz alone.

In the engine control station, Ordinary Seaman Herbert Blum watched as Chief engineer, Lehmann put the telephone down as 'carefully as if it was made of glass' and turned towards the men around him. 'We shall abandon the ship and sink her,' he said calmly with his usual, kind voice. 'I will forward the order. You may go now.'

It was the last time anybody saw Lehmann. Blum and his comrades left the engine control station. They intended to reach the battery deck and then continue to the main canteen. From there they could find a way to the shelter deck.

The British battleships reduced the range, reaching as close as 3,000 metres. The *Bismarck's* speed was reduced so much that the *Rodney* had to zigzag in order not to pass her. At such short range, the guns fired with the barrels trained more or less straight on the target. Tovey's tactic to close the range as quickly as possible had paid off. Considering the short range, the British expected to penetrate even the *Bismarck's* main belt armour and reach the vital engine rooms and the magazines, thus ensuring her rapid sinking. But the shells seem never to have reached these vital parts.[425]

The *Norfolk* and *Dorsetshire* had closed the range too, allowing them to fire several torpedoes. Still, the German battleship refused to sink. Tovey had already reached the limits of his fuel margins. He was also well aware that the Luftwaffe might intervene at any moment, and that perhaps German submarines might also be close by. 'Somebody get me my darts,' he exclaimed frustrated, 'let's see if we can sink her with those!'

In fact, Tovey could have spared himself the concern of sinking the burning enemy battleship. Slightly before 10.00 hours, the intercom telephone rang and Junack received the last order he ever received on board the *Bismarck*.[426] It was Oels' order to sink the ship that Lehmann passed on from the engine control station: 'Prepare her for scuttling.'

Junack ordered his men to place charges at the sea-intake valves and sent a few men to open the hatches at the shaft tunnels. He tried to reach Lehmann again, but this time the line was dead. Junack ordered a trusted officer to go to the engine control station to find out what had happened.

The destruction of the *Hood* had happened very quickly, with her crew of well over a thousand men losing their lives in an unbelievably short period of time. In contrast, the *Bismarck's* death struggle was long, as she continued to take hit after hit well after her crew had decided to scuttle her. Müllenheim-Rechberg had been correct when ordering his men to remain in the aft fire-control station. As long as the small turret did not receive a direct hit, they were safe from the splinters whizzing around outside. On the shelter deck, horrible scenes took place. As long as most men had been at their battle stations, with many well below the deck, they were fairly safe and casualties were limited. Once orders were issued to abandon the ship, the men moved up onto the open deck and many were simply slaughtered. Shells exploding on the ship's superstructures sent thousands of razor-sharp splinters over the deck. Some were so small that they did not cause more than superficial bleeding, other were large enough to cut off an arm or a leg. Some men were killed instantly. Blasts hurled men through the air, crushing them against walls, decks and gunwales or sent them over board. Many men fell onto the deck, tried to stand up despite being punch-drunk, only to be cut to pieces by splinters whizzing by.

The artificer Wilhelm Generotzky had just reached the upper deck, when he saw two Luftwaffe warrant officers who could not stand the thought of drowning. They shook hands, placed the muzzles of their pistols against their temples and made their small contribution to the blood bath taking place around them. 'If I had a gun,' he heard a warrant engineer next to him say, 'I would have done the same.'[427]

Shell hits from the British ships gradually turned the *Bismarck's* deck into something resembling a scrap yard. Hits higher up in the superstructures caused debris to fall down on the shelter deck. Headlights, davits and anti-aircraft guns were shot from their mounts, further increasing the shambles. In one of the secondary gun turrets, the crew had been trapped as a shell had destroyed the lock mechanism. Their screams were heard outside the turret, but all attempts to aid them were in vain. The damaged door could not be opened.

As casualties quickly mounted, the German doctors, medical orderlies and stretcher-bearers tried to help the wounded as much as possible. Debris on the deck severely hampered all movement and made the stretcher-bearer's work impossible. There was little the doctors could do, except aid a few of the wounded where they were found. However, the British shells could not see the difference between the doctors and combatants. The doctors worked until they too became casualties.

There was no longer any possibility of carrying out an orderly evacuation of the ship. Little more than scattered remnants remained of the *Bismarck's* boats. Men struggled to get the life boats and rubber rafts into the sea, but most of them had been damaged by the British gunfire and far too many were destroyed before they reached the water.

Corporal Georg Herzog, however, was lucky:

> I went down the ladder to the battery deck. I observed from here that comrades tossed inflatable boats over the side and jumped in after them. I personally, [along] with several comrades, tried to toss an inflatable boat overboard. But we did not succeed because a hit struck in our vicinity and splinter effects made the inflatable boat useless. I received a splinter (flesh wound in the calf of the

left leg). We then sought shelter behind turret 'D'. There was an inflatable boat behind turret 'D'. We untied this boat. Then we tossed the boat over the starboard side and jumped after it. I had luck on my side in immediately grabbing hold of the raft. Other comrades tried to swim to the raft. Only comrades Manthey and Höntzsch made it to the raft. All our efforts to fish out even more comrades were unsuccessful.[428]

Meanwhile, the men whose battle stations were located below sea level struggled to escape being trapped. Many of them never made it out, as routes were blocked by dented hatches, damaged bulkheads or destroyed ladders. Explosions and raging fires ravaged cabins and corridors. Gas from various burning materials was an invisible but deadly danger. On the battery deck, large groups of men were delayed beneath the shelter deck, as ladders could not carry more than a limited number of men. Panic rarely broke out, but while the men waited, they urged their comrades with shouts and curses. Oels and his company arrived at the main canteen and found almost three hundred men crammed next to a door leading aft. The hatch leading to the shelter deck was destroyed, blocking the exit and it was also impossible to move forward because of the raging fires. Evil-smelling, yellowish-green fumes filled the battery deck, causing the men who lacked gas masks to cough.

'Everybody must leave the ship!' Oels shouted. 'She will be sunk. You can not go ahead. It is all burning!'

These were his last words. A direct hit sent splinters raining through the compartment. Within a fraction of a second, the crammed room was turned into a slaughter house. More than a hundred men were mutilated or killed. Corporal Zimmermann had just arrived and saw how Oels and another officer were cut to pieces by the explosion.[429]

Ordinary Seaman Blum had reached the main canteen just before the shell exploded. The blast threw him down, but dazed he got on his feet again. Around him he saw fallen comrades and men with missing limbs tottering around. The blood floated around dead bodies, cut-off arms and legs and intestines, until it threatened to cover the entire floor. This nightmare, as close to a vision of hell as he could imagine, gave Blum strength. He climbed to the damaged hatch and managed to squeeze himself through the small opening and onto the shelter deck. The whistling and crashing from British shells replaced the sounds from the wounded.[430]

Corporal Zimmermann followed Blum. He too had managed to squeeze through the damaged hatch. 'I came out on the starboard side,' he recalled, 'and the first I saw was a heap of butchery. It was no longer possible to see what it had been. It was horrible.'[431]

During the *Bismarck*'s last moments, many painful farewells took place. Close friends were separated. Corporal Bruno Zickelbein was on the battery deck together with Seaman Hans Silberling, when the latter was ordered to report to the engine control station. The slightly older Silberling had been a kind of father figure to the 19 year old corporal and their friendship had been very strong. Silberling understood the implications of the order. He held out his hand to the corporal. 'This is the end,' he said. 'We will never see each other again. Give the people at home my kindest regards.' They shook hands; both men had tears in their eyes. Then Silberling disappeared and left Zickelbein alone.[432]

'When I came up into the open I saw things I never thought possible,' K-A Schuldt remembered. He had successfully struggled to reach the shelter deck. 'Everything was on fire; explosions could be heard or seen all over the ship. There were a hundred dead at least. Some without legs, arms, their heads.'

Schuldt ran across the officer in command of his station, sitting with his back against a wall. Both his legs had been shot off at the knees. He looked up at Schuldt and implored: 'Do you have a cigarette?'

Schuldt kneeled beside the officer. With trembling hands, he lit the cigarette. 'It was so sad I can hardly describe it,' he told. 'I gave him the cigarette and promised to take a message to his family if I myself was to survive.'[433]

Artificer Josef Statz had finally decided to abandon the ship, a decision strongly influenced by two of his comrades from the training period, Seifert and Moritz, who had appeared in the damage-control centre and urged him to follow. They made a demanding climb up the communications shaft, which was only 75cm wide and blocked with electrical cables that limited the space available to the crawling men. Finally they reached the mouth of the shaft, only to see that the fore fire control turret had been shot away. Statz found several of the men who had left the damage-control centre a few minutes before him. One of them was Lieutenant Jahreis, Müllenheim-Rechberg's friend. They were all dead.

At this moment, a shell struck not far away and threw the three men to the floor. A splinter hit Statz's shoulder, but he was not seriously wounded. Moritz seemed to be dead.

'Were you hit?' Statz heard a voice saying and discovered that Lieutenant Cardinal was on the bridge too, the same man that had claimed that the risk of a torpedo hit on the rudders was virtually nil. Statz had not seen him when emerging from the culvert. 'Just a minor bruise,' he said, 'but we must immediately get down on the deck.'

They were just about to leave the bridge they found that Moritz was still alive, but his chest had been split open by a splinter. Carefully they pulled the dying man into cover by the armoured gunwale. Statz had no idea how to help Moritz. He just rubbed Moritz's head, like a father trying to comfort his child. Moritz stared at Statz, forced a smile and said. 'Send my greetings to Cologne.' Shortly afterwards his eyes went glassy in death.[434]

Several shells hit alarmingly close. Seifert panicked. He tried to jump directly from the bridge into the water, but the distance was too great. He landed on some debris on the deck and was killed. However, Statz and Cardinal managed to reach the deck without further mishaps.

Below, in the engine room, Junack still waited impatiently for the messenger to return with the instructions for the demolition, but the minutes ticked away. Finally, Junack had to abandon any hopes that the messenger would come back. Either he was dead or something else had prevented him from returning. What should he do? The angle of the list increased. Thick smoke oozed forth from the boiler rooms, forcing the men to wear gas masks while working. Junack made the decision himself. He urged his men to discontinue their work and try to reach the deck. Then he instructed the Warrant Engineer to light the fuses. These two men were the last to leave the engine room.

At 10.15 hours, a shell fired by the *King George V* hit the base of the *Bismarck's* superstructure. It created a huge flame that swept all the way up to the bridge and set fire to a store of signal flares. They burst in a cascade of bright colours. On board the *Rodney*, Campbell saw how the a chain of explosions was set off throughout the enemy ship, throwing debris high up in the air and setting living as well as already dead men ablaze. He had already seen small groups of men jump into the sea and disappear. Now more and more men jumped overboard, trying to escape the hell on the *Bismarck*. 'Good God,' he exclaimed, loud enough for the men around him to hear. 'Why don't we stop?'

Almost simultaneously, the bells gave the signal for cease fire. Campbell looked at his watch. It showed 10.21 hours. He breathed a sigh of relief.

Tovey had decided that the *Bismarck* was so damaged that she would never again be of any use to the Germans, despite the fact that she still remained afloat. A German Condor reconnaissance aircraft had already been sighted and the British commander believed a Luftwaffe attack could occur at any moment. Also, he had to break off the action, or else the remaining fuel might not be sufficient to take his ships back to the British bases. He ordered that the other ships should follow the flagship, which surprised the commanders of the respective ships. Would the action be broken off while the *Bismarck* remained afloat? Somerville had finally launched a group of 12 Swordfish aircraft which soon reached the scene of battle, but stayed at a respectful distance. They could see innumerable men swimming in the water abaft the enemy ship. 'The gun duel between the ships was almost over,' one of the airmen recalled. He gazed at the scene from his observer seat. 'The *Bismarck* had turned to a smoking cauldron, rolling in the waves. She was still making headway with a few knots.'

The airmen saw the *Rodney* and *King George V* turn north and four minutes after Tovey had broken off the action, Somerville inquired what was going on. He was told that Tovey was low on fuel and returning to harbour. *Bismarck* was still afloat. The ships that had torpedoes left should try to sink her with those. 'Can't sink her with gunfire,' the Admiral concluded.

Only the *Dorsetshire* still had any torpedoes. Commander Martin had awaited the order to torpedo the burning wreck. He soon received it, from Wake-Walker on board the *Norfolk*. The *Dorsetshire* closed the range to the *Bismarck* to deliver the coup de grâce.[435]

In the starboard boiler room, Chief engine room artificer Schmidt reversed the pumps and opened all water-tight hatches nearby. He could hear Junack's charges detonating at the engine control station not far away. Obviously, he urgently had to reach the deck. A seaman arrived and shouted 'Everyone on deck!'

Meanwhile Junack and his subordinate worked their way upwards in the ship. As they passed the middle and upper platform decks, they expected to see frantic activity, but these spaces were deserted and the noise from the British firing had disappeared. 'The lower decks were brilliantly lit up,' he recalled, 'A peaceful mood prevailed, such as that of a Sunday afternoon in port, – the silence only broken by the explosions of our demolition-charges below.'[436]

The scenes became much worse when they reached battery deck, where most of the lights were out and groups of panic stricken men tried to find a way up through the smoke filled corridors. Junack was lucky. He encountered a group of seamen trying to get through a partially blocked hatch leading to the shelter deck. By persuading the men to take off their life vests, they managed to squeeze through the opening and one by one reach the deck.

At this stage, the ship was listing considerably, so much so that parts of the deck were below water. Men trying to leave the doomed ship crammed the deck. Junack could hear cries of distress, screams of pain, the sough from the flames and rumble from inrushing water, but for a moment was consumed by the irrelevant discovery that the cloud cover had broken up. He had not felt the sun on his face for many days.

Two powerful detonations rolled over the sea, as torpedoes from the *Dorsetshire* hit the doomed ship on the starboard side. These were followed by a third explosion on the port side a few minutes later. Junack joined a large group of people near the aft batteries. Several other officers were there too, among them Müllenheim-Rechberg, as well as hundreds of seamen and non-commissioned officers. Thick smoke obstructed visibility, but Junack could still see the ensign at the aft mast blowing in the wind.

Müllenheim-Rechberg ordered the men to inflate their life vests and prepare to jump into the sea. He and his men had remained in the fire control turret until the British fire ceased, but little time remained if they were not to sink with the ship. The list increased further. After a final salute to the ensign the men jumped into the sea.

Junack tried to instill some confidence into the men around him. 'Don't worry, comrades,' he shouted to them. 'I will be taking a Hamburg girl in my arms again!' Then they jumped into the cold water, but many did not jump far enough. The waves threw them back against the hull and knocked them unconscious.[437]

Junack never saw the fate of Lindemann, but some sailors in the water had a glimpse of two figures gradually working their way forward along the shelter deck. It was Lindemann, closely followed by his orderly. While the ship sank deeper and deeper, and the bow gradually raised, the Captain gesticulated to the younger man that he should save himself by jumping into the sea, but he refused and dutifully followed his commander. When both of them reached the stem, Lindemann stood at attention and moved his hand towards his white cap. The scene engraved itself on the memory of the men who witnessed it – 'as if taken from a book, but I saw it with my own eyes' – and then the ship rolled over and began to sink.[438]

Müllenheim-Rechberg swam until he was far enough from it not to be sucked down when it sank. He checked himself and turned around to see the *Bismarck* capsize:

> *The whole starboard side of her hull, all the way to the keel, was out of the water. I scrutinized it for signs of battle damage and was surprised to see no signs of any. Her port side had borne the brunt of the battle, and that side of her hull may have told a different story.*[439]

Before the eyes of the German seamen who had abandoned the ship, the *Bismarck* sank stern first. Small geysers of water pouring out left her hull and large bubbles of water developed in the oily water. A loud gurgling sound filled the air.

Then she was gone, as completely as if she had never existed. She took with her Lütjens, Lindemann, and perhaps as many as 1,400 seamen and officers, as well as all plans and dreams of successful cruiser warfare against British merchant shipping. No life remained on the *Bismarck* when she finally hit a volcano on the bottom of the ocean, almost five kilometres below the place where she had fought her last battle. She slid along the mountain slope before she settled in the sludge where she was to remain indefinitely.

For the men who had escaped sinking, another danger loomed large. The rough, cold and oily water was anything but benevolent. They struggled hard to keep their heads above the surface. The wounded suffered badly and their strength was rapidly sapped as they lost blood. The ice cold water first made their feet and hands numb, then legs and arms. Head after head disappeared below the waves, never to be seen again. Statz had jumped into the water together with Lieutenant Cardinal. For a moment they became separated, but somewhat later, Statz saw Cardinal again. However, the Lieutenant floated with his head at a strange angle, almost as if he was asleep. When the artificer swam closer, he realized Cardinal had shot himself in the head to avoid dying from drowning.

For a while, Statz believed he was the only one remaining, because he could not see any of his comrades in the waves. He tried to keep from swallowing the oily water and found some consolation in the fact that air contained by his leather jacket helped keeping him afloat. He wondered how many of the men had obeyed the general advice not to take off clothes before jumping into the water.

He did not know how long he had been swimming, when he saw the stem of a warship heading straight towards him. It was the cruiser *Dorsetshire* and behind her the destroyer *Maori* followed. They stopped, evidently to rescue survivors: A race against time began, as it was impossible to predict how long they would stay for fear of German submarines.

It took quite some time for the German seamen to swim near the cruiser, where the British crew had prepared scrambling nets, ropes and lifebuoys. Walter Fudge was one of the seamen who tried to help the distressed in the water. The *County*-class cruisers had a good reputation for stability, but only at speed. When immobile, they rolled violently. Merely to remain standing on the deck was very difficult and of course it was even more difficult to help the survivors in the water.

Fudge had been at his battle station, so he had not seen anything of the *Bismarck*. He was not permitted to go out on deck until the *Bismarck* had already sunk. However, when he saw hundreds of men swimming towards the *Dorsetshire*, a thought crossed his mind. 'It was only with the blessings of fate that it wasn't me there in the water, swimming for my life. In that moment I couldn't feel but pity for those men, and I can speak for the entire crew in saying we all felt the same. There was nothing of the usual 'you-shouldn't-have-messed-with-the-Royal-Navy'-attitude, only genuine compassion.'[440]

Seventeen-year-old George Bell, who served as Captain Martin's orderly, was of the same opinion. 'To be perfectly honest, there should have been a feeling of bitterness after the sinking of the *Hood*,' he recalled, 'but as soon as the rescue was begun, this was all forgotten. We were simply saving shipwrecked sailors.'[441]

Loops were tied at the lower end of the ropes and let down to the water to help the Germans. Some still had the strength to place the loop around their waist or feet, enabling the British to haul them on board. Others were exhausted by the swimming, their wounds and the cold water robbing them of energy. The reached the British cruiser in such dazed condition that they drowned, despite being able to touch the cruiser with numb fingers.

Müllenheim-Rechberg was among those who managed to reach the *Dorsetshire*. After several attempts, he grasped one of the ropes and put his foot into the loop. But he was so exhausted that he slid when he had reached the gunwale and fell back into the sea. By a stroke of fortune, he got hold of the same rope again and the same British seamen pulled him up once more. This time, Müllenheim-Rechberg did not try to get over the gunwale by himself. Rather he allowed himself to be dragged onto the deck. His immediate instinct was to assist the British seamen working to save the survivors, but he was quickly brought below deck.

Statz too was hauled on board. When he glanced at the water, he realized how many of his comrades had actually been swimming out there, not far from him. If Cardinal had not shot himself, he thought as a British seaman showed him where to go, he too would have been saved.

Generotzky had made several attempts to get hold of the ropes hanging down from the *Dorsetshire*, but every time the ship rolled and his hands had to carry all his body weight, he lost the grip and fell back into the sea. In the tumult someone stepped on his head and pushed him down, below the surface of the sea. A surge threw him onto the hull of the *Dorsetshire* and his leg was injured by the impact. Generotzky almost gave in, but when he saw that the British lowered further ropes abaft, he swam to them and grasped a rope with a loop. He managed to attach it and was pulled on board by two British seamen.

By then, about 80 German seamen had been hauled up on the *Dorsetshire*, among them Müllenheim-Rechberg, Junack, Schmidt, Blum, Statz and Generotzky, but hundreds still waited when the navigation officer on the *Dorsetshire* suddenly saw a small smoke puff emerge from the water about two nautical miles from the cruiser, on her starboard side. He immediately notified Captain Martin. After briefly considering the observation, it was agreed that the smoke probably came from a submarine. Although all the officers on the bridge were unanimous, it was Martin who had to take responsibility for the terrible decision. While the survivors near the hull of the British cruiser screamed loud enough to be heard on the bridge, and the officers around Martin watched their commander, he hesitated briefly. He weighed the risk of his ship being torpedoed against the knowledge that hundreds of seamen would drown. He had to give the highest priority to the security of his own ship. 'We have no choice,' he said to the officer on duty: 'Full speed ahead.'

The engine-room telegraph rang, the ship began to vibrate and the Germans in the sea saw how the water began to bubble as the propellers began to revolve. Terrified they raised their arms to the seamen working at the gunwale, shouted and pleaded to the men who a few hours earlier had been their enemies not to abandon them. British seamen beneath the deck could hear dull thuds as the Germans struck the hull with their fists. When the *Dorsetshire* gained speed, some of the Germans clung to the ropes, until their frozen hands were no longer capable of maintaining the grip. A few more Germans, who already were on the nets or about to be pulled up in the ropes, were saved, one of them after a British seaman climbed down the side of the hull and helped the exhausted man over the gunwale. Almost all the rest were lost.

In the cabin he had been taken to, the exhausted Müllenheim-Rechberg was exchanging his soaked clothes for the British clothes he had received, when he felt the vibrations from machines picking up speed and realized what was about to happen. He understood that the ship was about to sail, but could not understand why, as so many men remained in the water. He was quite convinced that no submarines were in the area and he ought to have heard the air raid alarm if Luftwaffe units closed in. 'I racked my brain,' he recalled, 'but the only thing that registered was horror that our men in the water, hundreds of them, before whose eyes the *Dorsetshire* was moving away, were being sentenced to death just when safety seemed within reach. My God, what a narrow escape I had.'[442]

'This dreadful situation,' Walter Fudge said, 'wasn't any fault of ours; neither was it the Germans.' It was the war![443]

CHAPTER 29

Epilogue

When the *Dorsetshire* and *Maori* sailed away from the scene where the *Bismarck* had fought her last battle, little remained as evidence of the drama that had taken place a few hours earlier. The manoeuvring warships had disappeared and the wind had swept away the cordite smoke from the guns. There was no noise of battle or alarms. Only the gently whistling wind and the splashing waves could be heard.

This was the sight that met Lieutenant Kentrat, commander of *U-74*, when his submarine approached to search for survivors from the *Bismarck*. After a while, he distantly saw a British cruiser and two destroyers, but aside from the enemy ships he did not see anything and soon the enemy warships had disappeared too. He searched all day long without any success and not until dusk was a raft with three German corporals found. It was Manthey, Herzog and Höntzsch. The three shipwrecked men were brought on board the *U-74* where they received blankets and food.[444] Kentrat continued to search for two more days, but he did not encounter any survivors.[445]

Another two men had survived on a raft of the same type as had saved Herzog and the other two. There had been more men on the raft, but one by one they lost consciousness after accidentally swallowing water polluted with oil, or were swept away by violent waves. Soon only five remained. They had seen the warships retire in the remote distance. Then they were alone. A German reconnaissance aircraft had flown over them at low altitude, made a turn and flown back in the opposite direction. The men on the raft did not know if they had been observed.

'I drifted with five men for about 2 more hours,' Corporal Otto Maus recalled. 'The air and the water appeared warm to us. In my estimation the raft capsized about 17.00 hours. Two comrades and I – Lorenzen and one from the prize crew command – managed to reach the raft again, while the others, a machinist corporal and a staff headquarters' corporal, both drowned.'[446]

As the darkness had arrived, Maus fell asleep briefly. When he woke up, he saw a man from one of the prize crews lying in a strange angle at the edge of the raft. He had drowned. Together with Lorenzen, Maus removed the life vest from the dead man and then let him disappear in the ocean. The raft was equipped with a signal pistol and they fired several flares, but it was all in vain. The dawn broke with slightly calmer weather, but no ship was to be seen. While the thirst and hunger grew, and the sunshine on their salt covered faces and hands made them sore, the day passed without any relief. When darkness again fell, they were convinced that no help would ever appear. But the end of their hardships was in fact near.

'Look!' Maus shouted and stirred up the dozing Lorenzen. 'A steamer!'

'My comrade woke me up with the scream,' Lorenzen recalled. He, too, could make out the ship against the dark horizon. 'The steamer instantly veered toward us.'[447]

When the German weather observation ship *Sachsenwald* arrived, she searched fruitlessly for more than a day, but all that was observed was a large patch of oil, wood debris, cloth and a few life belts, with dead bodies. At dusk on the second day, little hope of finding any survivors remained, but the flare fired by Maus and Lorenzen was seen from the bridge. The commander on board the *Sachsenwald* studied the light in his binoculars and found a raft with two men. He turned towards them and when the ship was close enough, a call was heard from the survivors: 'Are you Germans?'

'Yes,' the commander replied and was rewarded with weak cheers from the raft. Maus and Lorenzen were hauled on board the *Sachsenwald*, where they received food and drink, whereupon they fell into deep sleep. The weather ship searched all night and well into the following day. Thereafter it had to set course for a port, as virtually all the food had been consumed.[448] Maus and Lorenzen were the last survivors from the *Bismarck* to be found.

In London, Winston Churchill had just concluded a cabinet meeting and proceeded to the House of Commons with disappointing news. The battle at Crete developed in a very unsatisfactory way. A defeat and evacuation was only a matter of days away. When he addressed the assembly, he admitted that the intelligence from Crete spoke of a precarious situation. From Iraq and Libya too, discouraging reports had been received, although perhaps not fully as gloomy as the information from Crete. In order to alleviate the effect of this bad news, he reported optimistically on the signals from the Home Fleet. It was expected that the German battleship which had sunk the *Hood* might soon be destroyed. He had just finished his speech, when a secretary arrived with an urgent telegram. It was given to Churchill's Parliamentary Private Secretary, who immediately handed it over to the Prime Minister. The telegram could not have arrived at a better moment, even if Churchill had scripted the event himself.

'I crave your indulgence, Mr. Speaker,' he said as he rose from the bench, 'I have just received news that the *Bismarck* has been sunk' [449]

The House of Commons cheered and for a moment Crete, North Africa and the Middle East were forgotten. A day of defeat had been turned into a day of victory.

At King's Cross railway station in London, Ted Briggs said farewell to Bill Dundas and Bob Tilburn and climbed on board the train to his home in St. Panras, Derby. After arriving at Scotland in the *Royal Ulsterman*, they had first made a report to the Admiralty, whereupon they were allowed to go home while waiting for the Admiralty's investigation into the loss of the *Hood*. As long as the three comrades had been together, Briggs managed to maintain the façade of being a thick-skinned veteran, deceiving both himself and the others. But now, alone on the train, his nerve-racking experience caught up with him. Why had he survived when so many had died?

His mother had been informed that he would arrive and she of course went to meet him at the station. When the sinking of the *Hood* was reported by the BBC on 24 May, she had become one of thousands of parents, wives and relative who waited in dread for the confirmation that their relative had died, but merely an hour later she was reached by a telegram, saying that her son was alive, one of only three survivors. When she saw him step down from the train, the lingering doubts disappeared. Without uttering a word, she embraced him and then took him to a cab, bringing them both home to Nuns Street.

As Briggs sat next to his mother in the taxi and mechanically answered questions regarding how he felt, if he was hungry, or if he knew how long he could stay at home, the mental barriers that had sustained him this far began to crumble. When they exited the cab outside their home he burst into tears and began to shake and ramble incoherently. His mother would need almost a week to get him back into his old habits again.[450]

But the threat from the *Bismarck* was gone. For the ordinary person in Britain, the news probably rarely provoked little more than a quiet sigh of relief. The loss of the *Hood* had raised some alarming questions: was the Royal Navy no longer capable of fulfilling its duty to protect the British Isles from enemies on the continent? Now the misgivings vanished. The Royal Navy had won.

However, the final victory did not relieve Tovey, Wake-Walker and the other top ranking officers. As they were well aware of what had taken place during the operation, they clearly knew how close it had been. The same insecurity was most likely felt within the Admiralty. A sober analysis of the past days' events clearly showed that it was not only the actions, decisions and strength of the Royal Navy that resulted in the destruction of the *Bismarck*. Sheer luck also played a prominent part, as fortune favoured first the Germans, then the British.

However, susceptibility to chance was but one of the defects inherent in the idea of cruiser warfare. Since the beginning of the war, the results were meagre. Up until 31 December 1940, the Germans had sunk 4.5 million tons of merchant shipping. Submarines accounted for 57% of the sinkings, while the surface ships only contributed 12%. Air power was responsible for 13% and mines no less than 17%.[451] Of these weapons, clearly the surface ships had contributed least. Results hardly improved significantly during the first half of 1941. Despite their two-month voyage, the *Gneisenau* and *Scharnhorst* only sank or captured 22 ships with a combined capacity of 115,600 tons. Altogether, the large warships only sank 188,000 tons during the first six months of 1941.[452] As a comparison, German submarines and

airpower sent 575,000 tons to the bottom of the ocean in a single
month, April 1941. Even the German auxiliary cruisers, which were
much cheaper vessels compared to the large warships, inflicted losses of
191,000 tons during the first half of 1941.[453] A very dramatic
improvement was needed if the German surface ships were to have a
significant effect on the British war effort, but it appears wholly
implausible that they could have achieved such a success. With
hindsight, we know that the efforts of the German submarines, despite
their much greater success, were far from sufficient to bring Britain to
her knees.[454] The surface ships were even less likely to achieve such a
result.

Why were the cruisers so unsuccessful? Often, the German ships
were more powerful than their British counterparts, in speed as well as
endurance, which were crucial factors in the kind of warfare implicated
by the cruiser warfare strategy. The presence of fuel supply ships in the
Atlantic added to the German advantage.[455] The principle of caution
emphasized by Lütjens seems to have been wise, not least when
considering the events during the second half of May 1941. It is difficult
to see what else the Germans could have done to improve their chances.
That being the case, it seems that the strategy itself was flawed.

During World War II, German submarines sank an impressive total
of 14 million tons of merchant shipping. Such losses periodically
limited the flow of British imports, but did not curtail them entirely.
United States merchant ship more than offset the losses. Furthermore,
the losses inflicted by German submarines were diluted in a very large
merchant navy. At most, during a single month the Germans managed
to sink 10% of the commodities imported to the British Isles.[456] Even
if the Germans had managed to sustain that rate for several months, it
would have been insufficient to cause severe shortage. Again it must be
emphasized that the submarines were responsible for the vast majority
of the losses – German surface ships played a minor part in these
results. Hence, it seems clear that the Germans would have benefited
more from reducing the production of battleships and cruisers and
using the production capacity to build submarines. In fairness, it must
be admitted that the Germans had already began such a process well
before the *Bismarck* and *Prinz Eugen* left Gdynia. But battleships
carried more prestige than submarines and weapons that appear to
have political value in peacetime may prove less useful in war. The

German shift of priorities from surface ships to submarines was made after the war had began in 1939, but it would require some years before it had any significant impact.

The Germans seem to have nurtured hopes that a kind of 'system collapse' could be generated by their attacks on the British maritime trade but there is little evidence to support this belief.[457] The notion of the enemy as beholden to a fragile system, which will fall apart if a small but well aimed disturbance n is induced, was not confined to the German Navy. One of the best known examples is the U.S. Army air force, which developed the 'industrial web' theory in the interwar period. The theory postulated that the enemy economy could be ruptured by well-aimed attacks on certain nodes in the system. The concept did not prove successful during World War II, but the idea of the enemy as a fragile system has not been abandoned since World War II ended.

Possibly, the notion of a brittle system, which will collapse if it receives small but well-aimed damage, is alluring as it promises great results for little cost and effort. Perhaps the military was particularly susceptible to such ideas in the interwar period, when the horrendous memories of the costly battles of attrition during World War I were still vivid. Unfortunately 'system collapses' have been easier to envisage than realize. The leading officers of the German Navy were certainly misled by the idea, but it also served their purpose of providing them with a role and a strategy that could justify the navy's share of the defence budget and ensure their participation in a future war. Even though the British Navy had an overwhelming superiority in overall numbers, its many commitments would prevent it from using all its resources to engage German vessels, which according to Raeder's hopes could use the opportunity to strike against merchant shipping. However, in a critical situation, the British would have given priority to the protection of imports, not to the Mediterranean, the Indian Ocean or the Far East.

The difficulty of finding convoys is one of the major reasons why the cruiser warfare strategy failed. Unless a large number of ships was available to cover vast areas of the Atlantic, it was inevitable that the convoys would escape detection. Unfortunately, the German Navy had limited shipbuilding capacity, part of which also had to be used to repair ships returning from operations. Furthermore, the numerical inferiority was the very reason the Germans settled for attacking convoys. Had the German Navy possessed considerably more ships, it could have challenged British maritime superiority directly. Operation Berlin clearly showed how difficult it could be to find convoys and without finding them frequently enough, the Germans could never sink merchant ships at a rate sufficiently high to jeopardize the British imports. In a sense, the German concept had an inherent dichotomy: if both sides' search capabilities were low, the Germans would not sink enough merchant ships; but if both sides had good search capacity, the British would find the German raiders and eventually sink them. Thus, in order for the strategy to be effective the German ships had to radically improve their search capabilities, while the British made no progress at all. However, all trends pointed in the opposite direction.

Construction of the first German aircraft carrier, *Graf Zeppelin*, had been initiated in December 1936. Possession of such ships would have improved the German's capacity to search at sea, but Grand Admiral Raeder discontinued the project in April 1940, as it was estimated that the carrier would not be operational until the end of 1941.[458] The decision was probably correct. Several other German warship projects, which were also estimated to be completed too late, were discontinued. Simultaneously, the enemy improved his search capacity.

Possibly, one chance for the Germans to challenge British sea power may have existed. If the Kriegsmarine had waited until the *Tirpitz* was ready, and sent a combined force consisting of the *Bismarck*, *Tirpitz*, *Scharnhorst* and *Gneisenau*, it would have placed the Royal Navy in a very difficult position. As the Home Fleet did not possess an abundant number of battleships – the *Royal Navy* was committed to many parts of the world – a challenge like this would have been very troublesome for Tovey. During Operation Rheinübung he had been able to create two task forces, each with one battlecruiser and one battleship. However, considering the superior firepower and protection of the *Bismarck* and *Tirpitz*, it would have been very risky to send, for example, the *Hood* and *Prince of Wales* into battle against a German force of four capital ships. If Tovey had chosen to keep his four capital ships together, he would have narrowed the odds, but it is far from certain that such a force would have been equal to the four German ships. Considering the inferior protection of the British ships, the teething problems in the artillery of the *King George V* and *Prince of Wales* and the better fire control systems on the German ships, Tovey could very well have been at a disadvantage in such a battle. Furthermore, it would have been difficult for him to force the Germans to battle, if he kept all his capital ships together. Lütjens would have been allowed greater freedom to choose when and where to attack.

An operation comprising many German battleships was exactly what Lütjens advocated, but Admiral Raeder pushed for the curtailed Operation Rheinübung. Most likely, Raeder believed the risks were small. Consequently, according to his line of thinking, there was no need to wait for more battleships to be ready. The kind of operation preferred by Lütjens could have been conducted after Operation Rheinübung. There was some merit to Raeder's judgment. After all, the Germans had conducted several raids in the Atlantic since the war broke out and the only loss was the *Admiral Graf Spee*. Considering the speed and combat power of the *Bismarck*, Raeder found little reason to think that the outcome would be worse this time.

Obviously the sinking of the *Bismarck* meant that a very valuable ship had been lost, thus reducing the resources available to conduct cruiser warfare. The loss in itself could however be attributed to bad luck and mistakes in the initial phase of the operation, rather than shortcomings inherent in the concept. But the fundamental flaws in the concept remained, although perhaps Raeder did not see them. As already emphasized, the difficulty of finding convoys was a fundamental weakness, which prevented the Germans from sinking merchant ships at a rate sufficiently high to undermine the British war effort. This problem was in itself of decisive importance, but during the spring and summer of 1941 further difficulties loomed large. One of them was the radar on the British ships. It clearly reduced the chances of German ships reaching the Atlantic undetected. Aided by the radar, the Home Fleet might well close the Denmark Strait and the waters between Iceland and the Faeroes to German warships. With the radar on board the *Suffolk*, the British had caught up with the German lead in radar development. Her radar was approximately as good as the German EM II, perhaps slightly better. Several notes on the effectiveness of radar can be found in the *Gneisenau's* war diary for Operation Berlin. The Germans can hardly have been surprised by the British development of radar. The discussions during the planning of

Operation Rheinübung clearly show that the Germans did suspect the British might soon equip their ships with radar.

Grave as this was to the German plans, another circumstance, the British capture of *U-110*, was equally compromising. Soon after Operation Rheinübung, the British cracked the Enigma code used by the German Navy. This enabled the Royal Navy to track down the tankers and supply ships stationed on the Atlantic by the Germans. In order to deceive the enemy into thinking that their code was still secure, the Royal Navy decided to sink or capture only six of the eight ships at sea. However, by an unfortunate coincidence, the remaining two ships were accidentally encountered on 4 June by British warships.[459] Nevertheless, the Germans remained confident in the Enigma code. The Germans had been able to read British encrypted messages for years, but rarely had the weapons to take advantage of the information. The British, on the other hand, did not suffer from such limitations and the Royal Navy could use the Ultra intelligence to its advantage. With the loss of the tankers and supply ships, the Germans could not conduct operations in the Atlantic. It was a very severe blow to the German Navy, but, ironically, it was caused by perhaps the only problem they could have done something about had they known what had happened to their crypto systems.

To the German public the loss of the *Bismarck* was a national defeat, just as the loss of the *Hood* had been to the British. While the German people anxiously waited for the list of survivors to be revealed, letters and postcards from Adalbert Schneider and other men who had served on the *Bismarck* arrived, delayed greetings from men already dead. On 7 June the British Admiralty announced the names of those Germans who had been saved by the *Dorsetshire* and *Maori*. The Germans published the names of the five men saved by the *Sachsenwald* and *U-74*. The grim facts of the tragedy became evident. The *Bismarck* was gone, with almost her entire crew.

Early in June 1941, Raeder had a troublesome meeting with Hitler. The loss of the *Bismarck* had made the Führer dejected and irritable. The loss of the battleship was a major blow to German prestige, according to him, and the overall operation had been unsuccessful. The *Bismarck* was gone and the *Prinz Eugen* had put in at Brest on 1 June for maintenance. Of course, Hitler wanted to investigate the reasons for the failure. Raeder began with a few remarks and reminded Hitler that the Kriegsmarine had been allotted insufficient means, forcing him to take on the Royal Navy crippled from the outset. This disadvantage had not been made good, rather it had been aggravated as further British carriers and battleships were commissioned.

Hitler already knew all this and needed no lesson in history. 'Why did the *Bismarck* not return to Germany after sinking the *Hood*?' he asked instead.

Raeder argued that it would have been much more dangerous to return through the Denmark Strait, under threat of air attack and lighter vessels, than continue towards the Atlantic and turn towards St. Nazaire. Evidently, this had been Lütjens' intention and he had initially endeavoured to attract the enemy towards the planned submarine trap. He had to abandon the idea when it became evident that insufficient fuel oil was available to allow the wider route. 'Neither was the proposal from Marinegruppe West,' Raeder concluded, 'that the *Bismarck* would remain hidden for a few days, feasible anymore.'

'And the *Prince of Wales*,' Hitler said. 'Why did not Lütjens continue the action until this ship too had been sunk?'

To this question, the Grand Admiral replied that Lütjens' instructions told him to avoid engagements with enemy capital ships and to focus on sinking merchant ships. Taking on the *Prince of Wales* would have resulted in the *Bismarck* suffering further damage, which could not be justified considering the main aim of the operation. The fact that it subsequently became clear that the *Bismarck* had been damaged did not alter the soundness of the decision.

Hitler does not seem to have pressed Raeder too hard on the issue. His understanding of naval strategy was, as he himself admitted, quite limited and his interest in such matters remained low. Within a few weeks, he was to embark on his greatest project and there was no role for battleships, submarines or torpedo aircraft in it.

The role of the German surface fleet would soon be revised, a fact that did not escape the captured Lieutenant Commander Müllenheim-Rechberg. From the third storey in the building housing the 'Combined Services Detailed Interrogation Centre' in northern London, he could see the lawns, groves and the pond in Trent Park. The impression was so restful that he could have forgotten the war raging – but when he turned his head and looked to the southeast, the barrage balloons betrayed that Europe was still at war. After leaving the *Dorsetshire*, whose crew had treated him well, Müllenheim-Rechberg, like the other POW's from the *Bismarck*, had been transferred to the British Army. Finally he was moved to his present location, an interrogation centre known as Cockfosters.

As he spent long periods alone in his cell, Müllenheim-Rechberg had plenty of time to think about his time on board the *Bismarck* in port; the break-out; the battle in the Denmark Strait; and finally the terrible battle so few of his friends survived. Why had they failed? Had their voyage been of any service to the fatherland, and could the sacrifice of more than 2,000 German seamen during the operation ever be justified? Only one thing was abundantly clear to the young officer: he would have plenty of time to ruminate on these issues.

One of the British officers interrogating Müllenheim-Rechberg was Lieutenant Commander Ralph Izzard, previously correspondent for the *Daily Mail* in Berlin before the war broke out. Izzard first showed up in Müllenheim-Rechberg's cell in June, at about the same time as Raeder met Hitler. Despite being enemies, Izzard and the captured German officer got on well. As Izzard did not glean much information from Müllenheim-Rechberg, their conversations became numerous and often quite long. Müllenheim-Rechberg appreciated the talks, which broke the monotony of prison life and Izzard visited Müllenheim-Rechberg on different occasions on various days, sometimes even during the nocturnal air raids conducted by the Luftwaffe. He wanted to see how the prisoner reacted to the bombing attacks by his own countrymen. Together the two men listened silently to the noise from the distant bombs and anti-aircraft weapons.

One morning when Izzard entered the cell, Müllenheim-Rechberg immediately noted that something special had happened. 'Well, do you know,' the Englishman asked, 'that you're at war with Russia now?'

Müllenheim-Rechberg felt absolutely stupefied and at first did not know how to respond. He did not for a second believe that any scruples would prevent Hitler from breaking a non-aggression pact, but the sheer magnitude of the news was horrifying. A two-front war with all its consequences? 'No,' he finally uttered, 'How would I know?'

'Yes,' Izzard went on. 'Today Goebbels had to get up very early again and tell the German people that the Russians are still utter swine!'

Notes

[1] The consequences became painfully clear to Müllenheim-Rechberg: it would be a long war, and for him personally, it meant a very long imprisonment. Hitler's attack on the Soviet Union also had a profound and immediate effect on the German Navy. From this point, Germany's war would be predominantly a land war, in which the Navy and Air Force would increasingly become secondary to the Army. The era of large battleships was over.

[2] *Kriegstagebuch* ('war diary,' hereafter KTB) *Prinz Eugen*, 23 May 1941.

[3] Also, see S.W Roskill, *The War at Sea* (London: HMSO, 1954).

[4] Tim Clayton and Phil Craig, *Finest Hour* (London: Hodder & Stoughton, 1999), p. 70.

[5] G. Bidlingmeyer, *Einsatz der schweren Kriegsmarineeinheiten im ozeanischen Zufuhrkrieg* (Neckargemünd: Scharnhorst Buchkameradschaft, 1963), pp. 81-82.

[6] Actually, the *Deutschland* had already slipped by, but the British remained unaware that she was already close to German ports. See Roskill, *War at Sea*, p. 82, Bidlingmeyer, *Einsatz der schweren Kriegsmarineeinheiten*, pp. 64-66 and 82-85.

[7] Stephen Cashmore and David Bews, 'Against All Odds – HMS *Rawalpindi*,' Highland Archives, http://www.iprom.co.uk/archives/caithness/rawalpindi.htm...

[8] Bidlingmeyer, *Einsatz der schweren Kriegsmarineeinheiten*, pp. 83-87.

[9] U. Elfrath and B. Herzog, *Schlachtschiff Bismarck– technische Daten, Ausrüstung, Bewaffnung, panzerung, kampf und Untergang* (Freidberg: Podzun-Pallas, 1982), p. 6. Note that we have not used the percentages directly, as the overall weight is calculated differently for the British ships. To obtain comparable figures, we have calculated with an overall weight of 41,700 tons.

[10] V. E. Tarrant, *King George V Class Battleships* (London: Arms and Armour, 1999), p. 30.

[11] J. Brennecke, *Schlachtschiff Bismarck* (Munich: Kohlers, 1960), p. 115.

[12] Brennecke, *Schlachtschiff Bismarck*, pp. 97-98.

[13] As it is not possible to directly measure the power output of such machines, it is not surprising that different figures circulate. Figures are rather based on calculations of

steam pressure, speed attained and various other factors.

[14] Brennecke, *Schlachtschiff Bismarck*, p. 85.

[15] To penetrate armour, the bomb must not only be heavy, it must also strike at sufficiently high velocity, which was attained by dropping it from high altitude. However, the drawback was reduced accuracy.

[16] Tarrant, King George V *Class Battleships*, pp. 25 & 30; H.T. Lenton and J. J. Colledge, *Warships of WWII* (London: Ian Allan, 1980), pp. 18-21.

[17] Brennecke, *Schlachtschiff* Bismarck, p. 116

[18] Müllenheim-Rechberg, *Schlachtschiff* Bismarck, pp. 36-41.

[19] Although the British ships were fairly similar, as a consequence of the strategic situation, they were used differently.

[20] Bidlingmeyer, *Einsatz der schweren Kriegsmarineeinheiten*, pp. 124-126.

[21] Bidlingmeyer, *Einsatz der schweren Kriegsmarineeinheiten*, pp. 126-130; Roskill, *War at Sea*, pp. 288-290.

[22] Bidlingmeyer, *Einsatz der schweren Kriegsmarineeinheiten*, pp. 130-134, 146-147.

[23] Bidlingmeyer, *Einsatz der schweren Kriegsmarineeinheiten*, pp. 134-146.

[24] *Fuehrer Conferences on Naval Affairs 1939–1945* (London: Greenhill, 1990), p. 163.

[25] Bidlingmeyer, *Einsatz der schweren Kriegsmarineeinheiten*, pp. 146-148.

[26] Bidlingmeyer, *Einsatz der schweren Kriegsmarineeinheiten*, pp. 148-156.

[27] For details, see Anlage 1 zu flotte GKdos 50/40 A1, 'Allgemeiner Befehl für die Atlantikunternehmung,' Bundesarchiv-Militärarchiv, Freiburg (hereafter referred to as BA-MA) RM 92/5246.

[28] G. Rhys-Jones, *The Loss of the* Bismarck (London: Cassell, 1999), pp. 33f.

[29] Rhys-Jones, *The Loss of the* Bismarck, pp. 33f.

[30] KTB *Gneisenau*, pp. 11-12.

[31] KTB *Gneisenau*, pp. 11-12.

[32] The instructions for the communications were given in the document Flottenkommando B.Nr. 10/41 Chefs, 12. Januar 1941, 'Nachrichtenanordnungen des Flottenkommandos für das Unternehmen Berlin,' BA-MA RM 92/5246.

[33] The operations order is available as an annex to the *Gneisenau*'s war diary; see KTB *Gneisenau*, 2. January – 22. März 1941, p. 11.

[34] Müllenheim-Rechberg, *Schlachtschiff* Bismarck, p. 49.

[35] Müllenheim-Rechberg, *Schlachtschiff* Bismarck, p. 49.

[36] Slightly different figures can be found, probably as 'too poor accuracy' is partly a matter of judgement.

[37] Müllenheim-Rechberg, *Schlachtschiff* Bismarck, p. 54; Elfrath and Herzog, *Schlachtschiff* Bismarck – *technische Daten*, pp. 18-22.

[38] Brennecke, *Schlachtschiff* Bismarck, p. 176.

[39] Müllenheim-Rechberg, *Schlachtschiff* Bismarck, pp. 50-51.

[40] Müllenheim-Rechberg, *Schlachtschiff* Bismarck, pp. 219f.

[41] Robert C. Stern, *Battle beneath the Waves: Uboats at War* (London: Cassell, 1999), pp. 95-96.

[42] Müllenheim-Rechberg, *Schlachtschiff* Bismarck, pp. 208-213.

[43] KTB *Gneisenau*, 22–23 January 1941.

[44] KTB *Gneisenau*, 24 January 1941; Rhys-Jones, *The Loss of the* Bismarck, p. 35.

[45] Rhys-Jones, *The Loss of the* Bismarck, p. 35.

[46] KTB *Gneisenau*, 25–27 January 1941; Flottenkommando B.Nr. GKdos 50/41, 21. Januar 1941, p. 3, BA-MA RM 92/5246.

[47] KTB *Gneisenau*, 25–27 Janaury 1941; Flottenkommando B.Nr. GKdos 50/41, 21. Januar 1941, p. 3, BA-MA RM 92/5246.

[48] Rhys-Jones, *The Loss of the* Bismarck, pp. 36-37.

[49] KTB *Gneisenau*, 27–28 January 1941.

[50] KTB *Gneisenau*, 28 January 1941.

[51] KTB *Gneisenau*, 28 January 1941.

[52] KTB *Gneisenau*, 28 January 1941, also, see the war diary of the machine room, 'Flottenkommando B.Nr. GKdos 50/41, 21. Januar 1941, BA-MA RM 92/5246,' p. 41.

[53] KTB *Gneisenau*, 28 January 1941, also, see the war diary of the machine room, 'Flottenkommando B.Nr. GKdos 50/41, 21. Januar 1941, BA-MA RM 92/5246,' p. 41.

[54] Rhys-Jones, *The Loss of the* Bismarck, pp. 37-38.

[55] KTB *Gneisenau*, 28 January 1941.

[56] Roskill, *War at Sea*, p. 373.

[57] Roskill, *War at Sea*, p. 373; Rhys-Jones, *Loss of the* Bismarck, pp. 38-39.

[58] Rhys-Jones, *Loss of the* Bismarck, pp. 40 and 43.

[59] KTB *Gneisenau*, 28 January – 1 Februaury 1941.

[60] Rhys-Jones, *Loss of the* Bismarck, pp. 40-41.

[61] Bidlingmeyer, *Einsatz der schweren Kriegsmarineeinheiten*, p. 165.

[62] KTB *Gneisenau*, 3–4 February 1941.

[63] KTB *Gneisenau*, 3–4 February 1941; Rhys-Jones, *Loss of the* Bismarck, pp. 43-44. Note that Rhys-Jones has given ranges that are not supported by the *Gneisenau*'s war diary. Probably Rhys-Jones has mixed up angles with ranges, which were given in a somewhat unusual way by the Germans.

[64] KTB *Gneisenau*, 4–5 February 1941.

[65] KTB *Gneisenau*, 4–6 February 1941; Rhys-Jones, *Loss of the* Bismarck, pp. 44-45.

[66] KTB *Gneisenau*, 8 February 1941; Rhys-Jones, *Loss of the* Bismarck, p. 45.

[67] KTB *Gneisenau*, 8 February 1941.

[68] KTB *Gneisenau*, 8 February 1941; Rhys-Jones, *Loss of the* Bismarck, p. 46.

[69] Rhys-Jones, *Loss of the* Bismarck, pp. 46-47.

[70] Roskill, *War at Sea*, p. 374.

[71] The large German surface ships had been given fairly similar silhouettes, making identification more difficult for the enemy.

[72] KTB *Gneisenau*, 9–10 February 1941.

[73] KTB *Gneisenau*, 10 February 1941.

[74] KTB *Gneisenau*, 11 February 1941.

[75] KTB *Gneisenau*, 11–15 February 1941.

[76] KTB *Gneisenau*, 16–19 February 1941; Rhys-Jones, *Loss of the* Bismarck, p. 49.

[77] KTB *Gneisenau*, 18 February 1941. On the evening of 5 February, the two battleships tested their radar equipment. It was shown that it successfully detected the other ship at ranges up to 18,000 metres. If the angle of the ships was advantageous, detection could be made at ranges up to 22,000–23,000 metres. See KTB *Gneisenau*, 5

February 1941. On 23 February the *Gneisenau*'s radar found the *Scharnhorst* at a distance of 25km; see KTB *Gneisenau*, 23 February 1941.

[78] Rhys-Jones, *Loss of the* Bismarck, pp. 49-50.

[79] Rhys-Jones, *Loss of the* Bismarck, pp. 46 and 50.

[80] KTB *Gneisenau*, 20-21 February 1941.

[81] The description of the actions on 22 February is based on an annex to the KTB *Gneisenau*. For some reason, the actions are not described in the regular war diary. The annex is found on page 133 and onwards in BA-MA RM 92/5246.

[82] BA-MA RM 92/5246, p. 133f.

[83] BA-MA RM 92/5246, p. 133f.

[84] BA-MA RM 92/5246, p. 133f.

[85] BA-MA RM 92/5246, p. 133f.

[86] BA-MA RM 92/5246, p. 133f and KTB *Gneisenau* 22–26 February 1941.

[87] KTB *Gneisenau*, 28 February 1941.

[88] KTB *Gneisenau*, 28 February 1941.

[89] KTB *Gneisenau*, 28 February 1941; Erfahrungsbericht des Schiffsarztes Marineoberarzt Dozent Dr. Lepel über die Fernunternehmung des Schlachtschiffes 'Gneisenau' vom 22. I. – 22. III. 1941, BA-MA RM 92/5346.

[90] KTB *Gneisenau* 26–27 February 1941.

[91] KTB *Gneisenau*, 28 February 1941; Rhys-Jones, *Loss of the* Bismarck, pp. 55-57.

[92] One of the aircraft had been sent away on Lütjens' orders, when the ships sailed to rendezvous with the *Adria*. The aeroplane had flown to Trondheim, bringing a comprehensive report and plans for the future actions intended by Lütjens. Subsequently, the aeroplane had not been able to return to the *Scharnhorst*.

[93] *Kriegstagebuch der Seekriegsleitung 1939–1945* (Herford: Mittler & Sohn, 1990), vol 17, p. 393 (29 January 1941); KTB *Gneisenau*, 2–4 March 1941.

[94] KTB *Gneisenau*, 5 March 1941.

[95] KTB *Gneisenau*, 5 March 1941; Rhys-Jones, *Loss of the* Bismarck, p. 59.

[96] KTB *Gneisenau*, 5–6 March 1941. Also, see report on communications, p. 204 in file BA-MA RL 92/5246.

[97] KTB *Gneisenau*, 5–6 March 1941.

[98] KTB *Gneisenau,* 7 March 1941.

[99] KTB *Gneisenau*, 7 March 1941; Rhys-Jones, *Loss of the* Bismarck, pp. 60-61.

[100] Rhys-Jones, *Loss of the* Bismarck, p. 61.

[101] KTB *Gneisenau*, 7–8 March 1941.

[102] KTB *Gneisenau*, 8 March 1941; Roskill, *War at Sea*, pp. 375-6.

[103] *Kriegstagebuch der Seekriegsleitung 1939-1945*, vol. 19, p. 154, 158, 173; Rhys-Jones, *Loss of the* Bismarck, p. 64.

[104] *Kriegstagebuch der Seekriegsleitung 1939-1945*, vol., 19, p. 173; KTB *Gneisenau*, 8 March 1941; Rhys-Jones, p *Loss of the* Bismarck, p. 64.

[105] KTB *Gneisenau*, 8–12 March 1941; Rhys-Jones, *Loss of the* Bismarck, pp. 58 and 64-65.

[106] KTB *Gneisenau*, 12–15 March 1941.

[107] Bidlingmeyer, *Einsatz der schweren Kriegsmarineeinheiten*, pp. 190-198.

[108] KTB *Gneisenau*, 15 March 1941.

[109] KTB *Gneisenau*, 16 March 1941.

[110] KTB *Gneisenau*, 16 March 1941.

[111] Roskill, *War at Sea*, pp. 376-377.

[112] KTB *Gneisenau*, 19–20 March 1941, Roskill, *War at Sea*, p. 377; Rhys-Jones, *Loss of the* Bismarck, pp. 67-70.

[113] Bidlingmeyer, *Einsatz der schweren Kriegsmarineeinheiten*, pp. 190-198.

[114] The *Scharnhorst* had three Arado 196 aircraft, the *Gneisenau* one.

[115] Brennecke, *Schlachtschiff* Bismarck, pp. 126-127.

[116] The directive can be found in Brennecke, *Schlachtschiff* Bismarck, pp. 137-143.

[117] Brennecke, *Schlachtschiff* Bismarck, pp. 138 and 152.

[118] Brennecke, *Schlachtschiff* Bismarck, p. 151.

[119] Brennecke, *Schlachtschiff* Bismarck, pp. 139-140.

[120] See the directive of 2 April 1941, in Brennecke p. 139. In his memoirs, Raeder gives a very positive description of Lütjens' ability to command operations of the kind envisaged; see E. Raeder, *Mein Leben*, Band I & II (Tübingen: Schlichtenmeyer, 1956–1957), vol. II, p. 262.

[121] Brennecke, *Schlachtschiff* Bismarck, p. 150.

[122] *Kriegstagebuch der Seekriegsleitung 1939–1945*, vol. 20, p. 44 (4 April 1941).

[123] *Kriegstagebuch der Seekriegsleitung 1939–1945*, vol. 20, pp. 72 and 90 (6 and 7 April, 1941); Brennecke, *Schlachtschiff* Bismarck, p. 145; L. Kennedy, *Pursuit: The Sinking of the* Bismarck (London: Cassel, 2001), p. 28.

[124] *Kriegstagebuch der Seekriegsleitung 1939–1945*, vol. 20, p. 90 (7 April, 1941); p. 73 (6 April, 1941).

[125] Brennecke, *Schlachtschiff* Bismarck, p. 144.

[126] Brennecke, *Schlachtschiff* Bismarck, pp. 144-145 and 478.

[127] *Kriegstagebuch der Seekriegsleitung 1939–1945*, vol. 20, p. 115 (9 April, 1941).

[128] *Kriegstagebuch der Seekriegsleitung 1939–1945*, vol. 20, pp. 90, 143 and 163 (7, 11 and 12 April, 1941); Brennecke *Schlachtschiff* Bismarck, p. 146.

[129] Submarines were different, as they could be protected by bomb proof shelters. The cruisers and battleships were far too large for such buildings.

[130] The discussion can be found in *Kriegstagebuch der Seekriegsleitung 1939–1945*, vol. 20, pp. 156-159 (12 April, 1941).

[131] *Kriegstagebuch der Seekriegsleitung 1939–1945*, vol. 20, pp. 156-157 (12 April, 1941).

[132] *Kriegstagebuch der Seekriegsleitung 1939–1945*, vol. 20, pp. 156-159 (12 April, 1941).

[133] *Kriegstagebuch der Seekriegsleitung 1939–1945*, vol. 20, pp. 157-158 (12 April, 1941).

[134] *Kriegstagebuch der Seekriegsleitung 1939–1945*, vol. 20, pp. 126 and 137 (10 April, 1941).

[135] *Kriegstagebuch der Seekriegsleitung 1939–1945*, vol. 20, p. 127 (10 April, 1941).

[136] *Fuehrer Conferences*, p. 191 (20 April, 1941).

[137] *Kriegstagebuch der Seekriegsleitung 1939–1945*, vol. 20, p. 298 (21 April, 1941). See also Raeder, *Mein Leben*, vol. II, pp. 264-266.

[138] *Kriegstagebuch der Seekriegsleitung 1939–1945*, vol. 20, pp. 371-372 (26 April, 1941).

[139] *Kriegstagebuch der Seekriegsleitung 1939–1945*, vol. 20, pp. 371-3722 (26 April, 1941).

[140] *Kriegstagebuch der Seekriegsleitung 1939–1945*, vol. 20, p. 347 (24 April, 1941).

[141] The intention to use the period of new moon is also evident in the directive of 2 April; see Brennecke, *Schlachtschiff* Bismarck, p. 139.

[142] *Kriegstagebuch der Seekriegsleitung 1939–1945*, vol. 20, p. 347 (24 April, 1941).

[143] Rhys-Jones, *Loss of the* Bismarck, p. 82.

[144] Rhys-Jones, *Loss of the* Bismarck, p. 82.

[145] Brennecke, *Schlachtschiff* Bismarck, p. 149.

[146] For more on this, see Roskill, *War at Sea*, pp. 41-61 and 112-121.

[147] Roskill, *War at Sea*, pp. 8, 293-296.

[148] Tarrant, King George V *Class Battleships*, pp. 30-34.

[149] Lenton and Colledge, *Warships of World War II*, pp. 57-59; Roskill, *War at Sea*, pp. 268, 298, 307, 382, 396, 421-423, 426, 428-430, 433-434, 440, 491, 534.

[150] Roskill, *War at Sea*, p. 268.

[151] R. Grenfell, *The* Bismarck *Episode* (London: Faber & Faber, 1948), pp. 20f; Rhys-Jones, *The Loss of the* Bismarck, pp. 99 and 149.

[152] Roskill, *War at Sea*, p. 396.

[153] Roskill, *War at Sea*, p. 382.

[154] Brennecke, *Schlachtschiff* Bismarck, pp. 162-172.

[155] Müllenheim-Rechberg, *Schlachtschiff* Bismarck, pp. 85-86.

[156] *Kriegstagebuch der Seekriegsleitung 1939–1945*, vol. 20, p. 407 (28 April, 1941) and vol. 21, p. 168 (13 May, 1941).

[157] Müllenheim-Rechberg, *Schlachtschiff* Bismarck, p. 87, Brennecke, *Schlachtschiff* Bismarck, pp. 164-166 claims the visit took place on 12 May. However, the *Bismarck*'s war diary shows that 5 May is the correct date.

[158] Müllenheim-Rechberg, *Schlachtschiff* Bismarck, pp. 87-88.

[159] Müllenheim-Rechberg, *Schlachtschiff* Bismarck, pp. 88-89.

[160] Brennecke, *Schlachtschiff* Bismarck, pp. 167-169.

[161] Müllenheim-Rechberg, *Schlachtschiff* Bismarck, p. 81.

[162] L. Kennedy, *Pursuit: The Sinking of the* Bismarck (London: Collins, 1954), pp. 31-32.

[163] Stephen Budiansky, *Battle of Wits: The Complete Story of Codebreaking in World War II* (Penguin, London, 2001), pp. 249-250.

[164] Müllenheim-Rechberg, *Schlachtschiff* Bismarck, p. 81.

[165] Kennedy, *Pursuit*, p. 34.

[166] *Kriegstagebuch der Seekriegsleitung 1939–1945*, vol. 21, pp. 243 and 254 (17 and 18 May, 1941); Brennecke *Schlachtschiff* Bismarck, pp. 149 and 173.

[167] Stephen Roskill, *The Navy at War 1939–45* (London: Wordsworth, 1998), p. 126.

[168] Budiansky, *Battle of Wits*, pp. 340-341.

[169] Ronald Lewin, *Ultra Goes to War:The Secret Story* (London: Penguin Books, 2001), p. 206.

[170] KTB *Bismarck*, 18 May, 1941.

[171] KTB *Bismarck*, 18 May, 1941.

[172] KTB *Bismarck*, 18 May, 1941; Müllenheim-Rechberg, *Schlachtschiff* Bismarck, p. 92.

[173] Müllenheim-Rechberg, *Schlachtschiff* Bismarck, p. 92; Brenneke, *Schlachtschiff*

Bismarck, pp. 175-176.

[174] Brenneke, pp. 176-178; *Kriegstagebuch der Seekriegsleitung 1939–1945*, vol. 21, p. 292 (20 May, 1941).

[175] *Kriegstagebuch der Seekriegsleitung 1939–1945*, vol. 21, p. 272 (19 May, 1941).

[176] KTB *Bismarck*, 19 May, 1941.

[177] KTB *Bismarck*, 20 May, 1941, Müllenheim-Rechberg, *Schlachtschiff* Bismarck, pp. 93-94.

[178] Müllenheim-Rechberg, *Schlachtschiff* Bismarck, p. 94.

[179] KTB *Bismarck*, 20 May, 1941, Müllenheim-Rechberg, *Schlachtschiff* Bismarck, pp. 94-95. See also the translator's remark in B. von Müllenheim-Rechberg, *Slagskeppet* Bismarck (Höganäs: Wiken, 1987), in particular on p. 82.

[180] See the translator's remark in *Slagskeppet* Bismarck, p 82.

[181] Müllenheim-Rechberg, *Schlachtschiff* Bismarck, p. 95.

[182] Arnold Hauge, *The Allied Convoy System 1939-45: Its Organization, Defence and Operation* (Chatham, 2001), p. 132.

[183] Kennedy, *Pursuit*, p. 135.

[184] KTB *Bismarck*, 20 May, 1941.

[185] KTB *Prinz Eugen*, 21 May, 1941; Brennecke, *Schlachtschiff* Bismarck, pp. 180-181.

[186] KTB *Bismarck*, 21 May, 1941; Müllenheim-Rechberg, *Schlachtschiff* Bismarck, p. 98.

[187] Roskill, *War at Sea*, pp. 395-396.

[188] It has never been fully clear who in the Swedish intelligence service gave Lund the information. British sources claim a Major Törnberg, but no such person served in Swedish intelligence at that time. Possibly it may have been a Captain Ternberg. See translator's comment in *Slagskeppet* Bismarck, pp. 82-83.

[189] Kennedy, *Pursuit*, p. 35.

[190] Kennedy, *Pursuit*, p. 35.

[191] Kennedy, *Pursuit*, pp. 35-36.

[192] Grenfell, *The* Bismarck *Episode*, pp. 12-13; Kennedy, *Pursuit*, p. 39.

[193] JGDC/DLW, Interpretation of Report No. 1490, Public Records Office, Kew, London, *Battlefront: Sinking of the* Bismarck; Kennedy, *Pursuit*, pp. 41-42.

[194] Kennedy, *Pursuit*, p. 44.

[195] JGDC/DLW, Interpretation of Report No. 1490, Public Records Office, Kew, London, *Battlefront: Sinking of the* Bismarck; Naval Staff History, Battle Summary No. 5, 'The Chase and Sinking of the *Bismarck*,' Public Records Office, Kew, London, Adm 234/322, pp. 3-4; Roskill, *War at Sea*, p. 396.

[196] Kennedy, p *Pursuit*, p. 42.

[197] Naval Staff History, Battle Summary No. 5, p. 4.

[198] KTB *Prinz Eugen*, 21 May, 1941. We have presumed that the *Bismarck* could at most take on slightly more than 8,200 cubic metres of fuel oil (see for example the war diary of the machinery 6 May, 1941). At a speed of 17 knots, the *Bismarck* had an endurance of 8,900 nautical miles, so the voyage to Bergen represented about 10% of her range. Thus, she must have consumed about 800 cubic metres. She was also 200 tons below her maximum capacity when she left Gdynia.

[199] KTB *Prinz Eugen*, 21 May, 1941; KTB *Bismarck*, 21 May, 1941.

[200] *Kriegstagebuch der Seekriegsleitung 1939-1945*, vol. 21, p. 292 (20 May, 1941).

[201] Müllenheim-Rechberg, *Schlachtschiff* Bismarck, pp. 101-102.

[202] KTB *Prinz Eugen*, 21-22 May, 1941; KTB *Bismarck*, 22 May, 1941.

[203] KTB *Prinz Eugen*, 22 May, 1941; KTB *Bismarck*, 22 May, 1941.

[204] KTB *Prinz Eugen*, 22 May, 1941; KTB *Bismarck*, 22 May, 1941.

[205] Kennedy, *Pursuit*, p. 50.

[206] KTB *Prinz Eugen*, 22 May, 1941; KTB *Bismarck*, 22 May, 1941.

[207] Enclosure to Home Fleet letter 659/H.F.1325 of 30 May 1941, 'Report of Operations in Pursuit of the *Bismarck*,' p. 2, Public Records Office, Kew, London, ADM 199/1188.

[208] 'Report of operations in pursuit of the *Bismarck*,' p. 2

[209] 'Report of operations in pursuit of the *Bismarck*,' p. 2; Grenfell, *The* Bismarck *Episode*, pp. 29-30.

[210] Coastal Command, *The Air Ministry Account of the Part Played by Coastal Command in the Battle of the Seas. 1939–1942.* (Issued for the Air Ministry by the Ministry of Information; London and Tonbridge: Whitefriars Press, S.O. Code No. 70-411).

[211] Grenfell, *The* Bismarck *Episode*, pp. 32-33.

[212] Grenfell, *The* Bismarck *Episode*, pp. 33-34.

[213] Grenfell, *The* Bismarck *Episode*, pp. 34-35; *Sink the* Bismarck, documentary, History Channel, HMS Hood Association, http://www.hmshood.com/crew/remember/tedflagship.htm.

[214] David Mearns and Rob White, Hood *and* Bismarck: *The Deep-Sea Discovery of an Epic Battle* (Channel 4 Books, London, 2001), p. 67.

[215] Grenfell, *The* Bismarck *Episode*, pp. 34-35.

[216] 'Report of Operations in Pursuit of the Bismarck,' pp. 2-3.

[217] Mearns and White, Hood *and* Bismarck, pp. 18-20.

[218] , Mearns and White, Hood *and* Bismarck, pp. 20-25.

[219] Ted Briggs, *Flagship* Hood: *The Fate of Britain's Mightiest Warship*, H.M.S. *Hood* Association, http://www.hmshood.com/crew/remember/tedflagship.htm.

[220] Mearns and White, Hood *and* Bismarck, p. 68.

[221] KTB *Prinz Eugen*, 22 May, 1941.

[222] KTB *Bismarck*, 22 May, 1941.

[223] KTB *Prinz Eugen*, 23 May, 1941.

[224] KTB *Bismarck*, 22 May, 1941; *Kriegstagebuch der Seekriegsleitung 1939-1945*, vol. 21, p. 323 (22 May, 1941).

[225] Lenton Colledge, *Warships of World War II*, p. 17; Roskill, *War at Sea* ,p. 75; Kennedy, *Pursuit*, pp. 50 and 231.

[226] KTB *Bismarck*, 23 May, 1941.

[227] KTB *Bismarck*, 23 May, 1941.

[228] Müllenheim-Rechberg, *Schlachtschiff* Bismarck, pp. 112-3; KTB *Bismarck*, 23 May, 1941.

[229] Müllenheim-Rechberg, *Schlachtschiff* Bismarck, pp. 112-3; KTB *Bismarck*, 23 May, 1941.

[230] Müllenheim-Rechberg, *Schlachtschiff* Bismarck, p. 113

[231] Naval Staff History, Battle Summary No 5, pp. 3f.

[232] Kennedy, *Pursuit*, p. 43.

[233] Roskill, *War at Sea*, pp. 396-397 and map between these pages; Naval Staff History, Battle Summary No. 5, p. 5.

[234] Roskill, *The Navy at War 1939-45*, p. 128.

[235] Roskill, *The War at Sea*, pp. 396-397 and map between these pages.

[236] Grenfell, *The* Bismarck *Episode*, pp. 38-39; Kennedy, *Pursuit*, pp. 53-55.

[237] Kennedy, *Pursuit*, p. 54.

[238] Grenfell, *The* Bismarck *Episode*, p. 40.

[239] Grenfell, *The* Bismarck *Episode*, p. 40.

[240] Grenfell, *The* Bismarck *Episode*, p. 40.

[241] Grenfell, *The* Bismarck *Episode*, p. 42.

[242] Rhys-Jones, *The Loss of the* Bismarck, p. 104.

[243] Müllenheim-Rechberg, *Schlachtschiff* Bismarck, p. 113.

[244] Grenfell, *The* Bismarck *Episode*, p. 43; Roskill, *The War at Sea*, p. 397; Müllenheim-Rechberg, *Schlachtschiff* Bismarck, pp. 113-114; Naval Staff History, Battle Summary No. 5, pp. 5-6.

[245] Müllenheim-Rechberg, *Schlachtschiff* Bismarck, pp. 113-114.

[246] Müllenheim-Rechberg, *Schlachtschiff* Bismarck, pp. 113-114; Naval Staff History, Battle Summary No. 5, pp. 5-6; Kennedy, *Pursuit*, pp. 57-58.

[247] 'Report of operations in pursuit of the Bismarck,' p. 3; Grenfell, *The* Bismarck *Episode*, pp. 43-44.

[248] Our estimate of the *Prinz Eugen*'s fuel oil is based on the fact that she had 3,233 cubic metres when leaving Bergen (KTB *Prinz Eugen*, 21 May, 1941) and 2,466 at 08.00 hours on 23 May (KTB *Prinz Eugen*, 23 May, 1941). Thus she probably had about 2,100 cubic metres at 20.00 hours on 23 May.

[249] Using all her fuel oil capacity of 3 950 cubic metres, the *Prinz Eugen* could steam at 32.5 knots for 60 hours. See P. Schmalenbach, *Kreuzer* prinz Eugen *unter drei Flaggen* (Hamburg: Koehlers, 2001), p. 43. See also previous note.

[250] Brennecke, *Schlachtschiff* Bismarck, pp. 209-210.

[251] Brennecke, *Schlachtschiff* Bismarck, pp. 209-210; KTB *Prinz Eugen*, 23 May 1941, Müllenheim-Rechberg, *Schlachtschiff* Bismarck, p. 115.

[252] Rhys-Jones, *The Loss of the* Bismarck, p. 100.

[253] Roskill, *War at Sea*, p. 398, n. 2; Tarrant, King George V *Class Battleships*, p. 48.

[254] R. Hough, *The Longest Battle: The War at Sea 1939–1945* (London: Pan Books, 1986), p. 95.

[255] Naval Staff History, Battle Summary No. 5, p. 7; Kennedy, *Pursuit*, p. 71.

[256] Grenfell, *The* Bismarck *Episode*, p. 46.

[257] J. H. Wellings, *On His Majesty's Service* (Naval War College Press, Newport, 1983), pp. 189 & 197.

[258] Naval Staff History, Battle Summary No 5, p. 6; Kennedy, *Pursuit*, p. 106.

[259] Rhys-Jones, *The Loss of the* Bismarck, p. 106; KTB *Bismarck*, 24 May, 1941.

[260] Kennedy, *Pursuit*, pp. 71f; Rhys-Jones, *The Loss of the* Bismarck, pp. 106f.

[261] Rhys-Jones, *The Loss of the* Bismarck, p. 115.

[262] Briggs, *Flagship Hood*.

[263] Naval Staff History, Battle Summary No. 5, p. 7; Roskill, *War at Sea*, map

between pages 396 and 397.

[264] Naval Staff History, Battle Summary No. 5, p. 7.

[265] Naval Staff History, Battle Summary No. 5, p. 7; Roskill, *War at Sea*, p. 401.

[266] Naval Staff History, Battle Summary No. 5, p. 7; Roskill, *War at Sea*, p. 401; Grenfell, *The* Bismarck *Episode*, p. 48; Kennedy, *Pursuit*, p. 72.

[267] Rhys-Jones, *The Loss of the* Bismarck, p. 107; KTB *Bismarck*, 24 May, 1941.

[268] Rhys-Jones, *The Loss of the* Bismarck, p. 107.

[269] Rhys-Jones, *The Loss of the* Bismarck, p. 117.

[270] Naval Staff History, Battle Summary No. 5, p. 7; Roskill, *War at Sea*, p. 401; Tarrant, King George V *Class Battleships*, pp. 30-33.

[271] 'Biography of Bob Tilburn,' H.M.S. *Hood* Association, http://hmshood.com/crew/biography/bobtilburn_bio.htm.

[272] Briggs, *Flagship* Hood.

[273] Kennedy, *Pursuit*, pp. 80f.

[274] Board of inquiry on the loss of HMS *Hood*, PRO, ADM 116/4352, p. 24.

[275] Müllenheim-Rechberg, *Schlachtschiff* Bismarck, p. 121.

[276] Briggs, *Flagship* Hood.

[277] Coastal Command, The air ministry Account of the Part Played by Coastal Command in the Battle of the Seas.

[278] Board of inquiry on the loss of HMS *Hood*, p. 25.

[279] Kennedy, *Pursuit*, p. 86.

[280] It has often been argued that the *Hood* blew up after a shell penetrated her weak deck armour. The thesis may well have been nourished by the pre-war fear. Still, it seems quite unlikely as an explanation. It seems that the range was about 15,000 metres when the fatal shell was fired. At that range, the *Bismarck*'s guns needed very little elevation to hit the target, only about 8 degrees and the shell would strike a horizontal surface at an angle of only 10 degrees. At such an angle, it is very difficult to penetrate deck armour. Only if the target had rolled considerably, would a penetration have been possible. It would have been different at the range when the battle was begun, but the disastrous hit occurred when the range had closed to about 10,000 metres. Thus it seems that Holland's plan worked as intended. Unfortunately the dangers were not over. The *Bismarck*'s guns fired with higher muzzle velocity than the British guns: for example, the *Bismarck* fired with a MV of 850 m/s (see Elfrath and Herzog, *Schlachtschiff* Bismarck – *technische Daten*, p. 22) compared to the *King George V's* 754 m/s (see Tarrant, King George V *Class Battleships*, p. 31). This meant that the German shells followed a lower trajectory and could penetrate more vertical armour than the British guns, but it also meant that the German shells hit deck armour at a less advantageous angle. The difference between German and British guns should not be exaggerated, but perhaps Holland assumed that the German guns' ballistic properties were similar to their British counterparts. If so, he probably believed the Germans were able to penetrate the deck armour at a shorter distance than was actually the case, but he may also have underestimated the range at which they could penetrate the side armour.

[281] The British turrets were called A, B, X and Y from fore to aft.

[282] William, J. Jurens, The Loss of HMS *Hood*: A Re-Examination; and Mearns and

White, Hood *and* Bismarck, pp. 199-200.

[283] Board of inquiry on the loss of HMS *Hood*, p. 27.

[284] Coastal Command, The Air Ministry Account of the Part Played by Coastal Command in the Battle of the Seas.

[285] Mearns and White, Hood *and* Bismarck, p. 207.

[286] Kennedy, *Pursuit*, pp. 87, 93.

[287] Müllenheim-Rechberg, *Schlachtschiff* Bismarck, pp. 122-123. Müllenheim-Rechberg does not give the name of the assistant and we have not been able to figure it out.

[288] Müllenheim-Rechberg, *Schlachtschiff* Bismarck, pp. 121-122.

[289] *Sink the* Bismarck.

[290] Müllenheim-Rechberg, *Schlachtschiff* Bismarck, p. 122.

[291] Mearns and White, Hood *and* Bismarck, p. 207.

[292] Mearns and White, Hood *and* Bismarck, p. 202.

[293] *Sink the* Bismarck.

[294] Rhys-Jones, *Loss of the* Bismarck, p. 132.

[295] Mearns and White, Hood *and* Bismarck, p. 127.

[296] Kennedy, *Pursuit*, pp. 91-92.

[297] Naval Staff History, Battle Summary No. 5, p. 10; Roskill, *War at Sea*, p. 407.

[298] Naval Staff History, Battle Summary No. 5, p. 10.

[299] Naval Staff History, Battle Summary No 5, Map 2; Grenfell, *The* Bismarck *Episode*, pp. 76-77.

[300] Grenfell, *The* Bismarck *Episode*, pp. 67-70; Naval Staff History, Battle Summary No 5, Map.

[301] Kennedy, *Pursuit – The Sinking of the* Bismarck, pp. 108-109; Naval Staff History, Battle Summary No. 5, p. 9.

[302] Müllenheim-Rechberg, *Schlachtschiff* Bismarck, p. 128.

[303] Müllenheim-Rechberg, *Schlachtschiff* Bismarck, pp. 128-129.

[304] Brennecke, *Schlachtschiff* Bismarck, p. 257.

[305] Jack Taylor, 'I was there - We found only three,' H.M.S. *Hood* Association, http://hmshood.com/crew/remember/electra_taylor.htm.

[306] Hough, *The Longest Battle*, p. 97.

[307] Müllenheim-Rechberg, *Schlachtschiff* Bismarck, pp. 128-129.

[308] Müllenheim-Rechberg, *Schlachtschiff* Bismarck, pp. 128-129.

[309] KTB *Bismarck*, 24 May, 1941; Elfrath and Herzog, *Schlachtschiff* Bismarck – *technische Daten*, p. 22.

[310] KTB *Bismarck*, 24 May, 1941; Müllenheim-Rechberg, *Schlachtschiff* Bismarck, pp. 136-137.

[311] KTB *Bismarck*, 24 May, 1941; Müllenheim-Rechberg, *Schlachtschiff* Bismarck, pp. 136-137.

[312] KTB *Bismarck*, 24 May, 1941; Müllenheim-Rechberg, *Schlachtschiff* Bismarck, p. 137.

[313] KTB *Bismarck*, 24 May, 1941; Müllenheim-Rechberg, *Schlachtschiff* Bismarck, pp. 136-137.

[314] By 08.00 hours on 24 May, Tovey's ships had covered approximately 600 nautical

miles. The distance between Tovey and Lütjens was 300 nautical miles at that time. With the current courses and speeds, Tovey only closed the distance at a rate of one or two knots. At least 150 hours would pass before he could engage. At a speed of 28 knots, 4,600 nautical miles would be covered in 150 hours, a distance exceeding the endurance of the *King George V* by 50 % at the current speed. As she had already consumed part of her fuel oil, it was an obviously impossible situation. See Roskill, map p. 409; Rhys-Jones, *Loss of the* Bismarck, p. 133; Tarrant, King George V *Class Battleships*, p. 31.

[315] Rhys-Jones, *Loss of the* Bismarck, p. 132; Grenfell, *The* Bismarck *Episode*, pp. 67-68.

[316] Rhys-Jones, *Loss of the* Bismarck, pp. 135-136; Grenfell, *The* Bismarck *Episode*, pp. 76-77.

[317] 'Report of Operations in Pursuit of the Bismarck,' p. 4; Roskill, *War at Sea*, pp. 407-408.

[318] 'Report of Operations in Pursuit of the Bismarck,' p. 4; Roskill, *War at Sea*, pp. 407-409; Wellings, *On his Majesty's Service*, p. 198. Note that all these sources differ as to when the *Victorious* was detached.

[319] Grenfell, *The* Bismarck *Episode*, p. 84.

[320] Grenfell, *The* Bismarck *Episode*, pp. 83-92.

[321] Ludovic, *Pursuit*, p. 109.

[322] KTB *Bismarck*, 24 May, 1941; Müllenheim-Rechberg, *Schlachtschiff* Bismarck, pp. 138-139; Schmalenbach, *Kreuzer* Prinz Eugen, p. 126; Grenfell, *The* Bismarck *Episode*, pp. 90-91; Kennedy, *Pursuit*, p. 109f.

[323] Kennedy, *Pursuit*, p. 111.

[324] Naval Staff History, Battle Summary No 5, p. 14.

[325] Müllenheim-Rechberg, *Schlachtschiff* Bismarck, p. 142.

[326] Mark E. Horan, 'With Gallantry and Determination,' http://www.kbismarck.com/article2.html.

[327] Kennedy, *Pursuit*, p. 119.

[328] *Sink the* Bismarck.

[329] *Sink the* Bismarck.

[330] *Sink the* Bismarck.

[331] Müllenheim-Rechberg, *Schlachtschiff* Bismarck, p. 144.

[332] *Sink the* Bismarck.

[333] Kennedy, *Pursuit*, p. 120.

[334] Horan, 'With Gallantry and Determination'.

[335] KTB *Bismarck*, 24–25 May, 1941; Müllenheim-Rechberg, *Schlachtschiff* Bismarck, p. 145.

[336] *Sink the* Bismarck.

[337] KTB *Bismarck*, 24–25 May, 1941.

[338] KTB *Bismarck*, 24–25 May, 1941.

[339] Brennecke, *Schlachtschiff* Bismarck, pp. 268-272; KTB *Bismarck*, 24 May, 1941.

[340] Brennecke, *Schlachtschiff* Bismarck, pp. 268-269.

[341] 'Report of Operations in Pursuit of the *Bismarck*,' pp. 4-5; Grenfell, *The* Bismarck *Episode*, p. 96.

[342] Wellings, *On his Majesty's Service*, p. 199.

[343] Grenfell, *The* Bismarck *Episode*, p. 97.

[344] Grenfell, *The* Bismarck *Episode*, p. 97.

[345] Grenfell, *The* Bismarck *Episode*, pp. 91 and 97-99.

[346] Brennecke, *Schlachtschiff* Bismarck, pp. 284-286; Grenfell, *The* Bismarck *Episode*, pp. 97-98; Roskill, *War at Sea*, p. 409.

[347] Brennecke, *Schlachtschiff* Bismarck, pp 284-288.

[348] Grenfell, *The* Bismarck *Episode*, p. 98.

[349] Hough, *The Longest Battle*, p. 104.

[350] 'Report of Operations in Pursuit of the *Bismarck*,' p. 5; Naval Staff History, Battle Summary No. 5, p. 16; Grenfell, *The* Bismarck *Episode*, p. 98.

[351] 'Report of Operations in Pursuit of the *Bismarck*,' p. 5; Roskill, *The War at Sea*, pp. 408-410.

[352] Tarrant, King George V *Class Battleships*, p. 83; Roskill, *The War at Sea*, pp. 408-409.

[353] KTB *Bismarck*, 25 May, 1941.

[354] KTB *Bismarck*, 25 May, 1941.

[355] The positions of the British ships have been taken from Roskill, *War at Sea*, map after p. 408. The *Bismarck*'s exact position is not known, as her war diary was lost when the ship sank. The only position available is from the bearings taken when Lütjens' message was sent.

[356] KTB *Bismarck*, 25 May, 1941; Rhys-Jones, *Loss of the* Bismarck, p. 160.

[357] Kennedy, *Pursuit – The Sinking of the* Bismarck, pp. 130-131.

[358] Naval Staff History, Battle Summary No. 5, pp. 17-19.

[359] Kennedy, *Pursuit – The Sinking of the* Bismarck, p. 130; Rhys-Jones, *Loss of the* Bismarck, pp. 164-165.

[360] Wellings, *On his Majesty's Service*, pp. 204-207.

[361] Wellings, *On his Majesty's Service*, pp. 204-207.

[362] Wellings, *On his Majesty's Service*, pp. 204-207.

[363] An exhaustive discussion on the issue can be found in Rhys-Jones, *Loss of the* Bismarck, pp. 235-240.

[364] Kennedy, *Pursuit*, pp. 130-131.

[365] KTB *Bismarck*, 25 May, 1941; Kennedy, *Pursuit*, pp. 131-132.

[366] Müllenheim-Rechberg, *Schlachtschiff* Bismarck, p. 161.

[367] Müllenheim-Rechberg, *Schlachtschiff* Bismarck, p. 158. The speech is puzzling in one respect: Lütjens' claim that he had received orders to proceed to a French port. In fact, he made the decision himself. Perhaps the speech is not correctly reproduced. The only source is the memory of the five German seamen saved by *U-74* and the *Sachsenwald*.

[368] Müllenheim-Rechberg, *Schlachtschiff* Bismarck, p 165.

[369] Müllenheim-Rechberg, *Schlachtschiff* Bismarck, pp. 165-166.

[370] Rhys-Jones, *Loss of the* Bismarck, pp. 174-175.

[371] Naval Staff History, Battle Summary No 5, p. 19.

[372] Rhys-Jones, *Loss of the* Bismarck, pp. 164-165.

[373] It has been said that the relative in fact was Jeschonnek's son. If so, his family

name differed from his father, as no Jeschonnek has been found in the list of crew members on the *Bismarck*.

[374] Budiansky, *Battle of Wits*, p. 190.

[375] Rhys-Jones, *Loss of the* Bismarck, p. 168.

[376] Roskill, *The Navy at War 1939–45*, p. 136.

[377] Mary Kelly, *Secret Mission*, Irelandseye, http://www.irelandseye.com/aarticles/history/events/worldwar/secret.shtm

[378] *Sink the* Bismarck.

[379] *Bismarck*: The Report of the Scouting and Search for *Bismarck* by Ensign Smith.

[380] Kennedy, *Pursuit*, p. 152; Coastal Command, The Air Ministry Account of the Part Played by Coastal Command in the Battle of the Seas, 1939–1942.

[381] Philip Vian, *Action this Day* (London: Muller, 1960), p. 57.

[382] Kennedy, *Pursuit*, pp. 155-156.

[383] Rhys-Jones, *Loss of the* Bismarck, p. 182.

[384] Horan, 'With Gallantry and Determination'.

[385] Hough, *The Longest Battle*, p. 108.

[386] Kennedy*Pursuit*, p. 163.

[387] Müllenheim-Rechberg, *Schlachtschiff* Bismarck, pp. 170-171.

[388] Horan, 'With Gallantry and Determination'.

[389] Müllenheim-Rechberg, *Schlachtschiff* Bismarck, p. 177.

[390] Hough, *The Longest Battle*, p. 108.

[391] Mearns and White, Hood *and* Bismarck, pp. 141f.

[392] Kennedy, *Pursuit*, p, 169.

[393] Kennedy, *Pursuit*, p. 175.

[394] Müllenheim-Rechberg, *Schlachtschiff* Bismarck, p. 180.

[395] Kennedy, *Pursuit*, p. 172.

[396] Kennedy, *Pursuit*, p. 170.

[397] Brennecke, *Schlachtschiff* Bismarck, pp. 316-327; Müllenheim-Rechberg, *Schlachtschiff* Bismarck, pp. 187-193.

[398] William H. Garzke and Robert O. Dulin, '*Bismarck*'s Final Battle,' http://www.navweaps.com/index_inro/INRO_Bismarck_p2.htm.

[399] Brennecke, *Schlachtschiff* Bismarck, pp. 316-327; Müllenheim-Rechberg, *Schlachtschiff* Bismarck, pp. 187-193.

[400] Brennecke, *Schlachtschiff* Bismarck, pp. 316-327; Müllenheim-Rechberg, *Schlachtschiff* Bismarck, pp. 187-193.

[401] Brennecke, *Schlachtschiff* Bismarck, pp. 316-327; Müllenheim-Rechberg, *Schlachtschiff* Bismarck, pp. 187-193.

[402] 'Report of operations in pursuit of the *Bismarck*'.

[403] Müllenheim-Rechberg, *Schlachtschiff* Bismarck, p. 195.

[404] Garzke and Dulin, '*Bismarck*'s Final Battle'.

[405] Vian, *Action this Day*, p. 60.

[406] Dawn was just beginning when the *Maori* fired her last torpedoes at a range of almost 9,000 metres. It was virtually impossible to hit at that range.

[407] Müllenheim-Rechberg, *Schlachtschiff* Bismarck, p. 226.

[408] Müllenheim-Rechberg, *Schlachtschiff* Bismarck, p. 212.

[409] Müllenheim-Rechberg, *Schlachtschiff* Bismarck, pp. 212-214.

[410] *Sink the* Bismarck.

[411] Müllenheim-Rechberg, *Schlachtschiff* Bismarck, p. 222.

[412] Müllenheim-Rechberg, *Schlachtschiff* Bismarck, p. 222

[413] Müllenheim-Rechberg, *Schlachtschiff* Bismarck, p. 222.

[414] Müllenheim-Rechberg, *Schlachtschiff* Bismarck, p. 222.

[415] Kennedy, *Pursuit*, p. 200.

[416] *Sink the* Bismarck.

[417] Müllenheim-Rechberg, *Schlachtschiff* Bismarck, pp. 222-223.

[418] Rhys-Jones, *Loss of the* Bismarck, p. 204.

[419] Müllenheim-Rechberg, *Schlachtschiff* Bismarck, p. 248.

[420] 'WW2 Cruiser Operations,' http://www.world-war.co.uk/index.php3.

[421] Müllenheim-Rechberg, *Schlachtschiff* Bismarck, pp. 224-225. When the wreck of the *Bismarck* was discovered 1989 it was revealed that the parts above the armoured turret of Müllenheim-Rechberg's instrument had been cut off by a direct hit.

[422] The *Rodney* had two torpedo tubes below the waterline.

[423] Kennedy, *Pursuit*, p. 203.

[424] Kennedy, *Pursuit*, p. 208.

[425] Garzke and Dulin, '*Bismarck*'s Final Battle'.

[426] Sometimes, Tovey has been criticized for closing the range rather than fighting at longer range. It has been argued that the trajectories became so flat that the British shells only hit superstructures and the thick side armour of the *Bismarck*. It has been argued that at longer range the shells might have been able to strike the deck armour at such angles that it could have been penetrated. Such a theory appears shaky. First of all, the range has to be very long to achieve the striking angles needed, with the attendant poor accuracy. Considering the risks posed by German submarines and air power, combined with the grave shortage of fuel oil, a drawn-out battle was clearly undesirable. Furthermore, Tovey did not have the knowledge of the *Bismarck's* protection-layout to establish the optimum range for such a tactic. Rather he had to settle for a more reasonable solution. At shorter ranges, the penetration of battleship main guns was so great that armour plates had to be virtually impossibly thick to afford adequate protection. It was thus reasonable to assume that his ships would be able to penetrate the *Bismarck's* main belt at short range. Thus Tovey's tactic seems reasonable enough. The fact that the *Bismarck* did not sink is remarkable. Altogether, the *Rodney* and *King George V* fired 719 heavy shells and 2,157 lighter shells. It has been estimated that as many as one quarter of them may have hit the *Bismarck*. If so, it is understandable that Tovey said: 'This would have sunk a dozen battleships'. If as many as 150-200 heavy shells the *Bismarck*, it is much more than any battleship sustained. It suggests that the *Bismarck's* protection overall must be regarded as very good, an impression confirmed when the wreck was found in 1989.

[427] It has not been possible to establish exactly when the event took place, but about, or just before, 10.00 hours seems most plausible.

[428] Müllenheim-Rechberg, *Schlachtschiff* Bismarck, pp. 259-260.

[429] The Battleship *Bismarck*.

[430] *Sink the* Bismarck.

[431] Kennedy, *Pursuit*, pp. 209f.

[432] *Sink the* Bismarck.

[433] Müllenheim-Rechberg, *Schlachtschiff* Bismarck, pp. 235-236.

[434] *Sink the* Bismarck.

[435] Müllenheim-Rechberg, *Schlachtschiff* Bismarck, pp. 239-240.

[436] There has been a kind of dispute after the war on what actually caused the *Bismarck* to sink. From the German side it has been claimed that the crew sunk her, while the British have questioned this and instead emphasized the torpedoes fired by the *Dorsetshire*. Nevertheless, it seems beyond doubt that the Germans did scuttle their ship. The testimonials from the survivors are unanimous, irrespective of which ship saved them. When the wreck was found in 1989, it provided strong evidence that the *Bismarck* must have been scuttled. The hull was very well preserved, which means that it must have been completely waterfilled very early on its way down to the bottom of the ocean, or else it would have imploded under the pressure from the surrounding water. A ship that is not sunk by the crew will contain much air, unlike a properly scuttled ship which is quickly filled with water. At depths like 5,000 metres, the pressure from the water is enormous and no hull can withstand such pressure, unless it is filled with water inside. Thus the torpedoes from the *Dorsetshire* may well have hastened the process, but the *Bismarck* would nevertheless have sunk.

[437] B. Fitzsimons (ed.), *Warships of the Second World War* (London: BPC Publishing Ltd, 1973), p. 18.

[438] Mearns and White, Hood *and* Bismarck, p. 150.

[439] Müllenheim-Rechberg, *Schlachtschiff* Bismarck, p. 254.

[440] Müllenheim-Rechberg, *Schlachtschiff* Bismarck, p. 254.

[441] Told personally by Walter Fudge to the authors, via email.

[442] *Sink the* Bismarck,

[443] Müllenheim-Rechberg, *Schlachtschiff* Bismarck, p. 263.

[444] Walter Fudge, personal correspondence with authors.

[445] Kennedy, *Pursuit*, p. 216.

[446] It still remains unclear if it was U-74 that caused Captain Martin to break off the rescue action, or if it was just a mistaken observation. It seems however likely that the cruiser observed by Kentrat was indeed the *Dorsetshire*.

[447] http://www.kbismarck.com/

[448] http://www.kbismarck.com/

[449] Kennedy, *Pursuit*, pp. 216f.

[450] Roger Parkinson, *Blood, Toil, Tears and Sweat: The War History from Dunkirk to Alamein, based on the Cabinet Papers of 1940 to 1942Die Wende im U-Boot-Krieg.*

Index